Teenager on First,
Geezer at Bat,
4-F on Deck

ALSO BY JAMES D. SZALONTAI

*Close Shave: The Life and Times
of Baseball's Sal Maglie* (McFarland, 2002)

Teenager on First, Geezer at Bat, 4-F on Deck

Major League Baseball in 1945

JAMES D. SZALONTAI

McFarland & Company, Inc., Publishers
Jefferson, North Carolina, and London

LIBRARY OF CONGRESS CATALOGUING-IN-PUBLICATION DATA

Szalontai, James D., 1974–
　　Teenager on first, geezer at bat, 4-F on deck : major league baseball in 1945 / James D. Szalontai.
　　　　p.　　cm.
　　Includes bibliographical references and index.

　　ISBN 978-0-7864-3794-8
　　softcover : 50# alkaline paper ∞

　　1. Baseball — United States — History — 20th century.
2. Baseball players — United States — History — 20th century.
3. United States — Armed Forces — Sports — History — 20th century.　I. Title.
GV863.A1S97　　2009
796.3570973'09044 — dc22　　　　　　　　　　2008044746

British Library cataloguing data are available

©2009 James D. Szalontai. All rights reserved

No part of this book may be reproduced or transmitted in any form or by any means, electronic or mechanical, including photocopying or recording, or by any information storage and retrieval system, without permission in writing from the publisher.

On the cover: Floyd Caves "Babe" Herman

Manufactured in the United States of America

McFarland & Company, Inc., Publishers
　Box 611, Jefferson, North Carolina 28640
　　www.mcfarlandpub.com

Table of Contents

Preface   1

Introduction   5

1. The 1945 Season Approaches   23
2. Jolly Cholly and His Over-the-Hill Gang Win the Pennant   31
3. The Defending World Champions   41
4. Controversy in Brooklyn   53
5. The Bucs Stop Here   61
6. The Giants Race to the Top of the Senior Circuit   67
7. The Braves Load Up and Fall Down   81
8. The Doleful Deacon and the Colorless Reds   91
9. Look Away: Ben Chapman and the Faltering Phils   102
10. The National League Campaign   113
11. Hammerin' Hank and the World Champion Tigers   150
12. War Heroes, Knuckleballers, and a Spy   172
13. The Spirit of St. Louis   190
14. Marse Joe and the Bronx Bombers   202
15. The Boy Manager and the Holdout   213
16. Jimmy Dykes and the Pale Hose   223
17. Catfish, Boo, and Mr. Yawkey   234
18. Connie Mack, Bobo, and the No-Hit Wonder   242

19. The American League Campaign	253
20. The World Series	289
21. Return to Normalcy	293
Appendix A. The National League Teams	295
Appendix B. The American League Teams	301
Chapter Notes	307
Bibliography	315
Index	319

Preface

World War II baseball conjures up images of ball games with a multitude of poor plays, played by men who should be retired or in the bush leagues, or possessing some physical ailment that prohibited them from serving their country in the military. But the game disintegrated neither entirely nor abruptly; it was a systematic decline and as pre-war major leaguers joined the armed forces in greater numbers every year, the quality of play declined until the final wartime season, 1945, when major league baseball was played at a level that resembled the bush leagues. This book examines World War II baseball by observing the 1945 season, when the quality of play was at its nadir. Major league baseball was the most distorted during that wartime season and is most representative of people's impressions of how wartime ball was played. The book examines the teams, players, pennant races, World Series, and the various obstacles that organized baseball had to overcome to continue operation.

The student of wartime ball will certainly be familiar with some of the stories in this book about players like Pete Gray and Bert Shepard. But he will most likely learn a great deal more about many of the other players, managers, teams, and games of the final wartime campaign. There are many details about players' backgrounds and careers that haven't been discussed in other books—players like Peanuts Lowrey, Red Schoendienst, Babe Herman, Clyde Sukeforth, Tommy Holmes, Jim Tobin, Red Barrett, Doc Cramer, George Case, Rick Ferrell, Paul Schreiber, Jeff Heath, Tony Cuccinello, Joe Cleary, Dave Ferriss and George "Catfish" Metkovich. The reader will also learn about the intimate details of the 1945 season such as when Connie Mack, the normally mild-mannered manager of the Philadelphia Athletics, tore into his team during spring training. Or how losing began to affect the health and decision-making of managers like Mel Ott and Joe McCarthy. The exhilarating pennant race in each league is thoroughly examined: The Chicago Cubs didn't secure the flag until the second to last day of the season; in the American League, the Tigers held off second-place Washington with a pennant-clinching victory on the season's final day. The 1945 World Series was sloppy but entertaining, just like the regular season that preceded it.

A number of obstacles had to be overcome for Major League Baseball simply to continue operating in 1945. There were, notably, various pressures and restrictions placed on the game by the government. One consequence of this was that games were occasionally postponed or halted because a team had to catch a train by curfew. A draft policy that discriminated against athletes who should have been classified 4-F had a deleterious affect on the game and depleted the rosters even more. And as the curtain rose on the 1945 campaign the country was still in mourning over the loss of President Franklin D. Roosevelt, one of the game's great supporters and the man who helped rally the country out of the Depression and through the tough times of the war. Opening Day, 1945, was not a day for celebration as the patrons at the various major league parks around the country took time to honor the former president. Fighting continued in Europe and in the Pacific, and it would be months before World War II would end. Despite the hardships in the country the game continued, and if it was played at a noticeably lower level than prewar standards, it provided the citizens with entertainment and a diversion from the more serious issues of the day. The institution of baseball and the United States itself were better off because the game continued during the war. To close down the national game would have adversely affected the psychological well-being of the nation and would have sent the wrong message to both the Nazis and Japanese. Furthermore, the servicemen abroad were in favor of baseball's continuation, and it gave them something to look forward to when they returned home. Organized baseball also helped aid the war effort in a number of ways, including raising funds, providing free tickets for servicemen, and collecting supplies.

There were many players in 1945 who if not for the war would likely never have played major league baseball. Players such as Jorge Comellas, John "Fats" Dantonio, Lefty Scott, Fred Daniels, Joe Buzas, Bob Maier, Walt Chipple, Fred Walters, Mike Milosevich, Bobby Wilkins, and Sandy Ullrich. There were old-timers, too, who came back during the war and played one last season in 1945 — men like Jimmie Foxx, Babe Herman, and Clyde Sukeforth. The rosters were so depleted that managers Leo Durocher of the Brooklyn Dodgers and Joe Cronin of the Boston Red Sox felt compelled to play despite being well past their prime. (Both men wrote their names in the Opening Day lineup, but neither one of them lasted more than three games.) Teenagers such as Granny Hamner, Tommy Brown, and Carl Scheib were getting an opportunity to play on big league diamonds, and so were youngsters like 22-year-old George Kell. The remaining prewar stars, players like Lou Boudreau and George Case, played with a various number of ailments, serving as a positive example for their teammates and helping their franchises at the gate. Players too old or too young to play big league ball under normal conditions helped the game move forward. So did the career minor leaguers and the 4-Fs and everyone else who put on a big league uniform in 1945.

This book is not the first to examine some aspect of World War II baseball, and it won't be the last, either. Many of the terrific books about wartime ball are listed in the bibliography. Each has made a significant contribution on the subject. I have relied on these and several other books, many of which only briefly take up, if at all, the subject of wartime ball. These histories, biographies, and memoirs provided a greater understanding of the players and managers of 1945. Books, articles, newspapers, and even Internet sites provided important information about the war's effect on the players, the fans, and Organized Baseball in general. It is hoped that the book will appeal both to the scholar of the game and to the general reader.

Introduction

By the fall of 1941, war clouds began to overshadow the United States. German U-boats had attacked U.S. vessels, and we had retaliated, but there was still no declaration of war. Everything changed on December 7, 1941, when the Japanese attacked Pearl Harbor and war no longer could be avoided. Baseball's future, like that of many other institutions, was uncertain. The baseball establishment heard the dreadful news in Chicago, where they had gathered for the winter meetings. Baseball pledged its "complete cooperation" to the war effort when National League President Ford Frick wired President Franklin Roosevelt on December 9. He ended his communication by saying, "We are yours to command."[1]

The baseball moguls had to look no further than what had transpired during World War I to become concerned. A paltry muster of under 100,000 men represented the regulars in the United States Army. To rectify the problem a draft was quickly enacted for males between the ages of twenty-one and thirty; later, those men between the ages of eighteen and forty-five were also considered. Few resisted the war, since patriotic fervor was running high, based in part on the romanticization of the Civil War in song and print. However, free speech was curtailed. Those who dared to criticize the war or the leaders of the country were jailed under the Espionage and Sedition Acts. One citizen observed, "It became criminal to advocate heavier taxation instead of bond issues, to state that conscription was unconstitutional though the Supreme Court had not yet held it valid, to say that the sinking of merchant vessels was legal, to urge that a referendum should have preceded our declaration of war, to say that war was contrary to the teachings of Christ."[2] By the end of World War I approximately 1,300,000 Americans were involved in combat and many of them participated in the horrific trench warfare. More Americans would die of disease (57,000) than would die in combat (49,000). While over 100,000 American soldiers perished in the conflict, another 230,000 were wounded.

Hank Gowdy, the Boston Braves catcher, was the first ballplayer to enlist in World War I in June of 1917. He fought in some of the war's bloodiest battles, at Chateau-Thierry, St. Mihiel, and in the Argonne. The 1917 season ran uninterrupted with only a few players going off to war. The following season was a different story altogether. Baseball came under criticism for allowing fit men to play a boys' game while the slaughter continued in Europe. For the 1918 season, 140 games were scheduled, but only about 126 were completed by each team as the season ended on Labor Day. Attendance dropped by over two million in 1918, with only 3,080,126 customers going through the turnstiles. Twelve of the minor leagues were terminated by the 1918 season; only nine started, with the International League the only one to complete its season. On May 23, 1918, the federal government declared it was time for fit men to "work or fight."[3] A deadline was set for July 1 for able-bodied men to find employment in war-related jobs or be subject to the draft. Baseball was declared to be a "nonessential occupation."[4] The baseball owners asked that the players be exempted until October 15, but they only received an extension until September 1. However, none of the players from the Cubs or Red Sox were drafted so that they could have a competitive World Series.

Trouble surrounded the series. The Cubs and Red Sox players came together and threatened to strike, objecting to the dwindling World Series share, which would be the smallest ever. Attendance was abysmal and the players would receive a percentage of the gate, but they had been promised a winner's and loser's share of $2,000 and $1,400 respectively before the series. During the 1918 winter meetings, the owners agreed to a new distribution system for allocating World Series funds. However, the players were not consulted about this decision and therefore their opinions were disregarded. The two teams refused to take the field for batting practice in game five as dumbfounded Fenway Park patrons grew increasingly perturbed. The player representatives of the Red Sox (Harry Hooper and Dave Shean) and the Cubs (Les Mann and Bill Killefer) handled the negotiations. They argued that their unpopular stance was based on fairness and not greed. They attempted to get the owners to yield to their demands by threatening not to finish the series and even suggested giving their entire share to the Red Cross. The owners were unswayed by their threats since the laws governing baseball gave the owners almost unlimited power to do what they wanted. Furthermore, the players' stance was anathema to the business of baseball and therefore quickly dismissed. The players finally succumbed and took the field one hour after the scheduled start of the game. They finally realized that their demands would not be met: the owners were against them, they had very few rights under the laws of the game, the newspapermen were sympathetic with the owners' position, and therefore the fans were also against them.

The patrons were disgusted by a statement that was read on the players' behalf. They would play, "not because we think we are getting a fair deal, because we are not." They were playing for the fans who have "always given us ... loyal support, and for the wounded soldiers and sailors who are in the grandstand waiting for us." Baseball writers attacked the players as "mercenary-minded" and "devoid of reason," and said their actions were "downright stupid." William Phelon, editor of *Baseball Magazine*, wrote, "Interest in Boston seemed to evaporate after the players' strike." He continued, "The fans didn't seem to be with the noble athletes," who were "dead lucky" to receive any money at all.[5] The Red Sox won the World Series that year, but they would have to wait 86 years before they won their next World Series championship.

During the deadball era, gamblers were intimately close with the players, and the outcomes of many games came under suspicion. There have been dark clouds over the 1918 World Series because of speculation that the World Series was fixed. Allan Wood argues this in his book, *1918: Babe Ruth and the World Champion Boston Red Sox*, as he provides a chapter that raises questions about the Series' legitimacy. It has been written of Ban Johnson, the president of the American League, that he "had information that a professional gambler planned to fix the 1918 World Series between the Cubs and Red Sox but dropped the idea of an investigation when he was unable to raise sufficient funds to carry it out." Furthermore, Harry Grabiner, who was Charles Comiskey's secretary, suggests in his diary that the 1918 Series was fixed. Although concentrating primarily on activities after the 1919 World Series, Grabiner also provides a list of players who may have thrown games at the tail end of the 1920 season, thereby helping the Cleveland Indians win the pennant. Grabiner wrote "1918 Series fixer" next to the name Gene Packard. Packard had played with the Cubs during the 1916 campaign and for two games in 1917 and therefore knew several of their players well. Three of the Red Sox players who were on the 1918 squad would be suspected of undermining the integrity of major league baseball through alleged gambling and game-fixing activities in later years.[6] The National Pastime was a dying sport and an investigation would cripple it. The following year's fix was exposed in the World Series between the Chicago White Sox and Cincinnati Reds.

The gambling problem was exacerbated during the war when racetracks closed down and the gamblers flocked to the ballparks and the seeds of the Black Sox scandal of 1919 were sown. Christy Mathewson, the Reds manager, accused Hal Chase of throwing games in 1918. Charges were dropped despite the fact that three Reds players supported Mathewson's story. Fred Lieb once wrote of Chase, "Trouble always followed in his wake. It was an ill day for baseball when his name first appeared in a box-score."[7] Chase's charming personality belied his corrupt soul. Bill James wrote that his legacy is that "one man could so alter the ethics of the sport."[8]

World War I's impact on organized baseball was devastating and included some public relations disasters. One such was when Chicago Cubs pitcher Harry Weaver requested a deferment from his draft board based on the fact that "we have a good chance to win the pennant."[9] Jake Daubert of the Brooklyn Dodgers objected to the shortened season, claiming it was a violation of his contract.

Major League baseball, Daubert argued, could have finished the 1918 season with those players who were outside draft age.[10]

Many of baseball's stars served in the military during World War I, including Herb Pennock, Sam Rice, Harry Heilmann, Eddie Collins, Jimmy Dykes, and Rabbit Maranville. Two of the game's best pitchers suffered the most devastating maladies: Christy Mathewson and Grover Cleveland Alexander. Mathewson's lungs were permanently damaged when he inhaled poison gas. Alexander found himself hugging the earth in France, praying to God that one of the forty-six-pound shells flung by German howitzers would not land on him. His battalion was caught in the trenches as the Germans unleashed a hellish bombardment. The earth vibrated violently as the shells hit the ground. Alexander was scarred by the experience for the rest of his life, deaf in one ear, a broken man who was prone to drinking.

So with the disturbing precedent of World War I, the baseball owners had reason to worry as they heard the devastating news of Pearl Harbor in Chicago. The uncertainty lasted for weeks. Judge Kenesaw Mountain Landis, the commissioner of baseball, who had ruled baseball with dictatorial efficiency, made his move. He was a staunch conservative who in his days as a judge was famous for trying communists and socialists. His word was law and he feared no one. Landis even took on the Standard Oil Company of Indiana and fined them the exorbitant amount of $29,240,000 when they accepted rebates or bribes from the Chicago and Alton Railroad. When the case was appealed to the Supreme Court, the decision was overturned and the fine dismissed. Like many conservatives he despised Roosevelt and referred to him as "that bastard in the White House."[11] On January 15, 1942, he swallowed his pride and sent a note to the president saying in part:

> Baseball is about to adopt schedules, sign players, make vast commitments, go to training camps. What do you want it to do? If you believe we ought to close down for the duration of the war, we are ready to do so immediately.... We await your order.[12]

Two days later Roosevelt provided baseball with the "green light" to continue, saying, "I honestly feel that it would be best for the country to keep baseball going. There will be fewer people unemployed and everybody will work longer hours and harder than ever before. And that means that they ought to have a chance for recreation and for taking their minds off their work even more than before...."[13]

The real impetus behind the "green light" letter was said to be Washington Senators owner Clark Griffith and Robert Hannegan, the chairman of the Democratic National Committee and postmaster general in the president's cabinet. Griffith would visit the White House every year to give Roosevelt his opening-day pass, and they developed a good friendship. He encouraged the president to order teams to play more night games, a controversial subject during the times. Roosevelt followed Griffith's suggestion, stating that it would allow those who worked during the day to see a game occasionally.

One of the ancillary effects of World War II was the abandonment of the St. Louis Browns' plans to move to Los Angeles. The Browns went to the league meetings in Chicago expecting to have their plan formally ratified. Their attendance problem was atrocious; at the tail end of the 1933 season they attracted only 34 paying customers to a game. In 1935 they drew fewer than 81,000 fans to Sportsman's Park. The St. Louis Cardinals in contrast drew 506,084 spectators to their ball games during the 1935 campaign. Facilities were poor, and with no air conditioning in the steamy midwest park, the clubhouse resembled a sauna. The infield quickly became worn out since they shared the park with the National League Cardinals; it resembled a "dust bowl by July."[14] One fan recalled, "Before leaving the stadium, we had to visit the rest room. I distinctly remember thinking that the rest room smelled exactly like the elephant house at the St. Louis zoo."[15] The Browns pushed for increased night games in order to improve attendance, but many organizations thought that if they also had to construct light posts it would escalate costs significantly. It was also thought that the bright lights would perhaps impair the eyesight of the players. With travel restrictions being implemented, the Browns found their West Coast plan to be dead in the water.

Fourteen months before Pearl Harbor, American males between the ages of twenty-one and thirty-five were required to register with the Selective Service. Shortly after, on November 18, 1940, the draft numbers of Hugh Mulcahy, a tough-luck pitcher with the Philadelphia Phillies, and Hank Greenberg, the Detroit Tigers slugger, were chosen. The Phillies program in 1942 showed Mulcahy producing a "V for victory" symbol with two bats. He lost five years in the prime of his career to be in the service. Greenberg's presence would be missed in the Tigers lineup as they dropped from a first-place conclusion in 1940 to a fourth-place tie in 1941. Mulcahy was the first major league player to be inducted into the military, on March 8, 1941, when he showed up at Camp Edwards in Massachusetts. Then on May 7, Greenberg was also inducted after starting the 1941 campaign with the Tigers, batting .269 in 19 games. Of the nearly 5,000 players in the minor leagues only 193 of them were in the service by August of '41. Only three other major leaguers joined Mulcahy and Greenberg in the service in 1941. Therefore the quality of play remained very high. Each wartime season saw the talent on the field become worse and worse, culminating in 1945 when it was abhorrent. That final year was particularly bad because James F. Byrnes, director of the Office of War Mobilization, loosened the draft-eligibility standards and began drafting those players who were previously classified as 4-F.

While the healthy ballplayers were plucked by the military, the baseball owners filled their teams' uniforms with those who were too old or too young to be drafted and players who had some kind of disability and were labeled 4-

F. Several baseball stars of the 1930s came back and prolonged their careers with one more moment in the sun. They included Paul and Lloyd Waner, Stan Hack, Jimmie Foxx, Paul Derringer, Ernie Lombardi, Chuck Klein, Al Lopez, and Billy Jurges. Other old-timers were not exactly household names, like 42-year-old Clay Touchstone of the White Sox, 44-year-old Joe Heving of the Braves, and 46-year-old Hod Lisenbee of the Reds.

The youngsters included Art Houtteman, Billy Pierce, Cass Michaels, Ed Yost, Ralph Branca, and Granny Hamner. The most famous of these kids was Joe Nuxhall, the left-handed Cincinnati Reds hurler, who was only 15 years old when he toed the pitching slab in June of '44 at Crosley Field in his major-league debut. He lasted only two-thirds of an inning and left with a 67.50 ERA in his only appearance of the season. Nuxhall would not return to the majors until 1952 and went on to have a solid sixteen-year big league career, finishing with a 135–117 record and a 3.90 ERA. Tommy Brown of the Dodgers and Carl Scheib of the Philadelphia Athletics were only 16 years old.

The 4-Fs suffered from varying ailments: Curt Davis had an ulcer, Jack Kramer had asthma, Ted Wilks had stomach problems, Bill Voiselle had difficulty hearing, Mike Garbark had a hernia, Hal Newhouser and Russ Christopher both had heart problems, Red Schoendienst had vision problems, Paul Richards and Marty Marion had trick knees, Frank Mancuso had back problems, and Tom Sunkel and Jack Franklin were both blind in one eye. The pugnacious Leo Durocher had a punctured eardrum that he developed when he was hit in the head with a pitched ball in 1933. The *New York Daily News* declared, "LEO HAS HOLE IN HEAD." Dick Sipek, an outfielder with the Cincinnati Reds in 1945, was totally deaf, the first such player to play in the big leagues since William "Dummy" Hoy and Luther "Dummy" Taylor. He did not receive as much publicity as Pete Gray and did not attract as many fans to come through the turnstiles, but managed to hit .244 in 82 games. The most famous of the 4-Fs was Pete Gray, a one-armed outfielder with the St. Louis Browns in 1945. He batted .218 in 77 games, but some of his teammates thought that he held them back from winning another pennant in 1945. "To the fans," *Newsweek* reported, "Pete Gray is more than a one-armed player in the majors. To them, he seems the symbol of the disabled serviceman."[16]

Before Jackie Robinson smashed the color line in 1947 there were other ballplayers of dark pigmentation and African descent who clandestinely played major league baseball. Whether one was given the opportunity to play in the big leagues was largely determined by if he was light-skinned or dark-skinned. Such was the case with Cubans Dolf Luque and Martin Dihigo: Luque, due to his light skin, was allowed to play in the big leagues, while Dihigo, a dark-skinned Cuban, was banished to the Negro Leagues. Luque was known for his hot temper and endured unconscionable abuse: opposing teams taunted him with jeers of "Cuban nigger," and he retaliated with beanballs at their skull.[17] The beanball was also used strategically to force a plate-hugging hitter to move

Introduction

away from the dish. When facing Luque, the hitter had a dilemma: if he crowded the plate he may get a beanball or brushback pitch delivered his way, and if he didn't crowd the plate he didn't stand much of a chance of getting a hit.

Luque's major league career spanned from 1914 to 1935 and he compiled a lifetime 194–179 record with a 3.24 ERA. During this era in baseball, beanball pitchers were ubiquitous around the majors, and every good pitcher knew he needed to pitch inside to become successful. Unfortunately, when Luque did throw at batters and pitch inside it prompted the racially insensitive writers who followed him to portray him as an emotional, hot-blooded, violent and unintelligent pitcher. This was despite the fact that he was abused physically and verbally by opposing players during his career because his skin wasn't the right color for the bigots in the game. The number of batters a pitcher hit is not always a good indication of how often a pitcher threw inside. This is because if a pitcher has a reputation of throwing at hitters and pitching inside, then the batter may be reluctant to dig a proper toehold in the batter's box and may have his foot in the bucket, preparing himself to bail once the ball is delivered in his direction. But consider that Luque hit only 26 batters in his career, while Burleigh Grimes, who also had a reputation as a beanball pitcher, and played during the same time period as Luque (from 1916 to 1934), hit 101.

When Luque died in July 1957, Frank Graham reflected eloquently on Luque's career in *The Sporting News*. He found it hard to believe that Luque died of a heart attack because he was a clutch pitcher and his heart never failed him before. Luque was strong, durable and determined. He was a thinking man's pitcher who was a great competitor but who also had a "fierce temper." Graham wrote he "would have been at a loss" pitching in 1957, "when a pitcher must not hit a batter on purpose."[18] For Graham to suggest that pitchers did not intentionally hit batters anymore was an indication of how frequent the beanball and brushback were utilized during Luque's career in the major leagues. In 1957 there were still plenty of beanball pitchers around, including Sal Maglie, who learned how to become an effective pitcher from Luque.

When Clark Griffith was manager of the Cincinnati Reds prior to World War I he signed "olive-skinned flychasers" Armando Marsans and Rafael Almeida.[19] They were both considered dark-skinned and their presence caused great controversy in Cincinnati. With major league baseball in desperate need of talent during World War II, Griffith, now the Washington Senators' owner, sent scout Joe Cambria to comb Cuba for talent. Griffith was a frugal man who knew he could pay the Cubans and other Latin American players low wages, and he hoped that they would not become eligible for the draft. His finds included Camilo Pascual, Bobby Estalella, and Roberto Ortiz. Many of these players knew little English, had difficulty adjusting to America, and were flooded with racial epithets and beanballs at their heads. It was even rumored that Griffith had his players sign affidavits, attesting to their "racial purity," that they were Hispanic and were not African-Americans.[20]

Dark-skinned pitcher Tommy de la Cruz pitched for the Cincinnati Reds during the war, compiling a 9–9 record with a 3.25 ERA in 1944. Cruz was of African descent, prompting Pittsburgh Pirate scout Howie Haak to say, "Hell, Tommy de la Cruz was as black as they came!"[21] Despite his considerable talent, Cruz never pitched in the show after that season as owners around the majors criticized the Reds for hiring what appeared to be a black man, while the Reds tried to deny such allegations. Hi Bithorn pitched for the wartime Chicago Cubs in 1942 and 1943. In '43 he was 18–12 with a 2.60 ERA. Fred Lieb once wrote that he "might be entitled to be called the first black player to appear in a big league uniform."[22] Bithorn died mysteriously in El Mante, Mexico, on January 1, 1952. One story said he got into an altercation with a police officer who shot him, while another story rumored that he was a member of a communist cell when his important mission went terribly wrong.[23]

Ironically, at a time when the owners used light-skinned blacks, old-timers, teenagers, and the disabled, they still refused to tap the abundant talent of the Negro Leagues. The Negro Leagues prospered during the war since their players were less affected by the military draft. Many of the teams showed a profit for the first time. Leo Durocher observed that he had seen "a million good colored players," and would welcome them on his team if white ownership did not blacklist them. Commissioner Landis warned Durocher that such remarks were unacceptable.[24] The black press pressured baseball to integrate and occasionally were successful in getting the Negro League players to try out for big league teams, but with the outcome already negatively predetermined before they stepped on the field. Such was the case in April 1945 when the Red Sox gave a tryout to Jackie Robinson, Sam Jethroe, and Marvin Williams. As they went through their workout a voice echoed from the grandstand: "Get those niggers off the field!"[25]

Several of major league baseball's big stars set examples for military service, including Hank Greenberg, Bob Feller, Ted Williams, Harry Walker, and Stan Musial. Hank Greenberg had been discharged by the army on December 5, 1941. The Japanese attacked Pearl Harbor two days later and Greenberg reenlisted on December 9. He was determined to fight dictatorial regimes as they spread around the world while confronting racism at home. Greenberg declared, "We are in trouble and there is only one thing for me to do — return to the service." He continued, "This doubtless means I am finished with baseball, and it would be silly for me to say I do not leave it without a pang. But all of us are confronted with a terrible task — the defense of our country and the fight for our lives."[26] The country needed heroes like Greenberg early in the war when things did not go America's way.

He had played during the Depression years when anger and desperation filled the populace. Spectators took their frustrations to the ballparks and anticipated violent outbursts on and off the field. At a time when salaries were cut, ballplayers were lucky to have jobs and would do anything to keep them. A strong anti–Semitic undercurrent swept the country like a volcanic tide. Yankee outfielder Ben Chapman gave Nazi salutes to fans and umpires[27] and called the taunting fans at the Stadium, "Fucking Jew bastards."[28] Greenberg found himself in the center of the storm, enduring anti–Semitic remarks, particularly in 1938 when he challenged Babe Ruth's sacrosanct home run record. Opposing players and fans called him "Kike,"[29] "Jew bastard," and "Christ killer."[30] He had been given the opportunity to do nonlethal jobs in the military such as entertain the troops by playing ball, but after spending a significant amount of time out of harm's way, he demanded combat duty. Greenberg transferred to the Army Air Corps and spent time in China and India. When a B-29 was impaired he tried to help the crew but was blown off his feet as a bomb exploded. Luckily no one died; as he told reporter Arthur Daley of the *New York Times*, it "was one occasion when I didn't wonder whether or not I'd be able to return to baseball. I was quite satisfied to be alive."[31]

The farm boy from America's heartland, Bob Feller, also enlisted two days after Pearl Harbor despite having a draft deferment. He was in charge of an anti-aircraft crew on the USS *Alabama*, a massive 35,000-ton battleship. In December of 1942 he left the United States and did not return until April of 1945. In 1944 the *Alabama* provided anti-aircraft protection for carriers in the South Pacific. In a bloody battle in Saipan, the battleship was nearly hit by torpedoes, bombs, and kamikaze pilots. Feller worked out incessantly on the ship, keeping himself in shape, and when they went ashore he loosened up his thunderous arm. When he returned in the spring of '45 he played ball at the Great Lakes Naval Station.

Ted Williams, the real-life John Wayne, also had a draft deferment. He was in a situation similar to Feller's, supporting his divorced mother, and was classified 3-A in 1943. Before leaving for the war his major league batting average was .356. He hit .406 in 1941 and won the Triple Crown in 1942. He was young, full of confidence, some would say arrogant, but he could back up his cockiness with results. The fans taunted him without mercy, and he took what they said personally. Williams feuded with the press, especially Dave Egan of the *Boston Record*. Stubbornly he refused to tip his cap to the fans, saying, "Never, never will I tip my cap to those damned New England buzzards."[32]

His discipline at the plate was unmatched, as he refused to swing at balls out of the strike zone or hit the ball the other way when the infielders shifted to the right side. Williams's fielding was suspect, partially due to lack of effort. The memory of Pete Reiser running into rock-solid outfield walls haunted him, and he assured everyone that he would not get "killed" for some fly ball.[33] His volatile temper would often explode, and occasionally he would spit at fans or give them the finger. Many characterized him as being selfish and he was not considered to be a team player. Some thought his selfishness was directly correlated to the Red Sox' inability to win several pennants and a World Series championship while he was there. Moe Berg said, "The truth is Williams is a choker."[34]

Williams enlisted after the 1942 season, tired of the press who questioned his patriotism. "If I can make a success of flying, I'd just as soon stay in service — provided I could get a month off once in a while to go hunting," he said.[35] Williams joined the Navy and spent most of the war as a flight instructor in Florida. He missed three seasons while in the service during World War II. In 1952 he rejoined and saw combat during the Korean War, where his plane was shot down and he made a miraculous landing to the amazement of everyone. Despite his abundant patriotism and his willingness to give his life to his country, the fans and the press still attacked him. Dave Egan personalized his attacks in his column in order to boost circulation. Before leaving for Korea, Williams was honored at Fenway Park, and Egan wrote a disapproving column that said in part:

> It seems disgraceful to me that a person such as Williams now is to be given the keys to the city. We talk about juvenile delinquency, and fight against it, and then officially honor a man whom we should officially horsewhip, for the vicious influence that he has had on the childhood of America....[36]

This is a rather unseemly observation of a war hero.

After leading the St. Louis Cardinals to the World Series in 1943, Harry Walker was inducted into the Army. Sent to Fort Riley, Kansas, where he expected to play ball, instead he developed spinal meningitis and almost lost his life. When he recovered he went to Europe, and saw action during the Battle of the Bulge. Then his reconnaissance unit penetrated deep into Bavaria as the Germans were fighting their last desperate battles. They were ordered to hold a bridge against a German offensive. He was accustomed to patrolling the outer garden at Sportsman's Park but now he found himself on point in a Jeep with two machine guns to shoot the enemy. Walker recalled, "I just cut through the whole mess, and they were scattered everywhere, firing back and forth at you, and you're just out there on point like a sitting duck."[37] He saw the horrors created by Adolf Hitler, visiting an internment camp and observing its assembly-line butchery. "We saw people slaughtered like animals. We buried them by the hundreds.... We do not know what suffering is like."[38] When the Germans surrendered he was ordered to form a baseball team to entertain the troops. A ball field was built in Linz, and another one in the Nuremberg stadium where Hitler staged his massive rallies to propagandize his death machine. Now American GIs watched America's national pastime in this former bastion of hatred.

St. Louis Cardinals star Stan Musial led his team to consecutive pennants in 1943 and 1944 before being drafted. He was assigned to ship repair in Hawaii, which provided him the opportunity to play ball several times a week while a huge group of sailors looked on. Pete Reiser had pleaded with him to join the Army's Fort Riley team in Kansas. Instead he chose the Navy, serving for fourteen months. Musial recalled that many of those players at Fort Riley, "like

Harry Walker, Murry Dickson, Al Brazle, and Peter Reiser ... ended up in the Battle of the Bulge."[39]

As a player no one represented the mentality of a soldier on the field more than Pete Reiser did. The sickening image of him lying unconscious after running into the outfield wall was emblematic of his career. Eleven times he was carried off the field on a stretcher; nine times he regained consciousness in the clubhouse or hospital. He came back for more, took vicious beanballs in the head, and his remarkable talent disintegrated. Leo Durocher said, "Pete Reiser had everything but luck."[40] In the Army he led three teams to a championship and always played those games hard, as if he where standing in the outer garden at Ebbets Field. He was ambidextrous: in one game he damaged his right shoulder and threw with his left. When he returned from the Army the tragedy continued. In a June 4, 1947, game against the Pittsburgh Pirates, he met the wall again, his head striking violently. He lay stricken until he was again carried off the field. Dick Young of the *New York Daily News* described what happened: "I ran downstairs to the clubhouse and into the trainer's room where Doc Wendler, the team trainer, was examining Pete. Soon, the team doctor arrived, and then a priest. I don't suppose another ballplayer ever has received last rites in a ballpark, and that must be Reiser's distinction, instead of inclusion in Cooperstown."[41]

Many other players saw fighting overseas. Cecil Travis gave four years to the Army. He left his major league career at the Battle of the Bulge, suffering frostbite which essentially ended his career. John Grodzicki, a Cardinals pitching prospect, injured his right leg, impairing his baseball abilities. Many minor leaguers fought as well; some, like Augie Donatelli, could no longer play ball effectively after serving. His B-17 was among those that raided Berlin in March of '44. His plane was hit, and forced to evacuate, he broke his leg on the fall. He faced hard times in two different prison camps. He was beaten, tried to escape unsuccessfully, and when liberated weighed 130 pounds. Upon returning to the States he decided to become an umpire and eventually became one in the National League. His fate was much better than minor league pitcher Forrest "Lefty" Brewer. Brewer went to England to prepare for the D-day invasion as part of the 508th Parachute Infantry Regiment. He was among the 24,000 Allied paratroopers who parachuted into France to begin the invasion of Europe on June 5, 1944. The men he was with helped capture a road and fought for approximately eleven hours before they were overrun by Germans. As he ran for the Merderet River, he was hit by machine gun fire and was said to have died instantly.

Three of the most inspiring stories were those of Bert Shepard, Lou Brissie, and Phil Marchildon. Shepard played in the minors before the war, with the Chicago White Sox organization. In March of '44 his P-38 fighter was shot down north of Berlin, and by the time he awoke, the German doctors had already amputated his right leg. Shortly afterward, he was fitted with a wooden foot and began tossing the ball around in the prison camp. He was part of a prisoner exchange and soon found himself in Walter Reed Hospital in Washington, D.C. His intentions of playing ball again became known and Clark Griffith offered him a tryout. George Case later recalled, after Shepard played in a regular season game, "Bert was pretty damn good, it was amazing. He realized he was exploited to a certain degree, but he was grateful."[42] Shepard was kept on as a batting practice pitcher and worked in exhibition games, and there was that one major league game. In five and one-third innings against the Red Sox in early August of '45, he gave up one run on three hits. His ERA stands at 1.69 in the *Baseball Encyclopedia*. Shepard was an inspiration to disabled veterans that their dreams could be accomplished.

Lou Brissie had agreed to play for the Philadelphia Athletics after attending a Presbyterian college, but in December of 1942 he enlisted in the Army. Two years later he saw bloody combat with the paratroopers in northern Italy. The conditions were abysmal: soldiers situated in the valley had to walk through mud that often went up to their knees and made it almost impossible to keep dry. The thousands of soldiers in the mountains dealt with freezing temperatures and snowdrifts. On December 7, 1944, Brissie's squad had returned to the front lines after getting a brief respite from combat. But they got a harsh welcome back as shells began raining down from the sky. A shell exploded near Brissie, tearing his left leg open. He suffered two broken feet, his left leg was injured severely between the knee and ankle, his left ankle was injured, and his hands and shoulders were also damaged. He suffered shrapnel wounds all over his body and successfully persuaded the doctors not to amputate his leg. Twenty-three operations would follow. The recovery was long and strenuous, and after going through several army hospitals he was released in April of 1946, with his leg intact, but with a noticeable limp and a cane to assist him as he walked. The doctors didn't believe he would play baseball at a competitive level again, but he found one at the Greenville Shriner's hospital who helped him achieve his baseball goals. Through great perseverance he would make it to the big show: his best seasons were 1948 and 1949 when he compiled records of 14–10 and 16–11 for the Athletics. The 6' 4", 215-pound southpaw from South Carolina completed his seven-year big league career with a 44–48 record and a 4.07 ERA while pitching for the Athletics and Indians.

In 1942 Phil Marchildon went 17–14 for the Athletics and then he joined the Royal Canadian Air Force. He was a tail gunner in a bomber. In August of 1944 his plane was shot down. It looked like the end had come as he swam for four hours in Kiel Bay, Denmark, before a fisherman pulled him to safety. Marchildon was sent to a Nazi POW camp in Poland, where his health deteriorated because of the poor conditions and lack of food. Five of his crew members had died. He returned to the States in atrocious shape in 1945. Connie Mack held "Marchildon Night" at Shibe Park, where 35,000 fans watched him struggle through three innings.[43] The Athletics were a last-place team during the final wartime season, struggling to draw fans to the ballpark, and finishing last in the American League in attendance (462,631). Bringing Marchildon back to pitch was a sure way for Connie Mack to have a large crowd and make some money. When coach Al Simmons got a look at Marchildon he was adamant that the pitcher should not be exploited because he needed to recuperate and was in no shape to pitch in a major league game. But Mack wanted to honor the right-handed pitcher and also get a big payday. In the pregame ceremony Marchildon was given a $1,000 war bond and then he took the hill. He couldn't stop fidgeting and had what some called "war nerves."[44] The war hero stood in the center of the diamond, malnourished, changed by combat, shaking uncontrollably. It was a courageous effort until he left the game with a pulled groin muscle. Marchildon would rebound and have a 13–16 season the following year with a 3.49 ERA, and in 1947 he was even better at 19–9 with a 3.22 ERA. In 1948 he dropped to 9–15 with a 4.53 ERA. He then pitched in only eight more big league games during the 1949 and 1950 campaigns, finishing his nine-year career with a 68–75 record and a 3.93 ERA.

During the war, when nonessential travel was cut, Joseph B. Eastman, director of the Office of Defense Transportation, asked major league baseball to do its part. Commissioner Landis responded by ordering major league teams to locate their spring training sites east of the Mississippi River and north of the Ohio and Potomac Rivers, except for the two St. Louis teams, who were allowed to train in Missouri. So beginning in 1943 and lasting through 1945, the majors abandoned the comforts of the South for the difficult Northern climate. The Boston teams would train in the frigid New England weather during the 1943 and 1944 seasons before escaping to a slightly less hostile climate in 1945. The Red Sox prepared for the 1943 and 1944 seasons at Tufts College in Medford, Massachusetts, and then stayed in Atlantic City, New Jersey, in 1945 while doing much of their training in the adjacent town of Pleasantville. Boston's National League representative trained at the Choate Prep School in Wallingford, Connecticut, in 1943 and 1944, and then trained on the campus of Georgetown University in Washington, D.C., during the 1945 spring training season. The Dodgers trained at Bear Mountain, New York, the Giants at Lakewood, New Jersey, and the Yankees at Asbury Park, New Jersey, and then Atlantic City in 1944 and 1945. The Athletics were in Wilmington, Delaware, in 1943, and then moved to Frederick, Maryland, for the final two wartime training camps. The Phillies prepared for the 1943 campaign in Hershey, Pennsylvania, and then moved to Wilmington, Delaware. The Senators spent all three seasons on the campus of the University of Maryland. Several clubs found training camps in Indiana: the Cubs, White Sox, Reds, Indians, Tigers, and Pirates. And the St. Louis teams stayed in or close to Missouri: the Cardinals in Cairo, Illinois, and the Browns in Cape Girardeau, Missouri.

The facilities were often poor and the weather dreadful. Knowing that Americans were risking their lives in battle, players were discouraged from complaining. In 1943, the New York–New Jersey area experienced its coldest winter in years. *The Sporting News* reported that the Giants Carl Hubbell "did nothing in Lakewood but play Ping-Pong."[45] After the season Hubbell announced he was retiring as a player, refusing to train his arm in the frigid North. Many of the fields were flooded and players were forced to train indoors. For others it was simply too cold to go outside. Teams lucky enough to have an indoor batting cage were ahead of the competition. Billy Southworth, the Cardinals manager, said, "We're making the best of it, but a wooden gymnasium floor is no place to prepare to play baseball. I admit I'm relieved each time we get out of a crowded gym with all the players intact."[46] One of the reasons major league baseball chose to train in the North was to avoid having their players look pampered. As commissioner Landis declared, "I do not propose to have athletes lolling about on the sands in some semitropical climate."[47]

Wartime restrictions brought about rationing on tires, cars, sugar, gasoline, rubber, fuel oil, shoes, etc. Players were no longer provided private railroad cars and the menus were lacking in beef. With restrictions on wool, leather, and rubber, the baseballs became less resilient and inferior. The infamous "balata ball" was used for a short period during the 1943 season. The core was made of granulated cork and tests by the Cooper Union Institute of Technology found that it was 25.9 percent less resilient than the previous year's ball.[48]

Early in the war U-boats were torpedoing U.S. ships, leading to a coastal "dim-out" or "black-out" on April 28, 1942. To hinder German submarine activity the "dim-out" stretched along a 15-mile strip of the Atlantic coast.[49] U.S. tankers were usually targeted at night and it was believed that the bright lights made them more visible and more vulnerable to attack. Lights were allowed to be used at the Polo Grounds and Ebbets Field for only one hour as darkness approached. *The Sporting News* reported, "Army officials decided that the glare would invite trouble at sea and perhaps guide some suicide flier bearing a grim message from Dizzy Adolf...." The New York Giants and Brooklyn Dodgers decided to schedule "twilight" games for what was originally supposed to be a night game.[50] Twilight games started late in the afternoon and ended under the lights.

With nonessential travel cut, the public was encouraged to walk or take public transportation to games. Fans were asked to give blood. Clubs encouraged them to bring scrap iron, grease, old newspapers, cardboard boxes, and other items that could help the war effort to the park. When the Dodgers held "Kitchen Fat Day" in July '43, 4,512 women contributed 5,002 pounds of grease. In return for their generosity they were allowed to watch the ballgame for free.[51] The minor league Louisville Colonels held "Waste Fat Night," while the Cincinnati Reds held a "Smokes for Service Men" game. To gain entry into the ballpark, patrons had to donate cigarettes instead of producing a ticket.[52]

Servicemen in uniform were often allowed in free. Fans were told to throw back baseballs. When a fan refused his patriotic duty at Ebbets Field, the *New*

York Times reported, "Another pugnacious patriot threatened to punch him. Eventually the ball was returned after several ushers had kept the would-be combatants apart."[53] From 1942 to 1944 each major league team donated the proceeds from one home game to the Army and Navy relief funds. In 1942 they collectively raised $506,000, in 1943 it was $326,500, and $328,500 in 1944. A second All-Star game was held in 1942 to give the profits to war charities: the American League defeated the senior circuit, 3–1, on July 6 to earn the right to play Mickey Cochrane's Service All-Stars in Cleveland the following night. The American League won again, 5–0, as a paid crowd of 62,094 showed up to help raise over $100,000 for the Army-Navy Relief Fund and for the Ball and Bat Fund. War Bond All-Star teams were created to compete against Army baseball stars and raise even more money.

The Navy and Army put together baseball teams to entertain troops at home and overseas. Navy powerhouses were assembled at Norfolk, Virginia; Great Lakes, Illinois; and Pearl Harbor, Hawaii. The Army, however, dispersed its talent more widely and therefore its teams were not as potent. Baseball was also played in some of the more benevolent prisoner of war camps overseas.

Attendance dropped substantially during the war years. In 1940 major league attendance was 9.8 million, but by 1943 it reached a low of 7.5 million before rebounding the following two years with attendance figures of 8.8 million and 10.8 million respectively. Talent was more evenly dispersed around the majors, and some of the perennial losers like the St. Louis Browns and the Washington Senators became competitive. The Browns actually won the American League pennant in 1944 with an 89–65 record. Many of the minor league circuits were forced to shut down operations during the war.

The ballparks were resplendent with patriotic fervor. War heroes were honored before games as tanks and other military equipment were paraded. Patriotic songs were played, "The Star Spangled Banner" was performed before every game.[54] War Bonds and War Stamps were sold at the ballpark. Many Americans worked through the night in war plants producing weapons for overseas. To accommodate them, mid-morning games were scheduled. A lot of these games drew respectable crowds, like the 11,129 who showed up to see the second division Phillies host the Pittsburgh Pirates in an August '43 doubleheader. The game started at 10:30 A.M.

In the book, *Baseball Goes to War*, which is best known under its original title, *Even the Browns*, William Mead wrote, "Patriotic jingoism was the language of the day." Organized baseball identified itself with the war effort more than any other institution. Baseball officials and those who wrote about the game were eager to promote it as being uniquely American, an institution that the soldiers were fighting abroad to defend. Baseball was often referred to as the "national pastime," and that term was fully embraced by baseball officials, perhaps more than ever before. Mead wrote, "This stance contained an element of self-interest bordering on desperation." Major League officials and owners felt like they had to fully support the war effort by engaging in fund raising activities and other endeavors because otherwise they may be viewed as a frivolous and nonessential institution and perhaps be shut down, resulting in irreparable damage to the sport. Baseball provided a morale boost to the country and a recreational activity that Americans could fully embrace and be proud of.[55]

The Sporting News propagandized the plight of organized baseball in print. Hyperbole was rampant, with writers like Dan Daniel all too willing to compare the heated competition that took place on the diamond to military combat. An article by Dan Daniel that appeared in *The Sporting News* in February 1942 insisted that baseball was moving forward just like the military and it too is aware of the sacrifices that must be made and the dangers that it must deal with on the ground, in the air, and in the sea. *The Sporting News* wrote in an editorial that the Japanese had never fully embraced the game of baseball because if they had, they wouldn't have become a dictatorial and adversarial regime. During the early twentieth century American teams had traveled to Japan to entertain their citizens and teach them the game. But after Pearl Harbor, *The Sporting News* editors attacked the Japanese by writing that the Japanese hitters were not as successful as the Americans because they were weak and small in stature. They were jealous of the powerful American sluggers. Sportswriters furthermore asserted that the Japanese were arrogant. *The Sporting News* insisted that baseball was essential to the American war effort. They more than implied that baseball was God's game being played in God's country. *The Sporting News* implied that baseball was what made Americans civilized human beings and the enemy were intrinsically very different, mainly because they had not fully embraced baseball. In April of 1942 the magazine published a profile of Buddy Lewis, who had played for the Washington Senators before joining the Air Corps. The article stated that Lewis thought the "little brown men" that he would face in battle would not be any harder to hit than the junior circuit's left-handed hurlers.[56]

To play baseball was to do one's patriotic duty and while ballplayers did not make the same sacrifices as soldiers, *The Sporting News* informed their readers that they served their country honorably. In their January 15, 1942 issue, they insisted that Luke Appling, the excellent shortstop of the Chicago White Sox, who had a tendency to hit large quantities of foul balls, was doing a great patriotic service because the American League had adopted a policy for the upcoming season whereby they would collect foul balls and send them to military camps. In a typical hyperbolic analysis the newspaper predicted that Appling would hit even more foul balls than he had in previous years and probably spray one box of balls into the stands each time he came up. While collecting foul balls and giving them to soldiers may have appeared to be a small contribution to the war effort, it did send the message to the baseball viewing populace that sacrifices would have to be made. From 1942 to 1944 about 40 balls per game were retrieved from the stands for a total of 148,644 during those three seasons. Lester Thorpe was one of many citizens who were critical of this policy. He sent a letter to the *New York Times* expressing his opinion that the large amount of money that was allocated to the Army and Navy should make it easy for them to afford enough baseballs for their servicemen to use during their recreational time. Therefore, Thorpe claimed, major league baseball's policy was an unnecessary "scheme" to make the American people submissive to their government.[57]

Baseball undoubtedly played an important role during the war by helping improve morale on the home front; supporting the war effort; providing the servicemen overseas with something that they could look forward to; and showing people that baseball could persevere and overcome obstacles, so perhaps they, too, could overcome their difficulties in life. *The Sporting News*' conduct during the war was hyperbolic but it was also praiseworthy. There was great writing by writers who loved the game and who had a legitimate argument as to why baseball should continue. If baseball had shut down it could have had a devastating impact on the country. The world was unstable and the country's future was threatened by totalitarian regimes. Perhaps the writers at *The Sporting News* were also concerned about their own livelihood because if baseball was to be shut down then there would be no need for their newspaper to exist.

Ultimately the conduct of major league baseball and its players during those war years was among its proudest moments in the history of the National Pastime. And those who wrote about the game also made a great contribution in chronicling an important time in baseball's history.

❖ 1 ❖

The 1945 Season Approaches

The war was going well for the Allies until December of 1944, when the Germans initiated a counterattack into the Ardennes Forest in Belgium. The Battle of the Bulge ended any thought of concluding the war by Christmas, and U.S. government officials reconsidered the eligibility of those with medical discharges and those men who were 4-Fs. James F. Byrnes, head of the Office of War Mobilization, insisted that if 4-F athletes could perform on the field they could also perform in combat. A player may have a trick knee, for example, but "if it doesn't get tricky on a football field, the chances are it won't get tricky at Verdun or in Belgium."[1] President Roosevelt called for what was essentially a "work or fight" measure similar to the one implemented in World War I. Those who were previously classified 4-F were reexamined. Baseball even considered whether it should start the season as a result. High-level political figures like FBI Director J. Edgar Hoover and Senator Happy Chandler stood up for the players and against their being aggressively targeted for the draft.

Several lingering questions hovered over organized baseball during the early months of 1945. First there was uncertainty over whether the season would even begin and whether there would be a World Series once it did. Organized baseball would eventually receive the necessary approval of the U.S. government to continue its operations, including that of the Office of Defense Transportation. During this time of uncertainty, controversial ideas were proposed, such as when Col. Monroe Johnson of the Office of Defense Transportation wanted to combine the two leagues. The July All-Star game for Fenway Park was canceled due to travel restrictions. *The Sporting News* wrote in its March 1 issue, "To be sure, the major leagues have yet to solve their manpower problem. They have yet to find the men with whom to play their schedules. But there now is most definite, official information that Washington sympathizes with the game and is willing to give its aid, comfort and blessing, if baseball can muster the essential playing strength."[2] Despite the uncertainty and obstacles that faced organized baseball, government officials were going to do everything possible to ensure the continuation of the game. Congress was set to enact legislative measures that would benefit the major leagues.

The Sporting News praised Ford Frick, National League President, and to a lesser extent William Harridge, American League President, for asking the government to sanction the upcoming season. At the same time it rebuked the policies of the late commissioner Judge Kenesaw Mountain Landis, who wanted to "remain away from Washington" when the war began, a policy which could have provided "fatal results." Frick was responsible of informing government officials about the dire predicament which baseball was in. He went to Washington, D.C., about a dozen times to lobby officials about the need for government help, and he did so without any support from the commissioner's office. Leslie M. O'Connor, who had been Landis's secretary, insisted that Frick was making these appearances as the president of the National League, that his views were not representative of the entire baseball community, and that he certainly didn't speak for the commissioner. *The Sporting News* insisted that O'Connor was wrong, and thankfully government officials correctly recognized Frick as the representative of baseball and not just as conveying the wishes of the National League. They also asserted that if the major leagues had followed Landis's strategy there would have been no major league baseball in 1945. The misguided Landis policy would have brought "doubt" and "pessimism," and led to the cessation of activities throughout ballparks around the nation. Only months after Landis had died, *The Sporting News* did not hesitate to attack his destructive policies.

The Sporting News was particularly gratified that baseball had sought the help of the government. It editorialized that for three years it had warned baseball that to refuse Washington's help and not to seek its assistance was "absurd." It urged baseball to strongly consider the predicament of the nation as a whole and wrote that baseball officials should reflect upon the game's position and importance to the country. Americans were all united for a single cause, to stop totalitarian regimes and save the civilized world. Baseball had to work with the government to help solve its problems or else it may have to cease operations until the war was over, which would have a harmful effect upon the game. *The Sporting News* also said that for three years they had advocated for and educated baseball fans about baseball's importance to society. The nation, the servicemen, and the baseball community all demanded that games be played without interruption, since baseball was "honorable" and "moral" and was a strong supporter of the war effort.

The travel concessions offered by Frick and Harridge would eliminate as much as 25 percent of the travel miles from the previous year. *The Sporting News* was greatly chagrined that the All-Star game had been canceled, because war charities would be the true loser as a result. Frick helped guide the game through difficult times and *The Sporting News* speculated that Frick would be rewarded for his service by being named the new commissioner of baseball.[3] Frick would also be fondly remembered in later years because in 1947 he warned the St. Louis Cardinals that if they were going to strike and refuse to play games against the

Brooklyn Dodgers as a protest against Jackie Robinson's presence in the major leagues, then they were going to destroy the game. The National League office would support Robinson and suspend those players who refused to take the field. Players who participated in this stupidity would not be welcomed in the National League.

After Happy Chandler, Landis's successor, was forced to leave office on July 15, 1951, Frick would be named the new commissioner on September 20, 1951, and serve until 1965. During Frick's tenure as president of the National League he allowed the owners to run the game and did not interfere. He was precisely the kind of person the owners were seeking after the activist administrations of Landis and Chandler. As commissioner he served the game primarily as a promoter, administrator, and mediator, and acted in a manner of which the owners approved. Frick's actions during World War II seemed to contradict his belief as commissioner that outside influences should be restricted and that the leagues should solve their own problems. Bill Veeck even suggested that Frick's autobiography should be titled *Armageddon Is a League Matter*.[4] With Frick implanted as a servile commissioner the owners were allowed to follow whatever plans they wished with little interference. Some of these policies were disastrous, such as the bonus baby rule whereby teams paid large bonuses to 18- or 19-year-old prospects. As a result an estimated 60 million dollars was given to prospects in bidding wars, money that was much needed to help the crumbling minor leagues. Furthermore, this policy led to disharmony in major league clubhouses as veteran players resented the large sums of money given to unproven ballplayers while these kids wasted their time on the bench instead of developing their skills in the minor leagues. These problems could have been diminished if Frick had advocated for the implementation of a free agent draft. David Voigt wrote, "At a time when critical leadership was needed, Frick offered none."[5] While Frick's leadership style as commissioner was questionable, his actions during World War II as National League president were admirable.

On March 21, 1945, organized baseball was buoyed when Paul V. McNutt, chief of the War Manpower Commission, declared that those players employed in war plants and other essential work could play professional baseball for the upcoming season. However, other manpower problems were exacerbated. Ballplayers were now being drafted simply because they were professional athletes. Ron Northey of the Philadelphia Phillies was classified 4-F for the second time on January 2 for a punctured eardrum, high blood pressure, and a heart problem. Under normal conditions any one of those ailments would have exempted him from military service. His draft board wanted to examine him again two weeks later but he voluntarily tried to enlist in the Navy and was again turned down. Pressure was mounting on government officials, so they brought him back again for a fourth time. On January 29 he was sworn into the United States Army. Howie Schultz, the 6'7" first baseman for the Brooklyn Dodgers, had received a notice from the Washington Selective Service Headquarters, who canceled his 4-F classification. In doing so the Selective Service had disregarded the 6'6" limit simply because Schultz was a ballplayer. Danny Litwhiler and Hugh Poland were also singled out for the draft, among others.

Teams rosters were being decimated by the new draft policy, not only before the season but also as it progressed. Ken Raffensberger, the ace of the Phillies staff, was taken into the service on April 30 after starting the season with an 0–3 record and a 4.44 ERA. The previous year he had tied Charley Schanz with thirteen wins, the most on the team. The Cardinals' pennant hopes were hurt the following day when Walker Cooper went into the service.

As spring training proceeded, travel restrictions would lead teams to cancel many of their exhibition games. They were replaced by intrasquad and service games. Poor weather also severely curtailed spring training workouts. The St. Louis Cardinals faced this predicament when the Ohio River continuously overflowed into their camp in Cairo, Illinois. The mayor of Cairo called his fire and sanitation departments into action to get the practice field in playing condition. In an attempt to drain the water they dug ditches and used the fire pumps in the outfield, but these actions provided only nominal success. Owner Sam Breadon moved his team to Sportsman's Park on March 26 after the Cardinals were unable to train for over a week. Only two days into camp there had already been talk of moving the training to St. Louis, but Breadon kept his club in Cairo to accommodate the local fans. However, with his ballplayers unable to train for over a week, his hand was forced. Not since 1919 had the Cardinals trained for the season in their own ballpark. Other teams faced similar weather problems, such as the Cubs, who towards the end of March had three feet of water cover their practice field. It was their third flood since arriving in French Lick, Indiana, and they sought to continue training on higher ground.

Travel restrictions meant playing many intrasquad games along with contests against local college and service teams. Once the season began, teams would visit opposing cities less often. The Giants, for example, scheduled only three trips to cities like Boston and Philadelphia during the regular season in wartime. Ford Frick said that athletes traveled 6,485,395 passenger miles during the 1941 season and in 1945 they expected that it would be cut to 3,000,000.

The quality of talent in this fourth wartime season would be at its nadir. Ford Frick acknowledged there was an inferior talent pool but was also optimistic that the National League race would be exciting. As opening day approached he wrote a report for the Associated Press that read in part that our "best ball teams have gone to war, but there is every indication of a keenly competitive National League race here at home."[6] Once the war ended, attendance was bound to increase. Servicemen in uniform would again be allowed in free, and their attendance figures were estimated to double in 1945.

In 1942 pitcher Phil Marchildon of the Philadelphia Athletics described his atrocious infield as follows:

That team was a bad one. They couldn't make a double play if you hit a line drive. Dick Siebert, he had a brace on his knee, and the other guy on third base, Buddy Blair, he had a brace on his knee. They couldn't move very far, either one of them. There was a fellow playing shortstop by the name of Davis; he wasn't too much of a player either. Oh, boy. There was a challenge. You got quite a kick out of being able to win.[7]

The '42 Athletics had lost their second baseman Benny McCoy and shortstop Al Brancato to the service. Marchildon's description of his ersatz infield was only a harbinger of things to come as the war progressed. Each year, the quality of play would get worse and worse. It started with a trickle and developed into a flood. As the first wartime season commenced in 1942, well-known stars like Hank Greenberg and Bob Feller were among the sixty-one big leaguers in the armed forces. The next year saw Ted Williams, Joe DiMaggio, and Johnny Mize, in addition to a number of excellent pitchers and a surfeit of lesser-known big leaguers, enter the service. There were a total of 219 big leaguers in the military in 1943 as rosters began to be decimated. In 1943, for example, the Yankees lost future Hall of Famers Joe DiMaggio, Phil Rizzuto, and Red Ruffing, along with quality players like Tommy Henrich and Buddy Hassett. By 1944 the play on the field was abysmal and with the new draft policy in 1945 that targeted professional athletes it became even worse.

When the Japanese bombed Pearl Harbor there were about 5,800 professional baseball players; by the start of the 1945 season, approximately 5,400 of them were in the service. If they weren't in combat, they entertained troops by playing baseball, and some did both. Many of the players who didn't go into the service took war-related jobs back at home. Harry O'Neill caught in one game for the Philadelphia Athletics in 1939. That was his only big league appearance; on March 6, 1945, he gave his life on Iwo Jima. Elmer Gedeon, who batted .200 in fifteen at-bats for the 1939 Washington Senators, was killed in St. Pol, France, in April of 1944 when a German pilot shot his plane down. Two years earlier he had acted heroically when an Army bomber he was on crashed in North Carolina. Despite suffering broken ribs upon impact he returned to the bomber and pulled a fellow crewman to safety, suffering severe burns in the process, and subsequently spending three months in the hospital. Gedeon and O'Neill were among the almost fifty professional ballplayers who died in combat.

The owners sought to fill uniforms with players who hadn't played in the big leagues in years, and many who hadn't played even in the minors for a long time either. Teenagers, who if not for the war would have had no right to be on a major league team, now got their chance in the show. And there were the disabled players who served as role models to those in similar predicaments; some, like Pete Gray, helped the owners at the gate.

Several examples will suffice of the poor play that tarnished the major league diamonds and represented baseball in 1945: George Metkovich, the

Boston Red Sox' first baseman, made three errors in one inning. Pittsburgh Pirate fans were so disgusted with the play of their team that they threw pop bottles at the players one day, then ran onto the field and chased them with malicious intents. The Philadelphia Phillies lost sixteen in a row during one stretch and needed eight errors by the Boston Braves in a fifteen-inning game to break the streak. Errors became commonplace, not only of the physical kind, but also of the mental variety. The Phillies had eleven players thirty-five years or older. During the '45 season big league clubs employed at least sixteen players who were forty years or older. In addition there were several teenagers in the big leagues. It was reported that 384 major leaguers were in the service in '45. A small percentage of these players were discharged during the '45 season. They faced a decision: to return during the tail end of the season and perhaps risk looking inept since their skills were rusty, or to return to the big leagues for the 1946 season after a rigorous training regimen where they would be better prepared to play major league ball. Joe DiMaggio decided he would wait to get in playing shape instead of running the risk of being embarrassed against inferior competition. Others like Bob Feller and Hank Greenberg were among the ballplayers that joined their teams right away after being in the service. The returning ballplayers were at various levels of fitness, depending on if they were predominantly combat soldiers, held supportive positions in the service such as postal clerk, or simply entertained the troops by playing ball. Some marginal ballplayers improved their skills by playing for a service team, while others let their skills diminish.

Things were looking better for major league baseball as opening day approached, but then disaster struck the country. On April 12, President Franklin Roosevelt died of a massive cerebral hemorrhage while vacationing in Warm Springs, Georgia. Harry Truman was sworn in as his successor. Baseball had already been mourning the loss of its stern commissioner, Judge Kenesaw Mountain Landis, who had died on November 25, 1944. Roosevelt had been a strong ally of baseball, encouraging it to continue during the war with his "green light" letter and encouraging more night games. During the 1944 season the wartime restrictions were lifted for night baseball and a high number of nocturnal contests were scheduled in '45. When Clark Griffith had visited the White House to give him his yearly pass on March 12, Roosevelt said, "You've got to give me credit for night baseball."[8] He was proud of his connection to and influence on the game and would be sorely missed. Some big league teams canceled their exhibition games for up to three days after his death. It was believed that Truman would also support the efforts of organized baseball, since he had shown interest in the game and attended the 1944 World Series in St. Louis.

Making predictions before the season is risky because injuries and trades can significantly transform a club and affect its chances. However, making predictions during wartime was far more unreliable. J.G. Taylor Spink wrote in the April 12 issue of *The Sporting News*, "Pennant prophecy never is what might be called a safe enterprise."⁹ As they entered what would be the final World War II baseball season, making predictions was even more difficult because of the uncertain state of team rosters. Teams were going to have players coming and going throughout the season as they were discharged from the military or were called to service. However, the fans demanded that the experts make their predictions nonetheless for the upcoming season.

The Sporting News predicted that the St. Louis Cardinals would win their fourth straight pennant in 1945 and face the St. Louis Browns in the second consecutive all–St. Louis World Series. Although with the loss of Danny Litwhiler, Walker Cooper, and Stan Musial the Cardinals were going to have a much more difficult time winning the pennant. In 1942 they had a 106–48 record and only won the pennant by two games over Brooklyn. But in 1943 and 1944 they had identical 105–49 records and cruised to the pennant by margins of 18 and 14.5 games. Billy Southworth, the Cardinals skipper, was hoping that rookie Red Schoendienst would help spark the offense and compensate for the loss of the key veterans who were called to military service. The Pittsburgh Pirates, who had a strong second half in 1944, were picked to finish second. *The Sporting News* predicted that the Chicago Cubs would finish in fourth place. Additionally, for the second straight year they were picked as the team most likely to surprise the circuit with an excellent record. Charlie Grimm's squad would benefit from the fact that, unlike St. Louis, they didn't lose any quality players from the year before and their lineup was almost the same as in 1944.

In the American League the St. Louis Browns were chosen to win their second consecutive pennant. *The Sporting News* reckoned that St. Louis's American League contingent was battle tested coming off their successful 1944 campaign. Furthermore, as the season was about to commence the only player of importance that the Browns were missing from the previous year was Denny Galehouse, who went 9–10 with a 3.12 ERA in 1944. When predicting where each team would finish, the manpower shortages were a major factor in the decision-making process. The Detroit Tigers would enter the season without Pinky Higgins and Dick Wakefield, who had each made solid contributions the year before. Steve O'Neill's team was picked to finish third behind the Yankees because of their excellent starting rotation, led by Hal Newhouser and Dizzy Trout, who finished first and second in the AL in wins in 1944 with 29 and 27 wins respectively.

The Washington Senators finished last in the American League in 1944 with a 64–90 record, and in 1945 *The Sporting News* predicted they would finish in the same position as the doormat of the junior circuit. The Senators would be without the services of Stan Spence and Early Wynn for the upcoming season: Spence batted .316 with 18 homers and 100 RBIs in 1944, while future Hall of Famer Wynn had his breakout year in 1943, going 18–12 with a 2.91 ERA, and then 8–17 with a respectable 3.38 ERA during the following season. Despite the loss of Wynn, *The Sporting News* acknowledged that pitching would not be a problem for manager Ossie Bluege. Returning moundsmen Dutch Leonard, Johnny Niggeling, Roger Wolff, Mickey Haefner and rookie Marino Pieretti were all set to toe the slab for Washington. Despite their solid starting rotation, *The Sporting News* did not think much of their ballclub and characterized them as a "Second division club, barring miracles."[10]

Spink and his colleagues at *The Sporting News* made the following predictions. They were unsure whether the Washington Senators or the Chicago White Sox would finish last in the American League. Spink wrote that you could choose Washington in seventh place and the White Sox in last place or vice versa:

National League	*American League*
1. St. Louis Cardinals	1. St. Louis Browns
2. Pittsburgh Pirates	2. New York Yankees
3. Cincinnati Reds	3. Detroit Tigers
4. Chicago Cubs	4. Cleveland Indians
5. New York Giants	5. Boston Red Sox
6. Brooklyn Dodgers	6. Philadelphia Athletics
7. Boston Braves	7. Washington Senators
8. Philadelphia Phillies	8. Chicago White Sox

❖ 2 ❖

Jolly Cholly and His Over-the-Hill Gang Win the Pennant

The Chicago Cubs prepared for their season during wartime in French Lick, Indiana, which provided one of the better spring training experiences for the players. The White Sox also trained there during 1943 and 1944 before moving to Terre Haute in 1945. The two teams quarreled during their time together over who would use the golf course, which was the only playing field in close proximity. Jimmy Dykes, the White Sox manager, along with coach Muddy Ruel, sought out new training facilities and found several barns which could be used for batting practice, along with a park in West Baden. The teams stayed at the 700-room French Lick Springs Hotel. The hotel allowed the players to practice in the auditorium when it rained and the players reciprocated by allowing hotel guests to join them in doing their calisthenics. The resort town attracted many wealthy and famous people, including boxing champion Joe Louis, with its famous mineral baths, which had attracted visitors for years. Even though accommodations were adequate, this was still spring training in the North; as Phil Cavarretta recalled, "Boy, it was cold. But it was wartime, and things weren't easy. Whatever they asked of us, we did. I was thankful just to be in spring training. Think of those kids who had to get into the service."[1]

The players would run along the Lost River or through the woods and then head straight for the basement bathhouse for a steam bath or rubdown. During 1945 the government suspended railroad service to French Lick and Cubs coach Red Smith was forced to drive eighteen miles to Orleans, Indiana, to pick up the players. Exhibition games with the Cincinnati Reds at Fort Knox and Louisville, Kentucky, were initially canceled by an Office of Defense Transportation ruling.

Despite missing Bill Nicholson from camp, as the Cubs entered their third week of training, manager Charlie Grimm felt satisfied with the team's progress. Nicholson was content with his contract and sent word that he would be ready by opening day. Grimm was nervous when a few of his pitchers arrived late but the tension was eased when Bob Chipman, Claude Passeau, and Hank Wyse showed up in camp. Along with Eddie Hanyzewski and Paul Derringer those five pitchers were set to anchor the staff. Offensively the Cubs had a solid lineup with Mickey Livingston, Phil Cavarretta, Don Johnson, Len Merullo, Stan Hack, Frank Secory, Andy Pafko, and Nicholson slated to be in the starting lineup. The Cubs also had great depth, particularly behind the plate, where they had Dewey Williams and Paul Gillespie projected to back up Livingston.

Charlie Grimm had managed the Chicago Cubs from 1932 to 1938 and came back during the 1944 season. In 1935 he led the Cubs to the pennant and then left abruptly in 1938 mainly because of health problems. The Cubs had a 45–36 record when he departed and were in third place, then playing manager Gabby Hartnett guided them to the National League pennant as they finished the season with an 89–63 record. After relinquishing his managerial post, Grimm became a radio broadcaster. In June of 1941 he teamed with Bill Veeck, Jr. to purchase a Cubs minor league affiliate, the Milwaukee Brewers of the American Association. The team was on the brink of financial ruin when they took over, heavily in debt, and Veeck came up with various promotions to get fans to the ballpark. These gimmicks and promotions may have been frowned upon by baseball traditionalists but they were a hit with the fans. Grimm became manager of the Brewers in 1941 and remained in that capacity through the 1943 season. As his August 28 birthday approached in 1943 the press asked Charlie what he wanted, and he responded by saying that an effective southpaw hurler would make an excellent present. Veeck subsequently held a birthday party on the field for Grimm, and in addition to giving him a one-thousand-dollar war bond, he also gave him a left-handed pitcher by the name of Julio Acosta who made his appearance by stepping out of a birthday cake. Acosta, who had been purchased from Norfolk, turned out to be a fine pitcher: he lost his first game, fanning seventeen during a 13-inning affair, and then won his next three starts. He also saved some crucial games, helping Milwaukee win the pennant.[2] Grimm and Veeck sold the club in 1945 for a substantial profit.

Grimm's second stint as manager of the Cubs was from 1944 to 1949 but he never again duplicated the pennant-winning accomplishments of the 1945 squad. In 1952 he managed the Boston Braves and then moved with the club to Milwaukee, where he managed from 1953 to 1956, finishing in second place two times and third once. From 1957 to 1959 he was employed by the Cubs as their vice president. He returned as the Cubs skipper in 1960 but lasted only seventeen games to begin the season, compiling a 6–11 record after which he would never manage in the big leagues again. Philip K. Wrigley, the owner of the Cubs, inserted Lou Boudreau, who was the radio broadcaster for the Cubs' WGN radio station, as the manager and then placed Grimm behind the microphone. The move backfired in two directions: Grimm was not a good radio announcer, while the Cubs limped to a seventh-place conclusion with a 60–94

2. Jolly Cholly and His Over-the-Hill Gang Win the Pennant

Charlie Grimm, manager of the Cubs, is shown feeding a cub. He had an amiable, easygoing personality, and was well liked by his players. Grimm managed the Cubs until 1938, when he departed during the season because of health reasons. When he returned in 1944 he found a team that was too tight, overly critical of themselves, and unable to relax. Grimm changed the atmosphere in the clubhouse. In 1945 the Cubs captured the National League pennant but lost the World Series to the Detroit Tigers in seven games (George Brace photograph).

record. Grimm ended his nineteen-year managerial career with a 1,287–1,067 record.

He began his playing career in 1916 by batting .091 in 22 at-bats for the Philadelphia Athletics. He played for the St. Louis Cardinals in 1918 and then went to the Pittsburgh Pirates the following season, remaining with the club through the 1924 season. As an everyday player he batted over .300 during five seasons, including a career high .345 with the 1923 Pirates. From 1925 to 1936 he played for the Chicago Cubs and ended his twenty-year playing career with a .290 average. He grew up admiring Hal Chase and like his hero he would become an excellent defensive first baseman.

As he entered the 1945 season, in his ten years managing for the Cubs and Milwaukee Brewers he had never finished out of the first division. He liked to keep a light atmosphere around the clubhouse and wanted his players to have fun. Grimm insisted that his first responsibility as manager when he returned in 1944 was to make the players relax and make sure they did not take the game too seriously. Even if they made a plethora of errors, the sun would rise the next day and they would still be alive. Baseball is a "young man's game," and once it ceases to be fun it is time for a player to turn in his uniform. He encouraged his players not to dwell on mistakes and concentrate on doing better the next day. When he became manager of the ball club, he saw players who were too tense; who were afraid of making mistakes; who would not let go of the past, which would lead to future mistakes. During this period in baseball history this mentality was certainly understandable, considering there was little financial and employment security for major league players who were always looking over their shoulders at players who were eager to take their spot for little money.

Grimm was a player's manager who was well liked. He managed as he played: in a rhythmic, unflappable manner. One day Stan Hack tried to make it to third on a short hit to center field and was thrown out. When he got into the dugout Grimm went through a pantomime of a guy unwinding a rope, hanging it on a rafter and putting it around his neck. It loosened Hack up and he tripled his next at-bat. Hack enjoyed watching Grimm's antics along the coaching lines. Grimm had an ability to mimic the walk, talk, and other bodily movements of people. One day he was encouraged to do so by Hans Lobert, who was a coach with the Cincinnati Reds. The Reds hadn't been playing well and were hearing it from the fans. Lobert thought that if Grimm could make them laugh then they would temporarily halt the booing. Grimm agreed to do so and mimicked the actions of umpire George Barr after a play at third. He walked right behind him, imitating his unusual gait and when Barr caught on to the act, Grimm was thrown out of the game.[3] Later in his career Grimm used flags to wave runners around the bases. He also buried the lineup card in the ground and would dig it up to see who was hitting.[4]

Even though Grimm fooled around he kept firm control of his ball club.

2. Jolly Cholly and His Over-the-Hill Gang Win the Pennant

Don Johnson, the Cubs third baseman, recalls:

> As a manager the players had respect for Charlie because even though he was funny in the clubhouse, he really had control of a ball club. I remember a young knuckleballer.... He was having a rough time, and he got knocked out of the game ... went up to the clubhouse, packed his stuff in his duffel bag.... Grimm sat down by his locker and watched him. The kid started out the door, and Charlie said to him, "Listen, lad, if you go out that door ... you're not coming back."
>
> And you never saw a guy unpack his stuff so quick in his life.... Some managers would have called him an SOB and a quitter, but Grimm let you know darn well he didn't like what was going on without belittling you.[5]

Some managers like Leo Durocher tried to motivate by fear, intimidation, and by putting their players down. There were those like Grimm and Cincinnati's Bill McKechnie who built their players up. Grimm was a very positive manager, very articulate, always in a good mood, and insisted that his players be happy. As a player they said he was "baseball's only left-handed banjo player," not because he was a "banjo" hitter but because he actually played the banjo.[6] He was very artistic, a characteristic that he developed from his father, who was a painter and an amateur musician. He was one of four children: his brother William became a pianist while his sister Margaret was a musician. Although he was a great music lover and was quite gifted in playing songs, he could not read music and was not formally trained. Ed Balinger, a Pittsburgh sports writer, insisted that when Grimm was playing for the Pirates they approached a gifted Italian banjo player who was performing at their hotel. They asked if Grimm could play along. A concert was hastily put together and the Italian said that Grimm had a terrific ear for music and it was unfortunate that Grimm's inability to read music would hinder his progress. In addition to playing the banjo, Grimm also drew cartoons as a hobby.[7] While with the Milwaukee Brewers he would play music for the fans, which was reportedly not very good because the band included such musically challenged members as Bill Veeck. Grimm loved to give out nicknames, a habit he had had since he was a kid. For example, Heinz Becker was nicknamed "Heinz-a-Poodle" and "Bunions" because he had problems with his feet. Phil Cavarretta's nickname was "Philibuck."[8] Grimm's own nickname was "Jolly Cholly."[9]

After finishing no higher than fourth place earlier in the war, the Chicago Cubs struck gold and brought home the National League pennant in 1945. In 1942 they finished in sixth place (68–86) with Jimmie Wilson as manager. The following year they improved to fifth place (74–79); during the '44 season when Charlie Grimm took over as skipper they finished in fourth place (75–79); and they won the pennant in '45 (98–56). Grimm became the manager of the Cubs after the team began the 1944 season with a 1–9 record under Jimmie Wilson, and then fell to 1–10 when Roy Johnson lost the only major league game he managed.

At the bat the Cubs were led by Phil Cavarretta, who led the National

League in batting with a .355 average. The line-drive-hitting Cavarretta won National League MVP honors in 1945. Cavarretta said years later, "It was a big achievement for me. In order to win a batting title, everything has to go your way.... And even though it was a war year, you still had to work hard to get your hits. There was nothing easy about it."[10] The left-handed batting champion was also an excellent defensive first baseman who occasionally played the outfield. He was extremely hard-working and was admired by teammates and fans alike. Cavarretta was born in Chicago and as a boy he would try to sneak a ride to Wrigley Field on the el. Sometimes the Cubs would allow kids to earn entry into the ballpark by having them collect trash around its periphery and he often took advantage of this policy. Cavarretta had a twenty-two-year major league career in which he batted .293: twenty of those seasons were with the Cubs and the other two were also in Chicago with the White Sox. Entering the 1945 season he had already played with pennant winners in '35 and '38, but he was seeking to win that elusive world championship. During the three World Series he played in he batted a combined .317, including .423 in 1945.

The other good hitters on the club included Don Johnson, Stan Hack, Bill Nicholson, Andy Pafko, Peanuts Lowrey, and Mickey Livingston. Heinz Becker batted .286 in 67 games as a first baseman and pinch hitter. Some said he had the worst feet in baseball, but he was also known for being the only German-born player during the war. He was born in Berlin on August 26, 1915, and left the country when he was three years old. In Venezuela he once boxed on the same card as Luis Firpo.

Thirty-five-year-old Stan Hack was a former bank clerk who owned a ranch in Oregon which kept him busy during the off-season. In his first 38 games and 158 chances during the 1945 season he had yet to make an error while patrolling the hot corner. "Smiling Stan" Hack was a six-foot, 170-pound left-handed batter but right-handed thrower who almost always had a smile on his face and a pinch of tobacco in his left cheek. He trained hard during the off-season, pitching hay and building fences. Hack was skilled at flying airplanes and would wrangle steers. His manager called him "Stash" and he had to beat out 27-year-old John Ostrowski for the starting third base job during spring training. Hack always had competition for his job but nonetheless was willing to provide tips to the younger players. He realized that one day his skills would diminish and he wouldn't be useful to a major league team anymore. If he could help his replacement become a better player, this would benefit the ball club and give him a sense of pride that he did the right thing. He felt like he had a responsibility to give back and help the youngsters. He wasn't with the Cubs for a "quick killing, followed by a getaway." When his playing career ended he wanted to become a coach, preferably with the Cubs.[11] He finished the season with a .323 batting average, the seventh time in his major league career that he had batted .300 or better. He completed his sixteen-year major league career in 1947, leaving the game with a .301 lifetime batting average.

Hack felt a sense of loyalty towards the Cubs, having played his entire career with that team. Hack spent several seasons managing in the minor leagues in the Western League, International League, Pacific Coast League, American Association and the Texas League. In 1954 he became the manager of the Cubs when he replaced his former teammate Phil Cavarretta, who had angered the owner, Philip K. Wrigley, when he told reporters that the Cubs were a second-division outfit.[12] Hack managed the Cubs from 1954 to 1956, finishing no higher than sixth place. His major league managerial career ended when he managed ten games for the 1958 St. Louis Cardinals. In 1957 and 1958 Hack's primary responsibility with the Cardinals was as an infield and batting coach.

Harry Lee Lowrey, better known as "Peanuts," batted .373 on a crucial eastern trip in early July that propelled the Cubs to first place. He was raised in Culver City, California, across the street from the M-G-M and Hal Roach movie lots. Lowrey would watch the car of Clark Gable and be treated to ice cream by the likes of Joe E. Brown and Buster Keaton. In 1936 he signed a contract with the Pacific Coast League's Los Angeles Angels, for a $1 bonus. He was subsequently sent to the Catalina Island team and then to Moline in the Three-I League. In 1938 he was with Ponca City in the Western Association when his club won the league championship with one .300 hitter. That team was proficient in executing small-ball strategies such as stealing bases, sacrificing runners over and utilizing the squeeze bunt. The aggressive style of play which he learned at Ponca City made an impression upon him. He bounced around a few bush-league clubs before being acquired by the Cubs in the winter of 1941. In 1942 he batted .190 in 27 games during his first major league season, then improved to .292 in 130 games the following year. In 1944 he was in the Army but with potential left fielders such as Frank Secory, Eddie Sauer, Dom Dallessandro and Lou Novikoff on the roster, his services were not missed by manager Grimm. Before joining the Army he had a reputation as being a "clubhouse lawyer," a player who is incessantly complaining. But the Army made him less cantankerous and more mature. He was a holdout for the duration of the 1945 spring training and therefore nothing was expected of him for the upcoming season. Early in the season he saw little playing time. However, once in the lineup Lowrey would produce, batting .283 with 7 homers and 89 RBIs. The 5'8" and a half, 170-pound outfielder disdained his nickname because it was "outdated": "It was given to me by my uncle when I was one day old — and that'll be 27 years ago next month."[13]

After leading the senior circuit in home runs and RBIs in 1943 and 1944, Bill Nicholson slumped to a .243 batting average with 13 homers and 88 driven in. Despite his offensive shortcomings he was a reliable right fielder. He was also known for being the "No. 1 tobacco chewer" on the club despite never having purchased tobacco for years.[14] The bleacherites at Wrigley Field always supplied him with more than enough chew. Don Johnson provided great defensive play at second base and batted .302. He was particularly gifted at turning the double play. Mickey Livingston, their personable catcher, had been discharged from the service the previous winter when a head injury restricted his ability to wear a steel helmet. He batted .254 in 224 at-bats. Andy Pafko was a pleasant 24-year-old outfielder with a terrific arm and fine all-around defensive skills. He was quiet and unassuming but a dependable ballplayer who would become very popular with the Wrigley Field fans. In 1945 he was in his third major league season and eager to take the advice from the veterans on the team. At the bat he contributed a .298 average with 12 homers and 110 RBIs, which helped make up for Nicholson's offensive slump.

Charlie Grimm was asked by a reporter in August who he thought deserved the most credit for the Cubs' rise to the top of the National League. Grimm shocked many by insisting that Len Merullo played the biggest role in the Cubs' improvement as the season progressed. After the weak-hitting shortstop was inserted into the starting lineup on July 1, the Cubs won eleven straight and had taken over first place on July 8. They continued to win, emerging victorious in 33 of 39 contests by August 1. On the season Merullo batted .239 in 121 games. He improved the Cubs' ability to turn the double play with terrific footwork and had the confidence that was lacking in previous years. Merullo admired Billy Jurges while growing up and possessed a powerful arm. When the Cubs visited his hometown of Boston as a youngster he would work out with the team. Scout Ralph Wheeler recalled that Grimm was amazed by the youngster's strong throws to first, which made a strong impression on the Cubs skipper. Despite overtures by the Dodgers and Reds to acquire the services of Merullo early in 1945, the Cubs resisted the temptation of trading their talented but inconsistent shortstop. His parents were poor Italians from East Boston and Merullo was one of twelve children. Merullo found it difficult concentrating early in the 1945 season and was benched twice. He was still grieving over the death of his twin sons, who had died at birth, and his wife then became very ill. By the end of the season she had begun to recover, which eased his mind. Additionally, he was concerned about being taken by the military, but in late June he became a 4-F.[15]

Hank Wyse led the staff with his 22–10 record and 2.68 ERA. Claude Passeau was 17–9; Paul Derringer 16–11; Ray Prim 13–8; Hank Borowy was 11–2 with a National League leading 2.13 ERA; and Paul Erickson 7–4. The Cubs caught a break in late June when Hank Wyse was called up for a physical and rejected for the draft. He rejoined the club on July 1 in New York after a 36-hour train ride and pitched that afternoon, leading his club to a 4–3 victory. That was the day Merullo was inserted into the lineup and helped propel the Cubs to eleven straight wins. The durable Cubs hurler won four games during that streak, including the eleventh victory, defeating the Boston Braves by a 6–1 score at Wrigley Field on July 12. Wyse also ended Tommy Holmes' 37-game hitting streak on that day. His victory over the Giants on July 15 came on two days' rest: it was his sixth straight victory, each one a complete game, and his

2. Jolly Cholly and His Over-the-Hill Gang Win the Pennant 39

fourth win in eleven days. At this juncture of the season his record stood at 12–5. Wyse was a workhorse, pitching 278 and one-third innings in 1945, and was willing to push his body to the limits by asking Grimm to let him pitch on two days' rest. The Cubs ace had great stamina, paced himself very well, and had excellent control. Grimm said he threw his sinker "with effortless ease until he gets into a jam." When he got into a difficult situation, he could handle the pressure and "bear down" on his opponent by throwing an impressive variety of pitches: a screwball, a changeup, a curveball and a fastball. He had great control and could pitch inside when needed. He became a control pitcher through hard work. He built a pitching target in his backyard and would throw at it for hours at a time. Wyse was half Cherokee and learned to pace himself pitching in the oppressive heat in the Texas League.[16]

Ray Prim, who was nearing his 39th birthday, had never won more than three major league games entering the 1945 season but he gave the Cubs a surprising boost. From July 6 to September 9, Prim was 10–3 and with better support could have won all thirteen. He lost to Philadelphia, 2–1, on August 14. Prim threw a four-hitter but lost the game when Andy Seminick reached for a pitch he was trying to waste and hit a home run. The other losses during that stretch were the result of poor defense. Prim was called "Pop" by his younger teammates and up to June 27 had only one victory. Prim's hair had a gray and silver color and before returning to the big leagues in 1943 he had not made a major league appearance in seven seasons, from 1936 to 1942. He had an unspectacular six-year career with the Washington Senators (1933–1934), followed by the Philadelphia Phillies (1935), and then the Chicago Cubs in 1943, 1945, and 1946. He had a lifetime 22–21 record with a 3.56 ERA while starting 34 of his 116 games.

Paul Derringer was also approaching his thirty-ninth birthday but aged much better than Prim. He won his first four games of the season, which set him on the way to a 16–11 record. This was the last season of his brilliant career, which he finished with a 223–212 record and a 3.46 ERA. He was a prolific spender and possessed the best wardrobe on the team. He also sought the best restaurants. Claude Passeau had first joined the Cubs in 1939 and was an excellent pitcher for them, peaking with twenty wins in 1940, although a gunshot accident restricted him from fully extending the fingers on his left hand. Passeau was considered the wealthiest Cub on the roster. He is a "Raw-boned six-footer with bulldog jaws," wrote J.G. Taylor Spink in *The Sporting News*.[17]

Hank Borowy came to the Cubs from the Yankees near the end of July and helped put the Cubs over the top for the pennant. The Yankees put him on waivers after July 15, when he allowed Detroit Tigers pitcher Zeb Eaton to hit a grand slam homer. Eaton batted .250 on the season with two homers in 32 at-bats. Each of the American League teams passed on Borowy, along with four National League teams, before the Cubs took him on waivers. Many teams around the majors were upset that the Cubs, who had recently risen into first place, were able to secure the services of such a terrific hurler. The Cubs paid $97,000 for his services; the newspapers rounded up and stated that the Chicago Cubs had paid $100,000 for Borowy. Al Laney wrote in the *New York Herald Tribune* that "the Cubs seem to have bought the pennant, or come pretty close to it anyhow. You could also put it the other way around and say that the Yankees sold the pennant, but that probably is a little far fetched considering what else the Yankees have this year."[18] Because the Yankees could have taken Borowy's name off the waiver list even if claimed, many of the American League teams passed on him since they assumed that the Yankees' intentions to get rid of him were not honorable. Clark Griffith, known for being a skinflint, made the outrageous claim that he would have offered $100,000 for Borowy. Larry MacPhail, now part owner of the Yankees, called Griffith on his ridiculous claim and said, "Griff would not have paid a hundred grand for the pitcher if I had thrown in the *Queen Mary*."[19] MacPhail was a character who had fought in St. Mihiel and the Argonne offensives during World War I, where he became a captain. After the war had concluded he attempted to kidnap Kaiser Wilhelm with several of his colleagues.

It was Charlie Grimm who relaxed this club and ultimately served as the catalyst for their pennant-winning climb. The Cub players stated that the turning point of the season came when Grimm threw a party for the club at his farm on June 4. Soon after that, the Cubs began their climb, taking them to baseball's promised land.

❖ 3 ❖

The Defending World Champions

The World War II years proved tremendously fruitful for the St. Louis Cardinals as they won three pennants and two World Series titles. In 1942 they won the National League pennant (106–48) and then defeated the New York Yankees in the World Series. They won another pennant in 1943 (105–49), but the Yankees got the better of them in the Series. In 1944 they were world champions once again as they first cruised to the pennant (105–49) and then defeated their hometown rivals, the St. Louis Browns, in the World Series. They became the first National League team to win over 100 games for three consecutive seasons. In 1945 they would finish in second place (95–59), three games behind Chicago.

The Cardinals kept on winning under wartime conditions despite losing several exceptional and good players early in the war, like Enos Slaughter, Terry Moore, Jimmy Brown, Johnny Beazley, Creepy Crespi, and Whitey Moore. The Cardinals were the first team to develop a farm system and when players left the team they had a surfeit of bodies to replace them. Whitey Kurowski stated, "If you weren't in there [the lineup] they always had three or four guys waiting to take your place." Max Lanier said that during one period, "they had about thirty ball clubs, and they kept us hungry." Lanier observed that the competition was "murder."[1] The farm system had been the brainchild of Branch Rickey, who was the former vice president of the team. Donald Honig wrote, "And far-flung the Cardinal empire was: At one time it seemed every small town in America was sure of having two things—an A&P and a Cardinal farm team."[2] If a Cardinal ballplayer suffered an injury there were plenty of players willing and able to replace him. The surplus talent was often sold off to other clubs. It was a lucrative system, collecting between $2.5 and $3 million dollars in player sales at one point, according to Rickey.[3] Before the war years the Cardinals won pennants in 1926, 1928, 1930, 1931, and 1934. The Cardinals farm system played an integral role in making the team a world's championship-caliber outfit during the war. At a time when teams were desperate to find talented players to wear their uniform, the Cardinals had more options than their competition.

The 1942 season was a remarkably strong year for their minor league teams: their Sacramento club won the Pacific Coast League pennant; Rochester won the International League pennant. Columbus took the flag in the American Association and Houston in the Texas League. Buddy Blattner made his big league debut in 1942 for the Cardinals, going 1 for 23 (.043) in 19 games. He characterized the Cardinals' 1942 farm system as follows: "You probably could have taken the top players of our farm system and finished only behind the Cardinals and Dodgers in the National League and the Yankees in the American."[4]

Despite the great depth at the minor league level filled with prospects who were eager for a big league opportunity there were several of the organization's major league players who decided to hold out during the spring of 1945. This was a risky strategy because once the war ended and the players in the service returned it would not have helped a player's position with the club if he had perturbed the owner. During spring training Cardinals owner Sam Breadon already had a feeling that things were not going to be so easy in 1945. By late March he had received so much bad news that he was reluctant to answer the phone. He was disturbed by the large number of Cardinal players who were holding out. Frederick G. Lieb facetiously wrote that Marty Marion was holding out because he had spent the winter reading about how great he was. According to some scribes he was the best shortstop to walk between the white lines in a major league park since Honus Wagner had done so with the Pittsburgh Pirates during the dead ball era. Marion's demand for a pay raise had left Breadon "somewhat groggy."[5] His fine defensive skills helped him win the 1944 National League MVP award as he batted .267 in 506 at-bats. Seventeen-game winner Ted Wilks was also disappointed with his contract offer. By late March he had already returned three contracts without his signature. Harry "The Cat" Brecheen, Max Lanier, and young infielder John Antonelli were also unsigned. Ken O'Dea was missing from camp.

Breadon was consumed with additional worries: Danny Litwhiler and Johnny Hopp were set to replace Stan Musial. They were classified 4-F and it was assumed they were set to stay with the ball club. Then suddenly Litwhiler was drafted into the Army despite having no cartilage in his left knee and having been rejected by the military after six previous examinations. Hopp was reclassified 1-A and told to be ready for an immediate call to service. The outfield, which had been a strength of the 1944 squad, was a major problem area as the season approached. During spring training the unspectacular threesome of Debs Garms, Augie Bergamo, and Jim Mallory were expected to play the outfield once the season began. Garms had played in eleven major league seasons with the Browns, Braves, Pirates, and Cardinals and had won the 1940 National League batting title with a .355 average in 358 at-bats with the Pittsburgh Pirates. He was a good hitter during his career but possessed little power and would turn 38 years old on June 26. Furthermore, he was coming off a 1944 campaign in which he batted .201 in 149 at-bats for the Cardinals. Bergamo batted .286 in 192 at-bats in 1944 as a rookie, and Mallory's only season as a major league player was in 1940 when he batted .167 in 12 at-bats for the Washington Senators. This would have been a significant downgrade from the 1944 outfield that consisted of Musial, Hopp, and Litwhiler. Fortunately for the Cardinals, Hopp remained with the club in 1945 and followed his .336 batting average in 1944 with a respectable .289 during the final World War II season. Red Schoendienst was forced to play out of position and was moved to the outfield. The outfield was set when the Cardinals made a trade to acquire Buster Adams once the season began.

Breadon was expecting Walker Cooper to depart for service in April. Rookie infielder Red Schoendienst had a stiff arm that he injured in a game the previous season. Breadon also tried to assist Cardinal skipper Billy Southworth and worried about the flooding which consumed his practice field. "Oh, for a return to good old St. Petersburg," remarked Breadon.[6] St. Louis was hit particularly hard by military conscription in 1945 as Danny Litwhiler, Walker Cooper, Stan Musial, Fred Schmidt, and Max Lanier were all called into the service. Later their pennant chances were hindered when shortstop Marty Marion came down with an ankle injury during a critical juncture of the season.

Breadon's biggest problem developed during the second month of the season when pitcher Mort Cooper, Walker's brother, left the team demanding a higher salary. After 24 games St. Louis played only .500 ball with three of their pitchers hindered with sore arms and Marion with a bad ankle. Cooper had been a twenty-game winner during three consecutive seasons from 1942 to 1944, winning 65 games during that period. He was dissatisfied with his 1944 contract for $12,000 and Breadon refused to pay him more than $13,500 for the upcoming season. Former Cardinal pitcher Dizzy Dean was shocked to hear that Cooper was only receiving $12,000 and came to Cooper's defense. Dean was under the impression that Cooper was getting at least $17,500 and insisted he was worth $20,000. They had lost a significant number of players from the previous year and he expressed doubt whether they could win the pennant in 1945. If they didn't yield to the demands of Cooper then "they're in a helluva fix," said Dean. Despite winning the pennant for three consecutive seasons the Cardinals were not paying salaries that were commensurate with great teams with great players. Nick Etten, for example, had a contract for $15,000 from the Yankees.[7] The previous year, when Cooper had demanded $17,500, Breadon tried to make his pitcher feel ashamed and unpatriotic for demanding more money when young men from around the country were fighting overseas to preserve the American way of life. Breadon suggested that those parents whose boys were in the military would be dismayed to read about such salary squabbles.[8] With the two sides at loggerheads, Cooper was finally traded to the Boston Braves on May 23, 1945, for Red Barrett and $60,000. It turned out to be a

Walker Cooper (left) and his older brother Mort were not fond of Cardinals owner Sam Breadon. Mort wanted a significant pay raise above the $12,000 he received in 1944. Breadon was not accommodating, and Mort was traded to Boston on May 23. Mort was a 4-F because of a leg injury, but his brother Walker, an excellent catcher for the Cardinals, joined the Navy after the beginning of the 1945 season. He also got into salary disputes with Breadon and had an acrimonious relationship with him. (George Brace photograph).

terrific trade for St. Louis: Barrett was 23–12 on the season, winning twenty-one of those games with the Cardinals. Boston, meantime, was not too happy to discover that Cooper had a sore arm. Mort worked only 101 and two-thirds innings on the season and had a 9–4 record. Breadon was accustomed to pulling off great trades when his players squabbled over salary and had sent packing greats like Rogers Hornsby, Dizzy Dean, and Joe Medwick in previous years.

Billy Southworth managed the Cardinals in 1929 and then from 1940 to 1945. Later he managed the Boston Braves from 1946 to 1951. He had been a solid outfielder in a thirteen-year major league career and finished with a .297 average. Billy Southworth, Jr., was what minor leaguer Red Ermisch described as "the apple of his father's eye." He was well liked by all and considered a good big league prospect. The young Southworth was cognizant about his patriotic duty and served as an example to all when he joined the Army Air Corps in September of 1940, the first professional baseball player to enlist. He survived twenty-five bombing missions in Europe, wearing his father's Cardinals cap for good luck, and earned several medals for combat duty. Disaster struck when he came home: on February 15, 1945, his bomber was forced to make an emergency landing and crashed into Flushing Bay, killing Southworth, Jr. Billy's son was a lieutenant colonel and he was training pilots how to fly the B-29s when he tragically died.[9]

It was a long, painful, and frustrating wait until the body was found. Nearly six months after he crashed, the body was recovered on August 3 off Silver Beach in the Bronx. Southworth, Sr., had to leave his team while they were in Pittsburgh to bring the body home. Coach Mike Gonzalez filled in as the skipper while he was absent. His son, who had risen as high as Toronto in the International League and had served his country honorably and courageously in the war, was buried with military honors on August 7 in Columbus, Ohio.[10]

When Southworth, Sr., went to manage the Braves, things went bad, as he couldn't move past his son's death. He had been an alcoholic years before while managing in the bushes, only to be saved by Branch Rickey, who gave him the Cardinals managerial job after he had put his problem in the past. With the Braves he began to drink heavily again and show up in the clubhouse drunk, which would lead to his ultimate demise as a big league manager.[11] Southworth insisted his players conform to the team's standards and tried to get rid of those who did not. He had strict team rules, pushed his players hard, and even got into confrontations with some of them. David Voigt even wrote, "Reportedly, an inability to curb ... [sexual] adventuring prompted Joe McCarthy and Billy Southworth to resign their managerial posts."[12]

The 1945 Cardinals had the second best batting average (.273) in the senior circuit behind the Cubs, but they lacked power hitting, slamming only 64 home runs. Whitey Kurowski, Buster Adams, Johnny Hopp, Augie Bergamo, Ray Sanders, Red Schoendienst and Emil Verban led them at the bat. On the hill were Red Barrett, Ken Burkhart, Blix Donnelly, Harry Brecheen, George

Dockins, and Ted Wilks. Their 3.24 ERA was second in the league. This season was a temporary lull in the Cardinals' run towards greatness, for in 1946 with Eddie Dyer as manager they would win another World Series title, this time defeating the Boston Red Sox.

Red Schoendienst was in his rookie season in 1945. Despite being better suited as a second baseman or shortstop he played left field, batted .278 and led the league with 26 stolen bases. The 6-foot, 170-pound Schoendienst was a natural infielder and 1945 was the only season of his career where he spent the majority of his time in the outfield. In the minor leagues he was a shortstop but was blocked at the big league level from that position because of Marty Marion. Schoendienst grew up a Cardinal fan in Germantown, Illinois, and was first spotted by the Cardinals at Sportsman's Park in a tryout camp. Germantown was only 40 miles from St. Louis and Schoendienst naturally became a Cardinals fan rooting for his favorite players, which included Marty Marion, Terry Moore, and Enos Slaughter. Schoendienst achieved his success despite only partial vision in his left eye, the result of a childhood accident: he was hammering a nail and when he didn't strike it properly the nail flew up and hit him in the eye. The injury was so bad that the doctor was prepared to remove the eye but Schoendienst would not allow him to do it. The Army classified him 4-F until Dr. Alvin Mueller, the brother of former Cardinal outfielder Heinie Mueller, helped improve his vision to 40/100. Shortly afterward, in May of 1944, he was conscripted, but when his vision regressed he was discharged after eight months. He went back for treatments with Dr. Mueller and his vision improved significantly. Schoendienst batted .372 for Rochester in 25 games during the 1944 season before going into the Army. His responsibilities in the Army included training with a demolition unit at Camp Blanding, Florida, and at Pine Camp, New York. He played for the Pine Camp baseball team and injured his right arm and shoulder in his final game. Schoendienst was a right-handed thrower.[13]

Schoendienst became a switch hitter through hard work: when he batted left-handed, his right eye had a good view of the pitcher, and when he batted right-handed he would turn his head in such a way that he could see the delivery very well with his right eye. His swing looked identical from both sides of the plate. Schoendienst was a line-drive hitter who would go on to have a Hall of Fame career. Frederick G. Lieb observed that he had a "pleasant" face that reminded him of movie star Mickey Rooney. He predicted that Schoendienst would become a star himself and make the big money. He suggested that his readers learn to spell his name.[14]

Red, who was born Albert Fred Schoendienst on February 2, 1923, possessed great speed and the ability to gauge the pitcher's delivery to get a good jump. Manager Billy Southworth employed the hit-and-run more frequently than the stolen base and during the last three pennant seasons, 1942 to 1944, his club stole only 71, 40 and 37 bases respectively. Even though Schoendienst didn't have the green light to steal when he wanted, Southworth would allow him to steal frequently and the stolen base contributed heavily to several wins on the season.

Dick Schofield, who became Schoendienst's teammate with the Cardinals in 1953, said, "He didn't look smooth in the field, but he was as good as anyone."[15] Red was very proficient in turning the double play. In 1949 he established a record for consecutive errorless chances and then performed even better in 1950, establishing a new record. During six seasons in his career he led the National League in fielding average.

Schoendienst's cousin Paul was playing first base with St. Paul in the American Association in 1945 and his older brother Julius was in the Cardinals farm system before going into the military in 1942. His father, Joe, was a catcher in the Clinton County League in Illinois but had to retire when he injured his arm. Red played fifteen of his nineteen major league seasons with the Cardinals from 1945 to 1956 and from 1961 to 1963. He also played for the New York Giants (1956–1957) and Milwaukee Braves (1957–1960). Schoendienst helped propel Milwaukee to a World Series title in 1957 and a pennant in 1958. He was diagnosed with tuberculosis after the 1958 World Series and played only five games for Milwaukee in 1959. In 1960 he provided a more significant contribution, batting .257 in 68 games and 226 at-bats. He returned to the Cardinals in 1961 and batted .300 in 72 games and 120 at-bats. During the 1962 campaign he batted .301 in 98 games and 143 at-bats. He played in six games in 1963 and was 0 for 5 in his final big league at-bats. He had a career high .342 batting average and .405 on-base percentage in 1953. He led the National League in doubles in 1950 with 43 and his 200 hits with the Giants and Braves in 1957 led the circuit. He had a .289 lifetime batting average with a .337 on-base percentage. Red hit 427 doubles, 78 triples, and 84 home runs, had 1,223 runs scored and 773 RBIs. He stole 89 bases, 29.2 percent of them in his rookie season of 1945. Red was one of the greatest switch hitters in the game's history and was elected to the Hall of Fame in 1989.

One of the highlights of Schoendienst's career was when he hit a home run in the fourteenth inning to lead the National League to a 4–3 victory in the 1950 All-Star game at Comiskey Park. In his only at-bat of the game Schoendient stepped into the batter's box against the left-handed pitcher, Ted Gray. But instead of batting right-handed against the southpaw as he was accustomed to doing as a switch hitter, Schoendienst batted left-handed and hit the home run on a first-pitch fastball.[16]

Red managed fourteen seasons in the big leagues and coached in seventeen. He was the Cardinals' manager from 1965 to 1976 and managed briefly during the 1980 and 1990 seasons. In 1967 the Cardinals won the World Series over Boston, four games to three. And in 1968 they lost the World Series to Detroit in seven games. Schoendienst's final major league tally as a manager was 1,041 wins and 955 loses.

The banjo-hitting Emil Verban played second and batted .278 while his double-play partner, Marty Marion, batted .277. Marion was the slick fielding shortstop who held the infield together. He had great range and a strong arm. Billy Southworth said, "He is the best shortstop I've ever seen, and he is the main reason why the Cardinals are as good as they are."[17] Marion was deferred from military service because as a child he fell down a cliff, shattering his right thigh. The kids he had been playing with left him at the bottom of a twenty-foot bank when they saw the gruesome injury and the bone sticking out of his leg. After several hours his father went into the woods where they had been playing and found him. He was in a body cast for seven months and had to use crutches for a year after that. As a result his right leg was one inch shorter than his left. Marion's nickname was "Slats," and it was given to him by Burt Shotton because he was tall and thin, standing 6'2" and about 165 pounds.[18] He played his entire big league career in St. Louis with the Cardinals from 1940 to 1950 and with the Browns in 1952 and 1953. Marion batted .263 lifetime with little power (36 homers), and despite playing a position where range and foot speed are important, he only stole 35 bases in his career. His brother Red Marion played four games for the 1935 Washington Senators, going 2 for 11 with one homer. Eight years later he returned to the big leagues with the 1943 Senators, and batted .176 (3 for 17) in fourteen games.

Whitey Kurowski, their third baseman, also had a childhood injury that made his right arm four inches shorter than his left. He developed osteomyelitis, which was the same affliction that later hampered Mickey Mantle in his knees. Kurowski had one of his better seasons in 1945, batting .323 with 21 homers and 102 RBIs. He was built solidly at 5'11" and 193 pounds. Whitey, who was given his nickname because of his "snow white" hair, was born George John Kurowski in Reading, Pennsylvania, on April 19, 1918, a date that was usually very close to opening day of the major league season. He batted and threw right-handed and was a dead pull hitter at the plate. Marty Marion compensated for Kurowski's inability to cover a lot of ground and fielded a plethora of ground balls that a wide-ranging, complete defensive third baseman would have scooped up. Kurowski's arm wasn't that strong either.[19] However, when he got to the ball he was generally a good fielder and led National League third basemen in fielding average in both 1944 and 1946. In his nine-year major league career with St. Louis from 1941 to 1949 he batted .286 with a .366 on-base percentage and 106 home runs.

Buster Adams had his career year, batting .287 with 22 homers and 109 RBIs in 1945. Adams began the season with the Philadelphia Phillies and played fourteen games for them. He was traded to St. Louis on May 8 for John Antonelli and Glenn Crawford. In 1944, the six-foot, 180-pound, right-handed hitting outfielder batted .283 with 17 homers and 64 RBIs for the Phillies. Those final two wartime seasons were easily the best years of his career. When baseball returned to normalcy in 1946 he managed only a .185 batting average with 5

3. The Defending World Champions

homers in 173 at-bats for the Cardinals. He returned to the Phillies in 1947, his final big league season, and batted .247 with 2 homers in 182 at-bats.

Ray Sanders was a 6'2", 185-pound, left-handed hitting, but right-handed throwing first baseman. In his seven major league seasons he played for four pennant winners and two world championship teams with the Cardinals from 1942 to 1944 and with the Boston Braves in 1948. He batted .252 as a rookie for the Red Birds in 1942 and then hit for a .280 clip with 11 homers and 73 RBIs in 1943. Sanders had his best season in 1944, batting .295 with 34 doubles, 9 triples, 12 home runs, 87 runs scored and 102 RBIs. He also fielded superbly and led the league's first basemen with a .994 fielding average. In 1945 he contributed to the club with a .276 batting average with 8 homers and 78 RBIs. His numbers declined significantly in the first postwar season in 1946, as he batted .243 with 6 homers in 259 at-bats for the Braves. He broke his arm during the 1946 campaign and as a result he didn't play in the big leagues in 1947. He played in a total of fourteen games in 1948 and 1949, ending his major league career with a .274 batting average and a good .370 on-base percentage. On March 6, 1948, he was traded to the Brooklyn Dodgers as part of a deal that sent Eddie Stanky to the Boston Braves. However, he never played for the Dodgers and on April 19, 1948, he was returned to the Braves for a reported $60,000.

St. Louis's capable backstop Ken O'Dea was finally getting an opportunity to be a first-string catcher after being relegated to backup status for most of his career. When he broke in with the Chicago Cubs in 1935, future Hall of Famer Gabby Hartnett was the starting catcher. O'Dea had some good years with the bat in Chicago, hitting .307 (189 at-bats) in 1936 and .301 (219 at-bats) in 1937. From 1939 to 1941 he played for the New York Giants but never amassed more than 97 at-bats in a season as Harry Danning was having his best years for New York. On December 11, 1941, he was traded to the St. Louis Cardinals as part of a swap that brought Johnny Mize to New York. This time he sat behind Walker Cooper, who was hitting the ball with great proficiency for the Red Birds. But after Cooper departed for the Navy after only four games in 1945, O'Dea was given the starting job on a temporary basis and batted .254 on the season in a career-high 100 games and 307 at-bats. However, just as O'Dea was inserted into the starting lineup he was already receiving competition from rookie Del Rice, who had been called up from Rochester. Rice saw significant playing time as well, batting .261 in 253 at-bats. O'Dea's final major league season came in 1946, when he batted .157 in 89 at-bats for the Cardinals and Braves. He ended his twelve-year career with a .255 batting average.

Red Barrett led the National League with twenty-three wins in 1945 and Ken Burkhart won eighteen, finishing tied for third. Neither pitcher would ever again approach those numbers. Barrett came over from the Boston Braves in the Mort Cooper trade and gave the Cardinals a colorful figure that was reminiscent of the Gas House Gang days. Barrett was loquacious and humorous, possessing an eccentric personality. To many Barrett was a "screwball" but others saw a guy who enjoyed life to the fullest. He liked to hang out in jazz clubs and sing with the band. Barrett insisted that he had sung with jazz bands throughout the country. He had sung with Sammy Kaye, Tommy Dorsey, Skinny Ennis and Abe Lyman, who was a close friend of his. He most enjoyed singing in front of injured soldiers in hospitals to lift their spirits. During the previous winter he was part of the opera *Narcissus*, which was performed by the Los Angeles Philharmonic Theater. Barrett broke into the big leagues with the Cincinnati Reds in 1937 but saw little playing time due to his run-ins with manager Bill McKechnie. It wasn't until 1943 with the Braves that he got his first opportunity to pitch regularly in the majors. He was 12–18 that season and in 1944 he compiled a 9–16 record with a 4.06 ERA. In addition to leading the National League in wins in 1945 he also led the circuit in complete games (24) and innings pitched (284.2). Barrett was not a fast pitcher but had good control and knew how to work to a hitter. Frederick G. Lieb wrote, "He's a real product of the good old American melting pot, as Red has Scotch, Irish, Spanish, English and Swiss blood in his veins. Probably the Celt, Spanish and Swiss strains explain his wish to warble, dance and yodel."[20]

Rookie pitcher Ken Burkhart put together an 18–8 record in 1945 with a 2.90 ERA in what would be the only great season in a short major league career. Burkhart was what Oscar Ruhl called a "northernized Tennessean," having been born and raised in Knoxville, where he lived until he was 17, and then moving to Cleveland, Ohio.[21] He was almost twenty-one when he attended a Cardinals tryout camp in Columbus, Ohio, and was then invited to baseball school at Winter Haven, Florida. In Florida he competed with about 200 kids in front of the Cardinals' scouts and was subsequently sent to New Iberia, Louisiana, in the Evangeline League. He spent seven years in the bushes before making it with the big club in 1945. Burkhart probably would have made it sooner if not for a broken leg he suffered while sliding into second base with Columbus in 1942. It wasn't until 1944 that he returned to form, compiling a 15–9 record with Columbus, who finished in fifth place. With the Cardinals in 1945 he almost threw four consecutive shutouts as a starting pitcher, missing by two innings on August 25, although he did give up a run in a relief appearance during that streak. Burkhart pitched in 42 games on the season and started 22 of them, proving to be a durable pitcher.

Sylvester Urban Donnelly was better known as Blix, and the right-handed pitcher started his big league career with the Cardinals in 1944, compiling a 2–1 record with a 2.12 ERA while pitching mostly in relief. In 1945 at the age of thirty-one he started 23 of his 31 games and was 8–10 with a 3.52 ERA. He pitched in the big leagues until 1951 with the Cardinals, Phillies, and Braves and had a 27–36 lifetime mark with a 3.49 ERA.

Harry "the Cat" Brecheen earned his nickname because of his great fielding ability: when a ball was hit in his vicinity he would pounce on it quickly like a cat on a mouse. He was an intelligent pitcher with a plan of attack for each batter. The Oklahoma-born southpaw hurler had a good sense of humor and would help his teammates loosen up with a laugh. On the hill, Brecheen threw a variety of excellent curveballs. He was meticulous on the mound and often rejected a new baseball after quick examination. The home plate umpire would put the rejected ball in his pocket and later toss it back to Brecheen to test him. But once again he would reject the baseball.[22] Brecheen stood at 5'10" and 160 pounds. For six seasons from 1944 to 1949 he would win at least fourteen games for the Cardinals, including a career high of twenty wins in 1948. In 1948 he led the senior circuit in ERA (2.24) and strikeouts (149). In 1945 he was thirty years old and pitching in his fourth major league season: he compiled a 15–4 record and a 2.52 ERA. He spent eleven of his twelve seasons during his major league career with St. Louis's National League contingent, going 133–92 lifetime with a 2.92 ERA.

George Dockins was another left-handed pitcher on the staff, and he went 8–6 with a 3.21 ERA, pitching mostly in relief. He only appeared in one additional major league season, pitching in four games for the 1947 Brooklyn Dodgers.

Right-hander Ted Wilks began his major league career in grand style in 1944, going 17–4 with a 2.64 ERA. In his ten-year major league career he never again approached those numbers and in 1945 he fell to 4–7 with a 2.93 ERA. In 1944 Wilks pitched 207.2 innings but in 1945 he was limited to only 98.1 innings because of a sore arm.

The Sportsman's Park infield was known as the "Rockpile," because of its hard surface and the myriad pebbles that adorned it. Marion would incessantly pick up pebbles and throw them over his shoulder in an attempt to avoid bad hops. Due to the horrible playing conditions, good fielders were certain to make their share of errors. The outfield, with its uneven grass, also provided problems. Enos Slaughter said regarding the unpredictable bounces, "Sometimes you'd get hit in the throat, sometimes in the leg, sometimes in the stomach. You'd try to get in front of it and stop it, but, boy! it was tough."[23]

The Cardinals' home park was the center of a controversy in June. It was sparked by Sam Breadon, who made denigrating comments about the Giants' home ballpark, the Polo Grounds. Breadon said that the Giants' home runs were not authentic because it was too easy to slam a long ball down the short right field line. The Giant players retaliated, calling the visitors' locker room at Sportsman's Park "dirty" and saying Breadon ran the ballpark like a "pigsty." Phil Weintraub said, "It's the worst excuse for a major league field I ever saw. I've played in better Class D ball parks." Red Treadway observed that because of the unpredictable hops, there was a randomness to the game since whether a ball was fielded was often based on luck and not skill. Opposing ballplayers called Sportsman's Park "Dugan's Brickyard" because the uneven nature of the field gave the impression that it was paved with old bricks. The conditions were exacerbated because both the Cardinals and Browns used the park. Breadon replied by saying that his field couldn't be that bad since they won three consecutive pennants and two World Series titles using the park. The Giants complained that there were four showers but only three shower heads in the visitors' locker room and Breadon countered by saying he had not heard of any complaints. However, Breadon did concede that he had not visited the room in a long time. The Park superintendent said the showers were properly equipped at the start of the season.[24]

In 1945 Sam Breadon had his hands full but unlike previous years the manpower shortage got the best of the Cardinals and they were beat out for the National League flag.

❖ 4 ❖

Controversy in Brooklyn

The spark behind the Brooklyn Dodgers in 1945 was their scrappy manager Leo "The Lip" Durocher. He was a cruel, vulgar human being, and when he put on the uniform he was out to kill. Durocher was a gritty shortstop, who also played second, and had started his career with the New York Yankees in 1925. Later he played for the Cincinnati Reds, the St. Louis Cardinals (the Gas House Gang) and Brooklyn. Defensively he was solid but offensively his weak hitting earned him the nickname "All American Out."[1] Off the field he was impeccably dressed, wore perfume, was well groomed and hung out with influential people. He got into gambling problems, incessantly cheated on his wife, and in 1945 beat the hell out of a fan under the stands. As manager he wanted "hungry ballplayers who come to kill you," players who were out to intimidate the opposition by throwing beanballs at the batter's head, players who took vicious take-out slides and could handle themselves in a fight.[2] Players who were dirty like himself. He was a throwback to John McGraw, doing anything to win a game and get the edge. Beanball wars were numerous with him as manager, particularly with hated rivals like the Giants and Cardinals. He had a nasty mouth and volcanic temper and could verbally or physically break almost anybody down.

Even his own players were not immune from verbal abuse. Ed Stevens, a 20-year-old first baseman with a bright-looking future, was called up to Brooklyn in 1945 but refused to go. During spring training he was verbally attacked by Durocher and when he got the call to the big leagues he didn't want anything to do with him. However, Branch Rickey persuaded the youngster to change his mind and he joined the Dodgers. But instead of ceasing the verbal attacks and showing sympathy for the predicament of his talented prospect, Durocher continued the harassment when Stevens joined the Dodgers and would not even stop the following year. Stevens recalled that Durocher verbally harassed him from the first inning during one particular ugly incident and when Leo got tired he told coach Chuck Dressen to take over for a few innings.[3] In 1948 Durocher would send shock waves reverberating throughout major league baseball when he became the manager of the New York Giants.

Leo Durocher was caught up in heated arguments with umpires throughout the 1945 season but his biggest headache was of the legal variety. It happened during a June 10 game between the Dodgers and the Phillies at Ebbets Field when Durocher and a park officer took John Christian, a taunting fan, under the stands and beat the hell out of him with brass knuckles. Leo was in a foul mood and by the sixth inning he had heard enough criticism from the fan, who was escorted to a place where Leo and the park officer could bloody him up. Christian, a former paratrooper in the Army, went to the hospital with a broken jaw, black eye, and various head injuries. Durocher was charged with assault and faced jail time and possible penalties from organized baseball. Branch Rickey, the Dodgers president, came to his manager's defense, stating that the organization "will stand as a unit against indecent and vulgar remarks from those in the stands."[4] Evidently Rickey turned a blind eye to his manager's own vulgarity. Rickey called his players "fine gentlemen" and made the claim that "players have sensibilities and feelings and we must protect them against abuse."[5] Rickey blamed everyone except Durocher, stating that the park policeman had urged Leo to listen to the fan's taunting and then suggested he beat the hell out of him.

The aggrieved fan would eventually face a fixed trial, for the judge was a huge Dodger fan and Leo would be exonerated.[6] Christian admitted calling Durocher "a crook" and "a bum," and in turn Leo lied through his teeth and said he was appalled by Christian's "ungentlemanly" behavior. He added, "I never touched him." Durocher had thought about settling the case out of court, but his lawyers warned him against it, fearing that if he was not acquitted then his baseball career was in serious peril. After the trial, Judge Louis Goldstein, an ardent Dodger fan, was overjoyed, saying, "I am glad for the sake of the Brooklyn baseball team that their manager has been vindicated and that no discredit has been placed on the great American game of baseball."[7]

Leo Durocher was not only hated around the league but was also hated by his own players. If his teams were losing he would often lose interest and be more approachable, but when his teams were winning he was a scoundrel. After one victory in 1943 he rebuked pitcher Bobo Newsom, accusing him of crossing up his catcher Bobby Bragan with a spitter. He tore into the unsuspecting pitcher in front of a reporter and suspended him. The writer wrote an article describing the incident, which did not sit well with the players. They rebelled and veteran Arky Vaughan led the way, tossing his uniform at Durocher's feet and yelling, "Here. If you want his uniform, you can have mine, too."[8] Dixie Walker followed Vaughan's lead and offered his uniform as the mutiny had begun. The players stared down their skipper in blatant disrespect for Durocher's authority. Leo, in search of a scapegoat, informed the menacing ballplayers that the reporter was "a liar."[9] That season he also kicked Joe Medwick off the team. Actions of this kind only lost him respect among his ballplayers and it took him a year to regain control over his team.

4. Controversy in Brooklyn

One day he had Chuck Dressen, the third base coach, give Billy Herman the take sign in an obvious hitting situation. As a result he watched two strikes go by and then lined out to third. Durocher looked disgusted with his head in his hands and Herman fired the practice ball at second base towards the dugout. The throw skipped off the grass and nailed Leo in the head. Billy Herman said, "I didn't like Leo. He didn't treat all the players the same. He played favorites. He wasn't trustworthy; too often he didn't tell you the truth, and he would do everything he could to protect himself, no matter what it did to you."[10] A similar incident happened with the opposition when the Cubs' Hi Bithorn fired the ball at Durocher when he was sitting in the dugout between innings. Bithorn was fined by his manager, Jimmie Wilson, not for throwing the ball but for not hitting Durocher.[11] On another occasion Leo gathered the writers and told them his pitcher, Luke Hamlin, was "the gutless wonder."[12] Durocher had a huge ego and this was highlighted during the 1945 spring training in Bear Mountain, New York, when he had the practice field named "Durocher Field."[13]

Durocher described the game when he had played as "a form of warfare played under a set of rules that were not necessarily drawn up by the league officials and certainly not by the Marquis of Queensberry."[14] To carry out his managerial philosophy he sought players like himself who were willing to fight for everything they could get, regardless of the rules. Eddie Stanky was such a player and like Durocher he was hated around the National League. Stanky took advantage of his limited skills and did anything to acquire the edge: he'd slap the ball out of a fielder's glove or throw dirt in his eyes, distract the pitcher in the batter's box, and jump up and down while in the field to upset the batter. Off the field he was as nice as they came, but on the field he was an irritant to the opposition and played the game outside the rules. He said he would "spike my mother if it meant being safe on a close play." Thomas Kiernan wrote that "Stanky was scrappy the way Adolph [sic] Hitler was anti–Semitic."[15] He was the perfect type of ballplayer for Durocher because he would "come to kill you." Durocher wrote in his autobiography, "Now, Stanky's the nicest gentleman who ever drew breath, but when the bell rings you're his mortal enemy. That's the kind of guy I want playing for me."[16] Alvin Dark summed up Stanky as follows:

> Stanky couldn't hit, run, or field. He couldn't do anything except beat you. He would sit on you at second base.... He would pull on your shirt, step on you.... When he got on base he immediately filled his hands with dirt.... He wanted something to throw in the second baseman's face.[17]

Nobody expected much from the Dodgers in 1945, in part because of their poor showing in 1944. After winning the pennant in 1941 the Brooklyn Dodgers failed to duplicate that finish during the war. In 1942 they narrowly lost the pennant to St. Louis, finishing in second place with a 104–50 record. In '43 they were in third place (81–72); in '44 seventh place (63–91); and in '45 third place

(87–67). In 1944 things were so bad that Branch Rickey declared, "All I can say is that we will have a large number of human beings at the training camp."[18]

The 1945 Dodgers were third in the National League in batting (.271) but they only belted 57 homers; only Cincinnati and Philadelphia hit less, with 56. Dixie Walker, Augie Galan, Eddie Stanky, Frenchy Bordagaray, Goody Rosen, and Luis Olmo led at the bat. Dixie was the established hitting star of the Dodgers who had led the majors in batting in 1944 with a .357 average. He was the brother of Harry Walker, the hitting star of the Cardinals, who was in the service during the '44 and '45 seasons. Dixie was so beloved in Brooklyn that they called him the "People's Cherce," and he was always willing to attend events in the borough.[19] He had a great batting eye and was proficient at contact hitting, striking out only sixteen times in 607 at-bats in '45. He batted an even .300 on the season with a major-league leading 124 RBIs. Durocher liked him because he was a veteran among the kids and bush-league caliber players. Leo preferred veteran teams instead of inexperienced aggregations, with whom he had to be extremely patient.

One of those kids was Tommy Brown, who was rushed to the big leagues in 1944 after only three months at Newport News and was not far removed from the Parade Grounds in Brooklyn. Pee Wee Reese had entered the Navy and Leo tried the untested sixteen-year-old in his stead. Brown's throws were so erratic that he earned the nickname "Buckshot" while playing in the minor leagues. The sailors sitting behind first base brought their gloves to catch the wild throws and cheered Brown on when the ball was hit to him.[20] Once Brown fielded the ball at short and threw it into the upper deck. He played 46 games in 1944 and batted .164 and made sixteen errors in the field. In 1945 he batted .245 in 57 games, while making twenty-three errors. He hit two home runs in 1945, and when he hit the first one off Preacher Roe he became the youngest player to hit a homer in major league history at the age of seventeen. Brown played in seven more major league seasons, having an unspectacular career, batting .241. He was known for hitting prolific drives during batting practice but the games were a different story altogether. Brown said, "Some players, the war helped. They got to play. It hurt me 'cause I wasn't ready."[21]

Goody Rosen would finish the season third in the National League batting race at .325. Dodger coach Chuck Dressen helped Rosen correct a hitch in his swing and Arthur Daley would write in the *New York Times*, "Mr. Goodwin Rosen began to belt the whatsis out of the ball and in practically no time at all was crowding Tommy Holmes for the batting championship...."[22] Rosen would only play one more major league season after 1945, batting .333 (1 for 3) for Brooklyn in three games and .281 for the Giants in one hundred contests during the 1946 season.

The Dodgers had their share of memorable players in '45, including the elongated Howie Schultz, who was 6'7"; *The Sporting News* called him "The Leaning Tower of Flatbush."[23] Babe Herman came back for one last time to

4. Controversy in Brooklyn

entertain the crowd. Eddie Basinski, their shortstop, played the violin in the Buffalo Symphony during the off-season and would occasionally entertain the players. Les Webber was a pitcher who had once been instructed by Durocher to hit every Cardinal in the lineup. Mickey Owen played briefly in '45 and would always be remembered in Dodger lore for dropping the third strike from Hugh Casey with two outs in the ninth inning during the fourth game of the 1941 World Series. Owen carried the burden for losing that series. Years later Casey said that he had thrown a spitter but Owen insisted that it was a curveball.

Hal Gregg, who went 18–13 with a 3.47 ERA in what was his best season, anchored the pitching staff. Vic Lombardi, Curt Davis and Tom Seats each won ten games. Art Herring, Clyde King, Ralph Branca, Cy Buker, and Les Webber also made significant contributions on the hill. Their staff ERA was 3.70, third best in the league.

Fans in Brooklyn were overjoyed when Babe Herman, an old Brooklyn relic, returned to the club during the summer. He had last played in the big leagues in 1937, and subsequently played for Toledo in the American Association (1937), Jersey City in the International League (1938), and then the Hollywood Stars of the Pacific Coast League from 1939 to 1944, before apparently retiring for good after the 1944 season. Playing in the Coast League allowed Herman to stay close to his ranch in Glendale, California. Branch Rickey talked Herman out of retirement. Herman was initially told he would receive two weeks to get in shape but within a few days he appeared in a senior league game. He had difficulty reserving a plane seat to fly to the East Coast. While playing for Hollywood he had injured his knee and had been playing with a steel brace for two years.

Herman was a member of Wilbert Robinson's bumbling "Daffiness Boys" in Brooklyn before bouncing around a couple teams. During Herman's first go-around in Brooklyn from 1926 to 1931 he became known as the guy who "tripled into [a] double play,"[24] but in actuality he "doubled into a double play."[25] It was also legend that Herman was hit on the head by a fly ball but he vehemently denied it, saying, "Maybe the shoulder, but not the head."[26] Once Herman was in uniform in 1945 the Brooklyn faithful were extremely impatient and eager to see their hero emerge from the dugout and participate in the action. But Leo Durocher made them wait four days before he was called upon to pinch hit against the St. Louis Cardinals in the first game of a doubleheader on July 8 before 36,053 approving witnesses at Ebbets Field. The crowd roared when Herman emerged from the dugout in the seventh inning to hit for Eddie Stanky: he broke his bat swinging at the first pitch, then hit a single and fell down while rounding the first base bag. If Ray Sanders, the Cardinals first baseman, had been alert, then Herman would have been thrown out at first after collecting a single. It was the forty-two-year-old Herman's first hit as a Dodger in fourteen years. His last season with Brooklyn had been in 1931, when he batted .313

Babe Herman showing his batting stance. Herman was beloved in Brooklyn and with the poor quality of players in 1945 he was able to return to the Dodgers despite not having played in the major leagues since 1937. He was predominantly used as a pinch-hitter and did all right considering his circumstances. The 6'4", 190-pound left-handed hitter had torn cartilage in his knee and was 42 years old. Herman batted .265 with a .359 on-base percentage in 34 at-bats and appeared in 37 games (George Brace photograph).

with 18 homers and 97 RBIs. The Dodger fans had waited patiently for several days before Herman got to play, and Al Laney wrote in the *New York Herald Tribune*, "We declare that there never has been such a demonstration of affection in Ebbets Field."[27] There simply weren't enough seats to accommodate all the fans who wanted to see Herman make his first appearance. Hundreds of fans couldn't get into the ballpark, including many servicemen. The police were encouraging ticketless fans to move away from Flatbush Avenue so it wouldn't be so congested.

Herman batted .265 for Leo Durocher's team in thirty-seven games and thirty-four at-bats. In 1945 he would play his last major league season, finishing his career with an impressive .324 batting average with 181 home runs and 997 RBIs.

The Dodger fans were a devoted group who enjoyed their home games in the cozy environs of Ebbets Field. It was similar to other ballparks of its time in that it had been built in an urban area surrounded by a large population. The park was built to fit around the neighboring city streets, giving the structure its unique architectural shape. The short right-field fence ran adjacent to Bedford Avenue and was an inviting site for left-handed sluggers. The dimensions were as follows: 348 feet down the left field line, 389 to center, and 297 feet down the right field line. The park was a bandbox, a pitcher's nightmare.

The Dodgers and Giants continued their heated rivalry in 1945 with Brooklyn besting their rivals with a 16–9 record. Some of these games were memorable while others simply forgettable. Brooklyn made eight errors on June 7 as the Giants won 10–5. The baseball writers had a field day describing the bush-league play exhibited by the Dodgers. Bill Lauder Jr. wrote in the *New York Herald Tribune*, "Shakespeare wrote 'The Comedy of Errors' and the Dodgers stole the title and presented a farce before an audience of 18,885 at the Polo Grounds yesterday co-starring the Giants."[28] John Drebinger wrote in the *New York Times*, "Whatever indignities the Giants may have suffered at the hands of the Dodgers over a long and turbulent stretch of years were more than atoned for yesterday at the Polo Grounds when Leo Durocher's Flock tossed away a ball game such as hasn't fallen into Melvin Ott's lap in many a revolving moon."[29]

On June 18 it took the Dodgers thirteen innings to defeat New York, 2–1, at Ebbets Field. Howie Schultz drove home the winning run with two out in the thirteenth as he singled off Ace Adams. Harry Feldman of the Giants headed into the ninth with a 1–0 lead but a crucial error by Johnny Rucker would allow the Dodgers to tie the score. George Coleman described Feldman's pitches in the *Brooklyn Eagle*: "Half-speed balls, a dinky hook on the inside, a sharp break on the outside corners mixed with a fire ball every so often, all thrown with uncanny control...."[30] A bench-clearing brawl almost ensued after second baseman Eddie Stanky tagged Danny Gardella with an "uppercut technique" in the eighth inning. Both benches emptied but the brawl was thwarted. Gardella was livid over the tag and a "mob scene" soon surrounded him.[31]

On August 23, Ralph Branca tossed a four-hitter for a 4–1 Dodger win at the Polo Grounds before 39,694 fans. When Branca was growing up he dreamed of nothing more than playing with the New York Giants, but it never materialized. Sal Maglie was the loser for New York. Two hours before the game was scheduled to start, about 10,000 people were already in the stands, eagerly anticipating the interborough war. The Giants needed about 84,000 fans to go over the million mark in attendance for the first time in their history. Umpire Tom Dunn kicked Eddie Stanky out of the game. Stanky was still fuming over a call Dunn made against the Dodgers earlier in the week. As he went out to take his position at second base he had some choice words for the umpire and was quickly tossed. For their earlier squabble Durocher was fined $75 and Stanky $25 by National League president Ford Frick.

Brooklyn passed the one million mark in attendance but lost, 6–2, on August 26. The Giants' victory broke a seven-game losing streak to the Dodgers; they had also lost eight consecutive games at Ebbets Field. Augie Galan was given his own day by the Brooklyn faithful and received a shotgun, ten-gallon hat, and cowboy boots. When Galan was a boy he shattered his right arm and never told anyone about the injury. Because the injury did not heal properly he played with excruciating pain in his arm and elbow during his career. In 1937 he had a left knee injury, which he reinjured in 1938, and then again in 1940 when he ran into the wall while trying to track down a foul ball. His arm injury had become so painful by 1943 that he had to give up switch hitting and bat only from the left side, which wasn't nearly as painful as his right-handed swing.[32] Galan's secret became public during the war when he failed his examination for military service. He was a valuable player for Brooklyn in 1945, batting .307 with an excellent .423 on-base percentage while scoring 114 runs and driving home 92. In 1943 (103) and 1944 (101) he led the National League in walks, and then in 1945 he drew over one hundred walks for the third season in a row, finishing with 114. Galan was also versatile in the field, playing three positions in 1945: first base (66 games), left field (49 games), and third base (40 games). In a sixteen-year career that ended in 1949, he batted .287 with a .390 on-base percentage.

The Giants/Dodgers game on September 1 at the Polo Grounds was typical of wartime ball as the Giants made three errors in a 5–4 victory while the Dodgers made two. The crowd of 19,776 pushed the Giants to their highest attendance ever: they had now drawn 941,198 to the Polo Grounds, breaking the 1937 mark of over nine hundred and twenty thousand. Brooklyn drew 1,059,220 fans to Ebbets Field in 1945, which was slightly better than the Giants' 1,016,468 home attendance. Ott's club was only a game and a half behind third-place Brooklyn as the two clubs fought to see who would finish higher in the standings. Harry Cross wrote in the *New York Herald Tribune*, "They are really serious about the interborough strife and behave as if the title of the universe depended on the outcome."[33]

By season's end Durocher and the Dodgers could at least take solace in the fact that they got the better of their rivals and finished in the first division.

❖ 5 ❖

The Bucs Stop Here

The Pittsburgh Pirates were expected to contend for the National League pennant during the 1945 season. The only player missing from their 1944 starting lineup was Vince DiMaggio, who was traded to the Philadelphia Phillies for left-handed pitcher Al Gerheauser on March 31. They were also returning all of their best pitchers from the 1944 campaign. From 1943 to 1945 the Pirates conducted their training activities in Muncie, Indiana. When they arrived for the 1943 spring training the only reminder of their customary spring training facilities in San Bernardino, California, was a large potted palm located in the Hotel Roberts. They did their training in a small gym which was the only indoor facility they could find. However, when the weather was accommodating they trained on the field belonging to the Ball State Teachers College.

The Pirates were missing their colorful manager, Frankie Frisch, during the training season and Spud Davis temporarily assumed the managerial duties. Frisch was suffering from acute inflammatory arthritis which developed after his ambitious USO tour in Europe. He was eager to get back to work but had to wait till he could walk without a cane. Just the thought of managing with a cane made the old man cringe: "Can you imagine the riding I'd take from those birds if I ever showed up leaning on a cane? Phew! Would they give it to me!" Frisch was particularly amused when he heard that Leo Durocher, his long-time nemesis, was going to try to play second base for Brooklyn. "He'll last five games and collapse. Who's gonna back him up?"[1]

Frankie Frisch was an intelligent, baseball-savvy, fiery personality who managed the Pirates from 1940 to 1946. He had previously managed the St. Louis Cardinals (1933–1938) and later the Chicago Cubs (1949–1951). In his nineteen-year Hall of Fame career with the Giants and Cardinals he batted .316 and participated in eight World Series, batting .294. Frisch had a good childhood and was the son of a wealthy linen manufacturer. He began to develop his high baseball acumen while attending Fordham Prep and then Fordham University, where he was coached by Art Devlin. The "Fordham Flash" also excelled at football and basketball; Walter Camp placed him on the second All-American team in 1917 as a great halfback. Frisch broke in with the New York

Giants in 1919 and was managed by the iron-fisted John McGraw. Over time he proved to be an exceptional switch hitter and a daring base runner, and was known for his magnificent defensive plays as a second baseman. Despite the fact that his defensive style was aesthetically lacking he found a way to get the job done. Gordon Mackay wrote in the 1924 *Reach Guide*, "Frisch is one of the poorest fielders we have ever lamped but his terrific speed overcomes this in every game. Frisch can knock down more balls with his elbows, knees, chest and head, and by dint of his fleet recovery throw out the runner, than any nine men we know."[2]

John McGraw would chew out his players when they made mistakes, but Frisch would not take it and would fire back. McGraw and Frisch had similar personalities and that is perhaps why the Giants skipper was particularly hard on him. On the field Frisch played with "Cobbian intensity."[3] He had great leadership qualities and many thought he would succeed McGraw in New York as manager. However, Bill Terry took that job and Frisch later became manager of the Gas House Gang Cardinals, where he motivated his players by cursing them out and even engaged in fisticuffs with some of them. Depression Era baseball was rough. However, he was happy to escape the unyielding customs of John McGraw. Frisch wrote, "After those stern years with the regimented Giants, to be in a baseball group where everybody was happy and relaxed, having a good time, enjoying their work. We worked hard, all right, but it was different. There was nobody standing over you with a whip in his hand, telling you to do it his way, or else."[4]

Frankie Frisch (left), manager of the Pittsburgh Pirates, sharing a laugh with Dizzy Dean of the Chicago Cubs. The colorful pitcher played for the Cubs from 1938 to 1941 and then coached for them briefly during the 1941 season before leaving for a broadcasting job with the St. Louis Cardinals. Dean won 102 games during the span of four remarkable seasons from 1933 to 1936 while playing under player-manager Frisch with the Cardinals. Frisch led the Cardinals to a World Series title in 1934, but when he managed the Pittsburgh Pirates from 1940 to 1946 they were consistently a mediocre ball club. In 1945, the Pirates had a good but unspectacular season, finishing in fourth place with an 82–72 mark (George Brace photograph).

In 1940 Frisch led the Pirates to a fourth place finish (78–76);

they again finished in fourth place in '41 (81–73); in '42 they fell to fifth place (66–81); in '43 they returned to fourth place (80–74); and in '44 they improved to second place (90–63). The future looked bright towards the tail end of the season when their Albany farm club sent the following prospects to join the Pirates: Vic Barnhart, Al Gionfriddo, Bill Rodgers, and Leonard Gilmore. However, in 1945 the Pirates would not meet expectations and finished in fourth place (82–72). Frisch's ball clubs in Pittsburgh were consistently good but not great. Frisch was asked about how his team would do during the first wartime season and he responded, "I intend to play my youngsters as long as I can and when Uncle Sam calls them, I'll hope they bat .400 against the Japs and the Nazis alike."[5]

The 1945 Pirates performed well in many of the key offensive categories: they were tied for fifth in the senior circuit in batting average (.267), but were third in on-base percentage (.342) and second in slugging percentage (.377). They led the league in doubles (259), finished second in triples (56), and third in home runs (72). The Pirates scored 753 runs, which was the third best in the league, and their 81 stolen bases was only one behind the league-leading Boston Braves. Their 3.76 team ERA was the fourth best in the circuit.

At the bat the 1945 Pirates were led by Bob Elliott, Babe Dahlgren, Frankie Gustine, Al Gionfriddo, Jim Russell, and Johnny Barrett, among others. The best pitchers included Preacher Roe, Nick Strincevich, Rip Sewell, Max Butcher, Al Gerheauser, and Ken Gables. Elliott was a 6-foot, 185-pound third baseman, who was also capable of playing the outfield. He batted .290, slammed eight homers and drove in 108 runs. This was the seventh season of what would be a fifteen-year major league career in which he batted .289 with a .375 on-base percentage and a .440 slugging percentage. He drove in 100 or more runs during six seasons including the final three wartime seasons from 1943 to 1945. During his 1947 MVP performance with the Boston Braves he compiled a .317 batting average, a .410 on-base percentage, and a .517 slugging percentage. In 1948 he led the senior league with 131 walks, which was 41 more walks than his second best season in that category in 1949. Shortstop Frankie Gustine would play ten of his twelve major league seasons with the Pirates and batted .280 on the season. After a cup of coffee with the Pirates in 1944, Al Gionfriddo played in 122 games and batted .284 in 1945. He would later become famous for making a spectacular catch to rob Joe DiMaggio in the sixth game of the 1947 World Series while playing for the Brooklyn Dodgers. Babe Dahlgren was in his next to last season, playing with his eighth team, and batted .250, with 5 homers and 75 RBIs. When Lou Gehrig finally took himself out of a game to end his consecutive-games streak, it was Dahlgren who had replaced him. Jim Russell began his career with Pittsburgh in 1942 and batted .284 with 12 homers and 77 driven in during 1945.

Johnny Barrett contributed with a .256 batting average, with 15 homers and 67 RBIs while playing center field (75 games) and right field (57 games).

Barrett loved to utilize his speed and in 1944 he led the majors with 19 triples and led the National League with 28 stolen bases. In 1945 his triples dropped to only 4 but he did steal 25 bags. While playing in the minor leagues with Hazleton in 1938 he led the Eastern League in triples and also led the Pacific Coast League in triples during the 1940 season with San Francisco. Barrett was from Lowell, Massachusetts, and signed his first contract with the Red Sox, who sent him off to Mansfield in the Ohio State League. His .378 batting average was second in the league to his manager Dewey Stover. He also frustrated the batteries in the circuit by stealing 51 bags in 84 games. After a few more stops along the minor league ladder he played with the San Francisco Seals in the Pacific Coast League in 1940. His manager was Lefty O'Doul, of whom he recalled, "He is a great fellow; I've never played under any better. He taught me a lot, too. Lefty liked to run as a player, and he taught me how to capitalize on my speed." Barrett began his big league career with Pittsburgh in 1942, batting .247. He was a pesky hitter who generally began the season slowly. In 1945 he was enjoying his best early season success of his career. He had been rejected by the Army because of stomach ulcers. Frederick G. Lieb wrote, "He has brown hair and gray eyes, and his face is as Irish as the map of Eire. He's as left-handed as his old Coast hero, Lefty O'Doul, throwing and batting left-handed."[6]

Thirty-nine-year-old Lloyd Waner came back to the Pirates to end his great career. He batted .263 in nineteen at-bats to finish with a .316 career batting average. Lloyd was known as "Little Poison" and for years had teamed up with his brother, Paul "Big Poison" Waner, to amaze the Pittsburgh faithful with their proficient hitting. Another aging veteran on the team was Al Lopez, who batted .218 in 91 games. As a kid he played in the sand lots behind the cigar factories in Tampa, Florida, and was one of nine children whose parents had come to the country from Madrid, Spain. Lopez batted .261 in nineteen big league seasons and was an excellent defensive catcher. During his career he played under six managers who were eventually enshrined in the Hall of Fame: Wilbert Robinson, Max Carey, Casey Stengel, Bill McKechnie, Frankie Frisch, and Lou Boudreau. (Carey did not have a managerial career that would significantly augment his Hall of Fame credentials: he only managed in two big league seasons, with Brooklyn in 1932 and 1933, and they finished in third and sixth place respectively.) Lopez later became a manager himself, for the Cleveland Indians and the Chicago White Sox, and was also inducted into the Hall of Fame. He managed the 1954 Indians to a pennant and later accomplished this feat with the 1959 White Sox. Lopez was an extraordinarily nice man and Bill Veeck observed, "If Al Lopez has a weakness as a manager — and I said if — it is that he is too decent.... Al was completely relaxed. In the cool, calm way of his he squeezed every possible drop of talent out of his team. When I think of that season [1959], I think of a squibbling hit and everybody running."[7] The 1959 White Sox played small ball to win the pennant. They hit a major-league-low 97 homers but led both leagues with 113 stolen bases.

Rip Sewell awed the crowds with his "eephus" pitch, also known as the "blooper," "parachute,"[8] and "skyscraper,"[9] among other terms. The pitch is thrown overhand with a fastball motion and comes in slow and very high, usually reaching a height of 25 feet above the ground and ideally drops from the top half to the bottom half of the strike zone. The pitch became famous when Ted Williams hit a homer off Sewell's "eephus" in the 1946 All-Star game. Williams recalled, "It came to the plate like a pop fly."[10] Sewell had first used the pitch in an exhibition game in 1942 against the Detroit Tigers. He began throwing the ball after his foot was injured in a hunting accident. Rip couldn't pivot properly to generate enough power to throw hard so he developed this pitch. Dick Wakefield was the first to see the pitch with the count at 3–2. "Wakefield started to swing, then he stopped, and then he swung again and almost fell down when he missed," recalls Sewell.[11] Everyone had a good laugh watching Wakefield trying to hit the ball.

Sewell was Lloyd Waner's teammate for several seasons, including the final two wartime seasons. Paul Waner was also a teammate of Sewell's for three seasons (1938–1940) with the Pittsburgh Pirates. On June 19, 1942, he got his 3,000th hit off the pitcher while playing with the Boston Braves. Sewell won twenty-one games in both 1943 and 1944 but in 1945 he slipped to an 11–9 record and a 4.07 ERA. In a thirteen-year career that ended with the 1949 season he compiled a 143–97 record and a 3.48 ERA. He pitched right-handed but batted from the left side of the plate. He managed only a .203 batting average in his career but slugged six homers. Sewell began his career with the 1932 Detroit Tigers but didn't return to the big leagues until 1938 with Pittsburgh.

Elwin Charles "Preacher" Roe grew up a Cardinals fan in Arkansas and got to make his major league debut with them by pitching in one game in 1938. He subsequently was buried in the Cardinals farm system and didn't start his big league career in earnest until 1944, when he was 13–11 with a 3.11 ERA for Pittsburgh. In 1945 he improved to 14–13 with a 2.87 ERA and led the National League with 148 strikeouts. Later he suffered a head injury back home and when he returned to the mound his velocity had diminished, causing him to have dreadful 1946 (3–8) and 1947 (4–15) seasons. The difficulties that Roe experienced during those two seasons compelled him to change his approach to pitching: "I commenced thinking about pitching to spots, changing speeds, fooling them hitters instead of over-powering them, and, of course, I commenced to develop my wet one."[12] He threw his spitball with a fastball motion and squeezed the ball before his release. The ball tumbled down sharply as it approached the hitter.

In 1948 he joined the Brooklyn Dodgers and would become a memorable figure in Dodger history. For six consecutive seasons, from 1948 to 1953, he won at least eleven games for Brooklyn, including a career high twenty-two victories in 1951. From 1949 to 1951 he was one of the best pitchers in the National League as he compiled a 56–20 record. After consecutive eleven-win seasons in 1952 and 1953, he pitched in his final big league season in 1954 and was 3–4 with an uninspiring 5.00 ERA. Roe ended his impressive career with a 127–84 record and a 3.43 ERA. In 1955 he caused a commotion when he admitted to Dick Young of *Sports Illustrated* that he had frequently doctored the baseball during his career. Young wrote a revealing article titled "The Outlawed Spitter Was My Money Pitch." Roe stated, "I threw spitballs the whole time I was with the Dodgers." He added, "I wasn't the only one that did it. There are still some guys wetting 'em up right now."[13] The spitter was only one pitch in his repertoire, but after the article was published he said, "Some seem to think I threw a hundred spitters every game."[14]

Another interesting personality who pitched for the Pirates was Walter "Boom-Boom" Beck. After compiling a 2–4 record for Cincinnati early in the year he appeared in fourteen games for Pittsburgh and was 6–1. He had pitched in the Baker Bowl as a visiting player and with its tremendously short right field porch had acquired the nickname Boom-Boom for "one boom off of the bat, the other off the tin wall."[15] One day he was removed from the game and became agitated and threw the ball off the tin right field wall. His right fielder had been chasing drives all day and had momentarily shut his eyes. Beck threw the ball near his head and the right fielder hurriedly awoke, scampered after it, and fired it to second, thinking the ball was in play.

One of the highlights of the season occurred when the Pirates had a two-day celebration to honor the career of Honus Wagner. Wagner was now a coach with the ball club and the fans collaborated with the Pirates organization to raise $14,000 for him during those two days. Wagner was the greatest shortstop to ever play the game and ended his playing career in 1917 with a .328 batting average. At 5'11" and 200 pounds he had huge shoulders, powerfully built arms, and huge hands which he used to scoop up the ball with grace. He enjoyed beer but avoided hard liquor; he enjoyed cigars but disdained cigarettes. He had bowed legs which belied his fast running ability. Donald Honig wrote, "He did not have the aloof elegance of a Mathewson, the zany charm of a Waddell, the intensity of a Cobb, the majesty of a Ruth, the aristocracy of a DiMaggio, the lethal perfectionism of a Williams, the breathless excitement of a Mays. But for many witnesses, including John McGraw, who watched him close-up for twenty years, Wagner was the greatest of ballplayers, with Cobb the only other candidate in the running for the title."[16] Like many Americans, Wagner endured economic hardships during the Depression and was given a coaching job in 1933 with the Pirates. He worked predominantly with the rookies and would love to tell them stories of his accomplishments. Wagner was the symbol of the Pirates and the generosity of the fans in 1945 showed that.

6

The Giants Race to the Top of the Senior Circuit

The 1945 Giants had one of the more diverse groups of players on any major league roster and were led by their amiable player-manager Mel Ott. Five days before Pearl Harbor, Mel Ott was named the Giants skipper. He was a likeable, left-handed hitting slugger, who had first caught the eye of John McGraw when he was sixteen years old. With his peculiar style of hitting, lifting his right foot as the pitch approached the plate, and then having a proper level swing, he was ideal for the short porch in right field at the Polo Grounds. McGraw declared him to be the "most natural hitter" he had ever seen.[1] He expected high standards from his young prodigy. One day he had heard a rumor that one of his young long-ball hitters had escorted a lady to their room. The portly McGraw mistakenly tore into Fred Lindstrom and when he heard that it was Ott he refused to believe it. "It wasn't Ott! It was Lindstrom!" he yelled.[2] Ott's lifetime batting average would be .304 with 511 home runs and 1,860 RBIs.

Ott predicted instant success below Coogan's Bluff in 1942, saying they would finish in the first division. On December 7, John Drebinger of the *New York Times* described a press conference that was held at the Giants offices: "By his engaging frankness, even temper and pleasing personality, the 32-year-old 'boy wonder' of the Polo Grounds seemed to convince one and all that here indeed was a Major League skipper who would never be difficult to approach or interview."[3] Shortly after, Ott pulled off a major trade that brought the powerful slugger Johnny Mize to New York. It served notice that he would assemble a powerful lineup, capable of putting large numbers on the scoreboard.

Things went well that first year, as they finished in third place (85–67). Ott batted .295 and led the league in homers (30) and runs scored (118). However, the pressure took its toll, as he incessantly tapped his foot to the earth while in the outfield, thinking about his next move, which distracted him from the current moment. In a game against Brooklyn, he uncharacteristically took out Pee Wee Reese at second with a vicious take-out slide, to the consternation of everyone. Leo Durocher, the Dodgers manager, urged his pitchers to retaliate with beanballs at his head. Ott's obsession led him to toss and turn at night, making it difficult for him to sleep. The following year, the Giants were the doormat of the National League, as they compiled a repugnant 55–98 record. Ott batted a paltry .234. They were slightly better in 1944, a fifth-place finish (67–87) and a .288 average for Ott with 26 homers. Ott developed a reputation as a nice guy who did not have what it took to be a successful manager. He did not discipline players adequately, and his amiable personality helped lead to his downfall as manager. The fiery Leo Durocher was sitting with a reporter one day when he pointed to the Giants dugout and said, "Take a look at that Number Four there. A nicer guy never drew breath than that man there.... Walker Cooper, Mize, Marshall, Kerr, Gordon, Thomson. Take a look at them. All nice guys. They'll finish last. Nice guys. Finish last."[4]

Many skeptics doubted Ott's abilities as spring training approached in 1945. He had spent part of his winter with a USO tour, entertaining the troops in Europe, just beyond the bloody combat areas. The 82nd Airborne visited with the Giants skipper and if he had encountered the troops a couple of days later he would have been trapped by the German counteroffensive. "Every day here is like the Dodgers and the Giants at Ebbets Field. Only I wish it were only pop bottles being thrown," said Ott.[5]

The Giants trained at what was once the John D. Rockefeller estate in Lakewood, New Jersey. After Rockefeller's death in 1937 the facilities had been converted into public parkland. It was ten degrees warmer than the city and the pine trees helped shield them from the blistering wind. There was plenty of snow in 1944, and only eight exhibition games were played, prompting Ott to call his squad "the worst conditioned club in Giant history."[6] In 1945 the Giants stayed in the plush Rockefeller mansion since the hotels were full. It had heat, private rooms for the players, and seventeen baths. The infields were constructed out on the golf course. When the Giants showed up they were welcomed by a snow-covered practice field. During their first year in Lakewood, Ott had warned his team not to complain: "Don't forget this is not Miami and there's a war on. Grumbling will get out among the fans, and we can't afford that sort of thing."[7]

Those pitchers who would be competing for a spot in the rotation included Bill Voiselle, Harry Feldman, Ewald Pyle, Rube Fischer, Van Lingle Mungo, Ray Harrell, Loren Bain, Bill Emmerich, Andy Hansen, Jack Brewer, and Frank Seward, among others. The Giants had twenty-two pitchers on the roster and Ott declared, "We look pretty good. I think our club will do something in the National League race this season."[8] The infield was set with four regulars from the '44 squad: Phil Weintraub, George Hausmann, Buddy Kerr, and Nap Reyes. Ernie Lombardi was the backstop. The outfielders included Ott and Joe Medwick with Johnny Rucker and Red (Leon) Treadway fighting for the final outfield spot.

Ott was considered unexciting but the rest of his team was replete with

Ernie Lombardi played the final five seasons of his Hall of Fame career with the New York Giants from 1943 to 1947. He was traded from Boston to New York on April 27, 1943, and batted .305 in 295 at-bats for Mel Ott's last-place ball club that season. In 1944 and 1945 he hit .255 and .307 respectively. If the slow-footed Lombardi had possessed even average speed his lifetime batting average would have been considerably higher (George Brace photograph).

colorful personalities. Ernie Lombardi was an iron-footed catcher with a capable bat, perhaps best remembered for being knocked out cold in the 1939 World Series between the New York Yankees and the Cincinnati Reds. In a crucial moment in game four with the score tied at 4–4 in the tenth inning, Charlie Keller came lumbering around third base and slid violently into the waiting Lombardi, slamming his knee into the catcher's jaw. Lombardi was out cold and three Yankee runners touched home plate, giving them the victory. The writers criticized him, said he was asleep at the wheel, said he was "snoozing" and lazy.[9] He became the scapegoat for the series. The Yankees had won the first three games easily, but they said Lombardi cost them the series because he lay unconscious in game four. The play haunted him for the rest of his career. Lombardi was a large, powerful hitter, but slow as molasses. In Cincinnati's Crosley Field one day the right-handed-hitting slugger took the ball the other way, off the wall, and was promptly thrown out at first base. When he came to the Giants he had trouble finding a roommate because he snored; Voiselle became his roommate because he had difficulty hearing. In 1938 he was the National League Most Valuable Player, batting a league-leading .342 with the Cincinnati Reds. In 1942 he again led the league in hitting, batting .330 with the Boston Braves. He had twelve seasons when he hit ten or more homers and his career batting average stood at .306. Defensively he possessed a strong and accurate throwing arm. At 6'3" and 230 pounds he also blocked the plate well when a runner tried to score. But the rest of his catching skills were not so great and his slow speed made it difficult for him to catch a popup, to throw the batter out if he bunted, or to hold a runner to one base on a passed ball or wild pitch.

When things went bad for Bill Voiselle, when the crowd started to curse him and the boos began to echo around the stadium, he was impervious to their insults, hard of hearing as he was. He wanted to be a Marine, fight valiantly for his country overseas, but his ailment precluded his doing so. Several incidents impaired his hearing: the ball that slammed into his face, the blood vessel that was ruptured in his nose when he was picking up a log, and the time he almost drowned as a kid competing in a contest. There was that classic moment in 1946 when a furious Mel Ott called his team together to find out which players would jump to Jorge Pasquel's Mexican League. Voiselle, who was oblivious to the proceedings, sang, "South of the border, down Mexico way," before being told to shut up.[10] He was a big guy, 6'4", 200 pounds, who struggled in the bushes with losing clubs. One year he posted a 10–21 record for the Jersey City Giants. After a cup of coffee with the New York Giants in '42 and '43 he broke through, compiling a 21–16 record with a 3.02 ERA, while leading the league in games started (41), innings pitched (312.2) and strikeouts (161) in 1944. Some suggested he was lucky in '44, but Voiselle credited his success to "a fast [ball] and curve ball, an overhand and sidearm delivery, and, of course, a change of pace."[11]

6. The Giants Race to the Top of the Senior Circuit

Van Lingle Mungo was a 6'2", 185-pound right hander who played hard and lived hard. He could have been one of the greatest pitchers ever to toe the slab if it wasn't for his proclivity to have a good time and drink, thus neglecting his body. In 1934, when Giants skipper Bill Terry wondered aloud if Brooklyn was still in the league, it was Mungo who pitched the next to last game for Brooklyn, winning 5–1 against the hated Giants. Mungo's victory dropped the Giants out of first place, where they had resided since June 6, and when Brooklyn won again, 8–5, on the following day it secured the pennant for St. Louis. Casey Stengel, Brooklyn's manager, had asked his club to "avenge the worst insult ever perpetrated," in a brief meeting with his club before they played the Giants in the final two games of the season.[12] From 1931 to 1941 Mungo won 102 games for the Dodgers, 81 of them during a five-year stretch from 1932 to 1936. His temper was legendary. One day he trashed the clubhouse after losing a ballgame when Tom Winsett muffed a fly ball. "Pack up your bags and come to Brooklyn, honey. If Winsett can play in the big leagues, it's a cinch you can, too,"[13] he told his wife. It was rumored that he and Ernest Hemingway almost had a bloody duel: Mungo holding the baseball bat and Hemingway a sword. He helped start a riot when he became a minor league manager in 1946; he got into fisticuffs with opposing players and became so disgusted playing for the hapless Brooklyn Dodgers that he once demanded a trade, refusing to play with "a gang of semipros."[14]

Mungo hurt his arm in the 1937 All-Star game and began manipulating the ball to get by. He kept slippery elm in his sock; when the ball was in play and the attention of the umpires diverted he reached down and put some slippery elm on his fingers. In 1942 he became a member of the New York Giants but managed only a 1–2 record with a 5.94 ERA. In 1943 he was 3–7 with a 3.91 ERA. He missed the next year due to military service but got to pitch at Fort Bragg and Camp Atterbury. It was uncertain what kind of contribution he could make to the '45 Giants since he had not won at least ten games since 1936, when he was 18–19 for Brooklyn. On March 12 he signed his Giants contract and as in previous seasons predicted he would win twenty games. He was so eager the first day the Giants worked out that Ott said, "Listen, Van, take it easy."[15] Mungo looked good, in better shape than he had ever been due to the time he spent in the military.

Joseph (Ducky) Medwick had seen the vicious baseball wars that sprouted up throughout the country. He played with the Gas House Gang Cardinals of the 1930s. They were a tough, scrappy aggregation who hustled for everything they got, utilizing vicious take-out slides with spikes that cut, fisticuffs, obscene language, and playing mind games with the opposition to acquire the edge. Sportsman's Park was dilapidated, it was scorchingly hot, and they refused to wash their uniforms, showing the visiting teams that the conditions did not bother them. In the final game of the 1934 World Series at Briggs Stadium, Medwick spiked Marv Owen in the chest after hitting a triple. He trotted out to left field and had to avoid fruits, vegetables, and other debris thrown down upon him. The ironfisted commissioner Landis was there and he suggested that the combatants, Owen and Medwick, shake hands to appease the mob. Medwick declined and the crowd refused to allow him to safely take his position. Finally, Landis removed Medwick from the game, fearing his life was in serious peril.

When he was traded to Brooklyn in 1940, Bob Bowman of the Cardinals hit his old teammate Medwick in the head, causing a concussion. Attorneys became involved and the National League investigated. The Dodgers complained of "Beanball, Incorporated," an attempt by National League teams to kill their pennant chances by hitting their players in the head.[16] Brooklyn's skipper Leo Durocher would get revenge, like in 1942 when he ordered his pitcher to hit every batter in the Cardinals lineup. Those Dodger pitchers found $100 bills in their lockers when they went headhunting. Durocher was notorious for ordering his pitchers to "stick it in his ear,"[17] saying, "Give me some scratching, diving, hungry ballplayers who come to kill you."[18] In 1942 six of the National League teams took their frustrations to commissioner Landis, complaining that Durocher's pitchers were headhunters.

Medwick was born poor and that is part of why he developed his tough attitude, refusing to allow others to take what was his. He got into a number of memorable fights but as Johnny Mize said, "He knew who to pick on."[19] Medwick was a terrific bad-ball hitter, finishing with a .324 career average with 540 doubles, 113 triples, 205 home runs and 1,383 RBIs. He batted .337 for the Giants in 1944 and was looked upon as one of the important components of the 1945 squad.

Danny Gardella acted like a clown and was playing in the majors simply because many of the real big leaguers were overseas. In 1944 he batted .250 in 112 at-bats but his outfield play was woefully bad. He knocked around the bushes for many years. One day he decided to go fishing. While walking over a railroad bridge he heard a train coming, but instead of hustling to the other side he decided to hang over the side of the bridge. It was a slow freight and Gardella held on for his life for several minutes. In a road trip to Cincinnati in May of '45 he would scare Nap Reyes to death. Reyes left his room only to return finding a suicide note from Gardella saying he would kill himself because "life is too much for me."[20] Reyes scurried to the open window to find Gardella hanging over the side by his fingertips.

Gardella was a high-maintenance eccentric, eating dandelions in the outfield and walking on the top of Pullman cars. Phil Weintraub said, "Danny was very popular with the players, but he came into disfavor with Mel Ott."[21] On V-E day he put on a false mustache, combed his hair like Hitler, and then pretended he was the madman himself, scaring a maid to death. Fly balls were a dangerous proposition for Gardella and occasionally he was lucky he didn't get hit in the head. Early in the '44 season during a game against Chicago, he struggled with a fly ball, could not properly adjust his sunglasses and finished with his cap over his head, nearly getting "skulled." One observer said of a Gardella catch, "Danny made a sensational catch of an easy fly ball," while another added, "Gardella caught the ball-unassisted."[22] One person wrote in 1949, "Whenever a fly ball was struck in his direction, the fans shut their eyes and murmured prayers. Some of them prayed that Danny would catch the ball; the initiated prayed that he wouldn't get killed by it."[23] Harry Cross wrote in the *New York Herald Tribune* concerning the loquacious Gardella, "If his talent as a ball player was commensurate with his fluency as a talker he would burn up the league."[24]

The third definition of a "busher" in *The New Dickson Baseball Dictionary* is "any professional baseball player who lacks class."[25] Gardella was a "busher" in the true sense of the word, and many of them showed up on the radar screen during World War II. Arthur Daley wrote about his seemingly improved fielding abilities that went from abysmal to bad, in the *New York Times* on August 12, 1945:

> First rate? Ahem. Maybe we're traveling too fast. At present let's say that Dapper Dan is a very acceptable outfielder who is hitting solidly. No longer do spectators hold their breath when a fly ball wanders in the vicinity of the Gardella station. He's now practically certain to catch it. He's also learned enough about playing a ball off the wall so that he no longer resembles a dog chasing his own tail while in frantic pursuit of the elusive spheroid.[26]

On March 30, Ott announced that backup infielder Billy Jurges had signed his contract and would arrive shortly. Jurges had batted .211 in 246 at-bats in '44 but he was a smooth fielder who could capably backup at short or third. He was one of the old-timers on the Giants at thirty-seven years old and was about to begin his fifteenth big league season. Jurges had his problems off the field, living a rowdy life. The worst moment came when a girl shot him, but her bullets did not do any major damage. Two weeks later he was back in uniform. Jurges played hard: he was known for vicious take-out slides and was consumed with hatred on the diamond. He would get into fights frequently and became the target of beanball pitchers. He was one of the tough ballplayers who played under the amiable Mel Ott.

Jurges was an excellent shortstop in his younger days, playing for the Cubs from 1931 to 1938. He helped them secure three pennants but each time they lost in the World Series. He played for the Giants from 1939 to 1945 and then returned to the Cubs for his final two seasons. During four seasons (1932, 1935, 1937, and 1939) he led National League shortstops in fielding percentage and batted .258 in his seventeen-year big league career. After two subpar seasons with the bat, hitting .229 and .211 in 1943 and 1944, Jurges rebounded in 1945, batting a career high .324 in 176 at-bats. Joe King, a New York sportswriter, lauded Jurges's abilities in 1945:

Jurges stands out like a stake horse who has by some mistake been entered in the eighth race at Oriental Park. The fielding style, the finesse which the new lads cannot copy, is a treat to see. The strong arm that levels the ball across the infield is there. He knows where to be — automatically — when the play must be cut off or backed up. He breaks up a double play with artistry and employs the bat as a subtle weapon and not only as a bludgeon.

Those are the graces of yesteryear, and when in fleeting glimpses the fan of today is reminded of them, he is entitled for once to a full pardon when he pines for the good old days.[27]

Indeed wartime baseball was of the inferior sort. A total of 10,835 errors were committed from 1942 through 1945. The number of errors did not change substantially compared to prewar years but the fielders did benefit from lenient scoring. For the spectator to gaze upon the greensward and see a graceful major leaguer was special during the war and those players stood out.

Other key players for the Giants included relief specialist Ace Adams and infielders Buddy Kerr and Phil Weintraub. Adams led the league in games pitched for three consecutive seasons: 1942 (61), 1943 (70), and 1944 (65). He compiled a 7–4 record with a 1.84 ERA in 1942, was 11–7 with a 2.82 ERA in 1943 and was 8–11 with a 4.25 ERA in 1944. During the winter Adams worked hard on his peanut farm in Rome, Georgia, and considered playing ball his "vacation."[28] He was classified 1-A so there was a possibility he may be taken by the military sometime during the upcoming season.

Buddy Kerr was a lanky, 6'2", 175-pound shortstop who was looked upon highly by Mel Ott. He called him "potentially another Marty Marion."[29] He debuted with a .286 batting average in 27 games and 98 at-bats in 1943. In '44 he was the regular shortstop, playing in 150 games, batting .266 but booting 40 balls at shortstop. The young shortstop's skills were still developing, physically and mentally. In a game against Cincinnati on August 15, 1944, Kerr went to the second-base bag for a pickoff attempt but was slow in returning to his shortstop position when the ball was delivered, and the hitter bounced one through the vacated area. The Giants had more headaches later in the inning when Joe Medwick trapped the ball and then argued with the umpire while the winning runs scored. Both players were fined for "inexcusable mental errors."[30] Kerr was one of the Irish players that owner Horace Stoneham liked greatly. When Leo Durocher became manager of the Giants he recognized Kerr's limited abilities, saying, "I think mediocrity is the word for him." He wrote in his autobiography, "He didn't make errors but he didn't make plays either."[31] Durocher eventually persuaded Horace Stoneham to trade him so he could make room for his killer ballplayers. In December of 1949, Kerr was involved in a six-player deal that sent him to the Boston Braves and gave the Giants the excellent middle infield combination of shortstop Alvin Dark and second baseman Eddie Stanky. After batting only .209 for the Giants in 1949, Kerr hit .227 and .186 in 1950 and 1951, his final two big league seasons, finishing his nine-year career with a .249 batting average.

6. The Giants Race to the Top of the Senior Circuit

Phil Weintraub was working on his third tour with the Giants and had also played for the Cincinnati Reds and Philadelphia Phillies. He was a 6'1", 195-pounder, who initially started his career as an outfielder and was later converted to first base. Weintraub finished his career with a .295 batting average and an impressive .398 on-base percentage. He had retired after 1938 when he batted .311 for the Phillies, then changed his mind and went back to the minors. In '44 he landed a job with the Giants, batting .316 with 13 homers and 77 RBIs. During April of 1944 he caught a baseball thrown from a blimp four hundred feet in the air. On the last day of the month he drove in eleven runs in a game against Brooklyn, tying the American League mark for most RBIs in a game and one shy of the National League mark. When he walked into the clubhouse after the game Babe Ruth was waiting to congratulate him. That April 30 game was emblematic of the inept play which was showcased in big league parks during the war: the Giants defeated the Dodgers by a 26–8 score, beneficiaries of seventeen walks by Brooklyn hurlers. Mel Ott walked five straight times in the game and scored six runs while Ernie Lombardi drove in seven runs. This contest turned ugly late: after Leo Durocher, the Dodgers skipper, was thrown out in the sixth inning, he left the field trying to avoid the oranges and apples thrown in his direction. Joe Medwick, the Giants left fielder, was hit in the groin by a pop bottle. There were over 58,000 fans at the Polo Grounds on the eventful day. Not only did the Dodgers suffer an ignominious loss to their hated rivals, but the 26–8 defeat was the first game of a doubleheader. They won the second game.

When asked about the burdens of wartime ball Weintraub said, "You loved the game so much you didn't mind these things.... When we got hurt in those days, they said 'stick it in the dirt.' You were afraid to say you were hurt. You had an entirely different breed."[32] In 1945 he would experience his final big league season.

The Giants roster, like any other wartime team, was filled with "wartime" ballplayers and a few legitimate major leaguers. There were many players overseas whose loyalty was with the New York Giants. Hal Schumacher was among them. He was a great pitcher who compiled a 158–121 record with a 3.36 ERA in his thirteen-year major league career with the club. He was 12–13 with a 3.04 ERA in 1942 before going into the service and would not return until 1946, his final season. Well before he joined the Navy in January 1943, there were indications that his major league career would soon be put on hold. On May 27, 1941, Schumacher was locked in a competitive 1–1 pitching duel with Manny Salvo of the Braves at the Polo Grounds when the game was abruptly stopped after seven innings so they could listen to President Roosevelt address the nation in one of his fireside chats. Roosevelt's hearty voice echoed throughout the stadium as it was pumped into the Giants' home through the speakers above the centerfield clubhouse. The players and fans sat quietly for forty-five minutes listening to the speech in which Roosevelt declared that the United States would respond to the Nazis if they continued to wreak havoc on our shipping vessels while they were on their way to Europe. When the game resumed Schumacher was lifted and replaced with Carl Hubbell, whose single in the ninth inning gave the Giants a 2–1 victory.

When Schumacher first joined the Navy he spent about one year as a physical training officer before he became impatient and requested sea duty. Lieutenant Schumacher served on an aircraft carrier in the Pacific. Initially, he was an assistant air officer but then graduated to a higher rank because of his exceptional skills in nautical operations. During the early months of 1945, Stanley Woodward joined Schumacher on his carrier and observed that the former Giants hurler "has been through hell in her."[33] By this time "Prince Hal" had been on the carrier for over a year and had witnessed horrific combat. The carrier would sneak through island passages to support the fleet when Japanese air power was still very strong in the Philippines. Schumacher bravely withstood a vicious barrage by the enemy on December 18, 1944, when three of the fleet's destroyers were capsized. Schumacher's carrier was almost overturned as well, as the vessel was set on fire and planes flew off the deck as if they were made out of paper. The carrier barely survived and then was given less perilous duty.

As Woodward watched Schumacher perform his duties on the carrier he found it hard to imagine him pitching in the Polo Grounds or being associated with baseball in any way. He appeared to be a perfect fit for his current position, performing his duties as if he had been at sea his entire life. Once the war ended, Schumacher planned to pitch in the big leagues for another six seasons. However, a carrier was no place to practice one's baseball skills, and Schumacher's were likely to have diminished some since he walked on board. Since he had joined the Navy he hadn't played baseball but had played softball for the carrier's team. On the carrier the athletic activities were mainly restricted to volleyball and ping-pong. Schumacher was a participant in the poker game that began at 1915 hours and ended at 2330. They didn't play poker in the traditional way because almost everything in the deck was wild and the dealers would often make up their own games with unfamiliar names like "Roll'Em and Eniwetok."[34] Schumacher's stiffest competition in the poker game included a former Boston College professor named Bill Collins. Schumacher, like countless other ballplayers, sacrificed years of his career to serve his country.

Another Giant player eager to return was Harry Danning. He was an excellent hitting catcher, spending ten years with the club and batting .285. In 1942 he played his last season for the Giants: after being discharged from the Army in 1945 he wrote Horace Stoneham a letter saying, "I wish I could tell you that I was on my way to New York, but my legs are in such bad shape that I'll have to forget about ever playing ball again."[35]

The Giants played their home games at the Polo Grounds, a horseshoe-shaped ballpark that sat against Coogan's Bluff with home plate beneath the craggy cliff. It was a spacious 483 feet to the clubhouse in center field, meaning many mammoth shots died in the center fielder's glove, and 460 feet to the bleachers which were situated on the left and right sides of the clubhouse. However, it was only 279 feet down the left field line and 257 feet down the right field line. The double-deck, roofed grandstand went all the way around the infield; in center field there was a single-deck bleacher section. The upper portion of the left field deck hung over the lower deck by 23 feet while the double decks in right field were of equal distance. In the middle of the bleachers stood the Giant offices and players' clubhouse. Batting eyes were on the corners of the bleachers. The park could accommodate about 55,000 fans.

Businessmen and other well-known figures in society were often seen cavorting in the grandstand. Richie Ashburn of the Philadelphia Phillies said, "It never seemed to me that Giant fans were as involved emotionally or physically as some other fans. They never really affected a game, for example, at the Polo Grounds the way those fans at Ebbets Field could."[36] Giant fans had a certain classiness to them that was lacking at the claustrophobic bandbox in Flatbush. One person from Manhattan observed, "Dodger fans are vulgar."[37] Dodger fans were considered second-class citizens compared to Yankee and Giant fans. John Lardner wrote that the Dodger attraction was "brash, low, even buffoonish."[38]

In front of the clubhouse at the Polo Grounds stood the Eddie Grant memorial. Grant's final two seasons were with the Giants: he batted .277 and .208 in 1914 and 1915. He became a lawyer after his playing career and had received his degree from Harvard. He was a serious man with a sense of patriotic duty. One day while he was with the Giants they were playing a spring training game in Texas. The bench jockeys from the opposing team got on his case. Then he announced that his grandfather Ulysses S. Grant had already humbled the South with some memorable lessons. A riot almost ensued; however, Eddie was not related to the Civil War general, and had just made those comments to get them back.[39]

When World War I began he enlisted and soon became a captain. In France he was with the 307th Infantry Unit of the 77th Division. His superior officers were soon dead or wounded. Grant found himself leading the troops in hopes of rescuing Charles Whittlesey's "Lost Battalion," trapped behind German lines.[40] On October 5, 1918, in the Argonne Forest he was killed by a shell, the first major leaguer killed in that war. Grant was the most prominent big leaguer killed in World War I. The others included Bun Troy and Alex Burr. The Grant monument was unveiled on May 29, 1921, Memorial Day, deep in the center field of the Polo Grounds.

Horace Stoneham was the generous owner of the New York Giants. He had inherited the club from his father Charles A. Stoneham in 1936 and immediately placed his imprint on the team by dismissing club secretary James Tierney and replacing him with Eddie Brannick. When Charles originally bought the team in 1918, reporters described him as "a Wall Street broker," but he was really a gambler, bookie and ticket scalper.[41] In fact it was the notorious mobster Arnold Rothstein, who would be remembered for his nefarious role in the Black Sox scandal and in 1928 was shot to death during a poker game, who had helped arrange the sale of the Giants to Charles. Stoneham ran a service where he took stock orders but didn't execute them until the stock went down, and then pocketed the difference. Charles Stoneham's questionable relationships with those in the underworld worried some, and then John McGraw exacerbated the situation by trading for Hal Chase in 1919. Chase was no longer welcome in Cincinnati, where Reds manager Christy Mathewson accused him of throwing games in 1918. The American League also wanted nothing to do with Chase. John McGraw gave him one last chance and ironically Mathewson became a coach for the Giants in 1919. Mathewson and Chase never said a word to each other and Ray Robinson wrote, "Matty informed McGraw on a number of occasions that he thought Chase should have been as welcome as the bubonic plague at the Polo Grounds."[42] With New York out of the race towards the end of the season, Chase attempted to get Giant players to dump games for "easy money," and this finally led to his banishment for life by John Heydler, National League president.[43] The Cincinnati Reds, who had been liberated from the cancer that was Hal Chase, won the pennant and then the World Series in 1919. The Giants finished in second.

Horace Stoneham was a portly man who truly loved the game and his players, and would watch the games proceed from his office in the center field clubhouse, often with a drink nearby. Roger Kahn wrote, "His baseball intelligence seemed reasonably developed when he was sober, but Stoneham's drinking bouts were legend."[44] He would be remembered for embracing black players; the Giants were the second team to sign them, behind Branch Rickey's Dodgers. By 1948 he became worn out with Mel Ott's losing ball clubs and orchestrated the move that would bring Leo Durocher to the New York Giants. Later he would follow Walter O'Malley's Dodgers to the West Coast because of the dwindling crowds and the changing neighborhood, which hurt their bottom line.

The Giants sprinted to the top of the National League in 1945. They won 21 out of their first 26 games, which was the fastest NL start since John McGraw's Giants began the 1907 season with a 25–5 record. They found themselves at the top of the senior circuit after the first two months of the season. Then things fell apart, predominantly because their pitching began to falter. What had been an auspicious start to the season became a slow, tortuous, downward slide in June that had the Giants struggling to stay in the first division by the end of the month. Also leading to the Giants' fall was an incident that tore apart the team in early June. By the end of the year the Giants were a second-division ball club finishing in fifth place (78–74).

They dropped three of four in St. Louis from June 1 to 3. That disastrous first game with overcast skies and intermittent rain at Sportsman's Park served as a microcosm for the rest of the season. Bill Voiselle toed the slab for the Giants and was on top of his game, taking a 3–1 lead into the ninth inning. Mel Ott kept him in the game despite the fact that they sat through a fifty-three minute rain delay in the later innings. Protocol generally dictates that the starting pitcher is taken out in that situation, since he already has a high pitch count and would have to warm up again, resulting in far less productivity. Ace Adams was one of the better closers in the game and they would have been better off with the pill in his hands. There was one out and a runner on base when Johnny Hopp stepped into the batter's box. The count went to 0–2. Ott had instructed his pitchers that they were to waste an 0-and-2 pitch or face a $100 fine. Voiselle let loose a fastball that he would later contend was "high and away," but Hopp, a left-handed batter, reached for it and drove it to the opposite field into the left-center field gap.[45] Around came pinch runner Jack Creel to bring the Cardinals within one run while Hopp was hugging third with a triple. Ott was furious that the pitcher ignored his instructions, and stomped the earth in right field. Ray Sanders subsequently singled to bring home the second run and Whitey Kurowski won it with a triple of his own.

Mel Ott had become an overly serious man since becoming manager. He couldn't sleep at night, tossing and turning, always thinking about strategy. When it came to disciplining ballplayers he never quite knew how to do so appropriately. He was often too lenient, but in the case of Bill Voiselle, he acted like a pit bull destroying a slab of meat. Ott ran into the dugout and found Voiselle. He fined his ace pitcher not $100, but $500 for "disobeying pitching instructions."[46] Johnny Hopp witnessed Ott's explosion: "I was there when he came after Voiselle, just inside our dugout. Both teams used the same tunnel to get to the clubhouse. Ott exploded. He used every word in the book."[47] The clubhouse felt like a morgue as silenced draped the wartime ballplayers of New York. It was as if Ott's reaction paralyzed his once high-flying team, as the players could only shake their heads at their manager's reaction. And it wasn't the only time the notorious nice guy of baseball was overcome with anger and lashed out at his ballplayers. Perhaps the anger and frustration of not being able to win a pennant for his beloved Giants manifested at times in anomalous fits of rage.

Voiselle's record fell to 8–3 as a result. For the rest of the season he would only manage a 6–11 record. He had been 29–18 going back to the beginning of 1944 before that June 1 game. However, his brilliance upon the small hill in the middle of the diamond was no longer, and this game marked his demise. Voiselle was only making $3,500 and the fine hurt him in the pocketbook, although after much criticism Ott would give back the $500 fine. It was Ott who let his pitcher go back out after the rain delay. Voiselle was hurt by Ott's outrage, and said, "I pitched my arm off for him and the first chance he had, he cut my throat."[48] This game served as a harbinger for things to come as the Giants fell apart, going 2–10 to begin June. Al Laney wrote in the *New York Her-*

ald Tribune, "Voiselle said pitch got away, doesn't resent fine. Other Giant p's do, may cause trouble."[49]

However, the Giants manager did have at least one memorable game in 1945. On August 1, Melvin Thomas Ott stood in the batter's box waiting for the pitched ball from Johnny Hutchings in the third inning against the Boston Braves. Hutchings spun out of the windup and delivered the spheroid to the plate. Ott's eyes grew wide as he lifted his front leg as he was accustomed to do, and he sent the ball hurtling down the right field line. The ball bounced off the right field stands and back onto the field where Willie Schaefer, the Giants trainer, retrieved it. Ott took the grand tour around the bases for the 500th time in his major league career and his eleventh time this season. The Polo Grounds crowd of 22,098 erupted with cheers. Harry Cross wrote, "It is the game's good fortune to have a sportsman and gentleman of his integrity in its ranks."[50] Only Babe Ruth (714) and Jimmie Foxx (534) had more homers than Ott.

In the evening, there was a party for Mel Ott at Toots Shor's restaurant to celebrate his accomplishment. Sir Alexander Fleming was there, the Nobel Prize–winning bacteriologist from Scotland who had discovered penicillin. Shor sat with Fleming until Ott made his appearance and then he insulted the dignitary, saying, "Excuse me, Alex. I've got to greet someone who just came in who is really important."[51] It was one of many awkward moments for Ott and the Giants in another disappointing season.

Mel Ott led the 1945 Giants with a .308 batting average with 21 homers and 79 RBIs. This was his final major league season as an everyday player: in 1946 he appeared in only 31 games and batted .074, and in 1947, his last season, he played in only four games. Ernie Lombardi batted .307 with 19 homers; Danny Gardella hit for a .272 average with 18 homers; and Phil Weintraub also batted .272. Johnny Rucker (.273), Nap Reyes (.288), and Buddy Kerr (.249) also contributed offensively. The Giants led the majors in homers (114) and slugging percentage (.379) while their .269 batting average was fourth in the National League. Bill Voiselle led the pitchers with a 14–14 record with a 4.49 ERA. Harry Feldman (12–13), Van Lingle Mungo (14–7), Jack Brewer (8–6), and Ace Adams (11–9) also saw significant time on the pitcher's mound for Ott's team. New York had a collective ERA of 4.06, which was better than only the Phillies' abysmal 4.64 ERA in the senior circuit.

❖ 7 ❖

The Braves Load Up and Fall Down

The Boston Braves had not finished in the first division since 1934 when manager Bill McKechnie led them to a modest fourth-place conclusion (78–73). In 1938 Casey Stengel became their manager but failed to crack the first division in six seasons at the helm. Then Bob Coleman tried his turn as skipper, taking over for Stengel during the tail end of 1943 as they finished in sixth place and repeated that showing the following year. After 93 games (42–51) of the '45 season Coleman resigned and was replaced by Del Bissonette, who in his only try as a big league manager would finish the season with similar results (25–34). The Braves finished the season in sixth place with a 67–85 record.

Unlike Coleman, who had a brief major league career as a backstop, Bissonette experienced success in the big show as an everyday player. His five-year career as a first baseman with the Brooklyn Dodgers ended with a .305 batting average. He was beset by a number of ailments that hindered his playing abilities, including an arm injury which ended any hopes of pitching in the big leagues. Lefty O'Doul, his teammate with Brooklyn, once observed, "Del Bissonette is the gamest guy in baseball!" Bissonette was once beaned in the head by Leo Sweetland and came back the next day insisting to the worried doctors that his intense headaches were sinus troubles. The beaning took place in 1929 at Philadelphia's Baker Bowl and the ball reportedly bounced into the press box. Many years later Roscoe McGowen of the *New York Times* said, "I can still hear the thump." Bissonette didn't want to be taken out of the lineup, fearing that someone would take his job. One winter he had a series of "mastoid" operations, lost 30 pounds, later broke two fingers, and played through most of the season, only being taken out when he collapsed running the bases one day. He entered the hospital on New Year's Eve to have the operations and didn't leave until the spring training season was about to commence. The doctors urged him not to play, insisting that he was in no condition to endure a major league season, but Bissonette ignored the advice.[1]

In 1932 he lost 50 pounds after an infection developed as a result of an injury he suffered while playing volleyball. When his teammates visited him they found a man with a "gaunt face" and "shrunken body" who, when he returned to the Dodgers in 1933, was "a fighting shell of his former self." While in the hospital he insisted he would return, even though the doctors thought he might die and even brought in a representative of his church to administer the last rites. After missing 1932 he completed his major league career in 1933 batting .246 in 35 games. Ford Frick, who was then a baseball writer for the *Journal-American*, was critical of his colleagues when they didn't tell their fans about the comeback story of Del Bissonette. It was a heroic and dramatic story about a man who stared death in the face and came out on top. Additionally, Bissonette, like the rest of the country, found himself in financial trouble: he had made investments and amassed enough money to make the average citizen envious, but when the country fell into economic ruin after the 1929 stock market crash he lost his money.[2]

Del was impressive in his rookie season of 1928, batting .320 with a .396 on-base percentage with 30 doubles, 13 triples, 25 home runs, 90 runs scored, and 106 RBIs. He batted for a .281 clip in 1929, and then hit .336 with 16 homers, 102 runs scored and 113 RBIs in 1930. In 1931 he hit .290 with 12 home runs and 87 RBIs. In Bissonette's short career his numbers were truly impressive, and if he hadn't become ill he would have become much better known by the baseball public. He stood at 5'11" and 180 pounds and batted and threw left-handed. He was serious about his profession and worked hard to overcome the obstacles that hindered his progress. After his playing career was over Bissonette then became a bush league manager, winning four minor league pennants in his eight seasons before becoming the Braves skipper in 1945. His pennant with Hartford in the Eastern League in 1944 earned him a promotion as a coach with the Braves and finally as manager. Less than three months before his 73rd birthday, on June 9, 1972, he reportedly shot himself in the stomach and died several days later.[3]

The 1945 Braves had some long-ball hitters in their lineup, led by right fielder Tommy Holmes, who finished second in the National League batting race at .352, led the majors in homers (28) and drove home 117 runs. He also led the league in slugging (.577), hits (224), and doubles (47) in what would be his best season. His 125 runs scored was third in the National League behind Brooklyn's Eddie Stanky (128) and Goody Rosen (126). In 636 at-bats he struck out only nine times, which led regular position players. Additionally, he set a National League record with a thirty-seven game hitting streak. The streak ended on July 12 when the Cubs hurler, Hank Wyse, held him hitless in four at-bats at Wrigley Field. Rogers Hornsby previously held what was considered the modern National League record when he connected for a hit in 33 straight games in 1922. Joe DiMaggio set the major league mark in 1941 with his breathtaking 56-game hitting streak. During the streak Holmes batted .423 and collected 66 hits in 156 at-bats. Midway through the streak Holmes broke his bat, which he rarely ever did, and Bissonette traveled to his home in Maine to get an aging bat that Holmes began to use in the games. Holmes was small in stature but swung heavy bats; Bissonette's bat was like concrete and worked well.[4] He stood at 5'10" and 180 pounds.

Tommy began his hitting streak on June 6 as Boston won both ends of a doubleheader at Shibe Park against the Phillies by 15–1 and 7–3 scores. Holmes went 3 for 6 in the opener with a triple, two runs scored and two RBIs. In the second game he collected two more hits in five at-bats, hit one double and scored two runs. He batted in the two hole in both games behind leadoff man Eddie Joost. His 36th and 37th consecutive games with a hit occurred in Boston on July 8 as the Braves swept a doubleheader from the Pirates by 10–8 and 13–1 scores. Holmes went 1 for 4 in the opener with a run scored and one RBI. He was batting third in both games and his only hit in the second contest was a two-run homer in the fourth inning, part of a seven-run inning for Boston. During the streak he had eight three-hit games (21.6 percent), thirteen two-hit games (35.1 percent), and sixteen one-hit games (43.2 percent).

Holmes was originally signed by the New York Yankees, but like an unending number of minor league players in that organization, he found it was virtually impossible to crack the big show. George Weiss, the Yankees general manager, released Holmes from having an obscure bush league career in the Yankees organization and sent him to the Boston Braves. He debuted in 1942 batting .278, and followed that with .270 and .309 seasons. Holmes was a good listener and learned from the former Pirate great Paul Waner. Long-ball hitting was not the specialty for this left-handed batter, who had to deal with the spacious measurements at Braves Field and the strong wind that blew in off the Charles River. The Braves management would bring the fences in to about 320 feet down the line, making the distance 25 feet shorter. However, 1945 was the only season in which Holmes cracked more than thirteen home runs in his career.

Holmes was a 4-F with a sinus condition, but in 1945 the doctors flocked to him since he was a professional athlete. They concluded that Holmes wouldn't have much of a chance surviving in combat. One doctor observed, "If you go to England, you'll die."[5] The batting race was close, and he lost it to Chicago's Phil Cavarretta by three points. One of the reasons why Holmes did not surpass Cavarretta for the batting crown was a rookie pitcher for the Giants by the name of Sal Maglie, who had Holmes ducking fastballs at his head. Maglie said of Holmes, "If you were Italian, I wouldn't have decked you so many times."[6]

Thomas Francis Holmes was born in Brooklyn on March 29, 1917. He played ten of his eleven major league seasons with the Boston Braves from 1942 to 1951 and played one season with the Brooklyn Dodgers in 1952. He batted at least .309 for five consecutive seasons from 1944 to 1948. Holmes's lifetime batting average stands at .302 with a .366 on-base percentage. He hit 292 doubles,

Boston Braves fans had to endure another disappointing season in 1945 as the team finished in sixth place. But they got to witness the outstanding hitting exhibition put together by left-handed batter Tommy Holmes. Holmes put together a 37-game hitting streak and led the National League in hits (224), doubles (47), home runs (28), and slugging percentage (.577), earning him *The Sporting News* National League Player of the Year Award (George Brace photograph).

47 triples, and 88 home runs, and had 581 RBIs in his career. He struck out only 122 times in 4,992 career at-bats: he had a career high of twenty strikeouts in both 1943 and 1948. He struck out once every 40.9 at-bats, which is among the all-time best in major league history. Holmes was the manager of the Braves for part of the 1951 (48–47) and 1952 (13–22) seasons.

7. The Braves Load Up and Fall Down

There were two other Braves who also hit a high number of homers in 1945: Chuck Workman (25) and Butch Nieman (14). Workman had played briefly for the 1938 (two games) and the 1941 (nine games) Cleveland Indians before the war. He was an everyday player for the Braves in 1943, batting .249 with 10 homers and 67 RBIs in 615 at-bats while playing most of his games in right field. In 1944 he batted only .208 in 418 at-bats, and then in 1945 batted .274 while playing most of his games at third base. During his final major league season in 1946 with the Braves and Pirates, the left-handed-hitting Workman was able to produce only a .207 batting average in 193 at-bats. Butch Nieman, a left-handed-hitting outfielder, played for the Boston Braves during three wartime seasons from 1943 to 1945. In his three-year big league career he batted .256 with 37 homers. Phil Masi (.272, 7 homers), Carden Gillenwater (.288, 7 homers), and Whitey Wietelmann (.271, 4 homers) also produced offensively for the 1945 Braves. Masi was a catcher in the big leagues with the Braves, Pirates, and White Sox from 1939 to 1952. He had a .264 lifetime batting average with 47 homers. Offensively he was limited but he established himself behind the dish as an excellent defensive catcher and led the league in fielding average during the 1947, 1949, and 1950 seasons. Wietelmann played shortstop for most of his nine-year career in which he batted .232 with the Braves (1939–1946) and Pirates (1947). Except for 1943 (153 games), 1944 (125 games), and 1945 (123 games) he never played more than forty-eight games in a season. About a week before the 1945 campaign was set to commence, Wietelmann fractured the smallest digit on his left hand when he was hit by a line drive while throwing batting practice. Shortly afterward he had it amputated just below the second knuckle and was back in the Braves lineup towards the end of April. Boston smashed 101 homers during the 1945 campaign, which was second only to the Giants (114) in the National League. And their 721 runs scored was fifth in the senior league.

Besides the old players, the young players, and the disabled, there was a whole other group of men who were deferred from the draft during the war because they were supporting their families. Eddie Joost, a weak-hitting infielder for the Boston Nationals, was one such player. He stated: "I ... took my physical. The doctor told me that since the war was about to end and I had two children, he'd given me a six-month deferment. Otherwise I'd have gone to Germany for four years as part of the occupation forces. He said that if I had been trying to beat the draft, he'd have enlisted me." Joost had been voluntarily retired from the game and worked in a meat-packing plant in 1944 before he came back in '45, playing in 35 games and batting .248. Billy Jurges of the Giants made a hard slide into third one day and broke Joost's wrist. Joost thought he had received permission to go home only to find out he had been suspended without pay, which infuriated him. He insisted that he was blacklisted from major league baseball in 1946 because of his incident with the Braves at the tail end of the 1945 season and his frequent run-ins with managers like

Bill McKechnie in Cincinnati and Casey Stengel in Boston. He played for the Rochester Red Wings of the International League in 1946 and was told by their general manager that the owners of the major league teams had collectively agreed not to sign Joost.[7] However, he returned to the big leagues in 1947 and played until the 1955 season. In his seventeen-year major league career he batted .239 with a .361 on-base percentage and was predominantly a shortstop.

The Braves' frustration in 1945 was encapsulated in the disappointing performance of Mort Cooper. Cooper was traded from the Cardinals on May 23 for Red Barrett and $60,000 cash. Arm problems limited his contribution to the club as he won only seven games with Boston. By June, pitching had become so painful that he could only work about an inning before soreness developed and he could barely lift his arm. As a result he was moved to the bullpen, and only started eleven of the twenty games he appeared in as a Brave. Dr. Robert Hyland, who was the club physician for both the Cardinals and Browns, performed an operation on the pitcher and removed ten bone chips from his elbow. In 1941 Cooper had undergone a similar operation in which two bone chips were removed, and by the final World War II season the weary pitcher questioned whether pitching in the big leagues was worth the pain that he had to endure and the operations that were needed to fix the problem. Dr. Hyland assured Cooper that his arm would be fine after the surgery, and Cooper, who had led the National League in wins the year after his first surgery, had no reason to doubt he would return to his previous form. He insisted that if the Braves were fighting for a pennant he would have continued to pitch. Members of the Braves organization had insisted that Cooper go with an eastern doctor but he decided to stick with Hyland.[8] However, Cooper only had one more good season left, going 13–11 with a 3.12 ERA for the 1946 Braves. In 1947 he pitched in 18 games for the Braves and Giants, compiling an unimpressive 3–10 record and a 5.40 ERA. He pitched one game for the Chicago Cubs in 1949 during a failed comeback attempt. In his eleven-year career he had a 128–75 record with a 2.97 ERA.

When Frederick G. Lieb asked Cooper how it felt pitching against his former team, the hurler replied, "I am a ball player, and I'd strike out my own grandmother if that was necessary to win a game." Mort admitted that while he was recovering from his arm injury in St. Louis he found himself pulling for his old team while attending games at Sportsman's Park. He remained loyal to the Cardinals despite putting on an enemy uniform. Morton Cecil Cooper was born in Atherton, Missouri, on March 2, 1913, and had played for his home-state Cardinals since 1938 before being traded to Boston. Despite the setbacks and tribulations he encountered in 1945 he wished no ill will towards Red Barrett. He also showed no regret over the salary squabble which led to the trade to Boston. To Mort it was a "matter of principle." Sam Breadon, the Cardinals owner, placed a ceiling for his top-salaried players, but then added an extra $1,500 beyond the cap to Marty Marion's contract, which really perturbed

Cooper. Whatever bad feelings Cooper had for Breadon disappeared when Cooper requested tickets for some of his friends and had a cordial conversation with the Cardinals owner. Mort felt bad that he wasn't able to pitch for the Boston fans who had treated him so well. He thought the future of the organization was strong and added, "I'll bet you that in two or three years, they'll be right up there fighting for the pennant."[9] In fact, Cooper's prediction was correct, for in 1948 the Braves would win the pennant; however, he would not be part of that ball club.

The rest of the Braves pitching staff—Jim Tobin, Bob Logan, Johnny Hutchings, Nate Andrews, Ed Wright, and Bill Lee—were uninspiring. Their team ERA of 4.04 was sixth in the National League. Jim Tobin led the team in victories with nine, but also had fourteen losses in 27 games with the Braves. In August he was sent to the Detroit Tigers for cash and got the thrill of playing for the eventual World Series champions. Ed Wright was 8–3 with a 2.51 ERA in his rookie season. Logan, Hutchings, and Andrews won seven games apiece. Bill Lee was traded from the Phillies to the Braves on July 14 and went 6–3 with a 2.79 ERA for Boston after compiling a 3–6 record for Philadelphia. The oldest member on the squad was Joe Heving, who had gone 8–3 with a 1.96 ERA in 1944 for the Cleveland Indians. Heving already had a three-year-old grandson. After pitching in three games for Boston he called it quits midway through the season at the age of forty-four.

Nate Andrews was a six-foot, 195-pound right-hander, who had played briefly and unspectacularly for four seasons before the war with the St. Louis Cardinals and Cleveland Indians. In 1943 he had his breakout season, compiling a 14–20 record with a good 2.57 ERA and finishing third in the senior circuit with 283.2 innings pitched. He continued to pitch well in 1944, going 16–15 with a 3.22 ERA in 257.1 innings pitched. In 1945 he pitched only 137.2 innings and tallied a 7–12 record with a 4.58 ERA. In 1946, his final big league season, he went 3–4 with a 4.39 ERA in a total of ten games for the Reds and Giants, completing his career with a 41–54 mark and a 3.46 ERA.

Johnny Hutchings began his career with the Reds in 1940 (2–1, 3.50 ERA) and pitched for the Braves during five of his six major league seasons in 1941, 1942, and 1944 to 1946. He began the 1941 season with Cincinnati and was traded to Boston on June 12 for future Hall of Famer Lloyd Waner. Hutchings was a right-handed pitcher who threw mainly in relief during his career. In 1945 he started in only 12 of his 57 appearances and went 7–6 with a 3.75 ERA in 185 innings.

During Bill Lee's first six seasons in the big leagues with the Chicago Cubs from 1934 to 1939 he compiled a 106–70 record, including two twenty-win seasons in 1935 (20–6) and 1938 (22–9). He pitched briefly for the Cubs in 1947 and then ended his career with a 169–157 record and a 3.54 ERA in fourteen major league seasons. Lee was an imposing pitcher on the mound, standing at 6' 3" and 195 pounds, with a high leg kick that made his fastball deceptively fast.

After going 19–15 for Chicago in 1939, he fell to 9–17 with a 5.03 ERA in 1940 as his eyes began to fail him and he couldn't see the signs from the catcher. By 1942 he was wearing eyeglasses and improved to 13–13 with a 3.85 ERA. After Ed Wright's 1945 rookie season he played in four more major league seasons with the Braves (1946–1948) and Athletics (1952), finishing his career with a 25–16 record and a 4.00 ERA.

During spring training, manager Bob Coleman was planning to use right-handers Nate Andrews, Al Javery, and Jim Tobin in the starting rotation. Red Barrett or Tom Earley would join them as the fourth right-handed pitcher, and southpaws Charlie Cozart or Jimmy Wallace would also start. If this rotation had remained healthy and intact it had the potential of being one of the better pitching staffs in the senior circuit. However, Barrett and Tobin were traded during the season. Andrews pitched almost 120 fewer innings than the year before and his productivity declined.

Javery, who was 17–16 with a 3.21 ERA in 1943 and then went 10–19 with a 3.54 ERA in 1944, was a major disappointment during the final wartime season. The military had rejected Javery because of varicose veins. The 6'3", 183-pound hurler, who was nicknamed "Beartracks," was knocked around the senior league in 1945 as if the hitters were facing a batting practice pitcher. In 77.1 innings he allowed 92 hits and walked 51. He had a 2–7 record with a 6.28 ERA.

Tom Earley was a resident of Roxbury, Massachusetts, and had been discharged from the Navy in early 1945 in time for him to participate in spring training activities. In 1941, his fourth season with the Braves, he compiled a 6–8 record with an impressive 2.53 ERA while pitching mainly in relief. During the first wartime season he fell to 6–11 with a 4.71 ERA and then went into the military in 1943. He got to pitch for the formidable Norfolk Naval Training Station team while in the service. Coleman naturally surmised that because Earley had pitched so well during the last pre-war season he would dominate wartime hitters in 1945. However, he only pitched in eleven games, going 2–1 with a 4.61 ERA in his final major league season.

Southpaw Charlie Cozart had won eighteen games for Atlanta in the Southern Association during the 1944 season and made five relief appearances for the 1945 Braves, going 1–0 with a 10.13 ERA in eight innings during his only major league season. The other southpaw Coleman was relying on was Jimmy "Lefty" Wallace, who was made available during the training season because the Army discharged him when he injured his leg. Wallace had worked in nineteen games for the 1942 Braves, going 1–3 with a 3.83 ERA, pitching mainly out of the bullpen. He pitched in five games in 1945 and started three of them, going 1–0 with a 4.50 ERA. In 1946 he was only 24 years old and pitched in his final major league season, going 3–3 with a 4.18 ERA.

After spending the previous two spring training camps in Wallingford, Connecticut, the club moved to a more southern climate in 1945 and trained at Georgetown University in Washington, D.C., where medical students would often join the Braves in their workouts. Boston started the season slowly and never recovered: by June 1 they were already in seventh place, ten and a half games behind the first place Giants. John Quinn, the Braves general manager, tried to build a winner by making aggressive acquisitions once the season was underway. Not only did he pull off the Mort Cooper trade, he also acquired Joe Medwick and Ewald Pyle from the Giants for Clyde Kluttz. Brooklyn was desperately in need of catching help and was in the running to acquire Kluttz but their offer was insufficient. Jack Malaney playfully wrote, "Branch Rickey was willing to give only a weeping sales talk in exchange for Kluttz."[10] The Braves were suffering from a lack of pitching in June with Al Javery fighting a sore arm. Nate Andrews had left the team on a Western trip and was suspended. Additionally, infielders Dick Culler and Eddie Joost were suffering from injuries.

On May 16, when the Braves handed the Cardinals a double defeat at Braves Field, they were led to victory by two players who were getting their only opportunity to excel as major league players. Carden Gillenwater had played briefly for the 1940 St. Louis Cardinals (.160 in 25 at-bats) and the 1943 Brooklyn Dodgers (.176 in 17 at-bats). In 1944 he caught the eye of the Braves front office by hitting .296 with 19 homers and 70 RBIs for St. Paul in the American Association. Gillenwater patrolled the center field position for the 1945 Braves, hitting .288 with a .379 on-base percentage and slugging 7 homers while driving in 72 runs. He played in 144 games and had 517 at-bats. With the manpower shortages alleviated in 1946, Gillenwater struggled with a .228 batting average for the Braves and then played his final big league season with the 1948 Washington Senators, batting .244 in 221 at-bats. Despite only a .260 lifetime batting average, Gillenwater knew how to work the count and draw walks, finishing with a .359 on-base percentage. He not only provided some offensive punch for the 1945 Braves but also gave the team a good defensive center fielder, as he exhibited in the first game of a doubleheader on May 16 when he threw out the fleet-footed Augie Bergamo, who was attempting to go from first to third in the top of the third inning. Boston won that game, 5–4, in fourteen innings. Gillenwater then hammered an Al Jurisich delivery over the left field fence for a three-run homer to give the Braves an early lead in the second contest that they never relinquished, winning 4–1 before 3,082 witnesses.

Thirty-five-year-old Bob Logan went the distance for his first major league win in the nightcap. Like many left-handers of the day he was nicknamed "Lefty" and had been acquired from Indianapolis of the American Association. Before getting his opportunity with Boston he had played for the Brooklyn Dodgers, Detroit Tigers, Chicago Cubs and Cincinnati Reds. During the course of four seasons (1935, 1937, 1938 and 1941) with these clubs he had pitched in 23 games and had a 0–4 record. He played his final big league season in 1945, compiling a respectable 7–11 record and a 3.18 ERA.

One player who saw his only major league playing time in 1945 was Tommy

Nelson, who batted .165 in 121 at-bats. With the major leagues decimated by manpower shortages there were a lot of players like Gillenwater, Logan, and Nelson getting a rare opportunity to shine in the big show.

The Braves swept three games from the Cardinals on June 30 and July 1 and later won four of five from Pittsburgh to give the fans some hope. However, Boston then went into their worst tailspin of the season, culminating with Bob Coleman's resignation after a nine-game losing streak. His team was beset by myriad injuries, and in addition to losing his two ace pitchers, he had four infielders who were hurt at a critical juncture. Coleman initially went home to Evansville, Indiana, and then rejoined the team as a coach. Bissonette took over the club and was a fond admirer of his former manager Wilbert Robinson. He played a very aggressive style of baseball and his team took many chances on the bases. Furthermore, he was confident that he was not going to burn out like other managers had in 1945, like Coleman, Freddie Fitzsimmons, and Joe McCarthy. If he got angry he wasn't going to hold it in but instead would express his feelings to other people and let them know what he was thinking. Bissonette didn't believe in always making decisions by the book and would often rely on his gut feelings. As for landing the Braves managerial job, he felt he had it coming. It was a "tremendous break" to get the job, but he deserved it because he had taken managerial jobs in the bushes in places where no knowledgeable and experienced baseball man was available. "Now the huntsman is home," said Bissonette.[11] He insisted that he would never quit the Braves managerial position but instead would have to be fired. Unfortunately for Bissonette, those 59 major league games he managed at the tail end of the 1945 season were the only ones he ever managed in the big leagues.

Bissonette did have one moment that rekindled memories of an old Brooklyn tradition from Uncle Robbie's "daffiness boys." On August 1 the Giants defeated Boston, 9–2, but in the second inning two Braves found themselves occupying the same base: Carden Gillenwater rounded second and headed to the next station and was horrified to find that Butch Nieman was already occupying the third-base bag. Plays of this kind were certain to show up in wartime. Bissonette himself was involved in one infamous moment with the Dodgers in 1930. Babe Herman was on first when Bissonette hit a high fly ball to right field. Herman slowed down near the second base bag to see if the ball would be caught and as the spheroid cleared the wall for a home run, Bissonette raced past Herman and was called out. Herman, who had already participated in his share of misadventures during his career, was given the blame by the newspaper writers. However, in a 1945 interview, Bissonette had a much different recollection of the facts: he insisted that Herman had been tagging up at first base when he hit the fly ball.[12]

❖ 8 ❖

The Doleful Deacon and the Colorless Reds

After their third straight spring training at Indiana University in Bloomington, Indiana, the Reds were expecting to compete for the National League flag and were picked to finish in third place by *The Sporting News*. Instead they would endure a dreadful season in which they had difficulty putting together a sustained winning streak. The Cubs in particular feasted on Cincinnati pitching and won twenty-one of the twenty-two games they played against them on the season. The Reds' abysmal season was encapsulated in the first game of a doubleheader against the Phillies at Shibe Park on July 1. Cincinnati owned a 2 to 1 lead in the bottom of the fifth when Joe Bowman began to get hit hard. Manager Bill McKechnie replaced Bowman with Hod Lisenbee. Vince DiMaggio then gave the Phillies the go-ahead run with a force out. When catcher Al Unser tried to pick DiMaggio off first base, the ball ricocheted off Frank McCormick's glove and smacked him in the face. McCormick had to be removed from the game because too much blood was streaming from his nose. DiMaggio then tried to steal second and cut Eddie Miller with his spikes, opening a gash in Miller's left knee. Miller was helped off the field and subsequently missed the next two weeks. One inning, resulting in two injuries, was emblematic of the Reds' disappointing season.

The Giants defeated the Reds on August 14 to give Sal Maglie his first major league victory. Jesse Abramson discussed the hapless nature of the Cincinnati ball club when he wrote in the *New York Herald Tribune*, "Even Salvatore Maglie had to do little more than throw his glove on the Polo Grounds hummock yesterday to beat the harmless Reds...." The game took one hour and thirty-five minutes to complete, and Abramson added, "One can't watch the Reds much longer than that without falling asleep."[1] On September 12 only six hundred fans bothered to show up at Crosley Field, and Harry Cross wrote, "The game was played in an exclusive setting with only 600 paid witnesses in the seats. The bleachers offered a wonderful opportunity for secluded sunbathing, because there were only thirty-nine persons there, including the policeman."[2]

Cincinnati won the following day, 3–2, before a ladies' day crowd of 412 (281 paid). The boom in attendance since the end of the war had not reached the banks of the Ohio, and the Reds home attendance to this point was under 250,000. The Reds were in seventh place, thirty games out of first at that juncture.

The Cincinnati Reds had seen some good years and some bad ones during the war. In 1942 they finished in fourth place at 76–76; in 1943 they were second at 87–67; in 1944 they were third at 89–65; and in 1945 they would finish in seventh place at 61–93. They were managed by Bill "Deacon" McKechnie, who had led the Reds to a National League pennant in 1939 and a World Series championship in 1940. He was very experienced in running a ball club and in 1945 was managing in his twenty-fourth big league season. McKechnie was a stoic personality who never got too high or too low. He didn't curse and he didn't drink; he was unwavering, loyal, and patient, and led his club by stressing the fundamentals. The Cincinnati manager was temperate in his demeanor, rarely losing his temper, acting as a steadying force on a major league team. During spring training he kept the players in great shape with an arduous workout regimen. He would manage four pennant winners and two world championship teams during his twenty-five-year managerial career, which ended with the 1946 season. In addition to his great teams with the Reds he led the 1925 Pirates to a World Series championship and won the pennant with the Cardinals in 1928.

With his sober disposition he would occasionally find it difficult connecting with his players. Red Barrett was one player who never got along with his manager while playing in Cincinnati. McKechnie would judge the character of players such as Barrett from "the Deacon's angle." Barrett came from what he described as a "broad-minded, tolerant family," which was open to different perspectives and lifestyles. During his first day with the Reds he won a jitterbug contest in a Cincinnati nightclub named Kelly's. McKechnie was perturbed by Barrett's proclivity for hanging out in nightclubs, even though the young hurler didn't smoke or drink alcohol. Barrett insisted that the dancing helped keep his legs in shape, an important feature of a pitcher's makeup. His relationship with the Reds manager did not improve over time despite his never missing midnight curfew while a member of Cincinnati's major league representative.[3]

In another incident in late September 1939, McKechnie gave his durable hurler, Whitey Moore, instructions to get some rest because he may be needed in all four games of the upcoming series against the Cardinals which would decide whether they won the pennant. He was none too pleased to wake up the next morning to the *Cincinnati Enquirer's* headline that said, "Reds' Pitcher Escapes Death." He had drunk so much whiskey at a nightclub that he mistook the railroad tracks for a highway. An express train nearly hit Moore, and McKechnie was displeased when he had to get Moore out of jail at two in the morning. When they had a pregame meeting in preparation for that day's ball game, McKechnie showed his anger for one of the rare times in his career and even uttered a few curse words. He threatened to fine his troubled pitcher and desperately tried to find out what Moore was thinking when he decided to disobey his manager's orders. Many of the Reds players found the episode to be comical because they had never seen McKechnie lose his composure. Despite Moore's insubordination the Reds won the first two games of the series and won their first pennant since 1919, the year they beat the scandalous Chicago White Sox in the World Series.[4]

Despite not drinking himself, McKechnie allowed his players to drink in moderation. He was very kind and generous. When the team was playing well he would buy the players beer out of his own pocket. Bill Werber recalled that McKechnie encouraged him to have a beer after one game so that he would rehydrate himself. Werber referred to McKechnie as a "class act" who was well deserving of his 1962 Hall of Fame induction.[5] McKechnie had an unspectacular eleven-year major league career as a player which ended in 1920 with a .251 batting average. He was predominantly a third baseman but played all four infield positions and played two games in the outfield. His managerial career started in 1915 when he replaced Bill Phillips as the skipper of the Newark Peppers of the Federal League. Phillips had a 26–27 record as manager of the team, while under McKechnie they were 54–45 as they finished in fifth place with an 80–72 mark. From 1922 to 1926 he managed the Pittsburgh Pirates; in 1928 and part of 1929 he managed the St. Louis Cardinals. He then had some tough years in Boston with that city's National League ball club from 1930 to 1937, including an abysmal 38–115 record in 1935; then his fortunes improved mightily when he managed the Cincinnati Reds from 1938 to 1946. In 1946 the Reds were 67–87, finishing in sixth place. Under McKechnie they were 64–86, and then Hank Gowdy managed the only four games of his career, finishing 3–1. McKechnie's final major league tally as manager stood at 1,896–1,723.

By 1945 McKechnie had grown tired of the inferior product that was being showcased in ballparks around the country. When the Reds traveled to Boston to play the Braves on May 19, he showed his disdain for wartime ball during an interview at the Copley Plaza. An inquisitive reporter asked him what was wrong with the Reds. He responded, "We simply haven't got a ball club." By this time of the season the Reds were in seventh place, nine games off the pace. The biggest problem with most of the teams was the weak bench and lack of good backup players. McKechnie insisted that most teams could field a competent first unit, but if the starters got injured or had to leave the team, then the "replacements are pretty bad." Major league baseball was in poor condition, but despite its problems, "I suppose it's still baseball." McKechnie found some consolation in the fact that the fans still wanted the games to continue. He described Bob Logan, who had recently won his first major league game for the Braves, as a "fine boy-not too impressive on the mound, but he gets them out." McKechnie said that almost every pitcher who could simply throw strikes could win under wartime conditions. A pitcher with a good curveball could win 15 or 20 games.[6]

The Reds had played their home games on the intersection of Findlay and Western since 1884, predominantly in a ballpark called Crosley Field. There was a four-foot incline in left and left-center starting fifteen feet from the fence, forcing outfielders to run uphill to catch fly balls. The dimensions were fair all the way around: 387 feet to center, 328 feet to left and 366 to right. It was here that the first night game was played in the big leagues in 1935 despite many skeptics, including Commissioner Landis. One person observed, "The game became a strangely colorless, synthetic affair.... The consensus was clear: night baseball would never last."[7]

Frank McCormick, Eddie Miller, Al Libke, Al Lakeman and Eric Tipton led the Reds on offense. McCormick batted .276 with 10 homers and led the team with 81 RBIs. He was a slow-footed first baseman who was predominantly concerned about hitting and often made mental errors in the field. His lifetime average was .299 with 128 home runs. The 6'4", 205-pound, right-handed hitter had great bat control and plate discipline, for example, in 1938 he had 640 at-bats and struck out only 17 times, and then in 1939 had 630 at-bats with 16 strikeouts. He fanned only 189 times in 5,723 career at-bats. McCormick was always very efficient at the plate, getting the ball in play, and usually finishing with his foot in the bucket. He put together three outstanding seasons with the bat from 1938 to 1940, when he batted .327, .332, and .309. He led the senior league in hits in 1938 and 1939 with 209, and then in 1940 he was tied for the lead with Stan Hack with 191. In 1938 and 1939 he collected 40 and 41 two-base hits, and then in 1940 he hit a league-leading 44 doubles. His RBI totals during those three seasons were 106, a league-leading 128, and 127. But he soon developed a back injury which bothered him for the rest of his career and kept him out of military service. In 1944, despite his hitting .305 with 102 RBIs and a career-high twenty home runs, the fans at Crosley Field booed him without mercy, confident in their belief that McCormick was not putting forward his best effort. After the 1945 campaign he was sold to the Phillies and played for them in 1946 and 1947 before finishing his career with the Boston Braves in 1947 and 1948. Bill Werber, who was McCormick's teammate with the Reds from 1939 to 1941, found him to be a "fine fellow" with a "pleasant disposition."[8]

On this weak-hitting team it was their excellent defensive shortstop, Eddie Miller, who led the Reds in home runs with thirteen despite playing in only 115 games. Miller batted .238 lifetime in fourteen big league seasons and hit for occasional power, hitting thirteen or more home runs during four seasons. The Reds had a collective batting average of .249, and only the Phillies were worse in the senior league at .246. They tied the Phillies for the fewest homers with 56.

Outfielder Al Libke was in the rookie season of what would be a two-year major league career and batted .283. He also got to pitch in four games and did not allow an earned run in four and one-third innings. Al Lakeman became the starting catcher midway through the season and batted .256 with 8 homers. The 6'2", 195-pound, right-handed hitting backstop, was a backup for most of his career. His 76 games and 258 at-bats in 1945 were career highs in a nine-year career.

Eric Tipton, in his final major league season, batted .242 and played left field. He had played sparingly before the war with the Philadelphia Athletics, and then in both 1943 and 1944 he played 140 games and batted .288 and .301. He went to college at Duke and was nicknamed "Dukie" and "Blue Devil."

In this otherwise dull season for the Reds, outfielder Dick Sipek provided a refreshing addition to the squad. He was the first deaf player in the big leagues since his mentor Luther "Dummy" Taylor toed the slab for the New York Giants in his final season of 1908. In a nine-year major league career pitching almost exclusively for the Giants, Taylor compiled a 116–106 record with a 2.75 ERA and had a career-high twenty-one wins in 1904, tied for the fourth best in the National League. Taylor was Sipek's house-father at a school for the deaf in Illinois and it was because of his recommendation that Sipek got his first opportunity in pro ball with Birmingham of the Southern Association. Besides Taylor the only other deaf player to play in the big leagues was William "Dummy" Hoy, who participated in fourteen major league seasons, ending his career in 1902 with a .288 batting average. Hoy persuaded the home plate umpires to raise their right hand when the pitcher threw a strike so he could tell what decision was rendered by the arbiter.

Sipek batted .244 in 156 at-bats in '45, seeing most of his time as a pinch hitter, although he played the outfield in thirty-one games. He was twenty-two years old, very sociable, and very popular with his teammates. Sipek tried to allow people to understand his disability and even taught his teammates sign language. One day there was a close play and Sipek flashed the sign for a dirty word at the umpire who had called him out. The umpire was unaware of what had happened, while the Reds bench couldn't stop laughing. Even in the bushes his teammates liked him. One day in Memphis after a game a few sailors began to mock him as he walked ahead of them; when he turned around his Birmingham teammates were beating the hell out of the instigators.[9]

One of Bill McKechnie's biggest problems was the catching situation. During his first four seasons in Cincinnati from 1938 to 1941, future Hall of Famer Ernie Lombardi was an excellent receiver. Ray Lamanno did an adequate job as a rookie in 1942, batting .264 with 12 homers and 43 RBIs in 371 at-bats. Ray Mueller was a durable starting catcher in 1943 and 1944 who had acquired his nickname "Iron Man" by catching a record 155 games in 1944. He also produced at the plate, batting .286 with 10 homers and 73 RBIs. Mueller departed for military service in 1945 and Al Lakeman saw most of the action behind the plate, appearing in 76 games and having 258 at-bats. Lakeman had played for the Reds since 1942, but appeared in only 43 games during his first three seasons. He appeared in only one big league game in 1944, playing most of the season at Syracuse, not as a catcher but as a first baseman. In 1947 and 1949 Lakeman played briefly in the big leagues as a first baseman. Lakeman was born in Cincinnati on December 31, 1918, and played nine major league seasons, compiling a paltry .203 batting average. Also filling in behind the plate were Al Unser, Joe Just and Johnny Riddle. Unser batted .265 in 67 games and 204 at-bats in his fourth and final major league season. His son Del Unser would have a solid big league career from 1968 to 1982, batting .258 in 5,215 at-bats, which was 4,877 more than his father. Just batted .147 in 14 games and 34 at-bats. He also played briefly for the Reds in 1944, hitting .182 in 11 at-bats. Those were his only two big league seasons.

Johnny Riddle gave the club a veteran presence. Riddle had managed Dick Sipek and some of the other Reds players as manager of the Birmingham Barons of the Southern Association in 1944. He gave the 1945 Reds a knowledgeable baseball man who knew the game well from his vast experience, most of which was in the minor leagues. His major league resume listed the 1930 Chicago White Sox as his first major league team, where he batted .241 in 58 at-bats. He didn't return to the big show until 1937, appearing in ten games for the Washington Senators and Boston Braves. Riddle batted .281 in 57 at-bats for the 1938 Braves and then hit .300 in 10 games and 10 at-bats for the 1941 Cincinnati Reds. His next major league game came in 1944, when he appeared in one game. In 1945 the 39-year-old Riddle was called into service once again, batting .178 in 23 games and 45 at-bats. While Riddle's experience was certainly an asset in guiding young players, his age was a detriment; as McKechnie said, "he's been around too long to catch every day."[10] Riddle's final big league appearances came with the 1948 Pittsburgh Pirates, batting .200 in 10 games and 15 at-bats. On August 20, 1948, Riddle, who was near his 43rd birthday, and Fritz Ostermueller, who was within one month of his 41st birthday, formed one of the oldest batteries in major league baseball history.

Johnny's younger brother Elmer was thirty years old in 1945 and had made his big league debut with Cincinnati in 1939, pitching two scoreless innings in relief during one game. Elmer Riddle had two spectacular seasons: in 1941 he was 19–4 with a major-league-leading 2.24 ERA. And in 1943 he went 21–11 with a 2.63 ERA; his twenty-one wins were tied for the National League and major league lead with Rip Sewell and Mort Cooper. However, in 1944 his record fell to 2–2 with a 4.05 ERA in only four starts. The right-handed pitcher had a calcium deposit in his pitching shoulder that hindered his ability to pitch effectively. On May 7 he had to shut it down and subsequently had an operation. When he returned in 1945 he was once again ineffective, going 1–4 with an 8.19 ERA while making twelve appearances and three starts. Elmer pitched only one more effective season in his big league career when he compiled a 12–10 record

Brothers Johnny (left) and Elmer Riddle are pictured with Indianapolis, an American Association outfit. The brothers also played together on the 1945 Cincinnati Reds. Johnny was 39 years old in 1945 and had played intermittently in the big leagues in a seven-year career that ended with the 1948 Pittsburgh Pirates. His younger brother Elmer had problems with his pitching shoulder early in the 1944 season and had to shut it down on May 7 for season-ending surgery. Elmer's 1945 record indicated that the injury may have lingered into the final wartime season, as he compiled only a 1–4 record with an 8.19 ERA in 29.2 innings. On June 24 he pitched in his first game of the campaign, a loss in the first game of a doubleheader against Pittsburgh at Crosley Field (George Brace photograph).

and a 3.49 ERA for the 1948 Pittsburgh Pirates. However, the following year he was 1–8 with a 5.33 ERA in his final season. He had a 65–52 lifetime record and a 3.40 ERA.

The Reds lost several key pitchers who were with the club in 1944. The team was unable to compensate for the loss of Clyde Shoun, Jim Konstanty, Harry Gumbert, and Tommy de la Cruz. In 1945 they were led by Ed Heusser, Joe Bowman, Bucky Walters, Howie Fox, and Vern Kennedy, among others. Heusser stood at six foot and one-half inch tall and weighed 187 pounds. The right-hander had his breakout season in 1944, his sixth big league campaign, going 13–11 with a National League-leading 2.38 ERA. In 1945 he was 11–16 with a 3.71 ERA. Bowman began the 1945 season with the Boston Red Sox but was released after an 0–2 start and a 9.26 ERA. With Cincinnati, his sixth major league team in eleven seasons, he went 11–13 with a respectable 3.59 ERA. The 1945 campaign was the final one of his career; he finished with a 77–96 lifetime mark and a 4.40 ERA. Howie Fox stood at 6'3" and went 8–13 with a 4.93 ERA in his rookie season. Vern Kennedy, a former twenty-one-game winner with the 1936 Chicago White Sox, came over to Cincinnati after an 0–3 start with the Phillies and then went 5–12 for the Reds with a 4.00 ERA in his final big league season. Heusser and Bowman each won eleven games, but the pulse of the staff was Bucky Walters, who had led the league in wins in 1939 (27), 1940 (22), and 1944, when he was 23–8 with a 2.40 ERA. In 1945 he would slip to 10–10 with a 2.68 ERA. Walters was a quiet man who kept to himself; he worked quickly and strived in the big games. His repertoire included a fastball, curve, and sinker. Walters's unassuming personality fit very well with his manager Bill McKechnie.

In early August 1940 Walters was shaken to the core when Willard Hershberger was found dead in his room. Hershberger had committed suicide two days after a crushing ninth-inning loss to the Giants, and the grief-stricken catcher blamed the loss on himself. Ernie Lombardi was removed from the Reds lineup in late July as he nursed a painful ankle sprain, and Hershberger took his place. On the night of July 31, against the Giants at the Polo Grounds, he was behind the dish when Bill Terry's Giants pushed across four runs with two out in the last of the ninth against Walters to win 5–4. This was a devastating loss in the midst of a pennant race. Furthermore, many players were in a foul mood as they prepared to enter the mentally and physically draining dog days of August with its hot weather and high humidity. Hershberger had produced with the bat in 1939, batting .345 in 174 at-bats. In 1940 he also broke the .300 barrier, finishing at .309 in 123 at-bats before his life ended abruptly. Despite his success he was also a troubled young man: he would constantly worry about things; he collected guns and carried around a pistol; and he was haunted by his father's suicide. On August 1 Hershberger commenced the worrying, the self-doubt, and the self-hatred by blaming himself for Walters's loss, believing that he had let the team down and called the wrong pitches. In his next game, Hershberger could not deliver a hit in five at-bats and failed to step up and make a routine defensive play when it was needed. McKechnie asked Hershberger what was wrong and the Reds backstop told his skipper that he would be informed about his predicament after the game. In the evening he opened up to McKechnie and told him about his fears, about his father's suicide, and that he wasn't performing as well as he should and therefore letting the boys down. By the time McKechnie left his catcher he had cheered him up and thought he was feeling better. The next day Hershberger informed his roommate, Bill Baker, that he wasn't feeling well and would be a late arrival at the ballpark. A couple of innings into the first of two games on the day at Braves Field, the Reds skipper summoned a fan to see how Hershberger was doing. Charles Alexander described the suicide as follows: the fan had "discovered a gruesome sight: shirtless but otherwise fully clothed, Hershberger sat on the bathroom floor amid neatly arranged towels, his back against the tub, his throat slit, a safety razor nearby."[11] This was a premeditated action because Hershberger had taken out a life insurance policy before traveling east on the road trip. McKechnie admitted to reporters that Hershberger had told him why he was thinking about suicide, but said, "I will take it to my grave."[12]

Walters's sullen personality intensified as he was greatly affected by the death. The talented pitcher had a separate room for himself at the Copley Plaza Hotel on the trip. He was expecting his wife to join him in Boston but she failed to make the journey when their son developed an ear infection. Walters approached Bill Werber, the team's third baseman, and tried to persuade Werber to sleep in his room, fearful of spending the night alone because he was shaken by the tragedy. He moved all of Werber's personal items to his room just to make sure he showed up. Walters was a compassionate player who felt sympathy for the opposition. Once when he fanned Dolph Camilli of the Dodgers during three at-bats, he confided in Werber, saying, "I feel sorry for ole Dolph. He can't hit me." He wasn't being facetious either; Werber characterized his sentiment as being "genuine."[13]

Walters began his career as a third baseman with the Boston Braves in 1931, batting .211 in 9 games and 38 at-bats, and then batted .187 the following season in 75 at-bats. In 1933 he played for Boston's American League representative, improving to .256 with 4 homers and 28 RBIs in 195 at-bats. He began the 1934 season with the Red Sox and then became a member of the Philadelphia Phillies, hitting .260 with 4 homers and 38 RBIs in 300 at-bats. He hit eight homers on the season, slugging four with the Red Sox in 88 at-bats before coming to Philadelphia, the city in which he was born, on April 19, 1909. Walters pitched his first big league games in 1934, appearing in two contests as a hurler. The following year he was converted to pitcher on a full-time basis, going 9–9 with a 4.17 ERA. In 1936 the Phillies finished at the bottom of the senior circuit with a 54–100 record. Walters struggled on this poor team with an 11–21 mark and a 4.26 ERA. He improved to 14–15 the subsequent year.

After starting the 1938 season with Philadelphia he was traded to the Reds, finishing a combined 15–14. This was the start of seven consecutive seasons in which he would win at least fifteen games, including three seasons of 22 or more victories. He remained with the Reds until 1948 and then appeared in his final big league game with the 1950 Boston Braves. In sixteen seasons as a pitcher he was 198–160 with a 3.30 ERA. He was also one of the better hitting pitchers in the majors and hit a career-high .325 in 120 at-bats with the 1939 Cincinnati Reds. He batted .243 lifetime with 23 homers in 1,966 at-bats. Walters would later manage the Reds in 1948, going 20–33, and for most of the 1949 season as they finished in seventh place with a 61–90 record under Walters; they were 62–92 overall. He would later coach in the big leagues with the Boston Braves (1950–1952), Milwaukee Braves (1953–1955), and New York Giants (1956).

Walters, in his role as a veteran player, treated the young players with respect and would not belittle them as some others did. Hank Sauer, who began his big league career with the Reds, said, "He was the only player who treated me like one of the guys. No one else even talked to me. Bucky even bought me dinner." Walters would tell the younger players baseball stories and give them helpful advice.[14] Frank Baumholtz, who debuted with the Reds in 1947, admitted that even though the younger players looked up to Walters, he was not a "leader," and he didn't think there were any leaders on the team.[15]

In 1945 there were players getting an opportunity to perform in the big show who had never advanced to the higher levels of minor league baseball. Mel Bosser, a six-foot, 173-pound, right-handed pitcher, was one such player. When Bosser toed the slab at Philadelphia's Shibe Park on May 14 in his first big league start, the former Army Air Force corporal had never pitched higher than Class D before getting his shot with the 1945 Reds. Bosser was the winning pitcher as Cincinnati won, 5–4. He gave up five hits in seven and a third innings and struck out three. That was the good news; however, the bad news was that he walked ten batters. Walter "Boom-Boom" Beck pitched the final inning and two-thirds to secure the victory. On the season Bosser had a 2–0 record with a 3.38 ERA and six of his seven appearances were in relief. He walked seventeen batters in sixteen innings. On June 11 the Reds released him and Bosser never again pitched in the big leagues. If he had stayed on the club beyond June 15 he would have received a $2,000 bonus for signing. Although Bosser's record and earned run average were good, his inability to throw strikes earned him a demotion back to the bushes. When Bosser was sent down he did not complain and felt that he was given a fair shot.[16]

Among the aging players with the Reds in 1945 were Guy Bush and Hod Lisenbee. Bush was born on August 23, 1901, and had pitched for the Chattanooga club in 1944, compiling a 5–3 record. He began his career in 1923 with the Chicago Cubs and finished it with the Reds in 1945, pitching in four games with a 8.31 ERA. He finished with an excellent lifetime record of 176–136 with a 3.86 ERA. Hod Lisenbee, the elder statesman on the team, was born on September 23, 1898. He pitched with Syracuse in the International League in 1944, compiling a 15–15 record with a 4.06 ERA in 248 innings pitched. With the 1945 Reds he pitched in 31 games and was 1–3 with a 5.49 ERA.

Joe Nuxhall, who joined the Reds in spring training, was born on July 30, 1928, giving the Reds a large fluctuation in pitching ages. Nuxhall became the youngest player to make an appearance in a big league game when at age fifteen years, ten months, and eleven days, on June 10, 1944, he was called in from the bullpen when the Reds were getting hammered by the Cardinals at Crosley Field. Before being taken out of the game the petrified hurler yielded five runs on two singles, five walks, and a wild pitch, although he did manage to get two batters out in the process. That was the only game he pitched on the season and he had a 67.50 ERA. Nuxhall spent the 1945 spring training with the Reds before being farmed out. He didn't make it back to the big leagues until 1952 and finished a sixteen-year career with a 135–117 record. With Nuxhall missing from the big club in 1945, eighteen-year-old Herm Wehmeier replaced him as the youngest player on the team and was 0–1 in two games with a 12.60 ERA. He started both contests and pitched five innings on the season. After some more development in the bushes, Wehmeier would have a respectable big league career, finishing with a 92–108 record and a 4.80 ERA. During seven of his thirteen seasons he won at least ten games.

❖ 9 ❖

Look Away: Ben Chapman and the Faltering Phils

While the Phillies were preparing for the season in Wilmington, Delaware, their brain trust was busy acquiring new talent for the upcoming season. The three most influential members of the Phillies front office included most prominently owner Robert R.M. Carpenter, Sr., who was also a former vice president of the DuPont company and was married to a member of the DuPont family. His son Robert R.M. Carpenter, Jr., was president of the club. He was named to that position after his father purchased the team in 1943. Herb Pennock, a former big league pitcher, was the general manager of the club. Carpenter Sr. aggressively invested his money in his ball club and had spent over $250,000 on talent during his first two years. More than $50,000 of that was spent since the 1945 spring training had begun. This included paying for Vince DiMaggio's contract, which they acquired in a trade with Pittsburgh. Whitlow Wyatt was purchased from the Dodgers for $20,000. They gave $42,000 in bonus money to a number of young players during the winter. They also signed Jimmie Foxx and Gus Mancuso to healthy contracts. They invested $60,000 in their scouting and $60,000 more for the farm system.[1]

When many club owners were unwilling to spend large sums of money during the war, the Phillies aggressively tried to improve their ball club through acquisitions. However, not all of these investments proved successful. Whitlow Wyatt, for example, had five terrific seasons for Brooklyn from 1939 to 1943, winning 78 games during that stretch, including a career-high twenty-two victories in 1941 that was tied for the National League lead with his teammate Kirby Higbe. Before joining the Dodgers in 1939 Wyatt's major league career was a disappointment, plagued by arm problems and an inability to throw strikes consistently. Wyatt excelled for several seasons in Brooklyn but by 1944 his productivity declined sharply. He spent part of 1944 in the military and only pitched in nine games for Brooklyn, going 2–6 with a 7.17 ERA. The Phillies took a risk and gave the Dodgers $20,000 for his services on March 28. But in 1945, during Wyatt's final major league season, he compiled a 0–7 record and a 5.26 ERA in ten starts. He gave up 72 hits in 51.1 innings against inferior competition during that final wartime season.

The investment in the farm system would eventually pay off with a pennant-winning ball club in 1950. Herb Pennock had pitched for the Red Sox (1915–1922 and 1934) and then coached for them from 1936 to 1940. From 1941 to 1943 he was the supervisor of their farm system. He had watched Tom Yawkey, the Red Sox' owner, unsuccessfully try to buy a pennant by purchasing the contracts of established stars. He knew a quick fix wouldn't work with the Phillies; Carpenter, Sr., agreed with him and thus invested heavily in their farm system. When the Carpenters first took over the ball club in 1943 the Phillies' only working agreement was with Trenton, a Class B outfit in the Interstate League. But by the spring of 1945 they were planning to have eleven farm teams in the near future, having already added several farm clubs including the Utica Blue Sox in the Eastern League; the Wilmington Blue Rocks of the Interstate League; and the Bradford Blue Wings of the Pony League. By 1945 this once-depleted minor league system was showing some new life, and in 1948 they finally got a Triple A team with Toronto of the International League. Over a four-year stretch the Phillies gave out $1,250,000 in bonus money.

Heading into the 1945 season the Phils were already feeling the manpower shortage. Tony Lupien and Ron Northey were taken into the service. Two of their good minor league players, Les Scarsella and Hal Spindel, declined to leave their war jobs and join the club. Fred Daniels, who they had hoped would play second base, had a spinal infection. And their young shortstop, Granny Hamner, was expected to be taken into military service. Vince DiMaggio was brought in to add some pop but Stan Baumgartner observed that he "strikes out enough during the season to start a hurricane."[2]

The injuries continued once the season began. In June, Charley Schanz had "yellow jaundice."[3] DiMaggio had a leg injury; Coaker Triplett had a broken finger; Nick Goulish had an appendectomy; and infielder John Antonelli had an injured wrist. The injuries forced some players to fill in at positions they were unaccustomed to playing. When infielder Bitsy Mott went into the Navy, Jimmie Foxx was forced to play third base, and even catcher Andy Seminick played some third base during the season. When one of the infielders developed an ego, Herb Pennock made the following observation:

> I guess we'll have to put that guy in short pants again. His head is popping. The youngster may find himself in Utica. He laughs off his errors and his inability to cover more than a dime on the infield, although the truth is that he can't cover enough ground to be a Class B infielder in regular times. His hitting is about as healthy as a ration book after a steak dinner.[4]

Although Pennock did not say which of his infielders he was referring to, it may have been Garvin Hamner, who was sent down to the Atlanta Crackers of the Southern Association in June. However, it is more likely he was referring to Garvin's 18-year-old brother, Granny, who was a cocky, tough teenager from the streets of Richmond, Virginia, where he ran with a rowdy crowd that got into trouble. Pennock said the ballplayer might be sent down to Utica, and that is precisely where Granny spent most of the 1945 season. Eddie Sawyer, his manager in Utica, would later become the Phillies skipper during the 1948 season and lead them to a pennant in 1950. Also in June the Phillies purchased the contract of Dick Mauney, who had gone 16–7 for Atlanta in 1944, and then in the first of three major league seasons went 6–10 with a 3.08 ERA for the Phillies in 1945.

The Phillies played their home games at Shibe Park, which was located on Lehigh Avenue between 20th and 21st streets. The American League Athletics played there beginning in 1909 and the Phillies joined them in 1938 when they finally abandoned the decaying Baker Bowl. Michael Gershman wrote concerning the first day of the ballpark: "Philadelphians saw ... a dignified palace reminiscent of a bank or a library, with masses of pennants, ornamental scrollwork, and a fabulous French Renaissance cupola, which housed Connie Mack's office."[5] After renovations in 1925 the dimensions were 334 feet down the left field line, 468 feet to center, and 331 feet down the right field line. The park was kept in impeccable condition up until the 1950s when it began to decay. The New York Giants had considerable difficulty hitting homers in the ballpark during the early 1940s. Remarkably, Mel Ott had failed to hit a homer in Shibe Park entering the 1945 season. He observed, "It isn't a tough park, so far as measurements are concerned, but it always has been tough for me. For one thing there is something about the lighting that bothers me and I don't seem to see the ball as well as in other parks."[6]

If the Phillies ballpark deprived the Giants of their power hitting, Philadelphia's National League ball club was anything but potent when it came to winning games. From 1938 through 1942 they finished in last place with records of 45–105, 45–106, 50–103, 43–111, and 42–109. Their winning percentage ranged from .278 to .327. Before the start of the 1943 season, Chester Smith of the *Pittsburgh Press* wrote that the Phillies "didn't have enough talent to put up more than a fair battle in a class B league."[7] In 1943, when the Giants finished in the cellar, the Phillies graduated to seventh place, 64–90. In 1944 they were back in the cellar at 61–92. Once again they were destined for a last-place finish in 1945 (46–108). Freddie Fitzsimmons, a former pitcher with a corkscrew windup and a tantalizing knuckleball, managed the club through the first half of the season, while the caustic Ben Chapman took over as skipper on June 29.

Ben Chapman was one of those veteran ballplayers who had his career extended because of World War II. He was an outfielder with the Yankees during the first half of the '30s before being bounced around several teams. During the war he even pitched, going 5–3 for Brooklyn with a 3.40 ERA in 1944 and 3–3 with a 5.79 ERA in 1945 with the Dodgers and Phillies. He was traded to the Phillies on June 15 and two weeks later became their manager. Chapman was one of the scoundrels in the game, a devout anti–Semite, who gave Nazi salutes to fans and players. In 1933 he initiated a riot between the Yankees and Washington Senators when he went after second baseman Buddy Myer, a Jew. In December of 1938, when he was traded away from the Boston Red Sox, owner Tom Yawkey told him they were trading him because: "You're the number one Bolshevist in baseball."[8]

Chapman's temper was legendary. When a fan taunted him at Yankee Stadium, he chased him through the crowd. Catcher Birdie Tebbetts of the Tigers made an unflattering remark after Chapman struck out one day, and he dropped Tebbetts with a vicious punch. He threw the ball at an umpire after a close play. And there he was in 1947, as manager of the Philadelphia Phillies, casting unconscionable abuse upon Jackie Robinson. He ordered his players to go after Jackie and try to maim him in the field. The verbal abuse was nonstop: "Hey, coon, do you always smell so bad?" "Hey, nigger, why don't you go back to the cotton field where you belong?" and "Hey, snowflake, which one of those white boys' wives are you shacking up with tonight?"—among other vulgar comments.[9] National League President Ford Frick had to interfere and inform Chapman to cut it out. A photo op was set up showing Chapman holding a bat and standing next to Robinson. Chapman did not want to touch Robinson's skin, so he held out a bat for both of them to hold, but Robinson refused to hold it.

The calm before the storm. Ben Chapman of the Philadelphia Phillies surveys the playing field before the hostilities begin. Chapman was a volatile personality through much of his professional baseball career. He played for the Senators and White Sox in 1941 and then, with teams in need of players during the war, he resurfaced with Brooklyn in 1944 (.368, 14 for 38). Surprisingly, this former outfielder of American League teams made his best contribution on the hill, going 5–3 with a 3.40 ERA in 79.1 innings. In 1945 he went 3–3 with a 5.53 ERA on the mound before being traded to Philadelphia. With the Phillies he batted .314 (16 for 51), pitched in three games, and started his managerial career. Chapman is remembered not for his accomplishments as a talented outfielder with terrific speed, but his open hostility toward Jackie Robinson in 1947 (George Brace photograph).

Chapman argued in his defense that he was treating Robinson like any other rookie who had to handle abuse and affronts on his ethnicity. Philadelphia's controversial manager believed that verbally attacking Robinson on racial grounds was no different from attacking someone because he was Jewish, Polish, Italian or Irish. He said that Jackie "did not want to be patronized," that he wanted to be treated as an equal, and therefore was open to commensurate abuse. Harry Walker said that Chapman "fought hard and played hard all of his life. He gave a hard time to a lot of players. I remember he rode the hell out of Harry Danning when he was catching in New York, just to needle him because he was Jewish."[10] The only problem was, unlike other ballplayers, Robinson was instructed not to fight back, so the abuse was not commensurate. If someone said vile things about Chapman he could walk across the field, as he often did during his career, and beat the hell out of the instigators. If Robinson did the same thing there would have been repercussions that were far more serious than a fine or a suspension: the newspaper writers, fans, and owners who were against Robinson and did not want blacks to participate in major league baseball would have used it as an excuse to run him out of the major leagues and make sure that segregation persisted. Chapman and his team, replete with white Southerners, were determined to end Branch Rickey's great experiment single-handedly. In 1948 Chapman said to Jackie, "Robinson, you're one hell of a ballplayer, but you're still a nigger."[11]

Less than two years before becoming the manager of the Phillies, Chapman was suspended from organized baseball for one year after punching an umpire in the nose during the playoff as manager of Richmond in the Piedmont League. Chapman said, "You know how that happened. Richmond is a pretty hot town, it was a pretty hot series and Chapman is a pretty hot guy." He believed that to achieve what he thought was right it was more than appropriate to engage in fisticuffs and arguments. Ironically, when he became the manager of the Phillies in 1945 he insisted that he had mellowed and was not the volatile player he was as a young man who would retaliate every time he was insulted.[12]

The Phillies front office during the early 1940s was very chaotic. Freddie Fitzsimmons took over for Bucky Harris as manager during the 1943 season. William D. Cox, the Phillies owner, fired Harris because he called his players "jerks" and he couldn't properly motivate them.[13] The Phillies players were angered by the firing; they rallied in support of their former skipper and refused to take the field in their next game, until Harris told them to play. Harris fired back at Cox, "He's a fine guy to fire me — when he gambles on games his club plays."[14] The gambling allegations had legs, and Commissioner Landis banned Cox from organized baseball on November 23, 1943. Robert R.M. Carpenter eventually became the new owner. Cox himself had taken control of the Phillies in early 1943 because of problems with the previous owner, Gerry Nugent. Nugent was an intelligent baseball executive who ran the team on a shoe string-budget, making the best of the limited financial resources he had just to keep the organization afloat. But he was in debt to the National League, whose owners were tired of the predicament of this perennial second-division ball club. Nugent sold the team to the National League, who then sold it to Cox, hoping that he would provide some stability to the franchise.

Bill Veeck wrote in his autobiography that he wanted to buy the team and stock it with black players but Landis disallowed him to do so. But Veeck was either engaging in hyperbole or mendacity with his assertion. It is an apocryphal story that was frequently retold by historians until three SABR researchers—David Jordan, Larry Gerlach, and John Rossi—exposed Veeck's specious claim with a groundbreaking article in *The National Pastime*.[15] However, Veeck's support of the black ballplayer was legitimate and commendable, not in need of a fictional retelling. As owner of the Cleveland Indians in 1947 he purchased the rights to Larry Doby from the Newark Eagles of the Negro National League. Doby was a utility player that season, batting only .156 in 32 at-bats during the second half of the season. Like Jackie Robinson he faced unconscionable verbal abuse by fans and opposing players. Veeck received about 20,000 protest letters that were mostly violent, racist, and obscene in nature.[16] Despite Doby's inability to become an everyday player and his weak performance during his first season, Veeck stood by his mild-mannered ballplayer. Veeck's patience paid dividends in 1948 when Doby batted .301 with a .384 on-base percentage in 439 at-bats.

The star of the 1945 team was Vince DiMaggio, who batted .257 with 19 homers and 84 RBIs. The closest player on the team to DiMaggio in homers had only seven and in RBIs 60. He would not attain the same level of success as his younger brothers Joe and Dom, but on this club he stood out as a first-class player. Vince completed his ten-year big league career in 1946, finishing with a lifetime .249 average with 125 homers. Also making offensive contributions were Vance Dinges, Coaker Triplett, Jimmy Wasdell, Glenn Crawford, and John Antonelli. Dinges batted .287 while playing the outfield and first base. Triplett batted .240 with 7 homers in his final big league season. Wasdell batted .300 with seven homers and Crawford contributed a .295 batting average. John Antonelli played all four infield positions on the season (3B-109, 2B-23, 1B-1, SS-1) and batted .254. He was traded to the Phillies on May 8 along with Glenn Crawford as Buster Adams was sent to the St. Louis Cardinals.

The Phillies had two brothers on the team, Wesley Garvin Hamner and Granny Hamner. Garvin batted .198 in 32 games at the age of twenty-one and would play his only big league season in 1945. Granny, who batted .171 in 14 games, would have a seventeen-year career with a .262 lifetime average. Garvin was mainly a second baseman for the 1945 Phillies while Granny was a shortstop. Neither player was sure-handed defensively as Garvin made fifteen errors during the campaign while Granny was charged with eleven errors. There were many games early in the season when both Garvin and Granny were in the starting lineup and formed the Phillies double-play combination up the middle of the diamond. If they performed successfully at their respective positions then Phillies management was more than content to have them start the entire season. But their early season performance proved that neither Garvin nor Granny was ready to excel in the big show. When the curtain was raised on the 1945 season on April 17 the Hamner brothers were in the opening-day lineup. Brooklyn defeated Philadelphia, 8–2, at Ebbets Field. Garvin went 1 for 4 with one error and Granny was hitless in four at-bats. On the following day the Hamner brothers contributed to a 6–2 Phillies victory as they both went 2 for 4 at the plate. Granny had two RBIs, scored one run and committed one error in the field. On April 19, Garvin went 0 for 4 and Granny was 0 for 3 as the Phillies lost, 3–1, to Brooklyn. In each of those first three games against Brooklyn, Garvin batted in the sixth hole while Granny batted eighth.

On April 20 the Braves won, 6–5, thanks to a dramatic three-run homer by Butch Nieman with two outs in the ninth inning at Shibe Park in the Phillies' home opener. In the field the brothers participated in a 4–6–3 double play and Granny made two errors. Garvin went 1 for 4 at the plate with a run scored while Granny went hitless in four at-bats but did have one RBI. On April 22 more than 13,700 fans attended the doubleheader at Shibe Park and saw the Boston Braves take the opener by a 3–2 score; the Phillies rebounded in the nightcap, winning 7–6. Granny was charged with an error in the opening contest. Both brothers went hitless in the first game: Granny was 0 for 3 and Garvin was 0 for 2. In the second game, Garvin went 2 for 3 with a run scored while Granny was once again hitless, 0 for 4. On April 24, in a 5–2 Phillies loss to the Giants at the Polo Grounds, both Garvin and Granny went 0 for 3 and they were each charged with one error in the field. Two days later, in a 2–0 loss to New York, Garvin led off and went 1 for 3 while Granny was 0 for 1 with an error. At Braves Field on April 28 the Phillies lost, 8–7, as Garvin went 1 for 5 with one run scored and one RBI while Granny was 2 for 4 with a double, one run scored and one run driven in. On April 29 the Phillies and Braves split a doubleheader. Garvin was 0 for 7 in the two games with an error in the opener while Granny had three hits on the day with a double, a run scored and two RBIs. He was charged with an error in game two. The Hamner boys turned a 4–6–3 double play in the second contest.

On May 2 the Giants defeated the Phillies by a 9–8 score at Shibe Park before a meager crowd of under 1,750 fans. Garvin went 1 for 4 with two runs scored as the Phillies leadoff hitter while Granny batted eighth and went 0 for 4. Both Garvin and Granny made an error in the field. On May 5, Garvin was 1 for 8 in a doubleheader against Brooklyn. Granny had a particularly bad performance on this day. Phillies manager Freddie Fitzsimmons and Herb Pennock, the general manager, had given Granny every opportunity to succeed but their patience had worn thin by early May, and when they saw Granny commit three errors in the opening game his fate was sealed. It was obvious Fitzsimmons had lost confidence in the young man when he sent up Rene Monteagudo to pinch-hit for Granny in only the third inning. Perhaps he made the move to spare Granny from any more embarrassment on the day. Brooklyn won the opening contest, 10–1, and then won the nightcap, 12–8. There were six errors in the opener and in the second game there were nine errors, four by Brooklyn and five by Philadelphia, one of which was charged to Garvin. One name that was conspicuously missing from the starting lineup in the second game was Granny Hamner. Garvin played shortstop and Don Hasenmayer was sent out to start at second base. For Hasenmayer this was one of only eleven major league games he would ever play in during the course of two seasons, 1945 and 1946. He went 1 for 3 in the game with a run scored and one error. On May 8, Glenn Crawford was acquired in a trade with St. Louis and was immediately inserted into the starting lineup at shortstop. Garvin would continue to start but he was also destined to be removed from the starting lineup. Those games in which the Hamner brothers were inserted into the starting lineup were largely forgettable performances. It was apparent to Herb Pennock that both Garvin and Granny were not going to excel in the big leagues in 1945, and they both were sent down to the minor leagues.

In 1945 the Phillies used nine players at second base. Fred Daniels, who was also known as Tony, played the most games at the keystone position with 75. In his only big league season, Daniels batted .200 in 230 at-bats. Seven players would play shortstop for the Phillies during the season. Seeing the most action at the position was Bitsy Mott, who played shortstop in 63 of his 90 games during the campaign. Mott was a 5'8", 155-pound, right-handed batter who hit .221 in 289 at-bats during his only big league season in 1945.

The Phillies committed 234 errors in 1945, which was the most of any team during the war and the most in the major leagues since the 1940 Philadelphia Athletics made 238 errors. It was also the most in the National League since the 1936 Phillies were charged with 252 errors. Not surprisingly, the Chicago Cubs, a pennant-winning ball club, had the fewest errors in the majors in 1945 with 121. The Brooklyn Dodgers, a team that won 87 games, made 230 errors and committed the second most errors in the big leagues in 1945.

Granny had debuted in 1944 at the age of seventeen, making 9 errors in 21 games and batting .247. The Phillies signed him in September of 1944 and he went straight to the big leagues to finish the season with the team. Granny recalls, "We had a really poor club.... There were a few good players still around. But they were all getting older. We didn't get big crowds to watch us. So it wasn't too hard to break in."[17] The Philadelphia crowds were sparse but vocal and they booed the young kid without mercy when he made five errors during one game. His eyes welled up as he entered the dugout, fighting back the tears. Fitzsimmons, who was also the manager in 1944, challenged the fans to meet him in the dugout and settle the issue with his fists, but no one accepted the offer. Hamner would build his backbone in the minors. When sent down to

Utica in 1945 he kicked one in the field and challenged the fans who had booed him to a fight. A few of those young Phillies who played in 1945 would last until 1950, when they won the pennant. They included Granny Hamner, Putsy Caballero, and Andy Seminick.

Thirty-seven-year-old Jimmie Foxx was having one last day in the sun in 1945 before he would finally retire for good. He would bat .268 with 7 homers in 224 at-bats to finish his career with a .325 batting average and 534 home runs. Foxx was built as if he were chiseled out of stone and stood at 6 foot, 195 pounds. He had an affable personality and enjoyed the good life: fine cars, good cigars, and expensive whiskey. In 1945, when he was playing for that final paycheck, his reflexes had eroded to the point where he was endangering his health by walking between the white lines. One day, in 1942, he almost got skulled in Wrigley Field when the white ball came out of the white shirts in the bleachers and almost separated his head from his shoulders. However, by 1945 the caliber of talent he competed against was on a far lower level, and he was no longer playing for the Chicago Cubs, with their field's dangerous background for hitting. Like Ben Chapman, he even pitched, getting by with his fastball and screwball, compiling a 1–0 record with a 1.59 ERA in nine games for the Phillies. One day clothing was being collected outside the Polo Grounds for admission and John Drebinger of the *New York Times* wrote, "It was old clothes day at the Polo Grounds yesterday and what with the venerable Jimmie Foxx on third and the even more ancient Gus Mancuso behind the plate, it looked for a few moments as though some of the stuff the folks were leaving at the gate for admission had found its way onto the playing field."[18] Mancuso, the oldest member on the team, was approaching his fortieth birthday. This was also his final year, which saw him catching seventy ball games, and batting .199. His final career average stood at .265.

Like Ben Chapman, Jake Powell was another proud racist who coincidentally would finish his major league career by playing under Chapman towards the tail end of the season. He batted .194 in 31 games for the Washington Senators and batted .231 in 48 games for the Phillies in 1945. Powell was extremely fast, known for beating out an exorbitant number of bunts. He completed his career with a .271 average and 65 stolen bases.

Powell hated Jews and blacks. Early in the 1936 season he went after Hank Greenberg and broke Hank's wrist in a first-base collision. Greenberg only played twelve games that year. That same season Powell was traded from the Washington Senators to the New York Yankees, and when his new ball club traveled to Washington the fans threw bottles at him. Unperturbed, he picked up the bottles and tossed them back at the fans. In 1938 he started a Memorial Day riot by charging the mound against Red Sox hurler Archie McKain. Joe Kuhel and Powell started to fight one day when Kuhel's teammates on the Senators intervened and beat the hell out of Powell. Other memorable fights were against Joe Cronin and minor leaguer Eric McNair. In 1940 he chased a fly ball until he ran into the unyielding outfield wall and was knocked out cold. His skull was fractured as a result.

In 1938 he was a guest on a radio show before a game and declared that he found "pleasure" in "beating niggers over the head."[19] He told the audience he was a cop in the off-season, but that turned out to be a lie. Commissioner Landis suspended Powell for ten days. Landis, of course, kept blacks out of major league baseball during his reign as commissioner, but declared publicly, "There is no rule, formal or informal, or any understanding — written, subterranean, or sub-anything — against the hiring of Negro players by the teams of organized ball."[20] Westbrook Pegler of the *Chicago Daily News* criticized Landis's ten-day suspension of Powell as an attempt to "placate the colored clientele of a business which trades under the name of the national game, but has always treated the Negroes as Adolf Hitler treats the Jews." *The Sporting News* as usual came to organized baseball's defense and suggested that ballplayers were not intelligent enough to participate in unedited radio interviews. They wrote, "Powell was on the spot and was the victim of circumstances, which should not be held against him by the fans."[21] This was a sentiment that was also held by his manager, Joe McCarthy, who insisted that those who broadcast on the radio should not "pester players for interviews." While most of the country quickly forgot about the Powell incident, tolerating and encouraging verbal and physical assaults towards blacks, some fans in Washington and Chicago were motivated to protest his hate speech by throwing bottles and other objects at Powell when the Yankees came into town.[22]

Finally came the fitting end to his life in 1948. Powell found himself in a police station being booked for signing fake checks. The officers were questioning him when he reached for his .25-caliber pistol and shot himself. Before he put the fatal bullet through his head he declared, "To hell with all this. I'm going to end it all."[23]

The pitchers who led the hapless Phillies in 1945 were Dick Barrett, Andy Karl, Charley Schanz, Charlie Sproull, Dick Mauney, and Oscar Judd. Barrett was 8–20 with a 5.38 ERA in his final major league season. His twenty losses tied Bobo Newsom of the Philadelphia Athletics for the most losses in the majors during the 1945 campaign. Reliever Andy Karl was 8–8 with a 2.99 ERA and led the Phillies in victories. He also led major league pitchers by working in 67 contests. Charley Schanz and Charlie Sproull each won four games. Dick Mauney was 6–10 with a 3.08 ERA and Oscar Judd contributed a 5–4 record and a 3.81 ERA.

Hugh Mulcahy, who was the first big league player drafted for World War II, also put on the Phillies' pinstriped uniform. He hadn't pitched since 1940, when he was 13–22 with a 3.60 ERA and led the major leagues in losses. When he returned he was considerably underweight and had not fully recovered from an illness he had suffered in the South Pacific. In 1945 he was 1–3 with a 3.81 ERA in five games. Mulcahy was a very patriotic young man and was an inspiration to all servicemen when he was inducted into the Army on March 8, 1941, at Camp Edwards in Massachusetts and said, "Personally I think this conscription bill is a great thing for the young men of today." He thought he would be in the military for only one year and told reporters that it would take him a little longer to get into playing shape during the 1942 spring training.[24] Because of his tendency to lose ball games he was given the nickname "Losing Pitcher." Before he went off to war he reportedly said, "At last I'm on a winning team."[25] Mulcahy left his baseball career in the service, pitching in only sixteen games in 1946 and two in 1947 before his career ended with a 45–89 record and a 4.49 ERA.

For years the Philadelphia Phillies' managers, like those of other teams, had heard the "grandstand managers," who were eager to express their opinions about the general direction of the ball club, game strategy, and player personnel. Grandstand managers are fans that have a divergent opinion from the manager concerning the decisions that are made and generally express their disgust in a loud and forceful manner. In 1945, Herb Pennock, the Phillies general manager, officially sanctioned a "Grandstand Manager's Club." Freddie Fitzsimmons, the Phillies manager, said, "They have been yelling at me all year. A few more will make the party a little merrier and maybe they will help too. A thousand heads are better than one." To become a member of the new club, fans had to apply at the Phillies office or through the mail. They would sit in their own special section behind the Phillies dugout. Furthermore, their membership cards read "De Beste Stuurlui Staan Aan Wal," a Dutch phrase which translates into "The best pilots stand on the shore." These cards officially sanctioned the fans to second-guess the manager and to be critical of the front office. They could even suggest trades, complain about the food at the ballpark or criticize the uniforms of the team.[26] Regardless of whether there was a "Grandstand Manager's Club," the Philadelphia fans were not going to shy away from expressing their opinions.

❖ 10 ❖

The National League Campaign

The weather was unpleasantly cold on April 17, the opening day of the major league baseball season. Maurice J. Tobin, the governor of Massachusetts, not only used a glove when throwing out the ceremonial first pitch but also warmed up before doing so and then settled down to watch the Braves lose to the Giants, 11 to 6, at Braves Field. Only 5,702 fans attended the game. Ernie Lombardi paced the Giants with a three-run homer to center field and Phil Weintraub hit a two-run circuit shot. Bill Voiselle earned the victory while Al Javery took the loss. The winds were howling at Wrigley Field as the Cubs collected only four hits but were able to defeat the Cardinals, 3–2, behind the strong pitching of 38-year-old Paul Derringer. Don Johnson sent the 11,788 fans home happy when he won the game with an RBI single in the bottom of the ninth. At Ebbets Field, 10,996 spectators observed a quality start by Curt Davis as he went the distance in an 8–2 victory over the Phillies. Davis also collected two hits, including a home run. Ken Raffensberger was the losing pitcher in the first of only four starts and five appearances he would make on the season. Manager Leo Durocher wrote himself into the Brooklyn lineup and went 1 for 4 with a run scored and two RBIs as the second baseman. Durocher would only put himself into one more game on the season, which would be the last of his playing career. It had been rumored that Branch Rickey, the team president, had offered his manager a $1,000 bonus if he played in the first fifteen games. Durocher said, "I would not accept the $1000, even if it were offered to me."[1]

The best attendance in the majors on opening day was in Cincinnati, where a crowd of 30,069 saw the Reds win a thrilling 7–6 victory over the Pirates in eleven innings. The Reds scored six runs in the fifth inning, which was highlighted by Dain Clay's grand slam homer. Clay then won the game in the bottom of the eleventh with a bases-loaded single to give Hod Lisenbee a relief victory.

Ace Adams, the Giants reliever, was the beneficiary of four runs in the ninth inning as New York held on for an 8–4 win over Boston on the following day. Cincinnati had a four-run assault of their own in the eighth inning against Pittsburgh and they won, 6–0, behind Ed Heusser's eight-hit shutout. Philadelphia had a five-run fourth inning, and won 6–2 over Brooklyn. On April 19 it was Patriots Day in Boston and 1,793 fans showed up for the morning game but were disappointed to see New York score four runs in the eighth inning to win 4–3. Boston won the afternoon game, 13–5, behind the complete-game effort of Jim Tobin. Eddie Joost did not play in the doubleheader and was replaced by Steve Shemo at second base. Joost went 4 for 8 in the first two games of the campaign but suffered an injury to his right foot while sliding into second base during the season's second game and would be out of the lineup for a considerable length of time. Norm Wallen was called up from Indianapolis. Wallen, who was born Norman Edward Walentoski on February 13, 1917, in Milwaukee, appeared in four games during the season, batting .133 in 15 at-bats in his only big league appearances. At Ebbets Field, 4,099 freezing fans watched Hal Gregg yield one run on two hits and six walks while striking out seven as he pitched to his personal catcher, Clyde Sukeforth. Brooklyn won, 3–1, over Philadelphia. John Douglas, a left-handed hitting and throwing first baseman, joined the Dodgers and was expected to take over at the gateway station. He was recently discharged from the Navy and had played professional baseball for only one season, 1941, hitting .385 for Miami in the Florida East Coast League. Before being discharged in the middle of March he spent three and a half months at the Portsmouth Naval Hospital recovering from a knee operation. Douglas appeared in five big league games in 1945; he had nine at-bats, no hits, and two walks. At Wrigley Field, Walker Cooper found out he was going to be inducted into the Army and he went 4 for 5 as St. Louis defeated Chicago, 8–2. Pittsburgh defeated Cincinnati, 5–1.

A crowd of 12,640 paid their way into the Polo Grounds on April 20 to witness the Giants home opener. The spectators were not disappointed as the Giants defeated the Dodgers, 10–6, behind a pair of Phil Weintraub home runs. Many noticeable figures in military and civic life were there, including Mayor Fiorello LaGuardia, who tossed out the first ball. The music was provided by the 17th Regiment Band of the New York State National Guard. Harry Cross wrote, "It cannot be possible that all Giants-Dodgers games will be as circumspect as yesterday's. There wasn't a single squawk."[2] Outside the ballpark, a number of blacks were picketing, members of the League for Sports Equality, who were advocating for the inclusion of black ballplayers in big league baseball.

The Pirates also played their home opener on the 20th and defeated the Cubs by a 5–4 score before 9,449 spectators. Rip Sewell kept the opposition off balance with his blooper pitch and won his 100th big league game in the process. At Shibe Park, the Phillies had Private First Class John Rizner, a wounded veteran, throw out the first ball at their home opener. The game went ahead despite the rain as only 2,653 fans witnessed a thrilling 6–5 victory for the Braves. Charley Schanz began to tire in the ninth and with two outs served up a three-run gopher ball to Butch Nieman as the Braves took the lead and never relinquished it. Charlie Cozart was credited with the win, his only victory in a five game big league career.

At Sportsman's Park on April 22 the Cardinals and Reds split a doubleheader. Frank Dasso was the loser in the opener for Cincinnati and then earned the victory in the second game. In both games he made relief appearances, pitching four innings in the opener and one inning in the nightcap. Ted Wilks pitched a complete game in the opener in a 2–0 Cardinals victory. Bill McKechnie's squad sent a confident Bucky Walters to the mound in the first game. Walters was 6–0 against St. Louis in 1944. In the third inning he tried to stretch a double into a triple and was called out. The pitcher was visibly upset and argued violently with umpire Lou Jorda; after he shoved the arbiter he was thrown out of the game. The Reds won the second game by a 9–7 score and had strong offensive contributions from Eric Tipton and Steve Mesner.

On April 24, Mel Ott hit two, two-run homers, as the Giants defeated Philadelphia by a 5–2 margin. Butch Nieman exhibited more clutch hitting in Boston when he hit another three-run homer in the bottom of the ninth to give the Braves an 8–6 victory against Brooklyn. He had three homers on the season, each coming in the ninth inning. On the following day, Claude Passeau pitched a five-hit shutout and had two hits at the plate, including a homer, to give the Cubs a 4–0 victory before only 1,116 spectators at Crosley Field. The Cubs continued their winning ways by winning their fifth in a row on the 27th, 7–3, over Pittsburgh. Only 1,064 trembling fans braved the cold and Ed Heusser of Cincinnati tossed a four-hitter for a 2–1 win over St. Louis at Crosley Field. At Ebbets Field, Bill Voiselle won his third game in a 5–0 Giants victory. Steve Filipowicz leaned into one in the sixth inning, the ball went over the outfield fence and when one of the sailors failed to catch the ball it ricocheted back onto the field. Initially it was ruled a double, but when Mel Ott argued, umpire George Magerkurth changed it to a home run. Harry Cross observed, "That was just like putting a charge of TNT under the Dodger manager, Leo Durocher."[3] Durocher then had one of his volcanic explosions arguing the call.

National League umpire George Magerkurth was not immune to controversy, having had assault and battery charges dismissed after he had slugged a Cincinnati patron after the conclusion of a Reds/Braves doubleheader on July 19. With some persuasion the fan dropped the charges: Magerkurth had given the man $100 and written a letter apologizing for his conduct. The umpire had jumped the railing at Crosley Field to go after a fan who was heckling him but apparently hit the wrong guy. The presiding judge in the case, William D. Alexander, said, "I am glad that prosecution has been withdrawn. I'm an old baseball fan myself and I never saw a finer group of people than baseball fans...."[4] Magerkurth got into several scraps during his years as an umpire and was reprimanded with fines and suspensions. He was tough as nails, having been a professional boxer and fought seventy times. At Ebbets Field in 1940 a fan attacked him from behind and Magerkurth beat the hell out of him before he was separated from the assailant. The fan was a convict and had attacked the umpire to divert everyone's attention while his friend picked the pockets of the unsuspecting spectators in the stands. Magerkurth umpired during the tough 1930s when Billy Jurges said that some pitchers would "throw at you to kill you."[5] In 1939 Jurges and Magerkurth took turns punching each other in a fight. Magerkurth was intimidating and would not be pushed around. He even spat at players during confrontations. Hugh Casey became perturbed over a balk call one day and had the audacity to fire three consecutive balls at Magerkurth's skull. The pitcher's action only intensified the umpire's anger and failed to intimidate him.[6]

The Cardinals took a doubleheader from Cincinnati on April 29. Max Lanier won the opener, 2–1, while Mort Cooper started his first game of the season in the second contest and won 8–3. The Cubs dropped from first place when the Pirates took both ends of a doubleheader before 36,637 Wrigley Field spectators. Preacher Roe and Nick Strincevich were the winning pitchers as the Pirates ended the Cubs' six-game winning streak. In Ebbets Field, Dixie Walker hit a three-run homer to help the Dodgers defeat the Giants, 4–3. In Boston, the Phillies and Braves split a doubleheader.

On Tuesday, May 1, the National League standings were as follows:

	W L	PCT	GB
New York Giants	8–4	.667	—
Chicago Cubs	7–4	.636	.5
St. Louis Cardinals	5–4	.556	1.5
Boston Braves	6–5	.545	1.5
Brooklyn Dodgers	5–5	.500	2
Cincinnati Reds	5–6	.455	2.5
Pittsburgh Pirates	4–7	.364	4
Philadelphia Phillies	3–8	.273	4.5

It took the baseball owners until April 24, 1945, to name a replacement for the late Commissioner Judge Kenesaw Mountain Landis. Albert B. "Happy" Chandler, a former governor of Kentucky and now a senator, was named the new commissioner. Like Landis, he was also a lawyer, graduating from the University of Kentucky and then Harvard Law School. He declared, "Now that the war with Germany is virtually over I can conscientiously leave my other duties,"[7] and pledged that the game would be kept "clean."[8] Chandler was a strong advocate of the game during the war, defending its right to continue play, and this was in part why he was given the job. Shortly after being named commissioner he met with President Harry Truman and voiced his displeasure over the 4-F policy. Chandler denounced the practice of drafting 4-Fs only because they happened to play major league baseball and assured the public that President

Truman was looking into the situation. This was an issue that the new commissioner felt passionately about, believing that government officials were acting unethically and inconsistently in this matter, and insisting that if we couldn't have 400 or 500 of the four million 4-Fs to play baseball for the recreational health of the country then the United States couldn't defeat anyone.[9]

The baseball writers like Arthur Daley and Red Smith found Chandler to be refreshingly pleasant. As Red Smith would write, he was the "most relentlessly affable employee, most tireless handshaker, most indefatigable signer of autographs baseball has ever known. When he makes a speech, he recites poetry of the Edgar Guest stripe. When he makes a decision, his friends do not get worst of it."[10]

When Chandler got the job he believed he had a mandate from the owners to actively promote the game, including visiting ball clubs, making public appearances, and making the necessary decisions that would affect the game. While Landis was commissioner he took a policy role in running the game. He ran the office like it was his courthouse and kept the game on track by handing down firm rulings. Conversely, Chandler wanted to run the office like a politician. The owners believed he would follow their line, and be a figurehead while they ran things. However, they were woefully mistaken. It wasn't long before Chandler began to rub the owners the wrong way. Refusing to resign his Senate seat, he insisted that the owners sign a document with a pledge. It read they were "loyally to support commissioner" under all circumstances and not to criticize him.[11] Kenesaw Mountain Landis had left the office in an extremely strong position and Chandler demanded similar powers. He would lecture them, "You don't own the game.... The game belongs to the American people."[12] The owners would give him a short honeymoon period before things went bad. Before Chandler left office he would be known as the "Hillbilly Commissioner" and the "Bluegrass Jackass."[13] The owners were upset that he sanctioned the integration of major league baseball in 1947. The reserve clause was threatened when he blacklisted the players who jumped to Jorge Pasquel's Mexican League and lawsuits were filed. He signed a long-term television deal for the World Series and the All-Star game that the owners thought was too cheap and hurt them in the long haul. He also opposed Sunday night games. In 1947 he hypocritically suspended Leo Durocher for the "accumulation of unpleasant incidents detrimental to baseball."[14] Chandler would have to leave office before his term as commissioner would expire.

In early May the unseasonably cold and rainy weather was complicating the major league schedules. On May 3, all six big league games were postponed, including four National League contests. And on the following day five of the seven games were rained out. Additionally, the junior league contest in Chicago between the White Sox and Indians was postponed because of the cold weather. The Giants won a doubleheader from the Braves on May 5 as they extended their lead over second-place Chicago by a half game. At Sportsman's Park, Paul

Derringer improved to 4–0 as the Cubs won, 5–1, over the Cardinals before 3,032 fans. The Cincinnati versus Pittsburgh game was postponed due to wet grounds at Forbes Field. The game in Philadelphia was an artificial form of big league baseball as the Dodgers took two games from the Phillies, 10–1 and 12–8. The disappointed Shibe Park patrons not only watched their team lose twice but had to observe fifteen errors that were committed by both teams on the day. Butch Nieman was leading both leagues in hitting with a .432 batting average. Nieman along with Mel Ott and Ernie Lombardi led the senior circuit with four homers while Lombardi led the majors with nineteen RBIs. The Braves led the league in batting with a .279 team average, while the Giants had the best fielding percentage among the clubs at .978.

On Sunday, May 6, every major league team participated in a doubleheader. The Giants came from behind in the ninth inning to defeat the Braves, 4–3, in their opener as Phil Weintraub and Ernie Lombardi hit homers. The second game was stopped with a 1–1 tie in the eighth because of the rain. The Reds and Pirates split their twin bill at Forbes Field. Ed Heusser won the opener for the Reds, 3–1, while Rip Sewell led his team to a victory in the nightcap, 5–1. The Dodgers took another two games from Philadelphia at Shibe Park by 7–5 and 10–7 scores. In St. Louis, the Cardinals took two from the Cubs before a crowd of 13,718. Max Lanier and Mort Cooper earned the victories.

The war in Europe ended on May 8, V-E Day. Dwight D. Eisenhower accepted Germany's surrender in Rheims, France. The *New York Herald Tribune's* headline declared, "Today Is V-E Day: Truman, Churchill, Stalin to Proclaim War's End; Germans Surrender at Eisenhower's Headquarters."[15] Hitler didn't make it to the end, having killed himself eight days earlier. Americans celebrated but held back a little: they were still dealing with the death of Roosevelt, discovering the atrocities of the Holocaust, and fully aware that the slaughter continued in the Pacific.

Phil Weintraub's eighth-inning home run on May 11 propelled the Giants to a 4–3 victory over the Reds before a ladies' day crowd of 4,292 at the Polo Grounds. However, it was reported that only 426 ladies showed up. Those women who did walk through the turnstiles watched Van Lingle Mungo work himself into a bases-loaded jam with no outs in the top of the ninth inning. Ace Adams was summoned from the bullpen and allowed two to score before he recorded the final out to secure the victory. At Ebbets Field the ladies' day crowd was 5,901 as Tom Seats tossed a shutout and handed the Cardinals a 7–0 loss. It was the Dodgers' sixth straight victory and the first time they had whitewashed an opponent all season. Ben Chapman was no longer with the team and had returned to his home in Montgomery, Alabama, to take care of his wife, who was ill. Branch Rickey told Chapman that he should stay with his wife until she improved. Chapman rejoined the Dodgers on May 17. Only 811 spectators bothered to show up at Shibe Park on the 11th to watch the hapless Phillies lose to the Cubs, 7–1. Vince DiMaggio's second-inning homer gave the Phillies fans one of their only opportunities to cheer all day. Hank Wyse went the distance and allowed only five hits to earn the victory for the Cubs.

With additional travel restrictions being implemented it was almost certain that the All-Star game would be canceled and probably the World Series unless both pennant winners were from the same city. The government sent shivers up the sports world's spine when it was reported on May 12 that the American sports leagues would be fortunate if they played their entire schedules unless Japan was quickly defeated. J. Monroe Johnson, director of the Office of Defense Transportation, who delivered this unfortunate news, said that unless Japan surrendered within approximately the next six weeks, sports schedules would be drastically affected.[16] Furthermore, even with the end of the war in Europe, the continuation of the war with Japan brought about additional uncertainties for major league baseball. It was announced that 1.3 million servicemen would be discharged in the next twelve months, but many baseball players hadn't accumulated enough points that would qualify them for a discharge. And even if they had enough points they may still be needed for the war with Japan. The Detroit Tigers had been anticipating the return of Hank Greenberg, but after V-E Day he was sent to Europe to participate in a recreational program. Bill Dickey, who had not played for the Yankees since 1943, and Birdie Tebbetts, who had last played for the Tigers in 1942, were named the managers of the Navy and Army baseball teams, respectively. Neither player made an appearance in the majors during the 1945 campaign. With Mickey Cochrane reassigned to the Pacific, Bob Feller took over as skipper of the Great Lakes Naval Center team. The Great Lakes club had a reputation of fielding one of the best if not the best service teams during the war. By mid-May all these players, along with many others, were not expected to rejoin their clubs until the war against the Japanese was over.[17]

An enthusiastic crowd of 42,993 watched the Giants extend their winning streak to eight games by defeating the Cardinals, 4–3, on May 13. They received a fine pitching performance from Andy Hansen. St. Louis bounced back and won the second game, 6–5, as Bud Byerly earned the win with five relief innings after starter Mort Cooper had left the game. The Dodgers also won their eighth straight, defeating Cincinnati, 10–3, at Ebbets Field behind the fine pitching of Curt Davis before 27,200 fans. The Pirates won the first of two against the Phillies, 9–6, and then dropped the second game, 6–5. Boston defeated Chicago, 3–2, in a rain-shortened six-and-a-half-inning game, while the second contest was washed out. Boston's victory behind the pitching of Nate Andrews broke a five-game losing streak.

The Dodgers continued their winning ways, taking their tenth in a row by defeating Pittsburgh, 6–3, on May 15 and their eleventh in a row the following day. Pittsburgh finally ended the streak on the 17th with a 12–3 win behind the pitching of Nick Strincevich. The Pirates collected fifteen hits against four Brooklyn pitchers. Things turned ugly in this game when Pittsburgh's Johnny

Barrett slid into the keystone sack, spikes high, and ripped open Eddie Basinski's left knee during a play at second base. The fans became unruly and incessantly hurled epithets at the Pittsburgh center fielder. In the bottom of the third inning, Brooklyn pitcher Les Webber collided with Pittsburgh's catcher, Al Lopez, with a bang-bang play at home plate and umpire Jocko Conlan infuriated the Dodgers bench when he called the runner out.

Elsewhere on the 17th the Giants pushed across six runs in the eighth inning at the Polo Grounds before 7,147 witnesses to win 8–5. It was their twelfth win in their last thirteen games. Ace Adams received the win in relief of Andy Hansen. At the bat the Giants were led by George Hausmann, Mel Ott, and Phil Weintraub, who each collected three hits. Chicago's thirty-four-year-old veteran infielder Roy Hughes crashed into Billy Jurges in the Cubs' disastrous eighth inning and injured his left knee. They carried him off the field on a stretcher and he wasn't expected to return for several weeks. Hughes played all four infield positions in 1945 and batted .261 in 69 games and 222 at-bats. Making a rare appearance in the ninth inning for New York was Al Gardella, Danny's older brother. He made three putouts in the game. The 1945 season was the only big league campaign in which he participated: he went 2 for 26 (.077) at the bat in the sixteen games.

In Boston, Stan Partenheimer started for the Cardinals but was given an early hook when he was pulled after only two batters: Dick Culler got a one-base hit and Tommy Holmes drew a walk. The 5'11", 175-pound southpaw hurler had a brief major league resume which consisted of one ineffectual start with the 1944 Boston Red Sox when he was pulled after one inning, giving up two runs on three hits and two walks. Then in 1945 he appeared in eight games for the Cardinals, yielding nine runs in 13.1 innings for a 6.08 ERA. He attended Wooster College. His father Steve went to Amherst College and played one game for the 1913 Detroit Tigers, going 0 for 2. Ken Burkhart, a rookie pitcher who would compile an 18–8 record for the Redbirds, relieved Partenheimer and served up a three-run homer to Butch Nieman on his first pitch. But he would settle down and pitch nine innings for Billy Southworth's club, as they came from behind to win 7–4. The Cincinnati Reds won on the road in Philadelphia, aided by Frank McCormick's two-run homer in the eighth inning. Walter "Boom-Boom" Beck pitched a complete game for the Reds in the 4–2 triumph. The attendance for this Thursday game was a measly 1,281.

Brooklyn resumed their winning form on May 18 as the largest Ebbets Field crowd (31,334) of the short season were entertained in a Friday-night affair with the home team winning, 15–12, over Chicago. Left fielder Luis Olmo led the Dodgers with a three-hit game that included a grand slam homer and a triple. He scored three runs and drove in seven. Bill Hart and Goody Rosen also hit home runs for Brooklyn while Bill Nicholson and Andy Pafko hit long balls for the Cubs. Lee Pfund, who went 3–2 in 1945 with a 5.20 ERA in his only big league appearances, started for Brooklyn. The longtime major league

10. The National League Campaign

outfielder turned pitcher during the war, Ben Chapman, followed him to the bump and earned the win. Brooklyn's rookie southpaw, Vic Lombardi, worked the final two innings and gave up three runs in the ninth. The Cubs used four pitchers including a six-foot, 190-pound right-hander, who was born in Havana, Cuba, named Jorge Comellas. Comellas took the loss and went 0–2 in seven games with a 4.50 ERA in 1945, his only big league season. A war bond auction was held before the game and among the items auctioned off was the original manuscript of Frank Graham's new book, which was titled *The Brooklyn Dodgers: An Informal History*. Graham's book was published in 1945 by G.P. Putnam's Sons. John L. Smith, the president of Pfizer & Co., secured the manuscript with a $12,000 bid. In total $72,000 was raised.

In Philadelphia, the Cardinals went to the ninth inning trailing 8 to 7 but pushed across four runs in the final frame to win 11–8. This was a wild game with late-inning rallies by both teams. The Phillies themselves trailed 7–2 before pushing across six runs in the eighth. The Pittsburgh versus New York game was rained out, as was the Cincinnati versus Boston contest.

On May 19 all four National League games in New York, Brooklyn, Philadelphia, and Boston were postponed because of rain. The Sunday crowd at Ebbets Field on May 20 of 36,176 (33,708 paid) was the largest home crowd for Brooklyn since 1942. Thousands of fans tried to buy tickets to the sold-out game but were turned away. Brooklyn had seventeen hits in the two games while Chicago had sixteen. However, the Cubs were buoyed by a doubleheader victory over Leo Durocher's squad and were situated in fourth place, eight games out of first as a result. Chicago scored two unearned runs in the first inning of the opening game and three runs in the first frame of the nightcap. They won by scores of 4–2 and 4–1 behind the pitching of Paul Derringer and Hank Wyse, who each pitched complete games. In Philadelphia, the Cardinals won the opener, 6–2, and then Coaker Triplett hit a run-scoring double in the last of the ninth to give the Phillies a 7–6 win in the second game. The attendance for this game was a respectable 14,625, but that paled in comparison to the 51,340 (46,575 paid) who showed up at the Polo Grounds to watch the Giants and Pirates split a doubleheader. Bill Voiselle improved his record to 8–0 and pitched a complete game four-hitter to give the Giants a 5–1 victory in the first contest. Joe Medwick and Ernie Lombardi hit home runs. Preacher Roe tossed a three-hit shutout to lead Pittsburgh to a 4–0 victory in the nightcap. At Braves Field there were a total of 54 hits on the day as the Reds won the opener, 10–8, and then lost the second game, 9–4.

Despite losing to Pittsburgh by a 5–2 score at Forbes Field on the following day, the Giants enjoyed a comfortable three-and-a-half-game lead over second-place Brooklyn. In the only other National League contest on May 21, the Dodgers lost to the Cardinals, 4–0, at Ebbets Field as Blix Donnelly pitched a shutout. Dave Bartosch, the St. Louis right fielder, batted .255 in 47 at-bats and 24 games in 1945, his only big league season. He had one of the best games of his short career on May 21, going 3 for 5 as St. Louis's leadoff hitter with one run scored and one driven in. The Dodgers were hurt on May 22 when Mickey Owen received a notice from his draft board and was subsequently taken into the service. The next day more National League rosters were realigned when Mort Cooper was sent packing to Boston for Red Barrett and $60,000 cash. Cooper's intention was not to get traded but to increase his salary. He provided a terse comment: "I've been sold. Everybody's happy."[18] Also on the 23rd, Jimmie Foxx of the Phillies must have felt like a busher when he was tagged out by Bill Schuster, the Cubs shortstop. Foxx fell victim to the hidden-ball trick as he edged off second base, thinking that Claude Passeau, the Cubs pitcher, possessed the ball. Chicago won, 5–3, as Don Johnson, Bill Nicholson, and Peanuts Lowrey collected two hits apiece.

On May 26 the Cubs won, 2–1, over Philadelphia when former Cubs great Bill Lee walked three batters in a row to force in the winning run in the bottom of the ninth before 5,781 Wrigley Field fans. Paul Erickson gave up only four hits to earn the victory. The Giants scored five runs in the seventh before 1,414 Crosley Field fans to defeat the Reds, 5–1. Andy Hansen earned the win. The Dodgers ended a recent slump by initiating a sixteen-hit offensive for an 11–2 win against St. Louis. Brooklyn took a 4–0 lead in the first inning as the number two and three hole hitters in the lineup, Goody Rosen and Augie Galan, hit back-to-back home runs. The Dodgers scored four more in the fourth inning as Luis Olmo hit his second grand slam of the campaign. In 1945, Olmo had the best season of his career, batting .313 with 27 doubles, a National League–leading 13 triples, 10 homers, and 110 RBIs. Also on the 26th, Boston and Pittsburgh were rained out.

The Giants showed signs of wearing down by losing to the Pirates by a 16–4 score on the following day but had a six-and-a-half-game lead over second-place Brooklyn. Harry Cross observed, "The drive and aggressiveness of the Pirates embarrassed the Manhattan players from start to finish. At no time this season has the New York club looked as rheumatic as it did this afternoon."[19] The Pirates led the second game, 10–5, before it was halted because of a curfew in the eighth inning. In Cincinnati, Mort Cooper won his first game with the Braves with a 4–0 shutout. Bucky Walters returned the favor in the nightcap as Cincinnati won, 5–0. Ray Prim pitched the Cubs to a 6–1 win in Chicago while the second game was tied at 2–2 before being halted on account of darkness after eight innings. In the opening game Leo Durocher was told to exit the premises by the home plate umpire, Bill Stewart, when he questioned the balls and strikes calls of the arbiter. The Wrigley Field crowd of 38,133 enjoyed watching Durocher get the heave-ho and then booed him when he came out to argue Stewart's decision. At Sportsman's Park the Phillies scored a surprise doubleheader victory with quality pitching by Charley Schanz and Charlie Sproull.

Goody Rosen's two-run triple in the thirteenth inning led Brooklyn to a

6–4 victory at Forbes Field in Pittsburgh on May 31. Brooklyn utilized the services of two little-used catchers in this game: Stan Andrews and John Dantonio. Andrews went 2 for 3 in the game and Dantonio went 1 for 2. The 28-year-old Andrews was born Stanley Joseph Andruskewicz in Lynn, Massachusetts, on April 17, 1917. Before his final season in 1945 he had played briefly in the majors with the 1939 and 1940 Braves and the 1944 Dodgers. He batted .163 for Brooklyn in 21 games and 49 at-bats in 1945 before finishing the season with the Phillies, batting .333 in 33 at-bats. John Dantonio, known as "Fats," was born in New Orleans on December 31, 1918. He batted right-handed and stood at 5'8" and 165 pounds. He played in three games for Brooklyn in 1944, going 1 for 7, and then batted .250 in 47 games and 128 at-bats in 1945.

The Cardinals finished the month by defeating Boston, 9–4, at Sportsman's Park. They scored five runs in the first inning and forced Al Javery, the Braves starting pitcher, to be removed from the game in the opening frame as he only got one Cardinal to make an out. The Reds defeated Philadelphia at Crosely Field, 8–1, behind the fine pitching of Walter "Boom-Boom" Beck. The New York versus Chicago contest was rained out.

On June 1, the National League race looked as follows:

	W L	PCT	GB
New York Giants	26–11	.703	—
Brooklyn Dodgers	21–16	.588	5
Pittsburgh Pirates	19–16	.543	6
St. Louis Cardinals	20–17	.541	6
Chicago Cubs	18–16	.529	6.5
Cincinnati Reds	15–18	.455	9
Boston Braves	13–20	.394	10.5
Philadelphia Phillies	10–28	.263	16.5

The Phillies continued to play badly to begin the new month as they committed five errors in a 6–5 loss to Pittsburgh before 1,513 witnesses at Forbes Field. The Reds needed late-inning heroics by Frank McCormick, whose three-run homer in the bottom of the thirteenth propelled them to a 6–3 victory over Brooklyn. The Cardinals scored three in the ninth to defeat the Giants at Sportsman's Park by a 4–3 score. This was the game in which Bill Voiselle was suspended for failing to waste an 0 and 2 pitch to Johnny Hopp. It was the beginning of a downward spiral that would drop the Giants out of first place. The Boston versus Chicago game was postponed on June 1 because of the wet grounds. Phil Masi drove home the go-ahead run in the top of the tenth inning on the following day and Boston held on for 5–4 victory over the Cubs. Joe Heving won his final big league game in relief of Johnny Hutchings. Brooklyn currently had the best team batting average while the Giants were statistically the best fielding team in the league.

Cincinnati took a doubleheader from the Dodgers on June 3 to extend their winning streak to eight before 8,623 bundled-up fans at Crosley Field.

Joe Bowman and Frank Dasso went the distance for the Reds in the 6–2 and 2–1 victories. Eric Tipton started the nightcap for the hometown team in the left field station but he was removed from the game when Dodgers shortstop Eddie Basinski cut him open with his spikes during a play at second base in the second inning. The back of Tipton's head was cut open as he suffered a two-and-a-half-inch cut. The Giants dropped two games to the Cardinals, 11–3 and 8–2. It was unseasonably cold in St. Louis but the day was made more pleasant because of the good starting pitching of Red Barrett and Ted Wilks, who each went the distance. The spectators also witnessed a rare occurrence when Ernie Lombardi beat out a bunt. Lombardi hit a two-run homer in the opener and then went 2 for 4 in the nightcap. After losing 2–1 in the opener, the Cubs rebounded for a 3–1 victory over Boston before 9,110 freezing spectators at Wrigley Field. Pittsburgh defeated Philadelphia, 7–6, at Forbes Field in the first of two and had won twelve times in their last fourteen games. There was considerable friction in the opening contest because the players were frequently arguing with the umpires. In the bottom of the sixth, after a member of the home team was called out at home plate, three Pirates were banished from the game: manager Frankie Frisch, along with players Al Lopez and Al Gionfriddo. The second game was halted after six innings with the Phillies leading, 11–9. Pennsylvania's Sunday curfew law prohibited the teams from playing beyond seven o'clock in the evening.

While Boston was in Chicago on June 3 they received some disturbing news when pitcher Nate Andrews left the team without permission. He returned home to Rowland, North Carolina. John Quinn, the team's general manager, did not know why he left and he said that the pitcher would not be reprimanded until there was an explanation. There had been no indication that something was wrong with Andrews and his departure was a big mystery with the club.

With the aid of eight Dodger errors, the Giants vanquished their rival, 10–5, before 18,885 fans at the Polo Grounds on June 7. The Braves won two games from the Phillies to sweep their four-game series. Jim Tobin and Tom Earley pitched complete games for Boston in the 3–1 and 7–3 victories. Jack Creel earned one of his five major league victories when St. Louis defeated Chicago, 6–4. Joe Bowman pitched the Reds to a 7–3 win over the Pirates at Forbes Field. Cincinnati collected eleven hits on the day and benefited from five Pirate errors by Vic Barnhart, Lee Handley, Bill Salkeld, and two by Frankie Gustine. Shortstop Vic Barnhart saw his only significant major league playing time in 1945, batting .269 in 71 games and 201 at-bats. His father Clyde played for the Pirates from 1920 to 1928 and batted .295 lifetime. Lee Handley played in the big leagues from 1936 to 1941 and from 1944 to 1947. He played third base in 1945 and batted .298 in 312 at-bats. Bill Salkeld, a rookie catcher, batted .311 in 1945 with a .420 on-base percentage. In 95 games and 267 at-bats he hit 15 home runs and drove in 52. In his six-year big league career he batted .273. While Salkeld was playing in the Pacific Coast League many years earlier he was spiked by a base runner on his right knee as his shin guards were inadvertently moved out of their proper place. He spent three months in the hospital because of an infection that resulted from the injury and the doctors actually considered amputation at one time. As a result he couldn't squat like a healthy catcher and went down to catch the ball with one leg sticking out sideways.[20] (His grandson Roger Salkeld pitched in the major leagues for three seasons during the 1990s.) Frankie Gustine played mainly shortstop in 1945 and was in the seventh season of his twelve-year big league career in which he batted .265. In 1945 he contributed with a .280 batting average in 478 at-bats. In the June 7 game, Gustine was playing one of his twenty-nine games on the season at second base while Barnhart was the shortstop.

The Braves saw their best home crowd in years on June 10 as 30,095 fans watched them take a doubleheader from the slumping Giants. The Pirates also took two from St. Louis while Brooklyn won a rain-shortened game from Philadelphia, 10–4, that had four errors by the losers. Bill Nicholson hit a three-run homer in the eighth inning of the second game against Cincinnati to propel the Cubs to a doubleheader sweep.

A Forbes Field crowd of 15,126 watched Al Gerheauser lead Pittsburgh to a 9–3 win against Chicago on June 12. Gerheauser, a southpaw in his first season with Pittsburgh, went the distance, giving up nine hits and three walks. He also went 4 for 4 at the plate with two runs driven in. Gerheauser was 5–10 on the season with a 3.91 ERA. And his success at the bat was no fluke: in 1944 he batted .231 in 65 at-bats with one homer. During the final wartime season he hit .250 in 48 at-bats and then hit .333 during his final two big league seasons in 1946 and 1948 with 21 and 6 at-bats respectively. In 1943, his rookie year, when he compiled a 10–19 record and a 3.60 ERA for the Phillies, he also hit under .200 during his only season, batting .113 in 71 at-bats. He was credited with only two sacrifice bunts during his career.

When the Dodgers defeated New York, 7–4, before 15,013 Ebbets Field fans, the Pirates were only a game behind the first-place Giants. In Boston, Johnny Hutchings tossed a shutout for a 10–0 win over Philadelphia. Both the Braves and Phillies were in the midst of a streak: Boston had won eight in a row to move within three and a half games of New York in sixth place. The Phillies had lost fifteen in a row to break the ignominious team record for consecutive loses. The 1883 and 1936 Phillies had both lost fourteen in a row. While the 1936 Phillies were a last-place unit with a 54–100 (.351) record, the 1883 team was actually much worse, also finishing last with a 17–81 record for an abysmal .173 winning percentage. The 1936 Phillies actually looked quite good in comparison. The Cincinnati versus St. Louis game was rained out on June 12.

On the following day, June 13, the Phillies lost their sixteenth in a row in the first game of a doubleheader, 8–3, but then ended their losing streak by defeating Boston, 5–4, in fifteen innings in the second game. The second game was an absolute gift for Philadelphia as Boston committed eight errors: Shortstop

Whitey Wietelmann (3); pitcher Bob Logan (2); third baseman Dick Culler (1); center fielder Carden Gillenwater (1); and second baseman Steve Shemo (1). The Phillies scored two runs in the top of the fifteenth against right-hander Ira Hutchinson, who was in the final season of an eight-year big league career. Boston pushed across one in the bottom half of the fifteenth but came up short. Elsewhere on the 13th, Hal Gregg tossed a five-hitter for Brooklyn to give them a 3–2 win over New York. The only other scheduled game on the day in the senior league, between Cincinnati and St. Louis, was washed out.

On June 15 the Brooklyn Dodgers won their seventh in a row when their offense exploded for sixteen hits in a 9–8 victory over Boston at Braves Field. They also added some depth and experience to the catching position when they traded Ben Chapman to Philadelphia for Johnny Peacock, a left-handed hitting catcher. It was a good trade for Brooklyn because Chapman had a sore arm and would only pitch three more games on the season. Peacock played his final big league season in 1945. After batting .203 for Philadelphia in 33 games and 74 at-bats he hit .255 for Brooklyn in 48 games and 110 at-bats. With Peacock in the fold, the Dodgers released 43-year-old catcher Clyde Sukeforth. Sukeforth was also a left-handed hitting catcher who had played in the big leagues for the Cincinnati Reds and Brooklyn Dodgers from 1926 to 1934. However, with the acute manpower shortage in 1945 he returned to the Dodgers and batted an impressive .294 with a .345 on-base percentage in 18 games and 51 at-bats. Sukeforth remained with the organization as a scout. On May 25 when Sukeforth caught Curt Davis, a 41-year-old right-hander, it was one of the oldest batteries in major league baseball history.

Elsewhere on the 15th, New York defeated Philadelphia 7–5 at the Polo Grounds to end their six-game losing streak. Philadelphia's lineup was unimpressive and included players like Gus Mancuso, who was playing the seventeenth and final season of his career, batting a paltry .199 in 176 at-bats. They used three players in the game who only played in the major leagues during the 1945 campaign: Wally Flager, Fred Daniels, and Lefty Scott. There were three additional players who only played two major league seasons: John Antonelli, Glenn Crawford, and Vance Dinges. Outfielder and first baseman Jimmy Wasdell was one player in the lineup who performed well in 1945, batting .300 with 7 homers and 60 RBIs. On the 15th he played first base and went 1 for 2 with a double, a run scored and an RBI. Interestingly, the Phillies' best player in 1945, Vince DiMaggio, batted sixth and later in the series he batted seventh. This actually happened quite often early in the season. From 1940 to 1943 DiMaggio had hit 19, 21, 15, and 15 homers. His 1944 power numbers declined as he hit only nine homers, but he only played in 109 games for Pittsburgh and had 238 fewer at-bats than the year before. At Crosley Field the Cubs took two games from the Reds by 8–1 and 3–0 scores, while the first-place Pirates defeated the Cardinals in Pittsburgh by a 5–2 score. Right fielder Bob Elliott had a good day, going 3 for 4 with a solo homer and two runs scored.

On the 17th the Phillies swept a doubleheader from the Giants by 11–9 and 6–2 scores. Brooklyn took over first place with a 9–6 win over Boston in the first of two, while the second game was halted because of the curfew law with one out in the top of the eighth at Braves Field. In Cincinnati, the Cubs defeated the home team, 3–1, and then the second contest was washed out. Ken Burkhart and Ted Wilks broke the heart of Pirates fans when they led St. Louis to a doubleheader victory by 7–0 and 6–2 scores before 32,396 Forbes Field witnesses.

Dwight D. Eisenhower was triumphantly paraded through New York City on June 19, and after he was honored at City Hall it was off to the Polo Grounds to watch the Giants and Braves. It was a dreary afternoon, with rain pouring down, and if not for Eisenhower's presence the game most certainly would have been postponed. The players and fans gazed into the outer garden to witness Eisenhower's convertible enter through the center field gate precisely on schedule at 2:55. Those fortunate customers who sat within the bend of the horseshoe outfield stands saw him first and their enthusiastic reaction signaled the rest of the ballpark that their hero was about to enter. Everyone stood and cheered, acknowledging his gestures, as the car circled around the field. For most of the spectators in the stands this was their first opportunity to see the Supreme Allied Commander and they responded with great affection. Al Laney described Eisenhower as "a hero about whom no one in the world need have, or does have, the slightest reservation."[21]

The Polo Grounds was decorated in red, white, and blue. The country's colors were draped over the upper and lower boxes and flags were plentiful. Giants manager Mel Ott and Braves manager Bob Coleman gave Eisenhower a bat and two autographed baseballs in his box and then all the players had a picture taken with him. Eisenhower loved the game, having played at West Point, and informed the managers that he had also played professional ball under the alias of "Wilson" in Kansas. When the game started, he took out his pencil and tried to keep score, but well-wishers kept coming over to his box and eventually he let the program drop to the ground. Harry Cross wrote, "Everybody in the park wanted to shake hands with the famous warrior and at one time it looked as if most of them were doing it."[22] In the third inning the rain became heavy and Ike soon departed to watch the game in the center field clubhouse. This was a fortunate break because while he was watching the game from the stands the mayor of New York, Fiorello LaGuardia, kept bringing people over to talk with him. Now he could watch the game proceed with few interruptions. With the Braves leading 6–2 in the sixth inning, Eisenhower had to leave. He was not happy with the play of the Giants and told team owner Horace Stoneham, "What the hell has happened to the pitching since I went away to the war?"[23] There were 27,062 admirers of Eisenhower in the stands that day and many of them were more interested in seeing "Ike" than watching the baseball game. Boston held on to win the game, 9–2, as pitcher Jim Tobin and shortstop Dick Culler hit home runs for the victors. George Hausmann and Johnny Rucker hit home runs for the Giants: Rucker's homer was a thrilling inside-the-park job as the ball traveled to the far reaches of right field where the Giants bullpen was situated. Eisenhower couldn't have been too happy with the hitting, either, as the Giants failed to score after loading the bases with no outs in the third inning. By the end of the game the conditions were so bad that they were playing in mud.

When the Giants lost to the Braves on June 20 by a 15–10 score they dropped to fifth place in what was a rapid fall from the first division. Claude Passeau earned the win for Chicago in relief of Bob Chipman as they defeated Pittsburgh, 5–3. The Dodgers won a doubleheader from the Phillies by scores of 4–2 and 8–1. Art Herring and Curt Davis earned complete-game victories for Leo Durocher's squad. Pittsburgh ended a five-game losing streak with a 3–1 victory over Cincinnati on June 22. In a game imbued with hostility, the Braves defeated the Dodgers, 14–12, on the following day at Ebbets Field. Brooklyn's Augie Galan hit a three-run triple in the eighth inning, and when Eddie Stanky scored he was tripped up by Boston's hurler Ewald Pyle and fell down, face first, into the dirt. Dixie Walker, the on-deck hitter, quickly jumped on Pyle and they started to exchange punches as both benches cleared onto the field. Players on both teams inserted themselves into the hostilities and several more fights developed. When order appeared to be restored it took several Dodgers to restrain Walker from throwing another blow at the pitcher. Umpires Ziggy Sears, George Barr, and Tom Dunn did a good job in bringing an end to the fight in a timely manner. The game at Shibe Park that day was less entertaining as the Giants lost to the Phillies, 9–8, in eleven innings. Harry Cross wrote, "Senator A.B. (Happy) Chandler, the new commissioner of baseball, was at the game. There were also 3,700 local inhabitants, and the type of baseball played by both the Phils and the Giants was suggestive of the sandlots."[24] At Wrigley Field, the Cardinals came back from an early 3–0 deficit to defeat the Cubs, 6–4, as George Dockins earned the win with six and two-thirds innings of relief work. Lon Warneke, who was nicknamed "The Arkansas Hummingbird," made his first appearance with the Cubs since 1943 and worked a one-two-three ninth inning. In the final nine games of his distinguished career in 1945, he would compile a 0–1 record with a 3.86 ERA. His fifteen-year big league career ended with a 192–121 record and a 3.18 ERA. He became a minor league umpire during the following season and from 1949 to 1955 he was a National League umpire.

Johnny Hopp of the Cardinals was skulled by a Ray Prim fastball on June 24 and fell unconscious to the ground with a sickening thud. It happened in the opening game before 44,508 Wrigley Field fans; the two teams split the doubleheader. This was a time in baseball history when hitters did not wear batting helmets or have a proper batting eye and beanball pitchers were quite ubiquitous. Wrigley Field in particular was a dangerous place to hit a baseball as the white ball would come out of the white shirts in the bleachers and if the

10. The National League Campaign

batter failed to pick it up properly it could lead to a fatal injury. Hopp was lucky. Dr. S.C. Udel said, "He has a severe bump on the side of his head, but no concussion."[25] He was expected to rejoin the club in two or three days.

Nick Strincevich got the better of Harry Feldman on June 28 to give the Pirates a 3–1 win over New York. In Brooklyn the Cubs won, 11–8, getting fifteen hits off four pitchers. Eddie Stanky and Cubs catcher Mickey Livingston almost had a fight when Stanky cautioned the catcher concerning where he should toss the dirt. The Cardinals got the better of the Phillies, 6–1, behind the fine pitching of Ken Burkhart. Chuck Workman hit a two-run homer in the bottom of the ninth to give the Braves a 7–6 win over Cincinnati.

On June 30, Red Rolfe, the former New York Yankees third baseman, who ended his ten-year big league career in 1942 with a .289 batting average, was among the spectators at the Polo Grounds and witnessed the Cubs defeat the Giants by a 5–3 score. Rolfe was a graduate of Dartmouth College and when he left the Yankees he returned to the Ivy League to become the baseball and basketball coach at Yale. He attended the Giants game with several other college coaches and they insisted that their college players were almost as good as the big leaguers. In Boston, Tommy Holmes went 3 for 3, including a triple and a home run, and he also drove in four runs as the Braves defeated the Cardinals, 8–4. Cincinnati secured a 13–5 victory over the Phillies.

At the end of June the National League standings were as follows:

	W L	PCT	GB
Brooklyn Dodgers	39–24	.619	—
St. Louis Cardinals	36–27	.571	3
New York Giants	36–30	.545	4.5
Chicago Cubs	32–27	.542	5
Pittsburgh Pirates	33–29	.532	5.5
Boston Braves	30–31	.492	8
Cincinnati Reds	28–31	.475	9
Philadelphia Phillies	17–52	.246	25

Tommy Holmes was leading the major leagues in batting heading into July. Luis Olmo of Brooklyn had scored the most runs with 61. Ernie Lombardi led the National League with thirteen homers and was tied with Vern Stephens of the St. Louis Browns for the major league lead. Holmes continued his hot hitting by extending his hitting streak to twenty-eight when he hit two homers and had four RBIs as the Braves defeated St. Louis, 8 to 7, in the second game of a doubleheader on July 1. Boston also won the first game when Butch Nieman hit a three-run homer in the bottom of the tenth for a 6–3 win. At the Polo Grounds before 27,192 fans, the Giants split a pair with the Cubs. Van Lingle Mungo was the winner for New York in the opener as they won, 7–4. Hank Wyse won the second game, 4–3. The fans had to watch the game in unbearably hot conditions. Brooklyn lost the first of two with Pittsburgh, 4–3, at Ebbets Field when they left fifteen men stranded on the bases. They won the nightcap behind the strong pitching of Curt Davis by a 4–2 score. Philadelphia won their doubleheader from the Reds by scores of 3–2 and 8–6.

The Cubs pounded the Braves, 24–2, on twenty-eight hits on July 3. However, the day was not a total loss for Boston since Tommy Holmes extended his hitting streak with three more hits to increase his average to .402. Don Johnson and Phil Cavarretta had five hits apiece for Chicago. Nick Strincevich won his eighth game for the Pirates as they defeated Philadelphia, 10–3. The Giants and Reds also scored victories on the day. The Dodgers received news that Babe Herman would return to the club. Branch Rickey said, "All I want him to do is hit. Then he can walk back to the bench. I'm tired of seeing our pinch-hitters walk up there and strike out."[26]

The 4th of July was a dreadful day at the Polo Grounds as the Cardinals outscored the Giants 27–6 to win a doubleheader. The bunting near the Cardinals' bench even caught fire. Elsewhere, the Cubs took two games from Boston at Braves Field. The Reds won the opener at Ebbets Field before 27,316 spectators by a 4–3 score. Bucky Walters went the distance for Cincinnati and also collected two hits. Brooklyn bounced back in the second game behind the pitching of Hal Gregg to win 5–3. At Shibe Park the Phillies and Pirates split their holiday doubleheader: Philadelphia took the opener, 7–6, before losing the second game, 13–0. Tommy Holmes scratched out a hit on July 7 as Boston defeated the Pirates, 7–6. On the next day he was 1 for 4 as the Braves lost to Pittsburgh, 10–8, in the first of two. Then in the second game he led Boston to a 13–1 win when he hit his fourteenth homer to extend his hitting streak to thirty-seven. The streak ended in the first game of a doubleheader on July 12 as he went 0 for 4 against the Cubs' Hank Wyse.

Frank Sinatra sat behind the Giants dugout on July 8 at the Polo Grounds and watched Bucky Walters give up only five hits to lead the Reds to a 5–2 win in the first of two. Bill Voiselle earned his tenth victory of the campaign in the nightcap as New York won, 5–0. Between games a Latin-American delegation led by Fulgencio Batista, the former president and future dictator of Cuba, paid tribute to Cuban players Dolf Luque and Nap Reyes. Luque had pitched his final four big league seasons for New York's National League ball club from 1932 to 1935 and was currently a coach with the Giants. Nap Reyes would bat .288 in 431 at-bats and 122 games in 1945, which was his third major league campaign. Even a baseball neophyte would conclude that Luque was the more accomplished player as he received a bronze statue, while Reyes got two traveling bags which perhaps he used when he jumped to Jorge Pasquel's Mexican League in 1946. There were 26,896 spectators at the Polo Grounds on that day but more than 2,300 of them did not pay for a ticket. It was not unusual in 1945 to have several thousand people inside a ballpark who did not pay their way inside. This was largely because servicemen who showed up to the ballpark in their uniforms were allowed in without charge for many teams.

Since V-E Day the trains had become even more crowded with servicemen being discharged and coming back home. Two million servicemen were scheduled to be discharged within a year. With travel restrictions in place the All-Star game was canceled and in its stead teams scheduled exhibitions with the proceeds going to organizations like the Red Cross. On July 9, 41,267 showed up at the Polo Grounds to see the New York Yankees defeat the Giants, 7–1, in a seven-inning contest. A reported $50,518 was raised. Celebrities like Peggy Ann Garner, Bert Wheeler, and Jackie Gleason entertained the crowd. Commissioner Happy Chandler threw out the ceremonial first ball. Many other games were played, including at Griffith Stadium on July 10, where the Washington Senators defeated the Dodgers, 4–3, to raise $22,760. Bert Shepard, the inspirational war hero, pitched the first four innings for Washington and left with a 3–2 lead. The Red Sox defeated the Braves, 8–1, and raised $70,000. The bulk of the money was raised by forty-four wealthy fans who donated $1,000 apiece. Americans were coming back to the ballparks in droves. At the mid-season break the aggregate major league attendance reached 5,074,775. At the break the Cubs had a one-game lead over Brooklyn in the National League flag race. The Cardinals were also on their heels, only one and a half games behind.

With servicemen returning from the war it was becoming more difficult to travel by train, as major league clubs were accustomed to doing. When the Giants traveled from Chicago to Pittsburgh in July of 1945 they needed four different trains to get their players there. Often players could not find a place to sleep on the congested trains and would have to sit up all night. There were a few times where a game was suspended so that a team could catch a train. The game was then resumed at a later date, much to the consternation of the fans who wanted to see a complete baseball game. Sleepers were actually illegal in some places by decree of the Office of Defense Transportation. The situation had become so bad that Branch Rickey, president of the Brooklyn Dodgers, asked league president Ford Frick to help solve the problem. In mid–July the Dodgers were going to travel from Pittsburgh to Chicago, a 468-mile trip, and there were no sleeper cars available. Furthermore, the series finale in Pittsburgh on Tuesday, July 17, was a night game and they were going to play a doubleheader in Chicago the following afternoon. The players would most likely have to sit up all night and then play the next day when they were not completely rested. It was the fans who would also suffer because the quality of play could be affected if the players were not well rested. Sam Walters, Pittsburgh secretary, insisted that the Pirates would not change the time of the game to accommodate the Dodgers. They were expecting a good crowd for the night game and they did not want to lose revenue by changing the time and having a smaller crowd.[27]

The season resumed on July 12 as Brooklyn and Cincinnati split a doubleheader, as did Chicago and Boston. New York and Pittsburgh won their games on the day. On the 13th, Frank McCormick drove in the winning run with a single in the last of the ninth at Crosley Field to give the Reds a 6–5 victory over Brooklyn. He went 3 for 5 with a double and four runs driven in while batting cleanup. In St. Louis the Cardinals won a doubleheader from New York by 14–3 and 4–1 scores as Bud Byerly and Red Barrett pitched complete games. At Wrigley Field, Ray Prim pitched a four-hit shutout to give Chicago a 2–0 win over Boston. In Pittsburgh, Philadelphia won 11–9, as they completed a game from June 3. Then the Pirates won the regularly scheduled game by a 3–2 score in ten innings as Max Butcher went the distance. Butcher went 10–8 in 1945 with a 3.03 ERA in his tenth and final major league season.

Mort Cooper was booed loudly when he entered the ninth inning of the second game of a doubleheader at Sportsman's Park on July 15. Cooper earned the victory in relief as the Braves won, 5–3, to sweep the doubleheader. Carden Gillenwater drove home two in the top of the tenth to win the nightcap and had four RBIs in the game. Boston won the opener, 3–1, behind the strong pitching of Johnny Hutchings. The first-place Cubs solidified their lead by taking two from the Giants by 5–3 and 7–2 scores before 44,943 pennant-crazy fans at Wrigley Field. Hy Vandenberg and Hank Wyse were the winning pitchers. The Pirates won a doubleheader from the Dodgers by scores of 9–1 and 15–3 at Forbes Field. Jesse Abramson wrote, "A crowd of 24,390 had a hilarious afternoon watching Frankie Frisch's Buccaneers skip lightly into the first division."[28] Rip Sewell and Ken Gables earned the victories. The Reds also won a doubleheader at Crosley Field over the Phillies by 6–1 and 3–1 scores behind the pitching exploits of Bucky Walters and Vern Kennedy.

The Cubs had taken control of the National League race when they won thirteen of sixteen on a recent eastern trip and were back home playing in front of huge Wrigley Field crowds. When the Cubs split a doubleheader with the Dodgers before 42,797 fans on July 18 they had a three-game lead over the second-place Cardinals. Ray Prim pitched a seven-hit shutout to lead Chicago to a 5–0 win in the opener as the Dodgers committed five errors. Cy Buker earned a 9–5 Brooklyn win in the second game but needed help from Ralph Branca, who worked his way out of a bases-loaded jam in the seventh and then worked two scoreless innings. Branca had joined the Dodgers in Chicago from St. Paul.

After great uncertainty the World Series was "virtually assured" of being played when James Forrestal, Secretary of the Navy, and Admiral Chester W. Nimitz, commander in chief of the Pacific Fleet, requested that the World Series winner go to the Pacific and play against Army and Navy teams. Forrestal was very excited about the tour and suggested that it may convince more of the Japanese soldiers to surrender because they were interested in the scores and standings of baseball leagues and major league players. Commissioner Chandler declared that the World Series would be played because the servicemen were expecting it and therefore major league baseball was not going to disappoint the country's brave soldiers. It wasn't actually a new revelation that most servicemen were fond of baseball and were eagerly anticipating the fall classic, but Chandler made it appear as if it was big news and a final justification to play the World Series. He added that the transportation problems "can be worked

10. The National League Campaign

out satisfactorily." Chandler also said that he was enthusiastic about satisfying the demands of the services and that he'd make sure that the World Series winner or an All-Star team made the trip to the Pacific. Forrestal, in his July 16 letter to Chandler, suggested that the tour should be 90 days in duration and would be a significant enhancement to the servicemen's recreational program.[29]

Hank Wyse won his thirteenth game with a 3–1 win over Brooklyn on July 19. Two days later the Cubs defeated the Phillies, 5–3, behind the pitching of Paul Derringer. With an 8–3 victory over the Phillies on the 24th they increased their lead to four and a half games over St. Louis. Stan Hack and Andy Pafko led the Cubs at the plate. Wyse won his fourteenth game of the season over the Reds on July 26 as the Cubs won a hard-fought 2–1 victory. He walked two batters late in the game after going thirty-seven and one-third innings without allowing a free pass. Claude Passeau outdueled Bucky Walters for a 2–1 win on the 27th. Peanuts Lowrey drove home the winning run in the bottom of the tenth before 11,582 Wrigley Field patrons. Hank Borowy won his first game with the Cubs on July 29, winning the second game of a doubleheader, 3–2, over the Reds before 43,786 Chicago fans. Wyse pitched a complete game in the opener for a 4–1 win.

On Saturday, July 28, the Giants swept a doubleheader from Philadelphia at Shibe Park by scores of 2–1 and 8–2. Van Lingle Mungo improved to 11–5 with the victory in the opener but he tired late and had to be relieved by Ace Adams, who pitched two scoreless frames to secure the win. Jack Brewer, who had perhaps the best screwball in the senior league, went the distance in the nightcap. The most memorable performance on the day belonged to George Hausmann. Hausmann stood at 5' 5", and weighed 145 pounds. He batted right-handed and played second base. During his rookie campaign in 1944 he hit for a .266 clip in 466 at-bats, and then in 1945 he hit .279 in 623 at-bats. He hit only three homers in his three-year major league career, two in 1945. But on July 28, in the doubleheader against the Phillies, he accomplished a laudable feat. He reached base during all eleven trips to the plate: He had four singles, drew six walks, and reached first on a fielder's choice when he bunted. Hausmann stole two of his seven bases for the season on the day but scored only three runs. Fewer than 3,000 spectators paid money to witness the doubleheader but with free admission for servicemen and other notables there were 6,131 people at the game. This was the Giants' twenty-first doubleheader of the season, and they had won six, lost eight, and split seven.

While the Giants stole only 38 bags in 1945, which was last in the National League, they were very aggressive on the bases in July. In the second inning of their July 12 game against the St. Louis Cardinals at Sportsman's Park, the slow-footed Ernie Lombardi had a temporary bout of amnesia, forgetting that he lacked foot speed. The bases were loaded with no outs and Lombardi edged off second when Buddy Kerr hit the ball to shallow left field. Lombardi came lumbering around third and was out at the plate. But the Giants' aggressive base running paid off later in the game when George Hausmann scored on a one-base hit to shallow center field by Whitey Lockman. In the top of the tenth inning Lockman led off and collected his fourth one-base hit of the game. Then Phil Weintraub sacrificed him to second and Lombardi was passed intentionally. Mel Ott pulled Lombardi for pinch runner Johnny Hudson and two runs came across to score when Danny Gardella slammed an offering into right center for a double. New York won the game, 9–7. Johnny Hudson was in his seventh and last major league season in 1945. He had seen significant playing time with the 1938 Brooklyn Dodgers, batting .261 in 498 at-bats, and the 1939 Dodgers, batting .254 in 343 at-bats. He batted .202 in 50 games and 99 at-bats for the 1941 Chicago Cubs, then didn't return to the big show until 1945, when he went 0 for 11 in 28 games. He scored eight runs as he was often used as a pinch runner.

As July progressed, Danny Gardella, George Hausmann, Leon Treadway, Whitey Lockman, and Buddy Kerr were all thrown out for trying to take an extra base. On July 22 indecision and aggressiveness cost them as they lost two games to the Reds in Cincinnati. Mel Ott singled in the eighth inning of the opener and then he removed himself from the game and sent Johnny Rucker in to run for him. Phil Weintraub singled and Rucker advanced to third. Clyde Kluttz followed with a fly ball to Eric Tipton in left field, but Rucker froze at third and did not try to score when it appeared he would have been safe. The game was knotted at one in the twelfth inning when Hausmann doubled and then was caught off second and was called out as he tried to pilfer third base. Woody Williams's single scored Frank McCormick in the last of the thirteenth to give the Reds a 2–1 victory. Woodrow Wilson Williams had played briefly for the 1938 Brooklyn Dodgers (.333) and the 1943 Cincinnati Reds (.377) before playing 155 games in 1944, batting .240 in 653 at-bats and playing second base. He played his final major league season in 1945, batting .237 in 482 at-bats and failing to hit a home run.

July was a month in which Giant fans were cheering and also second-guessing their aggressive base running. Additionally, they had lost ground in the standings and their pennant hopes were quickly sinking.

On Wednesday, August 1, the National League standings were as follows:

	W L	PCT	GB
Chicago Cubs	58–32	.644	—
Brooklyn Dodgers	53–39	.576	6
St. Louis Cardinals	54–40	.574	6
Pittsburgh Pirates	49–46	.516	11.5
New York Giants	50–47	.515	11.5
Cincinnati Reds	41–47	.468	16
Boston Braves	42–52	.447	18
Philadelphia Phillies	26–70	.271	35

On July 18 the Boston Braves were given permission to install lights at Braves Field by the regional office of the War Production board. However, attendance was not a major problem for the Braves in 1945 because by late July they had drawn about 100,000 more fans to Braves Field than the previous year despite their getting off to a poor start and the horrible weather that they had to deal with. Night baseball to many was a sacrilege and represented a decadent form of the game. In July of 1944 major league teams were sanctioned to play as many night games as they desired. Ed Barrow, the president of the New York Yankees, said, "I am more convinced than ever that there is absolutely no future in electric-lighted play." Barrow went on to say how night baseball has had catastrophic consequences in the minor leagues and added, "It has ruined thousands of fine prospects."[30]

Al Laney of the *New York Herald Tribune* cautioned against having too many night games. With the war over in Europe, sports were going to benefit greatly with increased participation and attendance. Baseball schedules were becoming more "freakish." Laney believed that night baseball was beneficial for the game if "properly handled." However, it had led to the twi-night doubleheader which was a "horrible affair." Increasingly, there was a movement in the sport away from day baseball and some teams were already playing all night games except for Sunday. The exorbitant number of night games that were being played, the twi-night doubleheader, and even the Sunday doubleheader were bad for the game, according to Laney. These should be viewed as anomalies that the game tolerated during wartime when players who had no business participating in major league ball games got an opportunity, but with the postwar era about to commence, night games should be abandoned. The real players, after all, should be given the opportunity to play during the daytime and not be burdened by the illuminating but obtrusive arc-lights. Laney insisted that baseball was a daytime game and was a much different game when played under the lights. The Sunday doubleheader was also problematic and it was believed to be the reason why attendance was low on Saturdays. Doubleheaders had led to an uneven schedule and reduced the number of home dates for some teams to around 50 or 55 instead of what was once considered customary, 77 home dates. Because of this there were large gaps in the schedules where some teams wouldn't play for several days in a row. The Chicago Cubs' attendance record of more than 1.4 million fans couldn't be duplicated if there were so many doubleheaders. Laney advised baseball to return to the 77 home date schedule. There would always be a few doubleheaders on account of the weather and no team should play more than seven night games.[31]

Ironically, when Larry MacPhail first introduced night baseball its two biggest critics were Clark Griffith and Sam Breadon. But during the war their positions about night baseball had changed so severely that they both wished to play as many night games as possible and they would even play Sunday night games if they could get away with it. While these two owners were encouraging the ubiquitous implementation of night baseball, MacPhail was cautioning against it. In May of 1945 he said he was "extremely concerned over the unlimited growth" of night baseball. He insisted that it ruined the attendance during the day games and wanted to limit the number of night games to seven for each team. MacPhail acknowledged that the Yankees would probably install lights in Yankee Stadium after the war but they would "never play" more than seven nocturnal contests. Despite the perceived drawbacks of night baseball, MacPhail admitted that the added revenue he received as general manager of the Cincinnati Reds when he first played night games in the majors during the 1935 campaign gave the club financial stability so they could build a winner. Cincinnati won the NL pennant in both 1939 and 1940, although by then MacPhail had moved on to the Brooklyn Dodgers. The night games in Brooklyn helped him purchase the great players that were instrumental in the 1941 pennant-winning club.[32] At a time when baseball teams still traveled by train, night baseball took a toll on the players. For example, a team may play a night game in one city and then travel 500 miles to play a doubleheader the next afternoon. As of 1945 the only teams that lacked lights in their ballpark were the Yankees, Cubs, Tigers, and the two Boston teams.

The Chicago Cubs, who played all their games during the day, had continued to draw large crowds throughout the war, even when they had poor teams. Their bad teams would outdraw pennant-winning teams who played a large number of night games. In August of 1944 the New York Giants, who had lost twelve straight games, limped into Chicago to play the Cubs, who were barely hanging on to their spot in the first division, a fourth-place outfit, seven games under .500. The fans, however, were not dissuaded from coming to the ballpark as 42,445 fans showed up for the doubleheader. This was a typical situation for Chicago's National League outfit.

The Giants, Pirates, and Cardinals secured victories on August 1, while the Dodgers and Phillies were rained out at Shibe Park. The 4,044 women who gained entry into Wrigley Field by bringing cakes and cookies for the servicemen were dismayed to watch portly Max Butcher lead Pittsburgh to a 1–0 victory. But the Cubs returned the favor the following day, winning 1–0 behind Paul Derringer. Peanuts Lowrey doubled off Preacher Roe in the sixth inning to plate the only run. Phil Cavarretta began the month slowly but then drove in eight runs in an August 3rd twin bill. The Cubs were leading the major leagues in batting with a .284 team average. Chicago also had the best National League fielding percentage at .981. The St. Louis Cardinals were second in both categories, while Brooklyn had the worst team batting average (.227) and Philadelphia had the worst fielding percentage (.958).

On August 3, Hal Gregg, who had turned 24 years old on July 11, pitched a one-hitter in the opening game for a 5–1 Dodger win before 6,565 fans at Braves Field. The six-foot, three and a half inches tall, 195-pound right-handed pitcher was rebounding from his 1944 season, when he compiled a 9–16 record with a 5.46 ERA. In 1945 he improved to 18–13 with a 3.47 ERA. In the nightcap, Ralph Branca gave up four runs in two innings as Boston won, 5–3, behind

10. The National League Campaign

the pitching of Ed Wright. The Cubs defeated Cincinnati by scores of 11–5 and 9–1 at Crosley Field behind the pitching of Hank Wyse and Hank Borowy. A Forbes Field crowd that numbered 22,218 watched the visiting Cardinals win by a 5–1 score. Rookie southpaw George Dockins gave up six hits in the route-going performance and Johnny Hopp paced the offense with three hits. Philadelphia and New York were not scheduled on the day, but hooked up the following day at the Polo Grounds with the Giants winning, 5–4, in ten innings. Mel Ott and Clyde Kluttz hit homers and Ace Adams earned the win in relief. Vic Lombardi lost two games for Brooklyn against the Braves, one of the games was a continuation from a June 17 contest. The southpaw started the regularly scheduled game. In the bottom of the first he walked leadoff man Dick Culler. Lombardi threw to first in a pickoff attempt and umpire George Magerkurth gave a gesture while wiping the sweat from his forehead that made it appear as if he had called a balk and was informing Culler to advance to the midway. First baseman Augie Galan threw the ball to second baseman Eddie Stanky, but Stanky didn't tag the runner because he thought a balk had been called. The official scorer gave Culler a stolen base as a result. And naturally the Dodgers players argued vigorously. Joe Medwick's sacrifice fly would later score Culler. St. Louis and Cincinnati also secured victories on August 4.

Philadelphia's pitchers walked ten batters as they fell to New York, 14–5, on August 5 in the first of two. The second game wasn't decided until the thirteenth inning when Danny Gardella connected for a two-run homer and sent the home crowd to the exits in jubilation as the Giants won, 4–2. Bill Voiselle and Ace Adams were the winning pitchers. The slow-footed Ernie Lombardi beat out an infield single in the first game, to the astonishment of the Polo Grounds crowd. Brooklyn continued to be inconsistent as they shut out the Braves by a 7–0 score behind Art Herring's two-hitter, but then dropped the second game, 10–1. Chuck Workman hit a homer for Boston in the victory. The Cardinals and Pirates also split two games on the day. Red Barrett was the winner for St. Louis in the opener as they won, 10–3, while Fritz Ostermueller won the second game for Pittsburgh, 12–5. The Cubs kept on winning as Paul Erickson and Claude Passeau led them to a doubleheader victory over the Reds before 17,043 Crosley Field fans, including Commissioner Albert B. "Happy" Chandler. The Cubs kept up their pennant-leading pace on August 8 when they won two games from Boston at Braves Field. Finally they lost to Bill Lee and the Braves by a 7–3 margin on the 9th. Vince Shupe had four hits for the Braves and Butch Nieman hit his thirteenth homer of the season. On the following day, Boston won, 2–1, behind seven strong innings by starter Al Javery. Claude Passeau was working on a no-hitter on August 11 before surrendering a single to Boston's Phil Masi with two out in the eighth inning. He held on for a two-hit shutout as Chicago defeated Boston, 8–0, before 4,612 Braves Field spectators. Passeau struck out eight batters in the game and walked none.

Besides the hit to Masi, Passeau surrendered only one more hit in the

August 11 game to Morrie Aderholt. Aderholt was making his Braves debut as a pinch hitter in the eighth inning. In his fifth and final big league season he batted .217 for Brooklyn in 60 at-bats before going to the Braves and hitting .333 in 102 at-bats.

There were four shutouts in the National League on August 8. Hal Gregg pitched his first major league shutout as Brooklyn defeated Cincinnati, 1–0, at Ebbets Field. At the Polo Grounds the 46,805 witnesses were disappointed to see the Cardinals win, 3–0, behind the shutout pitching of George Dockins. Pittsburgh whitewashed Philadelphia, 4–0, behind the fine pitching of Preacher Roe, and then the Phillies returned the favor in the nightcap, 5–0. Dick Mauney, who would go 6–10 with a 3.08 ERA in his rookie season, pitched a shutout. At Braves Field, Chicago swept a doubleheader by 5–2 and 3–2 scores: Ray Prim went the distance in the opener, while Hank Wyse pitched all twelve innings in the second game.

The Flatbush faithful went home happy as Brooklyn gained one and a half games on Chicago when they defeated Cincinnati by 9–2 and 4–3 scores on August 9. The second game was decided when Babe Herman drove home the winning run with a pinch-hit single in the twelfth frame. First baseman Ed Stevens, who was recently recalled from Montreal, fielded well and went 3 for 5 in the second game with a run scored and an RBI. "Big Ed" Stevens was twenty years old in 1945 and batted .274 with a .376 on-base percentage and four homers in 55 games and 201 at-bats. He was from Galveston, Texas, and took great offense when someone wrote that he was from Houston during the season. As a young boy, Ed and two of his brothers collected thirty soup wrappers for a promotion and he thought he was going to receive a major league bat. But after keeping clean and making his mom happy but skeptical because he took three showers or baths a day, he was dismayed when he received the bat and it was of the drugstore variety. Furthermore, it broke on the first swing. Stevens was encouraged to seek a professional baseball career by his brother Mal, who was with Mobile in the Dodgers organization in 1945. Stevens, who spoke with a slow drawl, was happy to be sent to Johnstown, Pennsylvania, during the 1942 campaign. His interest in Johnstown was due to the fact that some veteran players had the audacity to suggest that the 1889 Johnstown flood was bigger than the Galveston hurricane of 1900. Stevens never did believe that story but had to see the place anyhow.[33]

On August 12 there were four doubleheaders in the senior circuit. Chicago traveled to Philadelphia and won two games from the Phillies by 4–3 and 12–6 scores. Phil Cavarretta, the captain and first baseman of the Cubs, collided with Fred Daniels at the gateway station in the opener and injured his right shoulder. He went to a nearby hospital where an examination was conducted and thankfully for the Cubs he didn't suffer a fracture. However, Cavarretta would be out of the lineup for several days. New York won their doubleheader from Cincinnati by 3–2 and 6–5 scores at the Polo Grounds. Mel Ott and Danny

Gardella hit home runs in the opener, while Ott connected for his second homer in the nightcap and Johnny Rucker also went deep. Cincinnati had lost nine straight games and twelve of their last thirteen. Brooklyn and St. Louis split their twin bill, as did Boston and Pittsburgh.

The Cardinals needed fifteen innings to defeat Brooklyn on August 13 as they won, 11–10, on Ken O'Dea's double, which sent Ray Sanders scampering across the plate with the winning run. Dixie Walker threw out runners at the plate in the twelfth and fourteenth innings. Red Barrett earned the victory for St. Louis in relief. Harry Feldman earned his tenth victory to give New York a 2–0 win over the Reds. Jimmie Wilson had taken over the managerial duties for the Reds while Bill McKechnie was home taking care of his ailing wife. Paul Derringer won his thirteenth as Chicago defeated Philadelphia, 4–1. Boston also emerged victorious, winning 6–4 over Pittsburgh.

After President Harry Truman dropped the second atomic bomb on Japan on August 9, the war ended in the Far East on August 14. The *New York Herald Tribune* declared, "Japanese War Ends: Truman Announces Unconditional Surrender; MacArthur Named Supreme Allied Commander."[34] Americans celebrated like never before and they continued to flock to major league parks for the rest of the season. On V-J Day the Phillies defeated the Cubs, 2–1, at Shibe Park behind the pitching of Oscar Judd. Judd hit a double and scored a run at the plate. The Cardinals and Giants also secured victories, while the Pirates won a doubleheader from Boston. However, the official V-J Day that was proclaimed by President Truman was on September 2, when the Japanese surrendered aboard the USS *Missouri* in Tokyo Bay.

The Cub juggernaut crushed the Dodgers, 20–6, on August 15 before 25,110 fans who were described as "men, women and children — with cowbells and V-J noisemakers and itinerant drummers and buglers." Chicago pounded out nineteen hits, including four homers, to give Hank Borowy an easy victory. Paul Gillespie had two of the homers, one of which was a grand slam in the first inning. Heinz Becker and Andy Pafko had the other two circuit shots. Chicago scored eight runs in the fourth and Jesse Abramson wrote, "The cowbells faded to a tinkle and were muffled altogether at the end; the musicians departed in mid-game along with thousands of others as the cheers changed to jeers.... the Dodgers ... proved they don't belong on the same field with a title-bound club."[35] Brooklyn rebounded the following day, 2–1, behind Tom Seats before 36,427 Ebbets Field fans. Al Laney wrote, "It was a fine setting for a good game of almost pre-war quality."[36] The Cubs won on the 17th, 4–3. Dixie Walker was incorrectly called out on a grounder for the final out of the game. Al Laney observed, "Brooklyn players and a large part of the crowd rushed and surrounded Tom Dunn, the first base umpire, making menacing gestures. What is technically known in Flatbush as a rhubarb was in the making, but since the game indubitably was over once Dunn had called Dixie out, dispersal was quickly accomplished."[37] The crowd booed vociferously when the umpires took the field on August 18. Among the 18,256 spectators at Ebbets Field was Ford Frick, National League President, who was there to make sure things didn't get out of control. Chicago collected twelve hits to win yet again, 7–3, as they won three of four in the series.

Sal Maglie won his second major league game and blanked the Pirates, 6–0, on the 18th. But then the Giants dropped a doubleheader at the Polo Grounds to Chicago on the following day. Ray Prim won the opener, 3–1, while Hank Borowy tossed an eight-hit shutout in the finale as Chicago emerged victorious by an 8–0 score. On August 20, Jimmie Foxx drove home the winning run with a ninth-inning single to lead the Phillies to a 4–3 win over Cincinnati. Only 950 fans paid their way into Shibe Park to see their miserable ball club in action. At Braves Field, Art Rebel led off the game for the Cardinals with a double and came around to score after Red Schoendienst singled and Buster Adams hit a sacrifice fly. Rebel went 2 for 4 in the game and drove in a run. The left-handed hitting outfielder played seven games for the 1938 Philadelphia Phillies and then returned to the big leagues in 1945 with the Cardinals, batting .347 in 72 at-bats and 26 games. Ken Burkhart won his fourteenth game with a seven-hit shutout as the Cardinals won, 2–0. Also on the 20th, the Giants defeated the Cubs, 9–3, as Van Lingle Mungo won his fourteenth game. And the Pirates defeated the Dodgers, 11–1, at Ebbets Field as the frustrated witnesses watched the home team commit seven errors.

George Hausmann's squeeze bunt with the bases loaded in the last of the ninth sent the winning run scampering across home plate as New York defeated Chicago, 4–3, on August 21. In Brooklyn, the Dodgers committed only two errors but they gave up eighteen hits and lost to Pittsburgh, 12–1. St. Louis won, 8–4, over Boston as Red Barrett won his eighteenth and Philadelphia won their fifth straight game with a 6–3 triumph over Cincinnati. The St. Louis Cardinals swept a three-game set from the Cubs on the 26th with a 5–1 victory and moved within two and a half games of Chicago. Red Barrett earned the win before 42,998 Wrigley Field patrons. It was the Cubs' fifth straight loss. On that same day the Dodgers passed the million mark in attendance with a 6–2 win over the Giants. Bill Lee won his fifth game for Boston as they defeated Philadelphia, 6–5, but the Phillies won the nightcap, 4–3, as Dick Barrett earned the win. A crowd of 9,797 viewed the Sunday doubleheader at Shibe Park. Pittsburgh won a doubleheader victory from Cincinnati by scores of 10–7 and 2–1.

With the Cubs clinging to a two-and-a-half-game lead over the surging Cardinals, manager Charlie Grimm decided to shake up the lineup. After leading the National League in homers in 1943 and 1944, Bill Nicholson had slumped to .253 with ten homers and was benched in late August. In 1945 Nicholson batted .243 with 13 home runs and 88 RBIs. He had 20 fewer homers than the year before and 34 fewer RBIs. Phil Cavarretta would play Nicholson's customary right field position while Heinz Becker filled in for Cavarretta at first base. Grimm said, "We have to get some hitting. Becker's ankles have been bad but

10. The National League Campaign

he has rested for a while and says he's ready to try for a regular job again."[38] Grimm celebrated his forty-seventh birthday with a 6–3 win over Pittsburgh on August 28 before 23,335 Forbes Field fans. Peanuts Lowrey hit a three-run homer in the fourth inning to give the Cubs a 3–2 lead that they never relinquished. Hank Borowy won his fifth game as a Cub. Becker was 1 for 5 at the first sack while Cavarretta was 1 for 4 in the game. They also gained a game on the Cardinals, who lost to the Reds, 3–2. The Cardinals lost again the following day, while Chicago shut out Pittsburgh, 2–0, as Heinz Becker led the attack with two hits, one of which was an RBI double. Starting pitcher Ray Prim wilted in the 91-degree heat and had to give way to Hy Vandenberg in the eighth inning.

Grimm's ball club lost on August 30 and then dropped the final game of the month in convincing fashion as the Cardinals defeated them 4–1 at Sportsman's Park. Harry Brecheen pitched a two-hitter and had two doubles and a sacrifice fly at the plate. Marty Marion was terrific in the field while Buster Adams and Whitey Kurowski hit homers. It appeared as if the National League flag race would come down to the wire.

On September 1 the National League standings were as follows:

	W L	PCT	GB
Chicago Cubs	76–45	.628	—
St. Louis Cardinals	74–49	.602	3
Brooklyn Dodgers	68–53	.562	8
New York Giants	67–57	.540	10.5
Pittsburgh Pirates	67–62	.519	13
Boston Braves	56–68	.452	21.5
Cincinnati Reds	49–73	.402	27.5
Philadelphia Phillies	37–87	.298	40.5

Johnny Hopp hit a ninth-inning triple to send the Cardinals home victorious on the first day of the month. George Dockins earned the victory over Claude Passeau in the 3–2 win. In Philadelphia, Vince DiMaggio elevated himself into the record books when he hit his fourth grand slam homer of the season in an 8–3 victory at Braves Field. He joined Frank Schulte, Babe Ruth, Lou Gehrig, and Rudy York, who also had accomplished the feat. The Cubs and Cardinals split a doubleheader on the following day, as did the Giants/Dodgers and Boston/Philadelphia. The Pirates took a pair from Cincinnati, 4–2 and 7–3, behind the pitching of Walter "Boom Boom" Beck and Nick Strincevich. Chicago extended their lead to four games when they took two from the Reds on the 3rd. They collected twenty-three hits on the day to win 7–2 and 7–1. The Giants drew their millionth customer to the Polo Grounds for the first time in their history as they took two from Philadelphia, 3–2 and 9–0. Sal Maglie threw a shutout in the second game, while Harry Feldman emerged victorious in the opener. The Cardinals continued to slump, dropping two games to the Pirates. Tom Seats started the first game at Ebbets Field and defeated Boston,

4–0, and then earned the victory in relief of Cy Buker in the second game, which ended at 4–3. Starting for Boston in the nightcap was Bob Whitcher, a former semi-pro from Lynn, Massachusetts, who had defeated the Braves twice during the exhibition season and impressed Boston's management so much that they signed him. Whitcher pitched three scoreless innings and then Brooklyn scored one run in both the fourth and fifth innings. Don Hendrickson replaced Whitcher with one out in the sixth inning and was the losing pitcher in the game. Whitcher, a 5'8", 165-pound southpaw, pitched six games for Boston in 1945, going 0–2 with a 2.87 ERA. In the tenth inning of the second game Boston's shortstop, Dick Culler, was picked off first, and when he advanced to second, Eddie Stanky, Brooklyn's second baseman, took the throw from Ed Stevens and slapped Culler across the face with the tag. Culler took offense to Stanky's tag and a fight developed between the two men and the benches cleared onto the field.

The only game scheduled on September 4 in the senior circuit was between the Cardinals and Pirates at Sportsman's Park. St. Louis held a 7–1 lead after five innings, but the Pirates scored five runs in the sixth, and in the ninth they pushed across two more runs. The Cardinals scored a run in the bottom half of the ninth inning to tie the game and keep their hopes alive. They remained knotted at eight until the bottom of the twelfth inning, when play was stopped after one pitch at 5:16. The Pirates had to catch a train back to Pittsburgh. Pirates manager Frankie Frisch used twenty players in the game, including six pitchers. Billy Southworth, the Cardinals' skipper, used sixteen players, including five pitchers.

Brooklyn defeated Pittsburgh by a 5–3 margin on the 5th at Forbes Field thanks to a two-run homer by Goody Rosen in the tenth inning. Umpire George Barr threw out Pirate manager Frankie Frisch and third baseman Bob Elliott. Elliott was fined $50 the following day for pushing the umpire in this game. Frisch was later fined $75 for insubordination when he refused to leave the bench after he was kicked out. Al Lopez broke Gabby Hartnett's major league record by catching his 1,794th game. And Pirates legend Honus Wagner was honored with his own night. Chicago took two games from the Giants at Wrigley Field by 5–2 and 10–2 scores. The Cubs continued to play well despite injuries to Phil Cavarretta, Don Johnson, and Heinz Becker. Cincinnati and Philadelphia split a doubleheader, while St. Louis defeated Boston, 4–2, behind the fine pitching of Harry Brecheen.

The New York Giants looked flat on September 6 and were impotent against the fine pitching of Chicago's Hank Borowy. Buddy Kerr was benched and replaced with Billy Jurges at shortstop. The 37-year-old Jurges, who contributed a .324 batting average on the season with a .405 on-base percentage in 176 at-bats, was predominantly a third baseman in 1945 but played shortstop eight times, a position that he had played during most of his career. Bill Nicholson hit a two-run homer to right field in the fifth inning and Chicago

10. The National League Campaign

won easily, 6–1. It was reported that Hi Bithorn was back with the Cubs. However, he never pitched with the club in 1945. Before going into the service, Bithorn compiled an 18–12 record with a 2.60 ERA in 1943. The second-place Cardinals split a doubleheader with Boston and were five games behind Chicago. At Crosley Field an embarrassingly low paid crowd of 346 was on hand to watch Howie Fox pitch a complete game in a 4–1 Cincinnati victory over the Phillies. At Forbes Field, Pittsburgh hitters hammered Brooklyn's starter Hal Gregg, who was ailing with a fingertip burn, and they won by a 17–5 score. Nick Strincevich, who went the distance for Pittsburgh, delivered a pitch to Luis Olmo in the top of the fourth inning and home plate umpire Tom Dunn called it a strike. Olmo disagreed with the umpire's decision, as did skipper Leo Durocher, who voiced his opinion from the dugout and was signaled by Dunn to exit the premises. Suddenly, Dunn was surrounded by Brooklyn players while Durocher and Olmo, who were both ejected, led the verbal assault. To exit the field, Durocher and Olmo had to go through the Pittsburgh dugout. While the argument was going on, the Pirate players put together a walkway for Durocher to follow by laying towels together on the ground. When Durocher was finished arguing with Dunn he was none too pleased to see what the Pittsburgh players had done and he kicked the towels and the equipment that were situated on the dugout steps. He reached into a box of baseballs and threw them in different directions. It was not a good day for Leo the Lip. Furthermore, Leo had to leave his club and return to New York for a court appearance. Chuck Dressen would lead the club while he was gone.

Sal Maglie hurled his third shutout of the season as he whitewashed the Cubs, 2–0, before a ladies' day crowd of 14,070 (7,670 paid) at Wrigley Field on September 7. He outdueled eighteen-game winner Hank Wyse. While Leo Durocher was in New York facing assault charges his Dodgers won, 3–2, at Forbes Field. Tom Seats earned the victory and improved his record to 9–5. Augie Galan was thrown out of the game when he kicked dirt on the umpire's shoes. Dixie Walker was tossed when he threw his glove in the air as he was going to right field between innings. George Dockins pitched a three-hit shutout to give St. Louis a 4–0 win over Boston at Sportsman's Park. In Cincinnati the Reds defeated the Phillies, 6–2, behind Joe Bowman, who worked eight and two-thirds innings. Mike Modak, who went 1–2 on the season with a 5.74 ERA during his only big league appearances, got the final out. Philadelphia took the second game, 8–6, as Dick Barrett earned the win. Barrett was born in Montoursville, Pennsylvania, on September 28, 1906. He debuted in the majors with the Philadelphia Athletics in 1933 (4–4, 5.76 ERA), and then played for the Boston Braves (1–3, 6.68 ERA) in 1934. He was out of the big leagues until 1943 when he reemerged with the Chicago Cubs, and after an 0–4 start he finished the season with the Phillies (10–9, 2.39 ERA). In 1944 he was 12–18 with a 3.86 ERA and then finished his career in 1945 with an 8–20 record.

On Saturday, September 8, a chagrined Wrigley Field crowd watched Harry

Feldman outduel Paul Derringer to give the Giants a 3–0 win before 10,394 spectators. Jim Mallory, who played four games for the 1940 Washington Senators and then 50 games for the Cardinals and Giants in 1945, batting .277 in 137 at-bats, left the New York club and took a job coaching football in North Carolina. Pete Coscarart, the Pittsburgh second baseman, who batted .242 on the season, drove home Bob Elliott in the twelfth inning to give the Pirates a 6–5 win over Brooklyn. Coscarart collected three singles, a triple, and three RBIs in the game. There were no other senior league games scheduled on the 8th. However, the Phillies received some bad news when they found out that Vince DiMaggio, who had crashed into the Crosley Field wall on the previous day, had a fractured right elbow and would not return that season. DiMaggio had turned 33 years old on September 6 and would only play one more big league season, appearing in 21 games for the Phillies and Giants in 1946 and batting .091 in 44 at-bats.

St. Louis kept the pressure on Chicago by taking two games from the Giants on September 9 before 20,704 fans at Sportsman's Park. The Cubs kept pace by winning a doubleheader from Boston and were three and a half games ahead of the Cardinals. Tommy Holmes and Phil Cavarretta were battling for the senior circuit batting title as the season came down the stretch. In the fourth inning of the second game, Holmes grounded to shortstop Len Merullo, who unleashed a low throw to first that eluded Cavarretta and went into the stands. Merullo was charged with an error on the play. But in an amazing sign of sportsmanship, Cavarretta informed official scorer Edgar H. Munzel of the *Chicago Sun* that Holmes was going to leg out a single and umpire Babe Pinelli was about to call the runner safe until the ball skipped past Cavarretta. Munzel then changed his decision and gave Holmes a hit.[39] Cavarretta would win the batting crown with a .355 batting average while Holmes was second at .352. Cincinnati took two games from Brooklyn while Pittsburgh and Philadelphia split a doubleheader.

On the following day the Pirates defeated the Phillies, 9–5, in a rain-shortened contest. The losing pitcher for Philadelphia was Izzy Leon, who went 0–4 with a 5.35 ERA in 14 games during his only big league season in 1945. Leon, who was born in Cruces, Cuba, on January 4, 1911, had actually played in the Negro Leagues from 1944 to 1948. Here was a player who apparently had a skin color that was light enough to allow him to get a trial in the big leagues during the final wartime season and was also welcomed in the black majors. The Cardinals were missing Marty Marion on the 10th, who was out of the lineup with a bad back, but they managed to win anyhow, 2–1, behind the fine pitching of Harry Brecheen before a Sportsman's Park crowd that numbered 7,439. Tom Dunn, the first base umpire, had to listen to criticism for much of the evening as he ruled on a few close plays. Johnny Rucker, the Giants center fielder and leadoff man, was kicked out of the game. The two runs scored when Bill Voiselle walked the bases loaded with two out in the fifth and then allowed a two-run single to Emil Verban. The Braves defeated the Cubs in Chicago by a 2–0 score as Ed Wright tossed a seven-hit shutout. The Dodgers emerged victorious against Cincinnati, 3–2, in a rain-shortened game.

Ed Sauer of the Chicago Cubs was the younger brother of Hank, who played with the 1945 Cincinnati Reds. He hit an infield single to bring home the winning run in the last of the ninth on September 11 as the Cubs defeated Boston, 5–4. Hank Borowy improved his record to 8–2 with Chicago and had completed all ten games he had started for the Cubs. St. Louis kept pace with a 6–5 win over New York and were only two and a half games behind Chicago. The Cardinals were the only team left with a legitimate chance of catching Chicago. The third-place Dodgers were ten games out and lost a ten-inning affair to Cincinnati, 5–4, but then won the nightcap, 11–6. The fourth-place Pirates solidified their position in the first division with a double defeat of Philadelphia, 5–4 and 5–1. Playing shortstop for the Phillies in both games was the little-used Ed Walczak. He went 2 for 4 in the opener and was hitless in three at-bats in the nightcap. Walczak was one of many players who would play briefly in 1945, his only major league season, and then was never to appear in the big show again. He batted .211 in 20 games and 57 at-bats.

Al Laney of *The New York Herald Tribune* jokingly assured his readers that there was no truth to a report that the Chicago Cubs, acting in a benevolent manner, would give Larry MacPhail a full World Series share if they happened to win the title. MacPhail was part of the Yankees ownership group and it was reported that he was responsible for allowing Borowy to leave the Yankees on a waiver wire deal. While it wasn't assured that Chicago would get their hands on the "swag," Laney insisted that their chances were very good that this would happen. The Cubs were a confident ball club as they approached the end of the season, and they not only believed that a World Series appearance was in their future but that they would bring home the title. Laney, like many of his colleagues, believed that without the insertion of Borowy into the Cubs' rotation, Chicago may have been several games off the pace, instead of sitting at the top of the senior circuit. When Borowy departed from New York's American League representative, MacPhail was adamant in his belief that Borowy could no longer pitch a complete game. But as of September 12, he already had pitched ten complete games for the Cubs and would pitch one more before the curtain was lowered on the 1945 campaign.[40]

Not only was Borowy compiling victories but he was a money pitcher, winning pressure-packed clutch games. This was the case on September 2 when Borowy toed the slab in hostile territory before 34,939 paid spectators at Sportsman's Park. This was the largest crowd to attend a Cardinals game in their home ballpark since August 13, 1939. These were the games that tested a pitcher's nerve: standing in the middle of the diamond, before a packed house, in the unrelenting St. Louis heat, desperately trying to hold off his rival. At this juncture of the season the Cardinals had won five consecutive games against the

Cubs and twelve of the fifteen games they had played against them. Chicago had a two-game advantage with seven games left to play against the surging Cardinals. Borowy yielded only five hits as the Cubs won, 4–1, in ten innings. However, they did drop the nightcap, 4–0, as Red Barrett pitched a one-hit shutout for St. Louis. The Cubs limped out of town, winning only one game in the four-game set, clinging to a two-game advantage that increased to four on Labor Day. If the Cubs had been swept in their four-game series against the Cardinals the pennant race may have taken a different direction.

The Cubs split a doubleheader with the Phillies on the 14th at Wrigley Field. But a Brooklyn Dodgers team that was extremely angry and was determined to impair the Cardinals' pennant hopes accomplished their goal and defeated the Cardinals in two games, 7–3 and 6–1. The Dodgers, who were scheduled to play the Cubs at Wrigley Field in a doubleheader on the following day, asked the Cardinals organization to move the twilight doubleheader to the daytime so that they could take the regular night train to Chicago. Sam Breadon, the Cardinals owner, refused the request and thought they would get a larger crowd for the twilight affair, but he was wrong as only 2,378 (2,103 paid) bothered to show up. Leo Durocher had been saving his two best pitchers, Hal Gregg and Vic Lombardi, for the doubleheader in Chicago on the following day, but with the Cardinals unwilling to grant the Dodgers' request he changed his mind and used them against St. Louis. Furthermore, the Dodgers had to play on a field that was saturated with water.[41]

The Dodgers were an angry team from the moment they arrived in St. Louis. Sam Breadon insisted that he had notified the Dodgers of a schedule change where the two teams would play a doubleheader on September 12. But according to the Dodgers they had never received notification until the day before, when they were in Cincinnati. Therefore their travel plans were interrupted and they woke up at 6 A.M. to catch a train out of Cincinnati. The day coach reportedly took eight and a half hours to travel to St. Louis. They skipped dinner and arrived at the ballpark about an hour before the twilight doubleheader was set to commence. They were so tired that they managed to get only two runs off Art Lopatka, who was making one of his eight major league appearances in his two-year career. St. Louis won the opener, 3–2, and Ralph Branca was saddled with the loss. Fortunately for the Dodgers the second game was rained out, as was the following day's games, setting up a doubleheader on getaway day.[42]

At Wrigley Field on September 15, a suspended game from July 20 was completed as Brooklyn won, 12–5. In the regularly scheduled game, the Dodgers rallied to score two in the ninth but the Cubs held on for a 7–6 decision. Successive singles by Goody Rosen, Augie Galan, and Dixie Walker plated the first run in the ninth after one out was recorded. Ed Stevens almost grounded into a double play but he touched the first base bag just ahead of the throw. Galan scored on the play but Walker was forced at second. Frenchy Bordagaray then singled past the first baseman, moving Stevens to second, representing the tying run. The crowd at Wrigley Field sensed the importance of the situation and urged Claude Passeau, who had relieved Hy Vandenberg in the ninth, to secure the victory. Hank Borowy started for Chicago but was removed for a pinch-hitter in the sixth inning. It was a cold, blustery day, with the crowd of 15,729 wearing overcoats and blankets to try to keep themselves warm. This was football weather, not the ideal conditions for the nation's pastime to be played in. Babe Herman, Brooklyn's beloved hero, stepped out of the Dodgers dugout to pinch hit for Tommy Brown with the tying run at second. Bill Lauder Jr. wrote, "Old Turkey Neck worked the count to two and two, then flailed futilely at Passeau's curve."[43] The Cardinals won their game over the Phillies and were three games out. New York and Cincinnati also won on the day.

A Sunday crowd of 41,478 attended the game at Wrigley Field on September 16 and watched the Cubs establish a new major league record by winning their eighteenth doubleheader. They defeated Brooklyn by scores of 3–2 and 4–2. Ray Prim won his thirteenth in the opener and Hank Wyse became the first Cubs pitcher to win twenty games since Claude Passeau in 1940. The Brooklyn hurlers were not nearly as talented as Chicago's. Ralph Branca, a 19-year-old right-hander, went the distance in the opener, yielding three runs on seven hits and four walks. After starting his career in 1944 with a 0–2 record in 21 games with a 7.05 ERA, he improved in 1945, going 5–6 with a 3.04 ERA. He started fifteen of the sixteen games he appeared in during the season. Tom Seats failed to make it out of the seventh inning in the second game as he allowed nine hits and four walks. Seats, a left-handed pitcher, played briefly for the 1940 Detroit Tigers (2–2, 4.69 ERA) and then played his last big league season in 1945, going 10–7 with a 4.36 ERA. Chicago's lead stood at four games and time was running out for Billy Southworth's ball club. In St. Louis, playing manager Ben Chapman sent himself up as a pinch-hitter in the top of the ninth inning of the opening game and cracked a two-run single as Philadelphia won, 4–3. Al Jurisich earned the win for St. Louis in the second game as they won, 10–3, at Sportsman's Park. Glenn Gardner pitched the final three and a third innings. In his only big league season Gardner compiled a 3–1 record and a 3.29 ERA. Augie Bergamo, the Cardinals leadoff man, went 4 for 5 in the second contest. At Crosley Field the Reds and Braves split a doubleheader while the Pirates and Giants also split two in Pittsburgh. On the 17th the Cardinals were three games behind Chicago when they defeated Philadelphia and the Cubs lost to the Dodgers.

A Sportsman's Park crowd of 25,068 watched the lead cut to two games on September 18 as the Cardinals defeated Chicago, 3–2. Red Barrett earned his twenty-second win. The Cardinals were still in the race because of their 14–4 record against Chicago on the season. Chicago won the second game of the series but the resilient Cardinals bounced back for a 2–0 win on the 20th. After two rainouts the Cubs extended their lead to two and a half games with a 6–5 win over St. Louis on September 25 at Wrigley Field. Hank Borowy earned the win but got some much-needed relief help from Ray Prim. It was Borowy's twentieth victory and it was reported that he became the first pitcher to win twenty games while pitching in both the American and National Leagues since Joe McGinnity won twenty-one with Baltimore and New York in 1902. McGinnity had pitched that season for two last-place clubs: the Baltimore Orioles had a 50–88 record in the American League, while the New York Giants were even worse, concluding with a 48–88 record in the National League.

The game on the 25th was played despite a continuous morning rain; an hour before game time it appeared unlikely that the game would be played. There was a "steady drizzle" when the gates were opened. Despite the unpleasant conditions a crowd of 21,138 showed up to watch their Cubs play this critical game. Al Laney observed that there was great tension in the ballpark and that the contest resembled the "decisive" game of the World Series.[44] The conditions were poor and not what they should have been for such an important game. The two starting pitchers on the day, Borowy and Harry Brecheen, had pitched well against their opponents all season. Brecheen was 4–0 against Chicago while Borowy was the only Cubs pitcher to defeat the Cardinals since he had joined the team. Stan Hack, who was generally a terrific third baseman, made a bad throw to second on a double-play grounder in the top of the first inning that opened the door for St. Louis. They scored two runs on singles by Whitey Kurowski and Ray Sanders to take an early 2–0 lead. But then Brecheen made an errant throw to first on Phil Cavarretta's roller in the bottom of the initial frame that allowed two runs to score to tie the game. Then for the first of two times on the day, Marty Marion, St. Louis's gifted shortstop, saved Brecheen from more damage when he made a brilliant play on Andy Pafko's liner that he turned into a twin killing. Chicago pushed across four runs in the seventh, which gave them a lead that they would not relinquish. Red Schoendienst made another error for St. Louis in the seventh, one of three on the day for the Cardinals.

St. Louis unleashed an eighteen-hit attack on the 26th and pounded seven Chicago pitchers for an 11–6 win. Ken Burkhart earned the win in relief of Red Barrett. St. Louis dropped a ball game to Pittsburgh on the following day, while the Cubs took two from the Reds before 4,403 Crosley Field spectators. When second baseman Don Johnson banged into umpire Babe Pinelli during a play at second base in the opener, it was feared that the Cubs may have lost their second baseman for an extended period of time. He was taken to the hospital, where he was diagnosed with a pulled muscle in his neck.

The hour glass was on empty for Billy Southworth's ball club, for the Chicago Cubs won the National League pennant on September 29, taking two games from the Pirates at Forbes Field, 4–3 and 5–0. Red Smith wrote that they played "in rain and cold and mist and mud," and the Cubs were determined to get that World Series "swag." The pennant-clinching first game had a dramatic finish: the Pirates had runners on second and third with two outs in the last of the ninth when Tommy O'Brien, a right-handed hitter who batted .335 in 161 at-bats during the 1945 campaign, was sent up to bat for the left-handed hitting Bill Salkeld. Then Charlie Grimm replaced the southpaw Bob Chipman with the right-handed pitcher Paul Erickson. Erickson struck out O'Brien with a curveball at 4:23 P.M. to clinch the pennant. The pitcher's cap flew off as he delivered the pitch and manager Grimm confessed, "I was dying. I was afraid Paul would stop his delivery to grab his cap. The balk would have tied the score." Red Smith described Erickson as a "gangling, white-haired twenty-seven-year-old pitcher from Zion City, Ill., whom the Cubs reclaimed from a milk route last June and earnestly endeavored to peddle to the Browns for $7,500 three weeks later...."[45] Hank Borowy earned his twenty-first victory of the season as the starter in the clinching game. Charlie Grimm was hoisted upon the shoulders of his players and given a ceremonial ride into the clubhouse to celebrate their first pennant since 1938. Only 4,016 fans paid their way into Forbes Field to observe the celebration. The Cardinals won a doubleheader from Cincinnati on the day, but it was too late.

The champagne was flowing in the evening as the Cubs had a dinner in honor of their pennant-winning ball club. After winning ten games with the Yankees, Hank Borowy won eleven more with Chicago. One of the many short speeches on the night was given by Charlie Grimm, who called Borowy the guy who "really won the pennant."[46] The Cubs ended their season on September 30, by defeating Pittsburgh, 5–3.

The final National League standings were as follows:

	W L	PCT	GB
Chicago Cubs	98–56	.636	—
St. Louis Cardinals	95–59	.617	3
Brooklyn Dodgers	87–67	.565	11
Pittsburgh Pirates	82–72	.532	16
New York Giants	78–74	.513	19
Boston Braves	67–85	.441	30
Cincinnati Reds	61–93	.396	37
Philadelphia Phillies	46–108	.299	52

❖ 11 ❖

Hammerin' Hank and the World Champion Tigers

The Detroit Tigers prepared for wartime baseball by training in Evansville, Indiana. In 1945 it appeared that the entire exhibition schedule would be canceled. The travel plans for them and their opponents were not in compliance with the standards established by the Office of Defense Transportation. Jack Zeller, Detroit's general manager, suggested the team walk 112 miles to the Chicago White Sox' camp in Terre Haute. Zeller told manager Steve O'Neill, "Have them carry their uniforms, bats, and toilet articles on their backs. The players are supposed to be athletes in good condition. There are a few million boys who aren't athletes and are walking from ten to twenty miles a day in training camps in this country and they're carrying something heavier than uniforms and bats." Steve O'Neill said that if they walked he would not join them: "I can't foot it that far."[1] They instead took a train to the White Sox' camp, played them in a few games, then hung around a few more days to practice before going to St. Louis to open the season. Dizzy Trout, who grew up nearby in Sandcut, Indiana, said he had a right to play wartime ball: "I'm sticking with the only job I know how to do. I consider the ballplayer who quits baseball and takes a war job just to stay out of the army a slacker."[2]

Steve O'Neill managed the Tigers and after finishing second in 1944 won the World Series in 1945. He was one of four brothers to play in the big leagues and was a very well liked and respected person around the game. Steve was successful in developing young talent like the explosive Hal Newhouser during his managerial career. He had a seventeen-year career as a major league catcher and batted .263 lifetime with a .349 on-base percentage, but he hit only thirteen home runs. In 1935 he became the manager of the Cleveland Indians, replacing the former pitching great Walter Johnson after 94 games. After a fifth-place finish in 1936 he graduated to the first division in 1937 as his team ended the season in fourth place. O'Neill had managed in the minor leagues with Toronto and Toledo before getting the opportunity to lead a big league team in 1935. However, in 1938 he was back managing in the bushes with Buffalo of the International League and remained there until 1940. In 1941 he was a coach with the Tigers and in 1942 he managed Beaumont in the Texas League. In 1943 he became Detroit's manager and from 1944 to 1947 had one first-place finish and three second-place showings. His last year with the Tigers was in 1948, when they were in fifth place. Then he spent two years leading the Boston Red Sox (1950–1951) and finished his managerial career with the Philadelphia Phillies (1952–1954).

The first two wartime seasons were not impressive for Detroit: in 1942 they finished in fifth place (73–81) with Del Baker as their manager. In 1943, with Steve O'Neill as the skipper, they again finished in fifth place (78–76); in 1944 they improved to second place (88–66); and in 1945 they won the pennant (88–65) and then defeated the Chicago Cubs in seven games for the World Series championship.

Detroit was fifth in the league in batting (.256) and second in earned run average (2.99). Rudy York and Roy Cullenbine were the big run producers, tied for the team lead with 18 homers, while Eddie Mayo, Doc Cramer, Bob Maier, and Hank Greenberg also contributed. Cullenbine was second in the American League with 93 RBIs while York was fourth with 87. York had the responsibility of filling Greenberg's shoes at first base during the war. The writers and fans got on him because he was inept around the bag, often looked horrible at the plate when guessing the pitch, and was a streaky hitter. He would drink and then fall asleep with a cigarette in his hand; Barney McCosky joked, "Rudy led the league in hotel fires."[3] In 1946 York was traded to the Boston Red Sox to make room for Greenberg at first base. In a thirteen-year career he batted .275 with 277 homers and in 1943 led the majors with 34 homers. He drove in 1,152 runs during his career and during six seasons had at least 103 RBIs.

Roy Cullenbine had a ten-year big league career in which he batted .276 with a .408 on-base percentage, hit a modest 110 homers, had 1,072 hits and 853 walks. He developed a reputation of working the count, content with taking the walk, and his 853 walks is a very high number for a batter who does not lead off nor hit the long ball with any authority. Also consider that there were only four seasons in his career in which he played over 140 games. He played in a total of 1,181 games in his career. The most homers he ever hit was 24 in 1947 and the second most was 18 in 1945. He hit 73 of his 110 homers, or 66.4 percent of his long balls, during his final four seasons from 1944 to 1947. Some people thought he was lazy because he didn't take the bat off his shoulder. Cullenbine started the season with the Cleveland Indians and came over to Detroit in a trade on April 27 for Don Ross and Dutch Meyer. He had a combined .272 average with a .402 on-base percentage and led the junior circuit with 113 walks.

Doc Cramer was an exceptional major league player, batting .296 in a twenty-year career with 2,705 hits. He was a banjo hitter and the most homers he ever hit was eight in 1933 with Connie Mack's Athletics. In 1945 he hit six

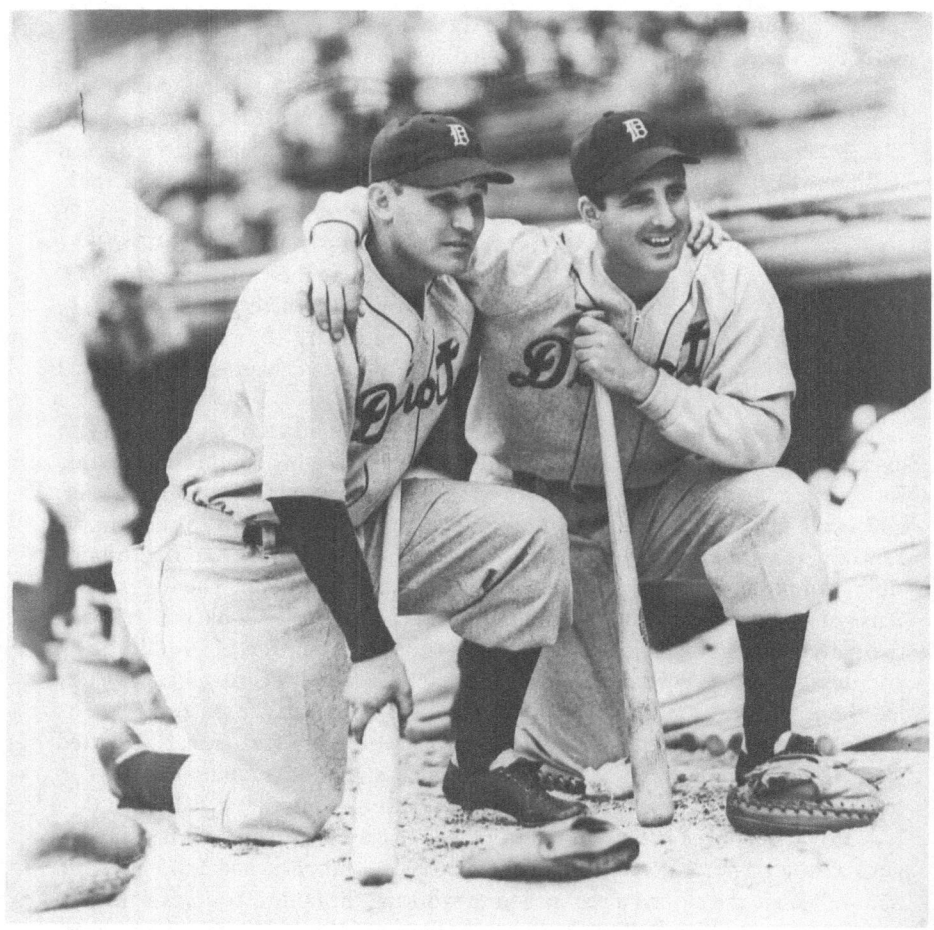

Detroit's power hitters Rudy York (left) and Hank Greenberg were a great nuisance to opposing pitchers during their careers. In 1940 York, who was formerly a catcher, became an everyday first baseman and Greenberg played left field. When Greenberg departed for military service early in 1941, first base became York's permanent home. Despite his 118 home runs and 504 RBIs from 1941 to 1945, the Detroit fans and writers would still often compare him to Greenberg. On January 3, 1946, he was traded to the Boston Red Sox for Eddie Lake, and Greenberg returned to the gateway position for the Tigers (George Brace photograph).

homers, including one in each game of a doubleheader against St. Louis on June 24. Cramer did not walk a lot either and seven times led the American League in at-bats. Despite turning 40 years old on July 22 he still covered the outfield very well and always possessed a great throwing arm. He patrolled the center field station for most of his career including the 1945 season.

Doc was born Roger Maxwell Cramer in Beach Haven, New Jersey, near Atlantic City. He acquired his nickname "Doc" because he rode around with the town doctor as a child. Cramer was extremely popular among his fellow players. Wally Moses, who played with Doc when he first came up with the Athletics, lauded his fellow flycatcher and said it was Cramer who taught him how to play the outfield. Cramer admitted the guidance wasn't out of charity but for "self-defense." He said that Moses's predecessor did not have much range in right field and Cramer felt he was covering two positions during that time. Therefore to make his job easier he decided to help Moses as much as he could with advice and tutorials on how to play the outfield. When a young outfielder named Ned Harris broke into Detroit's starting lineup during the first year of the war he was told by one of the veteran players to follow what Cramer did if he wished to become a good outfielder. Not only did he follow Cramer's steps in the field but also in the streets, hotel lobbies, and wherever else Doc went. This shortly became a source of amusement among members of the team, particularly when Cramer informed his teammates about his predicament. Cramer became so annoyed by Harris's activities that he considered physically harming him. However, a teammate stepped in and told Cramer that Harris had been advised and perhaps ordered to follow Cramer wherever he went.[4] Harris appeared in the major leagues during only four seasons with Detroit, from 1941 to 1943 and during one game in 1946. His best season was the 1942 campaign when he contributed to the team with a .271 batting average with 9 homers in 398 at-bats.

Cramer was discovered by Ralph (Cy) Perkins, who was working for Connie Mack's Philadelphia Athletics. Perkins had played under Mack for fifteen seasons with the Athletics: his first season was with the 1915 squad and his last with the 1930 team. During most of these seasons he was a backup but he was the team's starting catcher for a few years, including his 1921 season, when he batted .288 with 12 homers and 73 RBIs in 538 at-bats. In total he played seventeen big league seasons and batted .259. When he discovered Cramer, Perkins was in Philadelphia, but Sunday baseball was disallowed at that time so he traveled to Beach Haven to watch a semi-pro game. Cramer was pitching for Beach Haven that day and Perkins took notice. In addition to handling pitching responsibilities, Cramer also played shortstop and the outfield, proving to be a versatile and invaluable player. Perkins informed Connie Mack about the young hurler and Cramer was subsequently signed by the Athletics. He was sent to Martinsburg in the Blue Ridge League, and despite losing his first game as a starter to future major leaguer Clay Bryant, Cramer was given every opportunity to prove he could be a successful pitcher and he worked predominantly out of the bullpen. Bryant would have two memorable seasons in the majors, going 9–3 with the 1937 Chicago Cubs and 19–11 for them the following season with a 3.10 ERA. When Connie Mack examined the statistics from Martinsburg that season, what caught his eye was not Cramer's mound record but the .404 batting average he compiled while playing third base and the outfield.

At the insistence of Mack, Cramer henceforth became a full-time outfielder. Cramer's pitching record with Martinsburg was either 12–2 or 2–2 depending on the source. However, the 2–2 record makes more sense because otherwise Mack may not have switched him to the outfield. During this 1929 season, Cramer also got a cup of coffee with the Athletics, playing in two games. He failed to stick with the club the next spring, but batted .347 in 74 games for Portland in the Pacific Coast League. Cramer earned another call up to Philadelphia, this time batting .232 in 82 at-bats for the 1930 Athletics. In 1931 he batted .260 in 223 at-bats and then .336 in 384 at-bats the following year. In 1933 he became Philadelphia's regular center fielder and batted over .300 in both 1934 (.311) and 1935 (.332). From 1933 to 1935 he appeared in every game for the Athletics, proving to be a durable player. With the Athletics on June 20, 1932, and then again on July 13, 1935, he went 6 for 6 during a game, joining Ed Delahanty and Jim Bottomley as the only major leaguers to go 6 for 6 in two games.

In early January 1936, Cramer was traded to the Boston Red Sox and batted over .300 for four of the five seasons with the team from 1936 to 1940. However, during the 1940 season, Red Sox manager Joe Cronin took a liking to Dom DiMaggio, who batted .301 with 8 homers in 418 at-bats. Dom had the DiMaggio name, which impressed a lot of people, and he also had the ability to hit home runs. During Cramer's five seasons with Boston he experienced a power outage as he hit only one home run. Several weeks into the 1940 season Cramer was moved to right field to make room for DiMaggio in center and he disliked being forced to move without his approval. After the 1940 campaign Cramer was traded to Washington for Gee Walker. Walker was immediately traded in a six-player deal to Cleveland while Cramer batted .273 for the Senators in 1941. After the season he was traded to Detroit along with Jimmy Bloodworth for Frank Croucher and Bruce Campbell. Cramer would remain with the Tigers until 1948 when his career ended, playing only four games that final season. The 1945 season was his last as an everyday player. And on June 14 he collected his 2,500th hit.

Detroit's skilled center fielder enjoyed hunting, particularly fox hunting, during the off-season. His approach to fox hunting was not the traditional method: he drove in his car following his foxhounds until they found their prey and killed it. He had 14 foxhounds in his possession and the largest fox they ever killed weighed almost twenty pounds.[5] Cramer stood at 6 feet 2 inches tall and weighed 185 pounds. He batted left-handed but threw right-handed. For most of his career he batted out of the leadoff spot in the order. His birthday is listed in twenty-first century baseball encyclopedias as July 22, 1905. However, in a July 5, 1945, article by H.G. Salsinger in *The Sporting News*, Cramer insists that the records are wrong and that his birthday is actually July 22, 1906.

Cramer batted .275 in 1945 while second baseman Eddie Mayo hit .285 with 10 homers and 54 RBIs. In the middle of the infield the Tigers had a pair of thirty-five-year-olds: Mayo and Skeeter Webb. The war rejuvenated Mayo's career. He had been out of the majors since 1938 when he played only eight games for the Boston Braves. In 1943 he hooked up with the Philadelphia Athletics before coming to Detroit in 1944. His major league debut came in 1936 with the New York Giants and he got the opportunity to play in that season's World Series (1 game, 0 for 1). His double-play partner, Skeeter Webb, was Steve O'Neill's son-in-law, and the weak-hitting shortstop batted only .199. Bob Maier began the season in the outfield and switched to third base early in the campaign when Don Ross was traded. In his only big league season he batted .263. Chuck Hostetler made his big league debut at the age of forty in 1944, batting .298 in 265 at-bats. On September 22, 1945, he turned forty-two and was the oldest member on the team, batting .159 in 44 at-bats. Previously he had played ten seasons in the minors and some semi-pro ball.

In June, Hank Greenberg was discharged from the Army and joined the team. He did not spend his time in the service playing ball to entertain the troops but was on active duty in Europe, the Mediterranean, Egypt, India, and China. Unlike those who played a lot of ball during the war, Greenberg was coming into the game cold and the baseball public was unsure whether his skills had deteriorated. Jack Zeller, Detroit's general manager, said, "If he hits anywhere near his old clip we're the club to beat for the flag."[6] The writers were skeptical concerning what kind of contribution he could make to the club. Arthur Daley wrote in the *New York Times* that the older players were "going to find out that in baseball a man is 'old' at 34."[7] In 1944, Dick Wakefield gave the Tigers a boost when he rejoined the team on July 13, and Detroit went from seventh place to second place, missing the pennant by one game at season's end. They were hoping Greenberg would give them a similar lift in 1945. Greenberg silenced the critics by hitting .311 with 13 homers in 78 games. He batted .304 with two homers in the World Series. However, the subsequent year was a different story altogether; everyone would be back from the war and competition fierce. But he continued his success, batting .277, leading the major leagues with 44 homers and the American League with 127 RBIs. Ralph Kiner led the National League that year with only 23 homers. In 1947, his last season, now with the National League Pirates, Greenberg batted .249 with 25 homers.

As the Tigers were fighting for the pennant during the stretch run in September of 1945, Greenberg was contemplating retirement. He confessed to a friend that baseball was no longer enjoyable but had become a monotonous job. His legs were bothering him, perhaps because he hadn't played a full major league season since 1940 and because he hadn't gone through a rigorous spring training regimen to prepare for the season. Through his experiences during the war Detroit's patriotic slugger realized that there were more important pursuits than baseball, such as defending his country and protecting his family. Greenberg's talk of retirement may have also had to do with domestic considerations because he was planning to get married after the season.[8]

The pitching staff was anchored by Hal Newhouser and Dizzy Trout, with Al Benton, Stubby Overmire, Les Mueller, and Jim Tobin also making contributions. After going 29–9 in 1944, Newhouser won his second consecutive American League MVP by leading the majors in wins (25) and ERA (1.81) in 1945. Newhouser was a workhorse and in those two seasons he pitched a combined six hundred twenty-five and two-thirds innings. Many historians today disparage Newhouser as merely a wartime pitcher, but he did compile a 26–9 record with a 1.94 ERA in 1946. The game that helped fuel the stereotype that Newhouser was merely a "wartime" star gaining success against "wartime" players occurred on August 24 as Bob Feller returned to the Indians and pitched against Newhouser before 46,477 fans at Cleveland's Municipal Stadium. The Indians won, 4–2, behind Feller's terrific pitching. David Jordan wrote, "Nevertheless, the symbolism of the encounter struck many observers—the returning hero against the wartime wonder, Ulysses coming home to Ithaca — and the symbolic loss would come back to haunt Newhouser in later years, when people were busy denigrating his record."[9] When H.G. Salsinger of the *Detroit News* received a letter in September of 1945 asking about Newhouser's abilities against prewar hitting he defended Detroit's ace pitcher. While the letter writer from overseas insisted that Newhouser would not have attained the same level of success if there had not been a war, Salsinger countered by writing, "It is true that Newhouser has pitched against inferior batters in the last two years, but it is equally true that Newhouser has been supported by an inferior cast. The Detroit club has been correspondingly weak in batting and fielding. You see, it all evens up."[10]

Late in the season Newhouser was having a problem with his pitching shoulder and had to have X-rays taken at Henry Ford Hospital in Detroit. It was early September and his teammates had left for their final eastern trip of the season, beginning with a crucial seven-game set against the Yankees. The doctors informed Newhouser that there was no recognizable problem but Detroit's ace lefthander refused to believe it. He felt the pain and the discomfort in his shoulder and believed the doctors had done a poor job in their inability to provide a proper diagnosis. Although Newhouser showed up in New York for his scheduled start on September 7, it appeared doubtful that he could pitch effectively down the stretch and even more doubtful that the Tigers could win the flag without him. Detroit had taken three of the first five games in the series thus far and were clinging to a game and a half lead over Washington. Before the game Newhouser was given a shot of novocaine to relieve the pain in his shoulder. As he prepared to take the mound before the 13,607 paid spectators at the stadium he was told by Steve O'Neill that he would get an early hook if he got into trouble. When he broke off a curveball to Charlie Keller in the opening frame he felt a sharp pain shoot up his back. He then informed his catcher Paul Richards not to call any curveballs the rest of the game. The Yankees were looking for his great hook late into the game, unaware of his predicament, and when they finally realized that the curveball was no longer part of his pitching repertoire, Detroit had built a comfortable lead. Newhouser only threw fastballs and a change of pace after throwing that last painful curveball to Keller. In his first game back since being sidelined he registered a shutout as Detroit won, 5–0; he gave up only four one-base hits during the afternoon. It was Newhouser's sixth shutout and twenty-second victory of the season. Steve O'Neill did not perceive anything different in Newhouser. He playfully suggested that if Newhouser did indeed have an injury then every pitcher on his team should come down with the same ailment.[11]

Concerns over Newhouser's shoulder and back persisted till the end of the season and he wasn't in top form in the World Series. But he continued to provide one of the most courageous pitching exhibitions ever witnessed down the stretch in 1945. Newhouser's next scheduled start after the Yankee game was on September 11 but he was unable to take the hill because of his lingering shoulder problem. Dizzy Trout started instead and pitched a masterful two-hit shutout as Detroit blanked the Red Sox, 5–0. In Philadelphia on the following day, Newhouser warmed up for several minutes before shutting it down and informing O'Neill that he couldn't pitch that day. By the end of September 13, after the Tigers blew a 2–1 lead in the bottom of the ninth inning to Philadelphia to lose 3–2, they were clinging to a half-game lead over Washington. Newhouser's next start came against Washington at Griffith Stadium in the first game of a doubleheader on September 15. He pitched one scoreless inning before leaving the game. The newspapers said he left because of a back injury. It was a miserable day in Washington but despite the rainy weather, 22,949 partisans showed up to watch this critical doubleheader. After Newhouser left the mound in the first inning the rain became heavy and play was halted. There was an hour and six-minute rain delay and when play resumed, Stubby Overmire was the new Tigers pitcher. O'Neill said there was nothing wrong with Newhouser but that he wanted to be cautious and not have his ace pitcher warm up again, stiffen up, and risk additional injuries. He also wanted to use him on the following day. The Tigers won both games on the 15th. On September 16 the Tigers and Senators once again played a twin bill. Before the game Newhouser was given novocaine injections. Although it may have alleviated the pain, it also numbed his pitching shoulder, and may have affected his control. Joe Williams of the *New York World-Telegram* referred to Newhouser's injury as "a torn back muscle."[12] Newhouser and Roger Wolff hooked up in a pitcher's duel in the opening game with Wolff emerging victorious as Washington won, 3–2. Newhouser went the distance but worked out of trouble all day as he yielded nine hits, walked six, and left eleven runners stranded on the bases with Washington at bat. Detroit won the second game, 5–4, as Al Benton earned the win.

On Tuesday, September 18, the Senators won, 12–5, before 5,720 spectators in the final game of the series. Newhouser had a brief but ineffective relief appearance in the seventh inning and gave up a bases-loaded triple to George Case that gave Washington a comfortable 9–5 lead that they never relinquished. Steve O'Neill was desperate to win the finale, using nineteen players and six pitchers. But despite the loss Detroit left town winning three of five in the series and had a game and a half lead over the Senators. The Tigers went to Cleveland and dropped two games to the Indians, then returned home on September 22 to begin a homestand. Newhouser was on top of his game as he defeated the St. Louis Browns, 9–0, on four hits before the approving Briggs Stadium crowd. He also contributed at the plate with a double and triple, driving in three runs. Because of a poor scheduling decision by Washington owner Clark Griffith, who rented out his stadium to the Washington Redskins, the Senators ended their season on September 23, one game behind Detroit, who still had four games remaining.

Newhouser pitched brilliantly on September 26, tossing a shutout against Cleveland in the first of two at Briggs Stadium. He gave up seven hits, walked four, and struck out ten as Detroit won, 11–0. Once again Newhouser helped himself at the plate, collecting two doubles and a single and scoring two runs. He was a good hitting pitcher during the final two wartime seasons, batting .242 in 1944 and .257 in 109 at-bats in 1945.

The Indians threatened in the ninth and loaded the bases with no outs. Prince Hal reached back and struck out catcher Frankie Hayes for the first out. Then stepping into the batter's box was Elmer Weingartner, who was playing in what would be his only big league season in 1945. The hometown kid, who was born in Cleveland in 1918, batted .231 in 39 at-bats on the season. He batted right-handed and played twenty games at shortstop. Weingartner was a busher who was fortunate to have this opportunity. In his short major league stint he struck out eleven times in those 39 at-bats and had nine hits. On September 26, as he awaited Newhouser's delivery in the ninth inning, he had already collected one hit on the day, so he must have felt at least some confidence at the dish. But Weingartner hit into a double play and Newhouser's shutout was preserved. The first-game victory assured the Tigers of at least a tie with Washington, but they failed to clinch the pennant as they dropped the second game, 3–2.

For those historians and statisticians who are critical of Newhouser's wartime accomplishments and use it as a reason to argue that he was undeserving of his 1992 induction into the Hall of Fame, they may point to a game such as September 26, 1945, when Newhouser faced a Cleveland Indians batting order that may have had trouble being competitive in the International League in the prewar and postwar era. But Cleveland wasn't the doormat of the American League as Philadelphia was; in fact, after their two games on the 26th, they were in fifth place, ten games behind first-place Detroit, and two games over .500 at 73–71. Their lineup on September 26 in the first game of the doubleheader was as follows:

11. Hammerin' Hank and the World Champion Tigers

- Batting First — Dutch Meyer, 2B — Before the first wartime season in 1942, Meyer had played in a total of 70 big league games for the Chicago Cubs and Detroit Tigers. He batted .259 in 58 at-bats for Detroit in 1940 and then hit .190 in 153 at-bats in 1941. In 1942 he improved to .327 but batted only 52 times. He didn't play big league ball in 1943 and 1944, returning in 1945 and batting .292 in 524 at-bats for Cleveland. This was his only season as an everyday player in the majors and he hit seven of his ten career home runs. With everyone back in 1946 and the game once again operating under normal conditions, Meyer managed only a .232 batting average in 207 at-bats for Cleveland. It was his final big league season as he finished his six-year career with a .264 batting average. Before and after the war in 1940, 1941 and 1946 he compiled batting averages of .259, .190, and .232 which were each below his lifetime mark. Furthermore, his batting average dropped 60 points from 1945 to 1946.
- Batting Second — Mickey Rocco, 1B — He began his career in 1943 batting .240 and then hit .266 and .264 the following two seasons. In 1946 he hit for a .245 mark in 98 at-bats and subsequently never played another major league season. Rocco had the capability to hit for power, smacking a career-high 13 homers in 1944 and 10 in 1945. Like many wartime players, the left-handed batter, who was born Michael Dominick Rocco in St. Paul, Minnesota, on March 2, 1916, did not get much of an opportunity to show what he was capable of doing after the war.
- Batting Third — Jeff Heath, LF — Heath gave the Indians their second left-handed hitting slugger in their lineup and he was a legitimate major league player before the war. He broke in with Cleveland in 1936 and batted .341 in 41 at-bats and then hit .230 the following year, getting twenty more at-bats than in 1936. In 1938 the Indians finished in third place with an 86–66 record and Heath had his breakout season, batting .343 with 31 doubles, 18 triples, 21 homers, 104 runs scored and 112 RBIs. He led the majors in triples in 1938 and 1941 (20). His 1941 season was also great, hitting at a .340 clip with 32 doubles, 20 triples, 24 homers and a career-high 123 RBIs. During his four wartime seasons with Cleveland he batted .278, .274, .331, and .305. In 1946 he played for the Senators and Browns and held his own with a .278 batting average, 16 homers, and 84 RBIs in 482 at-bats. He batted .251 for the Browns in 1947; .319 for the Boston Braves in 1948; and then completed his career in 1949 with Boston by batting .306 in 111 at-bats. His lifetime batting average after fourteen seasons stood at .293 and his on-base percentage was .370. He hit 279 doubles, 102 triples and 194 homers. He was the only player in the Indians lineup on September 26 who was a true star under normal conditions.

- Batting Fourth — Les Fleming, RF — Batting cleanup was another left-handed hitter, Les Fleming. He started his big league career by playing eight games with Detroit in 1939 and then played two for Cleveland during the last prewar season in 1941. In 1942 he earned an everyday job, playing in every game for the Indians and batting .292 with 27 two-base hits, 14 homers and 82 RBIs. Fleming's impressive .412 on-base percentage was good enough to finish fourth in the American League. The 5'10", 185-pound first baseman drew 106 walks during the campaign and led the league in fielding percentage at his position. He didn't play in the majors during the next two years and returned to Cleveland in 1945, batting .329 in 140 at-bats while playing most of his games in right field. After the war he was thirty years old and hit .278 in 1946 and then .242 in 1947. He played briefly for the 1949 Pittsburgh Pirates and his career ended with a .277 lifetime batting average.
- Batting Fifth — Don Ross, 3B — Ross batted .260 for the Tigers in 265 at-bats in 1938 and then returned to the majors with Brooklyn in 1940, playing in ten games and hitting .289. He was with Detroit for the first three wartime seasons and batted .274, .267, and .210 in a moderate number of plate appearances. He began the 1945 campaign with Detroit and then was traded to Cleveland, where he hit .262. Ross lacked the ability to hit for power and hit a career high of three homers in both 1942 and 1946. He connected for twelve homers in his seven-year career. Just like Meyer and Rocco he played briefly in 1946 (.268 in 153 at-bats) and then his major league career was over.
- Batting Sixth — Pat Seerey, CF — He gave the Indians another power bat in their lineup, but unlike some of the other sluggers on the Tribe's roster he batted right-handed. During his seven-year career he played each outfield position for at least 100 games. He played left field the most often (291 games). Seerey could never hit for a good average during or after the war. But he could hit home runs and accumulated large numbers of strikeouts in his pursuit of the coveted long ball. He broke in with Cleveland in 1943, batting .222 in 72 at-bats and 26 games. The following year he batted .234 with 15 homers and 99 strikeouts in 342 at-bats. In 1945 at the age of twenty-two he managed only a .237 batting average but slugged 14 of Cleveland's 65 homers on the season. The Indians finished third in the American League in homers during the final World War II season. He also fanned 97 times that year. Seerey had his best season in 1946, batting only .225 but with 26 homers and 62 RBIs while striking out 101 times. In 1947 he hit only .171 but with 11 homers in 216 at-bats. He played briefly for the Indians in 1948 before being traded to the Chicago White Sox and hit a combined 19 homers on the year with a .231 average. Again he struck

out over a hundred times (102). He played four games for Chicago's American League representative in 1949 and his big league career was over at the age of twenty-six. Seerey was consistent throughout his career: a consistently poor average hitter but with the ability to hit for power, though he would accumulate large numbers of strikeouts.

- Batting Seventh — Frankie Hayes, C — In 1933 the Philadelphia Athletics finished in third place in the junior league with a 79–72 record. Hayes played three games for the Athletics that season and then batted .226 in 92 games and 248 at-bats during the 1934 campaign. By 1936 he was manager Connie Mack's starting catcher, batting .271 and hitting 10 homers. It was the first of six consecutive seasons he would hit at least ten round-trippers for Philadelphia. His career high in homers and RBI was in 1939 when he hit .283 with 20 long balls and drove in 83. In 1940 he compiled his best batting average at .308 with 16 homers and 70 RBIs in 465 at-bats. He split the 1942 season with the Philadelphia Athletics and the St. Louis Browns, batting only .248 with 2 homers in 222 at-bats. In 1943 his batting average dropped to .188 but in 1944, back with the Athletics, he hit for a .248 clip with 13 homers and 78 driven in while playing in all of his team's games. After beginning the 1945 campaign with the Athletics he was traded to Cleveland on May 29 for catcher Buddy Rosar and hit a combined .234 on the season, which was well below his .259 career batting average. Even though Hayes was only thirty years old in 1945 he was on the downside of his career. Perhaps the beating he took wearing the tools of ignorance led to his swift decline. In 1946 with the Indians and White Sox he managed only a .233 average in 335 at-bats. His fourteen-year career concluded with five games for the Boston Red Sox in 1947. If it wasn't for the war Hayes's major league career may have ended much sooner or he would have been a backup instead of a starter.

Major league teams were desperately trying to find capable catchers during the war. Those backstops like Hayes who had any talent whatsoever were expected to play every day and were worn out as a result. From the final day of the 1943 season with the Browns until April of 1946, Hayes caught every game and put together a streak of 312 consecutive games. His 155 games caught in 1944 is tied for second all-time for the most games caught in a season by a catcher, despite the fact that modern-day catchers have the longer 162-game schedule to surpass his mark. Ray Mueller of the Cincinnati Reds also caught 155 games that season. In 1945 Hayes caught 151 games for Philadelphia and Cleveland. He participated in 29 double plays that year, which ranks second on the all-time list for catchers behind Steve O'Neill's 36 double plays in 1916. During a time when catchers did not have the luxuries of the modern-day player, Hayes's durability was truly impressive.

- Batting Eighth — Elmer Weingartner, SS — His major league career consisted of those 20 games he played for Cleveland in 1945.
- Batting Ninth — Allie Reynolds, P — Reynolds put together an excellent 18–12 record in 1945 but unlike Newhouser was unable to produce at the plate, batting .094.

There were six players (Meyer, Rocco, Fleming, Ross, Seerey, and Weingartner) in Cleveland's lineup on September 26 who either never played before or after the war, were backup players during normal times and did not perform well, or in the case of Fleming was a respectable big leaguer at best. Seerey secured a spot on a major league roster in 1946 because of his power: his 26 home runs ranked fourth in the American League that season. But he also had major shortcomings such as his weak batting average and large number of strikeouts. Hayes's offensive numbers had begun to decline during the war even before the consecutive-games streak. If they had not been playing under wartime conditions his playing time would most likely have been curtailed. He played in 47 fewer games in 1946 than the previous year and his career ended in 1947 after only five games. Jeff Heath was the one player who could have been a star under normal conditions. Although his offensive numbers were still strong his body was beginning to hold him back: he played in only 60 games in 1944 and then 102 games in 1945 because of injuries.

The Cleveland Indians lineup was representative of the caliber of talent a pitcher had to face during that final wartime season. Under normal conditions most of those players were at best marginal big leaguers and some were very bad. Hayes was approaching the end of his career and Heath's body was breaking down. It was because of playing against these weak lineups that Donald Honig characterized Newhouser's 1944 season as "a lion with a carcass." He wrote about his 1945 campaign: "Again, he was a flashlight in a roomful of glittering candles."[13]

After failing to win the nightcap on the 26th and clinch the pennant, the Tigers traveled to St. Louis to play the final two games of the 1945 season. The Tigers limped into town after losing five of their last seven games and needed to win one of the two games against the third-place Browns at Sportsman's Park to clinch the pennant. If they suffered two setbacks then a playoff game would be necessary against the Senators at Briggs Stadium on October 1. O'Neill considered leaving Newhouser in Detroit so that he would be well rested for the playoff. But after much deliberation he decided that Newhouser had earned the right to participate in the celebration if they won. Additionally, Newhouser may be needed in the series and Detroit didn't want to face a well-rested Senators team. Throughout Detroit, in the bars, restaurants, and on the streets, people were more concerned about who was going to pitch against the Browns than about the strike in the oil industry which had affected the residents of the city. The Tigers' stretch run had allowed residents of the city to temporarily

11. Hammerin' Hank and the World Champion Tigers

forget about the labor disputes. There was a consensus among the populace that the Tigers would drop the first game on Saturday and then hope that Newhouser could go on Sunday and shut the door. However, if Newhouser answered the bell on Sunday he may not be able to pitch in the one-game playoff. There was certainly much for O'Neill to consider as they prepared for those final two games. Adding to the tension was a scheduling conflict: Detroit had planned to arrive in St. Louis on September 27, and after a good night's rest they would have a day off on the 28th to prepare for the series. But the Cleveland Indians, who were rained out in St. Louis on the 27th, were still staying at their hotel and played the following day as well. Therefore, Detroit could not check in until the 28th.

O'Neill was unsure who was going to pitch on Saturday and kept changing his mind. He said he would probably start Stubby Overmire. He surmised that right-handed hurlers Dizzy Trout and Al Benton might have trouble against Washington's left-handed hitters. Furthermore, Trout had been inconsistent lately and Benton had a swollen ankle, the same ankle that was reportedly broken early in the season. Except for Newhouser, O'Neill didn't have much confidence in his starting pitchers, and this was exemplified when he chose a man to pitch on Saturday who had not pitched in a major league game all season. In fact, he had not pitched since 1943 when he went 16–10 for Detroit. Virgil Trucks, who had recently been discharged by the Navy, was selected to start this critical game. While in the Navy, Trucks stayed in playing shape while stationed in Guam and accompanied a group of major leaguers around the islands in the South Pacific to entertain the troops with their ball-playing skills.

Hal Newhouser would earn inclusion into the Hall of Fame with a 207–150 lifetime record with 70 of those wins coming from 1942 to 1945. Trucks would finish his career with a 177–135 mark, and if he had not missed the 1944 season and all but one game in 1945 he would certainly have finished with over 200 wins and a record comparable to Newhouser's. Furthermore, consider that fellow pitchers Dizzy Trout and Newhouser improved considerably as the war progressed. Trout won 12 games in 1942 and then won 20 and 27 the next two seasons. In 1945 he had an 18-15 mark. Newhouser won 8 games during each of the first two wartime seasons and then won 29 and 25 during the final two wartime seasons. Trucks was 16–10 in 1943 and if he had pitched in the major leagues for a full season in 1944 and 1945 it is reasonable to assume that he would have won twenty games during each season. Trucks's career record may have been augmented even more if he hadn't had a drinking problem. Bob Cain said, "He drank quite a bit off and on, and I think that hurt his pitching." Trucks was not afraid to throw at a batter and sometimes the only motivation he needed to do so was if a batter got a hit. Ted Williams, for example, once got a hit off Trucks in Detroit, and the spirited right-hander nicknamed "Fire" told his teammates that Williams was going to get hit in the face the next time he came to bat. He didn't hit him between the eyes as he had predicted, but in the back.

Manager O'Neill pulled him from the game and an argument developed between the two men.[14] In 1952 Trucks finished with a 5–19 record for a Tigers team that finished in last place with a 50–104 mark. Two of his five victories were no-hitters which he tossed on May 15 and August 25. Collectively Trucks, Newhouser, and Trout were known as "TNT."[15]

The plans laid out by the Tigers were complicated even more on Saturday, September 29, when rain fell in St. Louis and postponed the game. A doubleheader was scheduled on the following day with the bleak realization for the Senators that a cancellation would give the flag to Detroit. League rules stipulated that games that were not played within the allocated time for the scheduled season were not made up; therefore if there was inclement weather on Sunday it would force a cancellation, not a postponement, and would mean that the Tigers had won the pennant.

The rain was still hovering around Sportsman's Park on September 30. The first game was set to commence at 12:30 central time but it began to rain at noon, forcing the game to begin an hour late. Starting pitchers Trucks and Nelson Potter warmed up three times before the game finally started. The groundskeeper and grounds crew earned their paychecks to get the field in playable condition. This game came down to the ninth inning when, trailing 3–2, Detroit rallied for four runs and secured the pennant with a 6–3 win. Trucks pitched well, yielding only one run in five and one-thirds innings, and during one stretch retiring fifteen consecutive batters. After giving up a double to Potter and surrendering a walk to Don Gutteridge in the sixth, Newhouser was given the call, and replaced Trucks on the bump. Then the Tigers ace walked Lou Finney on four pitches to load the bases. St. Louis's manager Luke Sewell then decided to lift the left-handed hitting Milt Byrnes for the right-handed hitting Mark Christman. Newhouser reached back and struck out the pinch-hitter. But George McQuinn followed with a prodigious drive into right center, and with the base runners vigorously rounding the bases as the ball hovered in the air, three runs were certain to score if the ball fell onto the earth. Doc Cramer, Detroit's center fielder, was able to track it down, catch the ball, and end the rally. Newhouser gave up the tying run in the seventh as the Browns knotted the game at two and then gave up another run in the eighth.

O'Neill decided that Newhouser, with his .257 batting average, needed to be pinched-hit for in the top of the ninth. His choice was Hub Walker, who before the 1945 campaign had not played in the big leagues since 1937 with the Cincinnati Reds. The five-foot, ten-and-a-half-inch, 175-pound left-handed hitter was 2 for 22 on the season, which translated into a .091 batting average. However, Walker came through with a single, increasing his final average to .130, and Red Borom would pinch run. Borom's major league career consisted of 7 games with Detroit in 1944, and then he batted .269 in 130 at-bats for the 1945 squad. Skeeter Webb bunted and Potter tried to get the lead runner at second but they were both safe. When Eddie Mayo followed with another bunt,

Potter played it safe and took the out at first. Cramer was walked intentionally to set up the double play, and then Hank Greenberg stepped into the box. With the count at 1 and 0, Greenberg smashed the ball down the left field line. It crashed into the bleachers just inside the foul pole for a grand slam homer. Al Benton pitched a scoreless bottom of the ninth to secure the pennant for Detroit. The players celebrated, but then such activities had to cease as they prepared for the second game. But now it was getting dark and it had begun to rain hard once again, and after a half inning the umpires decided to cancel this meaningless affair. O'Neill said regarding the day's games that he had never seen a game started under worse conditions.[16] The Tigers finished the season with an 88–65 record and had the lowest winning percentage (.575) for a pennant-winning ball club in major league history.

Newhouser's performance down the stretch in 1945 was courageous, inspirational, and heroic. Not only did he pitch in great pain with injuries to his shoulder and back, but the newspaper men often questioned his courage. They appeared to side with the medical community who could find nothing wrong with his shoulder, implying that Newhouser's problem was in his head and there wasn't anything the matter with him except, perhaps, an inability to handle the pressure of the pennant race. He had control problems early in his career but once his control improved, so did his record. He was a fierce competitor who hated to give up a hit at a critical juncture of a ball game. Al Rosen recalled getting a hit off Newhouser in 1950 and then being harassed as he rounded the bases with Newhouser following him with a menacing demeanor, calling him every curse word that came to mind.[17] Newhouser was Minnie Minoso's "idol," but this all changed when he hit a home run off him in the early 1950s: he was purposefully hit in the pocket his next time up. The impact of the ball hitting his pocket shattered his sunglasses. As Minoso made his way down to first, Newhouser let him have it with a verbal tirade.[18] Newhouser's temper was legendary and when he pitched he didn't want his teammates to joke around. He was all business out on the bump. When he wasn't verbally harassing batters who hit the long ball against him, he would just stare them down if they were fortunate enough to take Newhouser deep. On the mound, he would change speeds well, throw a blazing fastball and a hard curve. His pitching motion was aesthetically pleasing for many who witnessed him pitch. Dave Ferriss, who was a rookie for the Boston Red Sox in 1945, said he "had a smooth and stylish motion."[19] From 1946 to 1950 Newhouser won 26, 17, 21, 18, and 15 games. Beginning with the 1951 season his numbers began to decline, but he finished his career with four twenty-win seasons, two of which came during the war. In 1944 (29), 1945 (25), 1946 (26), and in 1948 (21) he led the American League in wins. He led the major leagues in strikeouts in both 1944 (187) and 1945 (212). His career high of 275 strikeouts in 1946 ranked second behind Cleveland's Bob Feller (348). The National League strikeout leader in 1946 was Johnny Schmitz of the Chicago Cubs, who only had 135.

Regardless of whether someone believes that Newhouser was worthy or unworthy of his 1992 Hall of Fame induction, there is no question that his performance during those final two wartime seasons is the reason why he has a permanent place in that hallowed institution. There are several players such as Hank Greenberg, Joe DiMaggio, Bob Feller, and Ted Williams who played no more than one wartime season and still earned their way into the Hall of Fame. Newhouser was a 4-F because of a heart ailment, and if he had not played during the 1944 and 1945 seasons he certainly would not have received serious consideration for the Hall of Fame. And it also should be considered that, even though the game returned to normal in 1946 because those who served in the military during some or all of the previous four seasons returned to the game, offensive numbers did not immediately return to prewar standards. This had to do with the fact that many of the returning vets had not played under major league conditions in several years and therefore their timing was off. In 1941 the American League's collective ERA was 4.15 and 5,902 runs were scored in the junior circuit. Then, of course, scoring plummeted during the war because of the poor quality of the baseballs and the poor quality of players around the majors. In 1946 the American League had a collective 3.50 ERA and there were 5,037 runs scored, which were both significantly below prewar standards. During the 1947 season the AL had a 3.71 ERA and 5,161 runs scored, and then in 1948 there was a significant jump as the junior league scored 5,841 runs and had a 4.29 ERA.

Paul Howard "Dizzy" Trout was a colorful pitcher who teamed up with Newhouser to give the Tigers a great pair of starting pitchers during the war. He was 20–12 with a 2.48 ERA in 1943 and in 1944 was 27–14 with a major league-leading 2.12 ERA. Trout led the majors that year with three hundred fifty-two and one-third innings pitched. He also led the junior circuit in games started (40); complete games (33); and shutouts (7). In 1945 he was 18–15 with a 3.14 ERA. As the Tigers were fighting for a pennant down the stretch, Trout also played a critical role in securing the flag. During one stretch he pitched in six games in nine days and won four of those games. At the plate Trout was anything but an automatic out and was one of several Tigers pitchers who knew how to handle the bat. In 1944 he hit .271 with 5 homers in 133 at-bats and then batted .245 with 2 homers the following year. On May 30, 1944, he connected for a game-ending home run against the Yankees in the first game of a twin bill. He connected for twenty homers in his career and only ten pitchers have hit more in major league history. Red Embree and Bob Muncrief each served up two gopher balls to Trout during his career. In his fifteen-year career on the hill, Trout compiled a 170–161 lifetime record with a 3.23 ERA. He spent most of his career with the Tigers from 1939 to 1952 and also pitched for the Boston Red Sox during the 1952 campaign before retiring. However, five years later he pitched so well in an Old-Timers game that he was signed by the Baltimore Orioles and pitched in two games for them in 1957. Trout threw very hard and like his teammates Newhouser and Trucks he would knock a guy down if they got a hit off him. Bob Cain said he was among the "meanest pitchers" in the game.[20] However, while Newhouser was loathed by many of his teammates for being inappropriately critical, too serious, and moody, Trout was an affable personality off the field who was well liked. His son Steve would also grow up to become a big league hurler.

Stubby Overmire contributed a 9–9 record and a 3.88 ERA in his third major league season, while Les Mueller was 6–8 with a 3.68 ERA. In August, Tommy Bridges returned to the Tigers after nearly two years in the Army. Bridges, who had a great big league career with a 194–138 record, appeared in four games and was 1–0 in 1945. The five-foot-ten-and-a-half-inch, 155-pound right-handed pitcher played his entire career with the Tigers from 1930 to 1943, and then after completing his military service pitched a total of only thirteen games in 1945 and 1946 before his illustrious career ended. For nine consecutive seasons from 1932 to 1940 he won at least twelve games, including three consecutive twenty-win seasons from 1934 to 1936 when he won 22, 21, and 23 games. Bridges played an important role on the pennant-winning 1934, 1935, and 1940 teams, and the Tigers won the World Series in 1935, defeating Chicago, four games to two. He had four victories in World Series competition and pitched well in each series. The Tigers heard that Bridges was joining the squad after they had dropped three games to Cleveland and they found the news to be encouraging. Bridges had the rank of sergeant in the Army; when released he was serving at Ft. Meade, Maryland, and had reportedly kept in shape by pitching for a service team. Joe Judge, a Washington Senators coach, had witnessed one of his games before he was released and believed he was throwing just as hard as he had in 1943 when he compiled a 12–7 record and a 2.39 ERA. Doc Cramer believed that Bridges' presence would help Detroit secure the pennant. Steve O'Neill was hopeful that he would make a contribution to the club. He felt they were fortunate to have his services for the stretch drive and said he would most likely be used in relief until he became comfortable with his surroundings.[21] However, Bridges was used sparingly, starting only one game and relieving in three.

He was born Thomas Jefferson Davis Bridges in Gordonsville, Tennessee, on December 28, 1906, and died in Nashville on April 19, 1968. Bridges was on the wrong side of thirty in 1945 and his best mound performances were in the past. In 1946 he posted a 1–1 record with a 5.91 ERA in nine games. Despite the fact that no big league club wanted his services after the first postwar campaign, he continued to pitch in the minors, posting a 33–25 record for Portland in the Pacific Coast League from 1947 to 1949. In 1950 he appeared in a total of eleven games for PCL teams San Francisco and Seattle, and then he became a scout for several major league teams: the Cincinnati Reds (1951), Detroit Tigers (1958–1960), and New York Mets (1963–1968). Bridges was a graduate of the University of Tennessee.

Also returning to the team after two years in the service was an imposing six-foot-four-inch, 215-pound right-hander named Al Benton. He was 13–8 with a 2.02 ERA in 1945. He won his first five starts, giving up one earned run and 22 hits in 45 innings. Benton joined the Navy in the fall of 1942 and got the opportunity to sharpen his pitching skills with a service team. He was the athletic director at the Naval Air Station in Norman, Oklahoma, where in two seasons he compiled a 27–9 record. George Halas, owner of the Chicago Bears, was also at the station before being sent overseas. Benton insisted that the amount of mound work he received while in the Navy was almost as much as he would have received if he had been pitching for the Tigers. Additionally, the competition he faced in the Navy was very impressive. He developed good control in the service, which he had previously been lacking. Early in his career Connie Mack soured on Benton and said he would not develop into a good major league pitcher. During his two years in Philadelphia (1934 and 1935) the only pitch he threw was a fastball, and it was just an average fastball. In 1938 he was sent to Detroit and soon developed a curve and what was his best pitch, the slider. Benton was Detroit's closer during their 1940 pennant-winning season, going 6–10 with a 4.42 ERA, and it was later calculated that he had seventeen saves. He worked all forty-two games he appeared in as a relief pitcher. However, he disdained relief duty and the uncertainty that came with it, such as having to begin warming up when the starter got into a jam and then having to cool down when the call to the bullpen never materialized. He characterized relief pitching as a "thankless job."[22] He persuaded his skipper to start him the following season as he went 15–6, starting 14 of his 38 games. In 1945 he started 27 of his 31 games.

Early in his professional career, while pitching for Oklahoma City in 1932, he earned a reputation as an iron man, working 21 innings over the course of three consecutive days and winning all three games. On the third day he worked six and two-third innings in relief, yielding only one hit and giving up no runs. Benton's biggest thrill in baseball as of 1945 was when he had two sacrifice bunts in an 11-run third inning on August 6, 1941, against Cleveland.[23] This wasn't all that surprising, in that he cherished each hit he received in the big leagues; despite being a bad hitter he desperately wanted to improve and to be known for his hitting prowess. In 1945 he batted .063 in 63 at-bats, which was not that far removed from his career .098 batting average. He spent his entire major league career in the American League, pitching for Philadelphia, Detroit, Cleveland, and Boston. His big league career spanned from 1934 to 1952; however, he didn't play during five major league seasons in that time period. After he posted a 4–3 record and a 2.39 ERA in 24 relief appearances for Boston in 1952 his career was over. He had a 98–88 record and a 3.66 ERA in his fourteen-year career.

After going 9–14 with the Boston Braves in 1945, Jim Tobin was traded to the Tigers in August and went 4–5 with a 3.55 ERA in his 14 games with Detroit.

Those fourteen games with the Tigers at the tail end of the final World War II season were the last big league games he ever pitched, as he finished his nine-year career with a 105–112 record. During his first year under the big tent he played for manager Pie Traynor's 1937 Pittsburgh Pirates, who finished in third place with an 86–68 conclusion. Tobin appeared in twenty games that season and compiled a 6–3 record. From 1937 to 1939 with Pittsburgh he compiled a collective 29–24 record during those three seasons before being traded to the Boston Braves. He hurt his arm in 1939 and decided that he needed to develop a new pitch. He had been experimenting with the knuckleball for years but didn't unveil it to National League hitters until 1940. The knuckleball works best when thrown into the wind so that the ball meets resistance as it tumbles to the plate. The knuckleball also works well at night and Tobin insisted that it is most effective during the nocturnal contests when the air is "heavy" and "the ball cuts up."[24]

The six-foot, 185-pound right-handed pitcher did not enjoy most of his six seasons in Boston, and when traded to the Tigers said he was "Happy and contented, at last!" He was unsatisfied and distraught about playing for Boston's National League club. Even if he pitched a great game he had a good chance of being saddled with the loss because his supporting cast was bad. In 1942, while pitching for a Braves team that finished in seventh place with a 59–89 record, Tobin was 12–21 and led the senior circuit in complete games (28) and innings pitched (287.2). In 1944 the Braves were a sixth-place outfit (65–89) as Tobin went 18–19 with a 3.01 ERA and led the circuit in complete games (28) for the second time in his career. With that much losing, "Life becomes futile," said Tobin. He tried to persuade the Boston front office to trade him but was unsuccessful for some time. There was tension and hostility between Tobin and the Braves front office. On August 9, 1945, John Quinn, the general manager, and Lou Perini, the owner, felt that they had to confront Tobin. They called him up and informed Tobin that he was the head of an "injurious mob" of about six players whose actions were hurting the team. John Quinn said that Tobin was a cancer on the team and did not care about the predicament of the ball club. Tobin thought the team made him the "goat," perhaps to divert attention away from the poor decisions of the front office and the poor performance of the team. Tobin did not take the rebuke without responding, and he told Quinn and Perini what he thought about them and their miserable ball club. Shortly after his falling-out with Braves management Tobin was sent packing to Detroit. With Boston he played before miniscule crowds. Like any pitcher, Tobin felt he needed offensive support to be successful, for his defense to turn double plays and for fly balls to be "caught occasionally." He was overjoyed that he now belonged to a club like Detroit that had strong defense, power hitting, and an excellent group of starting pitchers.[25]

On April 27, 1944, only 1,447 fans bothered to show up at Braves Field but that small contingent of loyal supporters watched Tobin pitch a no-hitter against Brooklyn. Like his teammate Dizzy Trout, Tobin was a threat to go deep while standing in the batter's box with a bat in his hand. He hit seventeen homers (16 as a pitcher) in his career: in 1942 he hit a career-high six homers while batting .246, and in 1945 he hit five, three with Boston and two with Detroit. On May 13, 1942, he became only the second pitcher in major league history to hit three home runs in one game, achieving the feat against the Chicago Cubs. He played a few games at first base for Boston in 1943 and also was used as a pinch-hitter. His brother John Patrick Tobin played for the Boston Red Sox during the 1945 season. It was his only opportunity to play in the big leagues during his professional career, batting .252 in 278 at-bats and playing most of his games at third base.

After Tobin was traded to Detroit he talked about the differences between the two leagues and the adjustment he had to make going over to the junior circuit after spending nine seasons in the senior league. He insisted that the American League had more power hitters and that they played more small ball in the National League, utilizing the stolen base more often. According to Tobin the National League had more hitters who were more likely to get one-base hits. Ultimately, he believed that the American League was the harder league to pitch in because of the desire to hit the long ball. Tobin said that he didn't discern any difference in the strike zone.[26] He had been in the American League for only a few weeks before making these assertions and seemed to be providing the traditional stereotypes of the two leagues.

Before the war the American League was certainly more powerful: the junior circuit collectively hit more home runs than the National League for eleven consecutive seasons from 1931 to 1941. During the seasons affected by World War II, from 1942 to 1945, the American League only led the National League in homers one time, in 1943. Furthermore, the National League led the American League in stolen bases during only one season, 1945. In 1943 the American League stole 242 more bases than the National League. During the four wartime seasons the American League stole 441 more bases than the senior league. In 1946 the American League hit more home runs and the National League stole more bases than the opposing league. The charts below show the home runs and stolen bases accumulated by each league during each wartime season.

Home runs hit in the National and American Leagues during the war:

Year	NL	AL
1942	538	533
1943	432	473
1944	575	459
1945	577	430

Stolen bases accumulated in the National and American Leagues during the war:

11. Hammerin' Hank and the World Champion Tigers

Year	NL	AL
1942	423	538
1943	384	626
1944	381	539
1945	527	453

The Tigers played their home games in Briggs Stadium at the corner of Michigan and Trumbull Avenues. Briggs Stadium, which was later called Tiger Stadium, was an intimate park with a signature upper-deck overhang. Briggs Stadium was known to have the best clubhouse accommodations for both the home and visiting teams. In 1945 the Tigers fans not only enjoyed their first-class ballpark but also a world championship team.

❖ 12 ❖

War Heroes, Knuckleballers, and a Spy

There were several former and current Washington Senators who made significant contributions in helping to win World War II. Moe Berg, former ballplayer, intellectual, and spy, contributed heavily to the Allied efforts. He graduated from Princeton in 1923 and later during his major league career he earned a law degree from Columbia. He made his big league debut with Brooklyn in 1923, batting .186 in 129 at-bats and playing shortstop. Then from 1926 to 1939 he played with the White Sox, Indians, Senators, and Red Sox and was predominantly a weak-hitting backup catcher. In a fifteen-year career he only played in 663 games and batted .243 with six homers. Players around the league said he was the "guy who could speak nine languages and couldn't hit a curve ball in any of them."[1] In 1934 he was in Tokyo with a group of major league All-Stars that included Babe Ruth, Lou Gehrig, and Jimmie Foxx. There he went to St. Luke's International Hospital, said he was visiting a patient, and went up to the roof, where he took photographs of military, industrial, and transportation installations.

Things didn't go well for the U.S. early in the war. Then on April 18, 1942, the United States struck the Japanese mainland when Major General James Doolittle led sixteen bombers in a raid of Japanese cities, including Tokyo. This gave a great morale boost to the country and its Allies. Later it was discovered that Berg's pictures had been used in the Doolittle raid to identify targets. Additionally, when the United States began to bomb Japanese cities with B-29s during the final few months of the war, Berg's films were also extremely helpful.

Berg was a savant, spoke at least eight languages, and voraciously devoured the newspapers in pursuit of more knowledge. When he played with the Washington Senators he kept a tuxedo in his locker because he was often invited to banquets and receptions. President Roosevelt looked for him when he attended a game at Griffith Stadium, and postmaster general Jim Farley pointed him out. Berg later joined the Office of Strategic Services and during the war gave radio broadcasts to the Japanese in their own language warning them what the U.S.

12. War Heroes, Knuckleballers, and a Spy

would do if the war progressed much further. He was sent to Germany to ascertain how far the Nazis had progressed in the development of the atomic bomb. Disguised as a Swiss graduate student, he was there under the pretext of touring the facility and receiving a lecture. In front of him stood Werner Heisenberg, who was thought to be Adolf Hitler's best-known and most influential atomic physicist. Moe had a gun under his coat and a cyanide pill to be used on himself if he killed the physicist. Berg was ordered to use the gun only if he concluded that the physicist's statements indicated he was helping Hitler develop an atomic bomb. However, Moe observed that this was not the case. Berg also parachuted behind German lines several times during the war to gather information.[2]

Before going off to war Buddy Lewis batted .291 or better in every full season he played in since starting his career in 1935. His best years were in 1937, 1939, and 1940, when he batted .314, .319, and .317 respectively. Lewis thought he should have been deferred because he was supporting his two parents, but he was not. He joined the Air Corps and would fly three hundred cargo missions in the China-Burma-India theater in a C-47. Buddy was honored with the Distinguished Flying Cross and Air Medal.

The way he left for the service was memorable. He had flown from Georgia to Washington and visited his teammates in his uniform at Griffith Stadium. Lewis informed them that he would give them a farewell salute they'd never forget. In the second game of a doubleheader in June of 1943 his DC-3 swooped in low from center field. He tipped his wing and almost hit the flagpole before leaving the ballpark. His teammates were overjoyed. George Case, who was in the batter's box, stepped out and threw his bat in the air, returning the salute.[3]

When he returned to the Senators in 1945, manager Ossie Bluege insisted that Lewis solved one of the problem areas of the ball club: an outfielder that can hit and could bat in the important third spot in the lineup.[4] Lewis hit his stride right away. Despite being hobbled by a charley horse when he was discharged, Lewis played in an exhibition game for Washington on July 26 against the New London, Connecticut, naval baseball team, and connected for a homer in his first at-bat. During his first at-bat in a junior league game, the pitcher stormed off the mound when two obvious strikes were called balls by the home-plate umpire. The umpire informed the hurler that he wasn't going to throw a strike to Lewis in his first at-bat back from the service. In Bill Gilbert's superb history of World War II baseball titled *They Also Served: Baseball and the Home Front, 1941–1945*, Lewis recalls that his first game back was in Chicago against Earl Caldwell with umpire Bill McGowan behind the plate.[5] However, Lewis's memory was off just a bit because his first game back was in Boston on July 27 as he went 0 for 2 and had two walks against Dave Ferriss. Although he failed to get a hit, Lewis hit the ball hard during his two outs. McGowan was one of the four umpires for the game. Washington won the contest, 3–1, and Ferriss's record fell to 17–3.

The trainer would give Lewis rubdowns to sooth his cold back but despite his ailments Lewis remained in the lineup down the stretch and gave the Senators the offensive production that was desperately needed. He regained his hitting stride right away in 1945, batting .333 for Washington in 69 games and 258 at-bats. He played three more seasons, finishing his eleven-year career with a .297 average. During Lewis's first five seasons in the big leagues from 1935 to 1939 he played third base but beginning in 1940 he was predominantly a right fielder. He batted left-handed but threw right-handed and stood at six feet one inch, and 175 pounds.

Before the war Cecil Travis had batted .302 or better in eight of his nine big league seasons. He batted .344 in 1937; .335 in 1938; and .359 in 1941 with a major league-leading 218 hits. Cecil returned in 1945 after serving over three years in the Army but never again regained his hitting skills. He batted .241 for Washington in 15 games; in 1946 he batted .252 in 137 games; and in his final season, 1947, he batted .216 in 74 games. About nine months before he rejoined the Senators he was with the Army's 76th Division at Bastogne in the Ardennes supporting the front line against a massive German offensive. The 101st Airborne figured most prominently in the defense and the Germans demanded the Americans surrender, but General Anthony McAuliffe replied by simply saying, "Nuts!"[6] Many of the troops were stranded in Bastogne for several weeks before reinforcements arrived. Travis's division provided relief near the end of the battle and then pursued the enemy into Germany. However, because of the bad condition of his frostbitten toes, he spent several weeks in a hospital in France before rejoining his unit. At Bastogne they tried to keep warm in the snow-covered earth, but all they could do was incessantly shake, particularly at night when they would freeze as the temperature dropped. There were no dry socks and not enough of the necessary equipment to go around. General George S. Patton visited his division one day and shook hands with many of the soldiers. Cecil didn't have enough points to go home when the war in Europe had ended, but when he volunteered to fight in the Pacific, he received a thirty-day furlough. While Cecil was at home, President Truman dropped the atomic bomb and the war with Japan ended. He suffered frostbite at the Battle of the Bulge like many others and his movement was hampered as a result. The medics noticed the poor condition of Travis's feet and if they had not acted in time he may have lost them. Unlike Buddy Lewis he never again regained his baseball skills. Many said his skills abandoned him because of the frostbite he suffered, but Travis disagreed, saying that his skills diminished because he had been out of baseball for too long.[7]

The Senators conducted their training camps during the war at the University of Maryland, where the several Latin players on the team had particular trouble coping with the cold weather. Walter Haight wrote the following about the Senators 1945 camp: "Ossie Bluege, the Senators' manager, has more problems than the little boy who failed in arithmetic last term. He has the outfield problem, the infield problem, the catching problem and the pitching problem. No matter how he adds up any column, they all seem to come out uneven."[8] Stan Spence, who was their only .300 hitter (.316) in 1944, was 1-A and was soon thereafter taken into the Army, missing the entire 1945 season. George Case had a shoulder operation in the off-season which he was still recovering from. Most of the outfielders were unproven while the infield was unsteady. Washington was picked to finish towards the bottom of the American League in 1945.

The dilution of wartime talent allowed the Senators to become legitimate pennant contenders. In 1942 they finished in seventh place (62–89); in 1943 second place (84–69); in 1944 they finished in the basement (64–90); and in 1945 they were back in second place (87–67). Bucky Harris was their manager in 1942 and Ossie Bluege started managing the club in 1943. Bluege managed the Senators until 1947 and was considered a loyal organization man to owner Clark Griffith.

Early in the season the Senators were getting excellent pitching but their hitting was anemic. George Case and George Binks were the only batters producing at the plate. Shirley Povich wrote, "Thus far they've been a team with first-division pitching and a last-place batting attack!"[9] Defensively, the Senators were doing a good job. Harlond Clift, Gil Torres, George Myatt, and Joe Kuhel were among the Senators not producing at the plate. Clark Griffith was trying to purchase Jeff Heath from the Cleveland Indians to bolster the offensive attack. A power hitter like Heath would have certainly improved the lineup.

When the War Department ended its policy of drafting 4-F ballplayers and the war in Europe ended, Bluege was hoping that many of the servicemen would be discharged and join his team. One area of concern was the catching position: Rick Ferrell was the starter and was an outstanding backstop ten years earlier, but in 1945 he was 39 years old and almost at the end of his career. He caught 91 games, while backups Al Evans and Mike Guerra did not instill confidence in their manager. It appeared that catcher Jake Early, who had last played with Washington in 1943, batting .258 with 5 homers and 60 RBIs, would return to the team. He would have given the club some experience at the position: in 1941 and 1942 he caught 104 games and then caught a career-high 126 in 1943. Additionally, at thirty years old and with less wear and tear on his body than Ferrell, at worst he would be platooning at the position and perhaps starting. Early was eager to return stateside to see his two children. As a member of the infantry he participated in combat in France and Germany. He never returned to the Senators in 1945, but thereafter played four unspectacular seasons in the American League with Washington and St. Louis before his big league career ended. While he had less wear and tear on his body than Ferrell he had to deal with the psychological trauma that came from war like any other combat participant.

While the Senators did not get the services of Early in 1945 to play a position that needed to be improved upon, they did get another pitcher, Walt Masterson. In his first four seasons in the majors as a member of Washington's American League aggregation, he compiled a 14–27 record from 1939 to 1942. In 1942 he was significantly better than previous years, going 5–9 but with a respectable 3.34 ERA. Masterson witnessed the destruction at Midway and Guam. Most civilians must have thought that a serviceman's discharge was a happy time, but Masterson candidly told a reporter that the adjustment was difficult. Military service "messes up your head," said Masterson. He thought that it must be strange for people to be in close proximity to a man who did not care whether he lived or died.[10] Despite Masterson's difficult readjustment to civilian life, he pitched for Washington in 1945, going 1–2 with a 1.08 ERA in four games and twenty-five innings. Shortly after he left the Navy he found himself starting against Bob Feller on September 13 before 24,606 fans at Griffith Stadium. He pitched a masterpiece against the future Hall of Famer and led Washington to a 4–0 victory in the distance-going performance to bring the Senators within a half game of first-place Detroit. The only two Tribe hitters to get a hit off Masterson were Al Cihocki and Frankie Hayes with their one-base knocks. Washington's returning hurler allowed two additional batters to reach first via the walk. The right-handed pitcher, who was born in Philadelphia, Pennsylvania, on June 22, 1920, would pitch fourteen years in the big leagues, compiling a 78–100 record and a 4.15 ERA.

As the season progressed, the Senators were hampered by a series of injuries to key players. However, Ossie Bluege kept his team in the race with a terrific managerial job. George Case had several injuries throughout the season. George Myatt played on an injured knee. Gil Torres played shortstop on an everyday basis despite being under the close supervision of a doctor. Rick Ferrell missed time with injured hands while Joe Kuhel missed time because of a fractured rib. The bench provided excellent support and filled in adequately for the injured players. Jose Zardon and Fred Vaughn in particular did a good job. When Jake Powell was benched, he quit the team and was soon playing for the Philadelphia Phillies. With a lack of power hitting, Bluege had his team running the bases aggressively and was particularly fond of the hit-and-run. He liked to utilize the hit-and-run with a hitter at the plate who was slow-footed, this was done to avoid a double play as the runner on first made it safely to second base while the batter tried to hit the ball through one of the vacated holes, depending on whether the shortstop or second baseman was covering the bag. Bluege truly did a remarkable job of managing in 1945, and almost took an injury-laden, mediocre ball club to the top of the junior circuit. By late August, Washington fans believed their team had a chance to win their first pennant since 1933. There had been some lean years since then: from 1934 to 1944 they had finished in the first division during only two seasons (1936 and 1943). Frank O'Neill wrote that Bluege's achievement in 1945 of bringing a team that was expected to finish buried in the second division to the brink of a pennant was a "minor miracle."[11]

In 1945 Bluege knew that the team's excellent performance was also a credit to his coaches, Clyde Milan and Joe Judge. Similar to Bluege, Milan had spent his entire playing career with Washington from 1907 to 1922. He was an outfielder with terrific speed who stood at 5'9" and weighed 168 pounds, batting from the left-handed side of the batter's box. Despite not being proficient in his capability to hit home runs (17) he knew how to manufacture runs with his speed. He stole 495 bases in his career and led the major leagues in 1912 (88) and 1913 (75). As a coach with the Senators he was particularly helpful in educating George Case about the intricacies of base stealing. Milan had spent one season as Washington's manager in 1922 as the club finished in sixth place with a 69–85 record. Critics said he was "too easygoing" and he was replaced with Donie Bush the following year. Milan was a playing manager in the bushes for New Haven in the Eastern League (1924) and Memphis (1925–1926). Then, with his playing career over, he became a coach with the Senators in 1928 and 1929, and then spent eight years managing for Birmingham and Chattanooga. He returned as a coach for the Senators in 1938 and remained their coach until his unexpected death during spring training in 1953. Milan had been laboring under the spring heat for two hours, hitting fungoes to the outfielders, when suddenly he collapsed to the ground, suffering a heart attack. He was dead in two hours.[12]

Bluege's managerial talents were exemplified in the defensive adjustment that he persuaded third baseman Harlond Clift to make. Clift batted only .211 on the season in 119 games and 375 at-bats. He hit eight homers during the campaign but seven of them came in the span of eleven days during a Western trip in July. The 5'11", 180-pound right-handed batter was playing what would be his final major league season in 1945, finishing his twelve-year career with a .272 batting average and 178 home runs. Most players who had been around the game for as long as Clift had been were intransigent, set in their ways, and unwilling to take advice from the skipper. But Bluege persuaded Clift to begin playing closer to the third base line to take away potential extra base hits. Clift had a tendency in the past to play way off the third base line but Bluege persuaded him to move significantly to his right while in the field.[13] Clift spent most of his career with the St. Louis Browns from 1934 to 1943 and then was traded along with Johnny Niggeling to Washington on August 18, 1943. Before the 1944 campaign commenced Clift fell off a horse and injured his right shoulder, so he played in only twelve games that season. Don Barnes, the St. Louis Browns owner, believed Clift was damaged goods by the time he went to Washington: he was unable to perform in the clutch, and the desire to win that burned deep within a ballplayer had been beaten out of him during all those losing seasons in St. Louis.[14]

Clift's backup in 1945, Hillis Layne, was also educated on how to play the hot corner. Bluege's knowledge about defensive positioning in the infield, particularly at third base, was developed by playing the hot corner himself for most of his big league career from 1922 to 1939. He spent his entire eighteen-year career with Washington, batting .272 with 43 home runs. He played all four infield positions but was mainly a third baseman. His younger brother Otto Bluege appeared in one game for the 1932 Cincinnati Reds, and then in 1933 batted .213 in 291 at-bats while playing most of his games at shortstop for a last-place Reds outfit (58–94).

The Senators were built around speed and pitching during the final wartime season. They led the major leagues with 110 stolen bases and a 2.92 ERA. However, they only banged out 27 homers; the Chicago White Sox were the only team that was worse with 22. To put that in perspective, realize that Tommy Holmes led the National League with 28 homers. At their home ballpark, within the spacious confines of Griffith Stadium, they hit only one home run all season, and that was of the inside-the-park variety, by Joe Kuhel on September 7. In 1941 there were 734 homers in the American League but in 1945 the league hit only 430. This was partially due to the poor talent dispersed around the league but also because the balls were in such poor condition and not conducive to long-ball hitting.

Washington batted .258 as a team, which was fourth in the American League. Buddy Lewis, Joe Kuhel, George Myatt, George Binks, George Case, and Rick Ferrell led the hitters. Case was a speed merchant who led the league in stolen bases six times during his eleven-year career. Collectively, the Senators easily led the majors with 110 steals; the Boston Braves were second with 82. Case was a 4-F because of an old shoulder injury and during the winter worked at an airplane factory in Trenton, New Jersey. He said the following about playing baseball in Washington, D.C.: "We had politicians in the clubhouse all the time. When he was a senator, Happy Chandler was in the clubhouse every home stand.... And during the war, you wouldn't believe the people we had. Generals Bradley, Wainwright, Secretary of State Stettinius. Eisenhower used to come in. It was really something."[15]

Case got six hits in a doubleheader in early July against the White Sox and took the lead in the batting race with a .341 average. He admitted to Shirley Povich that he would trade in all his base-running accomplishments for a batting crown.[16] In 1942 he had come somewhat close to accomplishing his goal, batting .320 and finishing fifth in the American League in batting. However, Ted Williams, coming off his .406 batting average in 1941, then hit for a .356 clip in 1942. Several injuries would hinder Case's performance as the season moved on and he finished short of the batting crown with a .294 average. Case not only utilized his speed on the bases but many of his hits were bunts that he legged out. The third baseman hugged the line and the shortstop moved deep in the hole when the right-handed Case came to the bat because he was a dead-pull hitter. However, in 1945 that strategy wasn't working as well and Case insisted that when fielders like Lou Boudreau and Cass Michaels would play him to pull he was successfully hitting the ball through the vacated areas in the infield. For years the corner infielders, particularly the third baseman, had crept in to guard against the bunt. Case tried to hit line drives at the third basemen who came in dangerously close but for the most part he was unsuccessful.

He had been nursing a shoulder injury for several years before finally having surgery at Johns Hopkins Hospital before the 1945 season. The shoulder was the reason why he was a 4-F; it would constantly pop out, making it difficult for Case to raise his arm and often too painful to raise it above his shoulder. He originally injured the shoulder early in his career when he overslid the second base bag and reached back, only to have his shoulder pop out. A few days later he thought the worst was behind him as the pain subsided. But the shoulder dislocated again when he was simply putting his coat on at Shibe Park and he was subsequently out of the lineup for three weeks. Case had two banged-up legs that were caused because of his aggressive base running. "I know I'm abusing my legs, but there's nothing to do about it," said Case. The fans and manager, Ossie Bluege, expected him to run and Case did not want to disappoint anyone. However, he wondered if the accolades were worth the punishment he was giving his body. During the 1945 season he also had a knee injury, sore thighs, and a sprained ankle that he injured when he was sliding for the motion pictures. After each game he took a bath and on road trips used about 25 pounds of Epsom salts. In 1945 he was a walking-wounded ballplayer, wearing a girdle to protect his thighs and a rudimentary brace on his left knee. Case didn't decide to have his shoulder operation until a late summer game in 1944 against the St. Louis Browns. He was incessantly bunting every Nelson Potter pitch foul and then the two players met down the first base line. Case recalled that St. Louis's star hurler called him "the worst name and I swung on him." That was the only punch he threw in the confrontation because his shoulder hurt too much. Case decided that it was best for him to have the operation because he didn't want to be placed in a position where he couldn't defend himself if he got into a fight or was attacked. He had the operation at Johns Hopkins Hospital and it was an intricate procedure: twelve inches of "gristle" was removed from his left thigh and used to repair his shoulder.[17]

George Case began his career with Washington in 1937 and remained with the club through the 1945 season. Then he played for Cleveland in 1946, batting only .225 in 484 at-bats, and ended his career with Washington in 1947 batting .150 in 80 at-bats and 36 games. The right-handed hitting leadoff man batted .282 lifetime in eleven major league seasons. He was a terror on the bases and led the American League in stolen bases for five consecutive years from 1939 to 1943 with 51, 35, 33, 44, and 61 steals. Additionally, his 28 steals in 1946 gave him another stolen-base crown, although his offensive numbers were well below his career average. During that 1946 season he experienced back spasms that were excruciatingly painful and made it difficult for him to stand. Case provided the junior league with an infusion of speed at a time when baseball strategy had become homogenized and the speed game was not utilized frequently around the majors. Case's career-high 61 steals in 1943 was more steals than five teams in the junior league and seven teams in the senior circuit that season. Case swiped 349 bags in his big league career. He compiled a lifetime .341 on-base percentage and scored at least 101 runs four times, including an American League-leading 102 runs in 1943. His career high was 109 in 1940.

In the outer garden he manned all three posts but was predominantly a left fielder. Early in his career he was a poor outfielder and felt he didn't deserve to be playing in Washington's outfield, home of future Hall of Famers Al Simmons and Goose Goslin and talented younger players like Taffy Wright and Mel Almada. He began the 1938 season platooning with Johnny Stone in right field but Stone's career ended as he developed tuberculosis, forcing him to retire. Washington's outfield that season consisted of three players who each batted over .300: Case, Simmons and Sam West. Bucky Harris, who was a player's manager, showed confidence in the young Case and let him develop into an excellent major leaguer. Three times in his career Case would bat over three hundred: 1938 (.305), 1939 (.302), and 1942 (.320).

His aggressive, daring base running changed the complexion of many games, such as a 3–2 win over the St. Louis Browns on September 7, 1945. Case went 1 for 3 on the day, scored two runs, and stole three bags. In the bottom of the first inning, Case got on first via a walk, stole second, and advanced to third on a grounder in the infield. He was hugging third with two outs, and he took off like a rocket when Bob Muncrief delivered the spheroid to catcher Frank Mancuso. Case's steal of home was successful, though Mancuso argued so violently that umpire Joe Rue was forced to kick him out of the game. Washington had a quick 1–0 lead because of Case's aggressiveness and the Browns were frustrated as a result. In the third inning Washington pushed across two more runs, and Case was instrumental in the first tally. He singled to left field and then stole second. The two hitters that followed hit fly balls to center fielder Milt Byrnes, and Case advanced to third and then across home plate on the two fly balls, scoring a run. But what was so special about this accomplishment was that neither fly ball was hit deep and most runners would not have even considered trying to take an extra base in that situation.

Case was a skilled small-ball practitioner, which included being a gifted bunter. When opposing catchers attempted to throw him out they were trying to catch a base stealer whose speed was comparable to that of a world class sprinter. According to Case, who was interviewed by Rich Westcott in his excellent book, *Diamond Greats: Profiles and Interviews with 65 of Baseball's History Makers*, he is the fastest man ever to circle the bases, accomplishing the feat in 13.5 seconds at Griffith Stadium.[18] This was a promotional event at Washington's ballpark: fans came out to see if he could break Hans Lobert's record, which he did. Case's memory was mostly accurate: he did break Lobert's record by three-tenths of a second on September 14, 1943, before a game between the Senators and Red Sox, and he circled the bases in the 13.5 seconds he remembered.

Lobert himself had set the record on October 9, 1910, in Cincinnati as a member of that city's National League ball club. Case's accomplishment, which was timed by competent AAU officials, appears to be much more impressive because he started with one foot on home plate, while Lobert's record was reportedly accomplished with a running start. When Case surpassed Lobert's time, was this a new record? According to an article in *The Sporting News* on July 12, 1945, Evar Swanson surpassed the mark of Lobert on September 15, 1929, as a member of the Cincinnati Reds with a 13.4-second performance. Then, as a member of the Columbus Red Birds, he surpassed that with a 13.3-second performance on September 20, 1931. In five big league seasons Swanson batted .303 and stole 69 bags, including a career-high 33 during his rookie year in 1929. For someone who was purportedly a speed burner he didn't take full advantage of his gift. Despite batting .306 for the 1933 Chicago White Sox, he stole only 19 bases in 144 games and 539 at-bats. During his final big league season in 1934 he batted .298 but stole a meager ten bags in 117 games and 426 at-bats.

Bill Veeck made Case the featured star in his first major league promotion in 1946. This time the witnesses saw Case race against Jesse Owens, the Olympic sprinter. Owens crossed the finish line just ahead of Case in a close and exciting race. But neither athlete was racing in the prime years of his career, and they had both slowed down because of age or injuries. These promotional races happened quite frequently and it allowed Case to earn some extra money to supplement his ball-playing salary. The only time the speedy outfielder lost a race while wearing a baseball uniform was against Owens. Case had the green light to run when he wanted, which was something that was rare during this time period. He considered the Tigers' Paul Richards, the hardest catcher to run on and Frankie Hayes the easiest. Despite his great base-running accomplishments his best experience as a major leaguer came with the bat when he collected nine hits in a doubleheader in 1940 to tie a major league record.[19] Case was born on November 11, 1915, as George Washington Case in Trenton, New Jersey.

First baseman Joe Kuhel exhibited terrific footwork around the bag and batted .285 on the season. Kuhel started his career with Washington in 1930 and was considered an excellent defensive first baseman. He completed his career with a .277 batting average in eighteen seasons with 131 homers and 1,049 RBIs. In 1933 he batted a career-high .322; in 1936 he drove in a career-high 118 runs; and in 1940 he connected on a career-best 27 homers. Kuhel did not run fast but was known as a good base runner. He stole 178 bags, including a career-high 22 in 1942, which was tied for third in the junior league. While he certainly put up some impressive offensive numbers during his career, his true talent was the defensive exhibition that he performed around the opening pillow. Shirley Povich knew a man who would pay his way into Griffith Stadium several times a week simply to watch Kuhel perform around the first-base bag. Kuhel was particularly gifted in his ability to handle errant throws from the infielders while keeping his toe on the bag. In many ways Kuhel was an anachronism, refusing to switch to the oversized first baseman's mitt that had become prevalent by the mid–1940s, and using a smaller mitt so that he would have that tactile sensation that perhaps was lacking in the newer mitts.[20]

When Kuhel first came up to the big show in 1930 he had to try to take the first-base job away from Joe Judge, who had been anchored at the position for Washington for nearly two decades. Judge played for Washington from 1915 to 1932 before finishing his career with the Brooklyn Dodgers and Boston Red Sox during the two subsequent seasons. For fifteen seasons from 1916 to 1930, Judge played at least 102 games as the club's first baseman. By the time Kuhel showed up in Washington the hourglass was almost empty on Judge's career. Clark Griffith, the Washington Senators owner, had a reputation of being frugal, but what he did for Judge on June 28, 1930, was truly generous. He persuaded Frank Navin, the Tigers owner, to agree that the revenues generated from the ticket sales beyond the first 9,000 admissions would be given to Judge on his special day. The crowd that day was about 18,000 in number and Judge walked away with $10,500, plus another $400 from the fans in Alexandria, Virginia.[21] When Kuhel took over the first-base job in Washington he was replacing one of the most popular players to ever walk between the white lines in the nation's capital.

Kuhel played for Washington from 1930 to 1937 before being traded to the Chicago White Sox on March 18, 1938, for Zeke Bonura. Clark Griffith immediately regretted the trade, knowing how important it was to have a competent defensive first baseman for a team to be successful. Bonura was considered a disappointment in Washington by many, including Griffith, as his batting average fell 56 points from his .345 mark in 1937 to .289 in 1938. However, Bonura continued to drive in runs at an accelerated pace and hit with power. For Griffith to regret trading for a guy who batted .289 with 22 homers and 114 RBIs is quite a statement. Bonura was traded to the New York Giants after the 1938 season. Kuhel's offensive numbers in 1938 (.267, 8 homers, 51 RBIs) did not even approach Bonura's. His numbers would improve over the following seasons and his defense was as good as ever. Kuhel, who batted and threw left-handed, spent six seasons in Chicago playing for the Pale Hose from 1938 to 1943. He was traded back to Washington on November 24, 1943, and batted .278 during the 1944 campaign but with little power (4 homers) in Washington's spacious ballpark. Like Griffith, Jimmy Dykes, the White Sox manager, regretted the trade because Hal Trosky, Kuhel's replacement at first base, performed significantly worse than he did with Cleveland in prior years. Kuhel was 39 years old in 1945. He batted .264 in 258 at-bats for the Senators and White Sox in 1946 and then his big league career was over after three games with the White Sox in 1947.

Kuhel didn't get along with *Washington Post* sportswriter Shirley Povich. Povich wrote, "He's a nice boy, but Kuhel and I aren't old pals." Kuhel was not afraid of letting people know how he felt and on one occasion he took a swing at Povich and a few other sportswriters. Kuhel was punished with a one-hundred-dollar fine. When he opened a letter from a fan on the following day it contained a fifty-dollar bill. The fan wanted to pay half his fine. He would have paid the other half, insisted the fan, if Kuhel had been able to hit Povich with his punch instead of missing the talented sportswriter.[22]

George Binks was hearing impaired as a result of a mastoid problem as a child that left him deaf in one ear. In his first full major league season in 1945 he batted .278 with 6 homers and 81 RBIs. In 1942 and 1943 he worked in a war plant and then batted .374 in 100 games for the 1944 Milwaukee Brewers. He was considered a very good fielder with a powerful arm, but on occasion would run into his fellow outfielders because he couldn't hear them. Frank O'Neill wrote about the outgoing ballplayer, "Binks is strongly individual in his predilections. He is the sort of fellow who prefers solitude in action. He does things. He is something after the temperamental model of Bob Meusel, except that Binks is not surly. He just acts for himself, and often times on impulse."[23] O'Neill went on to say that Binks set lofty goals for himself.

George Myatt, in his third season with Washington, contributed a .296 batting average and a .378 on-base percentage while playing most of his games at second base. Myatt began his career in 1938 with the New York Giants and played briefly for them during the 1938 and 1939 seasons, batting .306 and .189 respectively. He didn't play in the big leagues for the next three seasons and then caught on with Washington in 1943. His only significant playing time in the majors came during the 1944 (.284 in 538 at-bats) and 1945 (490 at-bats) seasons. He participated in a total of 27 games during the 1946 and 1947 seasons, and then his career under the big tent was over. Myatt teamed with George Case to give the Senators a potent stolen base combination. He stole 26 bags in 1944, which was third in the American League, and his 30 stolen bases in 1945 was tied with his teammate Case for second in the junior circuit.

Marino Pieretti and the four knuckleballers led the pitching staff: Roger Wolff, Mickey Haefner, Emil "Dutch" Leonard, and Johnny Niggeling. Alejandro Carrasquel also contributed on the hill with a 7–5 record and a 2.71 ERA. He was one of Griffith's Latin American ballplayers of dark complexion and even changed his name to "Alex" to Americanize himself and perhaps diminish some of the abuse he would take. However, the writers still called him "Carrasquel the Venezuelan."[24] Catcher Rick Ferrell had his hands full with the four knuckleballers. They threw the knuckleball in three different ways: Leonard and Haefner pushed off with two fingers, Niggeling released it off one finger, and Wolff used three fingers. Martin Quigley wrote, "How Rick Ferrell ... retained his sanity would make an interesting doctoral thesis on ways of coping with frustration."[25] Wolff compiled the best record with a 20–10 mark and a 2.12 ERA. Haefner was 16–14 with a 3.47 ERA. Leonard contributed a 17–7 mark and an excellent 2.13 ERA. And Niggeling had the only losing record among the foursome at 7–12 with a respectable 3.16 ERA.

When Roger Wolff was toiling in the bushes for ten years during the 1930s and early 1940s there was a predisposition against the knuckler. Most of the managers did not want knuckleball pitchers on their staff because the pitch was unpredictable and difficult to handle. When Wolff finally got his chance to play in the big leagues with the 1941 Philadelphia Athletics he was thirty years old. He started two games that season and lost both of them. In 1942 (12–15, 3.32 ERA) and 1943 (10–15, 3.54 ERA) he pitched well for an Athletics team that finished in the basement of the American League both seasons. As a member of the Senators in 1944 he fell to 4–15 and his earned run average skyrocketed to 4.99. The six-foot and a half, two hundred and eight-pound right-handed hurler won twenty games in 1945, pitched well in 1946 (5–8, 2.58 ERA), and then had a miserable 1947 campaign for the Cleveland Indians and Pittsburgh Pirates in his last big league season. Not only did catchers hate handling knuckleball pitchers but the umpires also hated to see a knuckleball hurler on the hill because the ball moved erratically, making it difficult to call balls and strikes. Umpire Cal Hubbard admitted that during one occasion in Boston, when playing manager Joe Cronin of the Red Sox sent himself up as a pinch-hitter, he gave the hitter a scouting report while performing his duties as the home plate umpire. Cronin asked Hubbard how he should approach Wolff. Wolff started many hitters with a small breaking curveball in hopes of getting a quick strike, and then he would pitch only knuckleballs for the remainder of the at-bat. Hubbard, who had pondered the question of whether the knuckler should be outlawed, told Cronin to be prepared for the first pitch curve. Wolff delivered the curve as he was inclined to do and Cronin hit a double.[26]

Johnny Niggeling also spent too many years in the bushes as major league teams avoided knuckleball hurlers. By the time he came up with the Boston Braves in 1938 he was approaching his thirty-fifth birthday. Before coming to Washington during the 1943 season he had pitched for the Braves, Reds, and Browns. His best season was in 1942, compiling a 15–11 record with a 2.66 ERA for St. Louis's American League representative. Niggeling's heroes were his teammates Rick Ferrell and Dutch Leonard. Ferrell was courageous because he called for the knuckler while other catchers were reluctant to do so. Early in Leonard's career many of his backstops would not call for the knuckler, but this all changed when Ferrell became his batterymate and he proved that a knuckleball pitcher can win.[27] Niggeling was old in 1945, almost forty-two, and he looked old as well. His face was sunken, he didn't appear to have an ounce of fat on him, and looked as if he had worked very hard his entire life. He stood at a height that was slightly above average at six feet and weighed somewhere in the neighborhood of 170 pounds. Niggeling pitched sixteen games in 1946 for the Senators and Braves and then his career under the bright lights was over. This was not the case for Mickey Haefner, the youngest of the knuckleball pitchers at thirty-two. In his first two seasons for Washington in 1943 and

1944 he went 11–5 and 12–15 respectively. He would pitch until 1950, finishing his eight-year career with a 78–91 record and a 3.50 ERA.

Dutch Leonard, born Emil John Leonard in Auburn, Illinois, on March 25, 1909, was not the oldest of the knuckleball pitching quartet of the Senators but he had played the longest and had the most distinguished career of the group. He came up with the Brooklyn Dodgers in 1933 and remained with the team until 1936. His career really took off when he joined the Senators in 1938 and Rick Ferrell became his catcher. With Washington from 1938 to 1946, he compiled a 118–101 record during those nine seasons. When he was traded to the Philadelphia Phillies in December of 1946 he compiled a 17–12 record in 1947 and then followed that with a 12–17 record the following year. He was involved in a four-player trade on December 14, 1948, that sent him to his final big league team, the Chicago Cubs. Leonard and Monk Dubiel were sent to Chicago in an exchange that sent Hank Borowy and Eddie Waitkus to the Philadelphia Phillies. From 1949 to 1953 he compiled a 26–28 record for the Cubs and then his career ended with an impressive 191–181 record and a 3.25 ERA.

Jim Tobin of the Detroit Tigers insisted that the knuckleball worked best at night and if Washington weren't playing so many night games their record would not be so good.[28] However, this was an opinion that was not held by Dutch Leonard, who pointed out that major league parks had rudimentary lighting systems that were inconsistent in their distribution of light. Leonard preferred day games and insisted that the hitter had the advantage in night games because home plate got more light than the other parts of the playing field. Where the defense is situated, the lights were not so good and many of the fielders were handling balls in the dark. Even a good defensive team can make large numbers of errors under the lights because they don't see the ball so well and they get a late jump on the ball.[29]

Rick Ferrell said the knuckleball was the "No. 1 enemy of catchers." The Washington backstop insisted that it was even more difficult to catch than a spitter. The problem with catching the knuckleball is gauging the break of the ball, which is inconsistent: it could break in or out, up or down. When catching the knuckleball there is always a sense that disaster is imminent. The catcher knows that at one point he will be unable to control the erratic pitch and he just hopes it doesn't happen at a critical juncture of the ball game. This was the case for Ferrell on the night of June 3 when the Senators faced off against the White Sox. Roger Wolff and Thornton Lee were in a scoreless pitcher's duel. In the eighth inning, Kerby Farrell of the White Sox hit a fly ball that should have been caught but instead it fell to the earth for a triple. With the runner at third who potentially could have been extremely important to the outcome of the ball game, Wolff delivered a knuckler that Ferrell was unable to handle and the runner scampered home from third to give Chicago a 1–0 lead. Ferrell was charged with two passed balls in the game but fortunately for the Senators they rallied to win the contest. Washington scored three runs in the bottom of the eighth and won by a 3–1 score.[30]

Ferrell believed that the fastball pitcher was the easiest pitcher to handle and the faster he threw the better it was for him. As a child he heard stories about how great a defensive catcher Gabby Street had been because he caught the flame-throwing hurler Walter Johnson, who was known for his explosive fastball. Many years later when Ferrell got the opportunity to talk with Street he asked him about his predicament with Johnson. Street assured Ferrell that catching Johnson was in fact very easy, contrary to the stories he may have heard.

The slugger who hits from the end of the bat has the most difficulty against the knuckler. Ted Williams, for example, was one hitter who would overswing at the pitch. Batters who choked up on the bat and would slap at the ball fared much better. Even though the catcher has great difficulty handling the knuckleball, the hitter has an even harder time trying to hit it. However, the base runner has a great advantage in trying to steal off the knuckleball pitcher, who is easy to run on. The knuckleball can also injure a catcher's hands. Ferrell's hands were beaten up, but a lot of the damage was done when he fought in twenty professional boxing matches in North Carolina.[31] He caught a knuckleball pitcher from a half-standing position and was patient, waiting for the ball to come to him, instead of reaching for it. As it was to be expected, Ferrell allowed a large number of passed balls (142) in his career, but so did contemporaries such as Frankie Hayes (139) and Ernie Lombardi (152).

Richard Benjamin Ferrell was born on October 12, 1905, in Durham, North Carolina. He began his Hall of Fame career with the St. Louis Browns in 1929 and would complete his big league career in 1947 with the Washington Senators. Ferrell played for the Senators from 1937 to 1941, and in 1944, 1945, and 1947. He batted .266 in 1945 in 286 at-bats and then batted .303 in 1947, his final big league season. He had a career .281 batting average with 28 homers and 734 RBIs in eighteen seasons. Ferrell had good plate discipline and bat control: he struck out only 277 times in 6,028 career at-bats. He drew 931 walks, including a career high of 75 in 1938. Ferrell didn't hit a lot of extra base hits and had a .363 slugging percentage but an impressive .378 on-base percentage. He got the opportunity to play with his brother Wes during five seasons with the Red Sox and Senators. Interestingly, both players were traded from the Red Sox to the Senators on June 11, 1937. The Senators received the two Ferrell brothers along with Mel Almada while Boston got the services of Ben Chapman and Bobo Newsom.

Rookie pitcher Marino Pieretti stood at 5' 7" and 153 pounds, and although he didn't rely on a knuckleball to be successful, he compiled a 14–13 record and a 3.32 ERA in 1945. In the off-season he killed cattle in a slaughterhouse in San Francisco; swinging the sledge hammer helped build up his strength and improved the velocity on his fastball. According to Pieretti the cattle would start

Perhaps Rick Ferrell didn't look like a catcher, standing at 5'10" and only 160 pounds, but he was strong, durable, and as tough as nails. The fearless backstop had the courage to call for the knuckleball when Dutch Leonard joined the Senators in 1938, which changed the course of Leonard's career. By 1944 Ferrell had his hands full with four knuckleball pitchers in the starting rotation: Leonard, Mickey Haefner, Johnny Niggeling, and Roger Wolff. While Ferrell's 1984 Hall of Fame induction remains controversial, what cannot be disputed is that he had a solid big league career (George Brace photograph).

running at him and then he would take the heavy sledge hammer and club the animals over the head. However, now that he had made it to the big leagues Pieretti said that he wasn't going to do any more killing and the slaughterhouse needed to replace him with a new employee. In 1944 he went 26–13 for Portland in the Pacific Coast League. Clark Griffith purchased Pieretti from Portland for $7,500 and made this decision without ever seeing him pitch or sending a scout to evaluate him. He figured if Pieretti could win 26 games in what he considered a Double-A league then he must be good.[32] Pieretti played six major league seasons with a 30–38 record and a 4.53 ERA. Griffith Stadium was a pitcher's park, which gave confidence to the Senators rotation. With Pieretti's help Washington finished the season only a game and a half behind Detroit and gave their fans much to be proud of in 1945.

By early August, Washington's 24-year-old hurler was sporting a 9–6 record. But four of his losses occurred because of the poor defensive performance behind him. In 1945 Washington had the most errors in the American League with 183; the only teams that were worse resided in the National League: Boston (193), Brooklyn (230), and Philadelphia (234). When Pieretti wasn't starting he asked his manager to use him in relief: he pitched in 44 games on the season and started 27 of them, while eating up 233.1 innings on the hill.

When Pieretti was a young man he was constantly trying to prove himself to scouts and managers in an attempt to find a team that would take him. He was persistent because he loved the game: he couldn't sleep at night, tossing and turning, while incessantly thinking about baseball. When he did fall asleep his dreams centered on baseball, and then when he woke up the next morning he was still thinking about the game he loved. He was born on September 23, 1920, in Lucca, Italy, and was brought to America when he was nine months old. His father was a carpenter and wanted his son to become a musician. The father's dream was partially accomplished in that Marino gained employment as an accordionist in San Francisco. However, he was working for the city's worst dance orchestras. His mother wasn't too pleased about Marino's passion for baseball: on one occasion she embarrassed her son when she walked onto the field during a game, pulled him from the batter's box, and then forced him to return home. She was upset because Marino missed his lesson with the accordion teacher.

Pieretti couldn't even make his high school baseball team. But these early failures and rejections made Marino stronger and gave him the mental toughness he needed to persevere and ultimately prove that he belonged. It was more than understandable that Pieretti would gravitate towards baseball. He grew up in the San Francisco Mission District, an area of town where kids had to protect themselves with their fists. However, it was also the part of town that produced baseball stars like Lefty O'Doul, Joe Cronin, Frankie Crosetti, and Tony Lazzeri.[33] Lazzeri had been the first Italian-American to make it big and then others followed. Soon sportswriters were suggesting that Italians had an inherent proclivity towards baseball that was lacking in other ethnic groups. Ugly stereotypes had long been disseminated about the Italians, and those who appeared to break away from these widely held beliefs were praised. *Life* magazine insisted that the Yankees' Joe DiMaggio "speaks English without an accent" and "never reeks of garlic."[34]

Marino married a Spanish girl named Flora Maeso. By August of 1945 they had a daughter who was eleven months old. Marino insisted that she got a bad break: because his child was female, she would never follow the career path of her father and pitch in the big leagues or even play baseball at a lower level.[35]

❖ 13 ❖

The Spirit of St. Louis

The Browns were known for the slogan, "First in shoes, first in booze, and last in the American League."[1] But in 1944 they won the American League pennant and then dropped the World Series to the Cardinals, four games to two. Their success symbolized the sad state the game was in during the war. If the authentic brand of major league baseball were being played they wouldn't have had much of a chance. While the Browns were preparing for the season in Cape Girardeau, Missouri, the baseball prognosticators thought they were a legitimate pennant contender. With the core of their team still intact, *The Sporting News* picked them to repeat in 1945.

Luke Sewell was the manager of the ball club. His first season with the club was in 1941 when he replaced Fred Haney and the team finished tied for sixth place (70–84). During the war the St. Louis Browns went from the outhouse to the penthouse. In 1942 they finished in third place (82–69); in '43 sixth place (72–80): in '44 they won the pennant (89–65); and in '45 they finished in third place (81–70).

Luke Sewell was born in Titus, Alabama, on January 5, 1901, and enrolled at the University of Alabama when he was fifteen years old. He played on the baseball team with his brother Joe; they were two of seven players on the 1920 and 1921 teams to eventually play in the big leagues. While at Alabama he also held arguably the most coveted position in the state, quarterback of the Crimson Tide football team. Another brother, Tommy, also went to the University of Alabama. Luke played twenty seasons in the major leagues as a catcher, spending most of his time with the Cleveland Indians from 1921 to 1932. Then he played for the Washington Senators (1933–1934) and the Chicago White Sox (1935–1938), then returned briefly to Cleveland in 1939 when his big league career appeared to be over. However, at the age of 41 he played six games for the Browns in 1942, collecting one hit in twelve at-bats for a .083 batting average. He completed his twenty-year major league career with a .259 batting average. Luke smashed only twenty homers in his career, including a career high of five with the Chicago White Sox in 1936. He struck out only 307 times in 5,383 at-bats, but that paled in comparison to his brother Joe, who struck out 114 times in 7,132 at-bats. His brother Joe had a Hall of Fame career with the Indians and Yankees, batting .312 lifetime with a .391 on-base percentage while playing most of his games at shortstop. Tommy appeared in one game with the 1927 Chicago Cubs and failed to get a hit in his only major league at-bat. Luke had an outstanding work ethic, and even as a player during the 1930s he held a second job, selling tires in the mornings and then playing ball in the afternoons.

Sewell managed the Browns beginning in 1941, when he replaced Fred Haney after a 15–29 start, and lasted until 1946, when he was let go after 124 games (53–71). Then he managed the Reds for three games in 1949. He remained as Cincinnati's skipper from 1950 to 1952 before being let go during the 1952 campaign after starting 39–59. He was replaced first with Earle Brucker (3–2) and then Rogers Hornsby (27–24) as the Reds finished in sixth place with a 69–85 record. While manager of the Reds he reportedly came up with the idea of having the grounds crew drag the infield in the middle of a game. This had a two-purpose effect: first, it assured that the infield had a smooth surface and the infielders could get good hops and avoid errors. It also allowed a longer time for the concessionaires to sell their goods to the public.[2]

Vern Stephens, George McQuinn, Mark Christman, Gene Moore, Milt Byrnes, and Frank Mancuso paced the offense in 1945. Catcher Frank Mancuso was the brother of major leaguer Gus Mancuso and had made his big league debut in 1944, batting .205 in 88 games. He batted .268 in 119 games in 1945. Frank was a veteran of the service, a second lieutenant who had broken his leg on his fifth jump as a paratrooper. The United Press reported, "The 25-year-old player, disappointed because he wanted to go overseas, believes it is his responsibility to help baseball weather the manpower crisis because he is convinced his ex-buddies want it to continue."[3]

Shortstop Vern Stephens was a wartime star who batted .289 in 1945 and led the American League with 24 homers. He made headlines the following year when he accepted a five-year, $175,000 contract to play in Jorge Pasquel's Mexican League. In Mexico he was treated like a king: "They couldn't do enough for me. I lived like a maharajah. No kidding. They'd run and get me everything I asked for. In fact, all the time I was there they were wonderful."[4] The Browns had initially offered him a contract of $15,000, which was $2,500 less than he had made the previous year, and because he didn't sign right away the offer went down to $13,000. Pasquel was trying to lure major leaguers, particularly those who were stars, to his Mexican League. He had some success luring marginal major leaguers, but Stephens was the biggest name he landed. However, Vern's wife didn't like Mexico and she helped concoct a plan to bring him back. A Browns scout, along with Stephens's father and Dick Muckerman, the president of the Browns, drove to Mexico. At the hotel they said they were sportswriters and visited the young shortstop. Vern was persuaded to return to America. So as not to raise suspicion Stephens left his clothes at the hotel and left with the three visitors. Two blocks from the border he exited the car and innocently walked across the bridge into the USA without being stopped. Since he was repentant and had come back before the season started, commissioner Chandler showed him mercy and did not blacklist him as he did with any other player who returned after the start of the season. Despite being treated like a king, he supposedly didn't like the cultural differences very much. When he returned he made the following statement:

> I came back because I wanted to be where I belong, in the good old USA. The Mexican League is far from being a major league. It is not fully organized. The parks are not good. The players, including those from the U.S., play to the best of their ability. But the league lacks that class we know up here in the big tent. Except at Mexico City, where they have a pretty fair diamond, the rest of the fields are not too good.... The scoreboards are ramshackle affairs and you don't know what other clubs in the league are doing because of poor telephone communication between league cities. And I missed my nice warm clubhouse shower after the games.[5]

Stephens was a womanizer, and like many of his teammates he liked to stay out late and drink. Luke Sewell, the Browns skipper, had to handle a lot of extravagant personalities on the ball club. They had several unrefined characters who were very tough and reckless ballplayers. Mike Kreevich, one of the Browns outfielders, had such a proclivity towards alcohol that the club got a priest to see him on a regular basis in hopes of keeping him sober.[6]

First baseman George McQuinn batted .277 with 7 homers. McQuinn stood only at 5'11" and 165 pounds but he was a powerful left-handed batter who hit 135 home runs in his career. During nine of his twelve major league seasons he hit at least eleven homers, including a career high of twenty in 1939. He played for four major league teams but spent most of his time with the Browns from 1938 to 1945.

Mark Christman also hit .277 but with 4 homers in 289 at-bats. Christman, who stood at 5'11" and 180 pounds, had a terrific day on August 5 at Sportsman's Park. He had seven straight hits, including two triples, against the Indians during a doubleheader. His streak ended in the sixth inning of game two when Ed Klieman delivered a pitch and he grounded out to shortstop Lou Boudreau. During his final at-bat on the day he was hit with a pitched ball and then stole his only base of the season. The next day Allie Reynolds delivered a vicious beanball that hit Christman in the head. St. Louis's third baseman was out of the lineup for an extended period of time as a result.

"Rowdy" Gene Moore batted .260 in his final major league season. In a fourteen-year big league career with six teams he batted .270 with a .333 on-base percentage. Milt Byrnes was in the last of his three-season big league career and batted .249 with 8 homers.

One-armed outfielder Pete Gray batted .218 in 234 at-bats in his only big league season and received the bulk of the media attention. He hit six doubles and two triples, but did not hit a home run. However, he was able to put the ball in play on a consistent basis, striking out only eleven times during the campaign. Gray was a fast runner but stole only five bases in eleven attempts. He was an excellent bunter as well and compiled a lot of his hits in the minor leagues by bunting down the third base line or dragging the ball down the first base line. In 1945 the infielders were playing in, hopeful of dissuading Gray from utilizing his effective strategy, and daring him to hit the ball past them. Gray held his 35-ounce bat down on the handle, and used his potent left wrist to swing the bat. He could handle a fastball but had difficulty against curveballs and changeups. Fielding was not so easy. After catching the ball he would slide it across his chest and down to his hand before jerking the hand backwards and unleashing the throw. He cut the padding out of his glove and only put two-thirds of his hand into it, with the smallest finger outside the glove. It took Gray slightly longer to throw the ball back into the infield than the normal outfielder. Many runners took advantage of his situation and would take an extra base. Gray played in 35 games in left field and 29 games in center in 1945.

Gray was born in Nanticoke, Pennsylvania, on March 6, 1915, under the name Peter Wyshner. He was of Lithuanian descent and his father worked in the mines in Nanticoke. Ethnic names like Wyshner were often frowned upon in American society during the 1930s and 1940s, so the family changed their name to Gray, hoping that it would be more palatable to the citizens of the country. As a child Gray was right-handed, but at the age of six his life was altered in a tragic accident. Gray and his friends hopped onto a delivery wagon and when it stopped he fell off as the wagon swayed uncontrollably. Gray got his right arm caught in the spokes and damaged it severely. He was rushed to the hospital but the surgeons could not save the arm. An amputation above the elbow followed and Gray's life would never be the same.

Gray loved the game so much that he was determined to achieve with one arm what most people could not achieve with two. He would play baseball whenever he could and worked hard to improve his skills. The future big leaguer was fiercely competitive and sensitive to how people reacted to his predicament. While playing as a teenager in his home town he aggressively slid into the catcher, knocking the ball from the backstop's hand. The catcher assured Gray that if he weren't handicapped he would punch him in the face. Gray then unleashed a vicious blow with his left hand, sending the catcher to the ground in great pain, grabbing his injured face. It was incidents like this that made Gray determined to overcome his disadvantageous position.

His love for the game was exemplified when at the age of seventeen he hitchhiked to Chicago to see his hero, Babe Ruth, play in the 1932 World Series against the Cubs. He was among the bleacherites at Wrigley Field in game three when Babe Ruth allegedly called his shot, predicting that he would hit a home run, by pointing his weapon, the bat, towards the outfield wall, while Charlie Root waited to deliver the pitch, standing on the small rise in the middle of the diamond. Gray saw Ruth and Lou Gehrig hit two home runs apiece on the day as the Yankees won, 7–5, before they went on to win game four to sweep the series. Seeing the two combatants, the best teams in their respective leagues, play in the World Series, and seeing his idol Babe Ruth, left a great impression on Gray and motivated him to work harder to achieve his goals.

Gray played for semi-pro teams in Nanticoke, Wilkes-Barre, and Pine Grove, Pennsylvania. But he surmised that if he was going to advance to higher levels he needed to go to New York, which was the baseball capital of the United States. He got in touch with Max Rosner, the manager and promoter of the Bushwicks, a semi-pro outfit that played in Brooklyn's Dexter Park. The Bushwicks were one of the best semi-pro teams in the country. Major league scouts watched their games and Bushwick alumni had graduated to play in the big leagues. Gray was so confident that he would perform well with the Bushwicks that he handed Rosner a $10 bill and told him he could keep it if things did not work out. He spent two years with the club and then got his first opportunity in organized baseball with Three Rivers in the Canadian-American League during the 1942 campaign.[7] The club agreed to sign him over the telephone without watching him play. The Three Rivers ball club was situated in Quebec, and when the manager picked up Gray in Montreal at a train station, he almost collapsed when he saw Gray's stump. It didn't take long for members of the community to spread the word about the new outfielder that was in town. During the first game he sat on the bench as the innings went by until they were losing 1–0 in the ninth. The chant of "We want Gray" reverberated throughout the grandstand. According to Gray, he was called upon to hit with the bases loaded in the ninth with two outs. The spectators "went crazy" as he prepared to hit, swinging two bats in his left hand. They called out his name in French. Gray hit a liner that fell upon the earth, down the right field line, to win the game. The fans threw money at him in admiration and he walked away with $700. However, the season went terribly wrong in late May when he fractured his collarbone, and he also suffered other injuries during the campaign. He played in only 42 games but batted an impressive .381. When he came to bat the outfielders would move over towards left field, uncertain as to whether Gray could pull the ball. Barney Hearn, who played for the Quebec Athletics in 1942, insisted that Gray could bat .350 simply on his bunting ability: "He'd drag down first base. Christ! The pitcher would scoot over there, and he'd bunt up the middle. He was a cutter!"[8]

The Three Rivers Foxes finished in sixth place in 1942 with a 56–66–1 record in the eight-team circuit. They were one of the two teams in the league who didn't have a working agreement with a major league team or with one of their higher classification affiliates. During that 1942 campaign the Canadian-American League, like other minor leagues, did everything they could to aid the war effort: the teams wore special uniforms, with the red, white, and blue colors of the country worn by the home teams. On the front of the uniform was the league's name and on the back a large, recognizable "V for victory" symbol. Money was raised by the teams and special games were played. Just like major league players who were drafted or volunteered for the war, minor league players also left in large numbers, and this had a deleterious effect on their playing careers.[9]

In 1943 Gray got a tryout with the Toronto Maple Leafs of the International League and insisted that he didn't make the team because of an illness. However, others said that he was bad-mouthing manager Burleigh Grimes while Grimes was in the vicinity. Grimes verbally tore into Gray and he was sent packing. He played the 1943 season with the Memphis Chicks of the Class A Southern Association. Playing at a higher classification than the previous year, he batted .289 in 126 games. In 1944 he batted .333 for Memphis and tied a league record with 68 stolen bases. He was charged with only six errors. At the bat he had 21 doubles, 9 triples, and 5 homers. Gray was the MVP of the Southern Association in 1944 and was given a watch and a $100 war bond for taking home the league's highest honor. By this time Gray had become a minor celebrity as his story was becoming well known throughout the country. There were movies made of Gray playing baseball. They were produced by the War Department and shown to wounded servicemen in the country and overseas. The St. Louis Browns' front office took notice of Gray's achievements and purchased his contract for $20,000.

Coming off his excellent year in Memphis he was optimistic about his chances in spring training and wanted to be treated just like everyone else. Luke Sewell insisted that Gray would not get any special treatment and would be treated just like any other ballplayer. To make the team he needed to produce and prove that he was deserving. Gray concurred with Sewell's sentiment: he didn't want any special favors. He was a private person who didn't like all the attention that was heaped upon him because of his disadvantageous position. Gray kept to himself and did not socialize with his teammates. He didn't like being called handicapped or to be looked upon as if he were the monkey at the zoo. Frederick G. Lieb observed, "Gray isn't loquacious; an interviewer has to draw him out. At times he gives a question considerable thought before replying. He freezes up if an interviewer is inclined to look upon him as a freak or curiosity." He did not want to be on the club merely to be a gate attraction. Sewell insisted that Gray would only attract paying customers to Sportsman's Park if he was a good ballplayer. Publicly the players, coaches, and manager all said the right things. But privately they had their doubts. Sewell would later admit that Gray did not belong in the major leagues and his presence upon the big league diamond was something of a joke. However, during the training season Gray impressed Sewell with his power, his timing at the plate, and his swiftness of foot. Gray was insecure about the situation but his roommate Al Hollingsworth reassured him that he wasn't being given this opportunity because of the manpower shortage.[10]

Once the regular season began the base runners were incessantly taking the extra base on him. A batter with excellent speed would hit the ball to Gray's outfield station and instead of getting a one-base hit like he normally would, he would keep going and would be standing on the midway with a double. Many of Gray's teammates insisted that his ineffective outfield play was the reason they lost between 6 and 12 games during the campaign. Gray took away playing time from legitimate major league players and they resented it. Mike Kreevich was in his twelfth and final major league season in 1945 and would bat .283 lifetime with a .346 on-base percentage. During the Browns' 1944 pennant-winning campaign Kreevich batted .301 in 402 at-bats. Kreevich thought that he should have been playing more than he was in 1945 and most of all resented being occasionally replaced by a one-armed outfielder. After batting .237 in 84 games he quit the team and was waived.[11] He was picked up by Washington on August 8 and batted .278 in 45 games and 158 at-bats for the Senators as they made their stretch run for the pennant.

Despite Gray's obvious limitations the scribes continuously lauded him almost as if it were their patriotic duty to do so. They were not simply lauding the great courage and resilience that Gray demonstrated in having a successful minor league career and making it to the big leagues; they were adamant that he was among the best players the Browns had. When the Browns traveled to Boston towards the end of May, Ed Rumill, the sports editor of the *Christian Science Monitor,* insisted that Gray was in the lineup "because he is one of the three best outfielders on the Brownie payroll." This was written despite the fact that the team employed outfielders Mike Kreevich, Gene Moore, and Milt Byrnes, each of whom was clearly a better player than Gray. During the season the Browns would also use Lou Finney and Chet Laabs in the outfield. They were both aging veterans but had performed successfully before the war. In a fifteen-year career that ended after playing four games for the 1947 Philadelphia Phillies, Finney completed his career with a .287 batting average and a .336 on-base percentage. In 1936 he batted .302 in 653 at-bats for the Philadelphia Athletics and also had a fine year with the Athletics and Red Sox in 1939, batting .310, and then hitting for a .320 clip for the 1940 Boston Red Sox. In 1944 he batted .287 for Boston, and after playing briefly for Boston in 1945 he was traded to the Browns in late July and hit for a respectable .277 average in 213 at-bats for St. Louis. He played most of his games in the outfield but also played first base. Chet Laabs had an eleven-year career in which he batted .262 with a .346 on-base percentage and smacked 117 home runs. From 1941 to 1943 he hit 59 home runs for the Browns, an average of 19.7 a season. His career high came in 1942 when he finished second in the American League with 27 home runs, nine homers off the pace of leader Ted Williams. In 1944 Laabs batted .234 in 201 at-bats and in 1945 he batted .239 in 109 at-bats. Babe Martin, a marginal major leaguer whose talents were somewhat comparable to Gray's, also saw significant playing time in the outfield for the 1945 Browns, batting .200 with 2 homers in 185 at-bats. During one juncture of the season when the outfield ranks became perilously weak, Don Gutteridge, the team's second baseman, who batted .238 during the campaign, was forced to play fourteen games in left field. Those were the only fourteen games he would play in the outer garden during his twelve-year career. It was clear that throughout the season the Browns had better players to play the outfield than Gray even if they had to play someone out of position. There was also hyperbole in the way the scribes described Gray's defensive prowess. Ed Rumill described his defensive play at Memphis in 1944 as "at-times-brilliant fielding."[12]

Pete Gray's best game in 1945 came on May 20 against the Yankees before the largest home crowd of the season at that juncture for St. Louis. There were 20,507 witnesses to the occasion at Sportsman's Park and they watched the Browns take both ends of a doubleheader by scores of 10–1 and 5–2 to sweep the four-game set. The Browns scored seven runs in the bottom of the first in the opening contest and Gray had two hits in the inning. Batting out of his customary lead-off spot, Gray went 3 for 5 in the opener with a run scored and two runs batted in. In the second game he went 1 for 3 with a run scored and made a nice catch off the bat of Bud Metheny. He wasn't charged with an error on the day and had nine putouts.

During spring training Gray said that he not only wanted to succeed to prove to himself that he belonged in the big show, but he wanted to do well for all the servicemen who were pulling for him and those well-wishers that had sent him letters. He was sensitive to the way he was being exploited and when offered $15,000 to appear in a movie about himself after the season had concluded, he refused the offer. Now that he had acquired big-league status, he was more famous than ever, and the circus atmosphere commenced. He was barnstorming in California and the fans were gawking at him as if he were a circus act. The two biggest attractions were Gray and Jess Alexander, a black outfielder with one arm. In 1946 Gray was back in the bushes, batting .250 for Toledo of the American Association. His final two minor league stops were with Elmira (1948) and Dallas (1949). Even though Gray did not have enough talent to succeed at the big league level, his .290 batting average in 1948 with the Elmira Pioneers of the Eastern League proved that he was a competent professional player at the minor league level.

In William Mead's outstanding tome on World War II baseball he vividly tells how Gray's life fell apart after his baseball career ended. When he was a boy he lived in a house that was envied by many in the community. But after his career concluded the house decayed, and by the fall of 1976 they still used a stove from previous generations. The house was saturated with dust. Gray drank too much and scoffed at the idea that he was some sort of hero.[13] It appeared that Gray would have been happier if the scribes had told the truth, that he was a hitter with no power who could barely hit over .200 under the big tent when the quality of play was poor. He would have certainly been happier if he had been treated like any other ballplayer, if fans and players hadn't mimicked his actions as if he were a freak show. Perhaps what galled him was that he was garnering so much attention while servicemen who fought overseas received few accolades, with rare exceptions like Ira Hayes, one of the flag raisers at Iwo Jima, who was honored in a pregame ceremony on opening day, 1945, in Washington. Pete Gray was born in Nanticoke and died there on June 30, 2002. Regardless of how he felt personally, what he achieved on bush-league diamonds and on the revered major league fields was truly impressive. It was a courageous accomplishment that spoke to Gray's resilient attitude and his willingness to never give up. He was an inspiration to servicemen around the country who had lost limbs in the horrific combat that they participated in. And he was an inspiration to others who found themselves in a similar situation because of a childhood accident or some other tragedy.

St. Louis had the third best earned run average in the American League at 3.14. And they were a balanced pitching staff, with five pitchers winning at least ten games: Nelson Potter (15–11), Jack Kramer (10–15), Sig Jakucki (12–10), Al Hollingsworth (12–9), and Bob Muncrief (13–4). Potter was 44–23 from 1943 to 1945. His first full big league season was in 1938 with Connie Mack's Athletics, when he went 2–12 with a 6.47 ERA. He wasn't much better the following year, compiling an 8–12 record and a 6.60 ERA. With the A's he tore the cartilage in his right knee, but the doctor botched the operation and later he had to have another to make it right. It was this unfortunate circumstance that had him pitching for Louisville in 1942 as a member of the Boston Red Sox organization. He won nineteen games for them and was subsequently sold to the Browns, where he flourished during the final three wartime seasons. To go along with a mediocre fastball he had a screwball, slider, and curveball. He pitched twelve seasons in the major leagues for five teams, and after going 6–11 for the Boston Braves in 1949, his career was over with a 92–97 record and a 3.99 ERA.

Al Hollingsworth was a six-foot, 174-pound southpaw, who was 37 years old in 1945 and was approaching the end of his big league career. He began his career with Cincinnati in 1935 and before joining the Browns in 1942 had an unimpressive career with the Reds, Phillies, Dodgers, and Senators. During the four war years from 1942 to 1945 he compiled records of 10–6, 6–13, 5–7, and 12–9. Hollingsworth was nicknamed "Boots," and completed his big league career after the 1946 campaign with a 70–104 lifetime mark and a 3.99 ERA. His lack of control held him back from being a better pitcher.

Jack Kramer was ten years younger than Hollingsworth and first appeared in the junior circuit with the 1939 Browns, compiling a 9–16 record and a 5.83 ERA. During the following two seasons he was not much better, and in 1942 he was out of baseball and aiding the war effort with a job in a war factory. He joined the Navy but was discharged during the summer of 1943 because of an asthma condition. With Toledo, which was one of the Browns' minor league affiliates, he won eight consecutive games and tossed a no-hitter. He made three relief appearances for St. Louis in 1943 and then returned to the Browns on a full-time basis in 1944 and went 17–13 with a 2.49 ERA. During the next three seasons he went 10–15, 13–11, and 11–16. In 1948 with the Boston Red Sox he had his best year in terms of winning percentage (.783), going 18–5 with a 4.35 ERA. He played a few more seasons with the Red Sox, Giants, and Yankees, and his career ended after the 1951 season with a 95–103 mark and a 4.24 ERA.

Bob Muncrief spent the bulk of his twelve-year major league career pitching for the Browns, starting with a total of three games during the 1937 and 1939 seasons, and then earned a full-time spot on the roster from 1941 to 1947. His career high in victories was thirteen, accomplished during the 1941, 1943, 1944, and 1945 seasons. Like that of his teammate Jack Kramer, his career ended in 1951: he pitched two games for the Yankees, his fifth major league team, and then his career was over with an 80–82 record and a 3.80 ERA.

Sig Jakucki had played briefly for the St. Louis Browns in 1936 and then bounced around the minors. A few years later he was out of organized baseball, and when the Browns tracked him down during the war, he was playing semi-pro ball in Texas. He was an incurable drunk and not the kind of person that fostered a salubrious clubhouse, but the Browns, like all teams, needed players, so they brought him back in 1944. In that pennant-winning season he was 13–9 with a 3.55 ERA, and in 1945 was 12–10 with a 3.51 ERA. On August 30 he was taken out of a game early and failed to make it through the third inning. He gave Luke Sewell some attitude while on the bench. Sewell answered back, "If you'd stay in condition, I wouldn't have to yank you." Jakucki replied by insisting that he was being singled out and constantly criticized because he liked to drink. The next day he showed up at the train station intoxicated and was told to go home. St. Louis coaches Fred Hofmann and Zack Taylor were reportedly threatened with bodily harm by the intransigent and out-of-control pitcher. Jakucki sneaked on the train anyway and was kicked off at a later stop when Sewell found out. Luke Sewell had taken enough: he kicked Jakucki off the team and ended his career. Sewell insisted that Jakucki would never play again for the St. Louis Browns and the front office backed him up. The Browns manager said that Jakucki was not in the proper condition because of his drinking habits. He had engaged in insubordination with his actions at the train station. And furthermore, Jakucki's absence from the team would make for a better working environment and a more harmonious clubhouse atmosphere. Sewell believed the Browns would do better without him.[14]

To replace Jakucki, the Browns called up three pitchers from Toledo: Cliff Fannin, Al LaMacchia, and John Miller. LaMacchia made the most impact, going 2–0 in five relief appearances with a 2.00 ERA. Those were the only two victories during his brief three-year major league career. He was 24 years old when he was called up in 1945. Fannin was only 21 and he was considered an exceptional prospect. He also had five relief appearances during the season with a 2.61 ERA. From 1946 to 1952 he would compile a 34–51 record for St. Louis.

The third pitcher called up, John "Ox" Miller, spun three complete games and won two. When Sewell ended Jakucki's career he wasn't telling some disruptive bench player that his services were no longer needed. When Jakucki was released he was the second best pitcher on the staff behind Nelson Potter. St. Louis finished only six games behind Detroit in the American League flag race, and Jakucki may have helped make up the difference. Furthermore, if the Browns hadn't relied on Pete Gray as a gate attraction, they could have won the flag.

Perhaps the most memorable game the Browns played in 1945 took place on June 20 against the White Sox at Sportsman's Park when a brawl erupted between the two teams. Karl Scheel, a batting practice pitcher for the White Sox, was taunting the Browns all day and engaging in aggressive bench jockeying. When Browns reliever George Caster was exiting the field in the eighth inning during a pitching change, Scheel antagonized the hurler and Caster in turn threw the ball into the White Sox dugout. Several Browns players then jumped into the White Sox dugout and worked over Scheel with their fists. Jimmy Dykes, the White Sox skipper, came out to argue for serious penalties for what Caster had done. That provoked the Browns to pour onto the field and invite themselves into the Chicago dugout, where they beat Scheel as best they could. Dykes had reportedly told catcher Frank Mancuso that he wasn't going to order Scheel to cease his behavior, but if the Browns wanted him to stop then they should do it themselves. However, the White Sox manager denied making these remarks and said he had informed Mancuso that Scheel was not leaving the bench. About a hundred fans rushed the field and congregated in front of the Pale Hose dugout to witness the hostilities close-up. Scheel would often personalize his attacks and he was persistent in his aggression. Earlier in the game Vern Stephens, the Browns shortstop, had thrown the ball in the direction of the White Sox dugout when he was called a name. Scheel was an ex–Marine who was an excellent semi-pro pitcher in Chicago before going into the service. He had started the jockeying in the prior series between the teams and then continued where he left off when the White Sox played the Browns on June 19. On the night of the brawl, he threw batting practice, while the Browns retaliated and verbally assaulted him. The fight left him bloodied and bruised with serious injuries to his face, legs, and back. Jimmy Dykes was also injured in the brawl with a bruised shin; his arm was cut, and a toe on his right foot was spiked.

As a result of the fight, Sewell was fined $250 and three of his players fined $100 apiece: Sig Jakucki, George Caster, and Ellis Clary. Browns management was upset when they found out none of the White Sox were fined. Don Barnes, President of the Browns, said, "Scheel used foul language toward the Browns. I have affidavits to that effect." Sewell stated, "The whole thing was regrettable, but you can't expect anybody to take what our boys took without doing something about it. They were invited into the White Sox dugout and they went." Dykes insisted that the fight could have been prevented if Sewell had intervened, and he added that the fight was the most "brutal" incident he had ever observed during his baseball career. The White Sox players said that Sewell encouraged his players to assault them.[15]

The players around the junior league seemed particularly gratified that Scheel received the beating that was coming to him. He had harassed other teams in the league, particularly the Indians and Tigers. Cleveland was the target of Scheel's ungentlemanly tactics when they visited Chicago for a three-game set beginning June 12. The acrimonious batting practice pitcher verbally attacked the Indians but they showed restraint and did not physically retaliate. But when word reached the Indians players that the Browns had pounced on Scheel and gave him a beating, they believed he had it coming and felt no sympathy for the man.

Gabby Street, the well-liked former catcher, who was broadcasting St. Louis games, said that the rhubarb reminded him of the old days when rowdy behavior was much more ubiquious.[16]

❖ 14 ❖

Marse Joe and the Bronx Bombers

In 1942 the Yankees won their second consecutive pennant with a 103–51 record, finishing nine games ahead of second-place Boston. Joe Gordon led the team's everyday players in batting at .322 and contributed 18 homers and 103 RBIs. These statistics helped earn him the 1942 American League MVP award. The major leagues were replete with Punch-and-Judy middle infielders, but Gordon possessed plenty of home run power, and during his first five big league seasons from 1938 to 1942 he hit home run totals of 25, 28, 30, 24, and 18. He was perhaps the best second baseman in the majors. Bill James labeled him as "the top second baseman of his time."[1] But while the statistics he compiled were impressive, the Yankees weren't about statistics; they were about winning. One day a writer asked Joe McCarthy why he liked Gordon as much as he did. McCarthy summoned the flashy keystoner and asked, "Joe, what's your batting average?" Gordon said he didn't know. McCarthy continued, "Well then, what's your fielding average?" Again, Gordon didn't know. McCarthy looked at the writer and declared, "That's what I like. All he cares about is beating you."[2] Gordon epitomized the selfless play of the ball club and the teamwork that was needed to form a cohesive unit. He would give himself up with a man on second and no outs by hitting the ball the other way; he always rounded the bag looking to take the extra base, and not being content; he did the little things that were necessary to win. The Yankees roster was full of players of this type. In 1943, Gordon had a bad year at the plate, batting only .249 with 17 homers and 69 RBIs. But most importantly, the team had achieved its goal and won the World Series. Joe was in the military during the 1944 and 1945 seasons and he joined a plethora of great Yankees who were now batting for Uncle Sam. It was these departures that led to the Yankees' decline, and by 1945 even the stately Yankees bore little resemblance to a prewar ball club.

Many people found enjoyment in the fact the Yankees had fallen into mediocrity as the war progressed. After losing the 1942 World Series to the St. Louis Cardinals, the Yankees took the 1943 World Series, four games to one. They

The heavy artillery of the Yankees, consisting of (left to right) Lou Gehrig, Joe Gordon, Tommy Henrich, Joe DiMaggio, and Bill Dickey, helped them have a championship caliber team before the war. Gehrig played only 8 games during the 1939 season when he was forced to retire because of his debilitating illness at the age of 35. During the war the Yankees lost Gordon, Henrich, DiMaggio, and Dickey to military service. New York won the pennant in 1942 and then the World Series in 1943, but by 1944 the manpower shortage caught up with them. They were no longer a championship outfit (George Brace photograph).

won the American League flag that season with a 98–56 record. In 1944 they fell to third place (83–71) and in 1945 dropped to fourth place with an 81–71 record.

The new Yankee ownership team of Larry MacPhail, Del Webb, and Dan Topping were hopeful they could win the pennant in 1945. MacPhail was known as a shrewd innovator when he was the general manager of the Cincinnati Reds and Brooklyn Dodgers. He was known for bringing about the first major league night game and the first televised game, and for broadcasting the entire schedule of a team, at home and on the road. Roger Kahn wrote that Topping and Webb "had no discernible social conscience," and the front office was comfortable with the all-white Yankees for years after Jackie Robinson integrated the game. Webb found satisfaction in that his construction company had built an internment camp for Japanese-Americans.³ MacPhail would eventually be at loggerheads with the rest of the ownership group. Larry tore into Topping: "You're just [the] guy who was born with a silver spoon in your mouth," adding, "You've never made a dollar in your life!" The younger Topping nailed him in the stomach a few times and threatened to throw punches to the head if the intoxicated MacPhail did not behave. MacPhail at one time told the wife of a player that her husband was a "bum."⁴ In 1948, Topping and Webb handed over $1.5 million to buy out MacPhail's interest in the Yankees.

After managing five years with the Chicago Cubs that included the pennant-winning season of 1929, Joe McCarthy became the Yankees manager in 1931 and managed them until May 24, 1946. When he took over the managerial reigns many were upset that Babe Ruth did not get the job. Slowly he gained the respect of the players and others around the organization. He helped foster the corporate image of the Yankees, insisting that his players dress nicely off the field by wearing a jacket and a tie. McCarthy led the Yankees to eight American League pennants during his time there. Seven of those eight seasons they went on to win the World Series. He would become extremely agitated when people said that his teams were so great that his only responsibility was to fill out the lineup. He was known to drink occasionally and tear into his players when he did. The eccentric personalities that he oversaw included Babe Ruth, Lou Gehrig, Tony Lazzeri, Lefty Gomez, Johnny Allen, Jake Powell, Ben Chapman, and Joe DiMaggio. And this group tested his patience. He had a great memory and was very attentive as to what was happening on the field. He never got along with MacPhail and would leave the club early in the 1946 season. Ironically, he came back to manage the Boston Red Sox in 1948, the logic being that the man who had once managed the Yankees perhaps would know how to beat them.

Joe DiMaggio once said of McCarthy, "He didn't do anything; he just managed. Joe wasn't too close to his players. I would say he was all business when it came to baseball. The only time he would really talk to the players would be out in the hotel lobby. He would be sitting with that big black cigar in his mouth, and he'd talk to anybody." DiMaggio also said, "All he demanded was that you give your best."⁵ Unlike other managers, McCarthy never made the big leagues as a player.

The first year in the North the Yankees trained at Asbury Park, New Jersey, where it was unbearably cold. The community was overflowing with residents during the summer but in the winter and spring only 14,000 were motivated to live there. In the clubhouse there was a hot stove that kept the players warm, but back at the hotel there was no heat due to a fuel shortage. When it was too cold the best accommodation they could find was a high school gym. McCarthy declared that training indoors did little to prepare a ball club for opening day. Like having part-time players, the aristocratic Yankees wanted nothing to do with this ersatz form of training.

In 1944 the Yankees moved to Atlantic City, where they used the 112th

Field Artillery Armory for indoor training. They constructed their baseball diamond on what had previously been a football field. The ball club did not even have a batting cage for indoor practice. In 1945 they could no longer use the armory as it was now being used to house wounded soldiers. After desperately attempting to find an adequate indoor facility they settled for an abandoned Navy aircraft hangar. The hangar was located beyond the left field fence of the field. It had a concrete floor and no heat, but the Yankees installed pot-bellied stoves. The team stayed at the Senator Hotel.

Ed Barrow, who now served the club as chairman under the new management, said that on the first day of spring training "our squad may consist of a manager, three coaches, and a flock of newspaper men."[6] Rud Rennie of the *New York Herald Tribune* struck a similar tone when he wrote that on the first day of camp the Yankees had: "Six players, two coaches, a batting practice pitcher, a trainer, a road secretary, a publicity man, a flock of reporters and George Weiss, an executive...."[7] The weather wasn't bad the first few days and they trained outdoors, unlike the previous year when they spent most of their time indoors. McCarthy showed up on March 13 and informed the writers, "It wasn't the weather that kept us indoors last season. It was the poor condition of the field. It was so soft it took a week to dry out after a rain. Now that the field has been surfaced, I'm sure we'll get on it a lot more than we did last year."[8]

The Yankees had a 7–7 spring record and played against a few teams whose training camps were conveniently located close to Atlantic City: the Boston Red Sox were training near Atlantic City in the town of Pleasantville, while the New York Giants were located in Lakewood, New Jersey. They also played the Brooklyn Dodgers two times before the season began, first at Yankee Stadium and then at Ebbets Field. Additionally, minor league teams Newark and Trenton, who were both situated in the Garden State, were also on the exhibition schedule. While the Yankees prepared for the 1945 season they also helped raise money for the war effort. On April 11 in Plainfield, New Jersey, a crowd of 1,332 paid to watch the Yankees defeat the Newark Bears, their International League farm team, by an 8–2 score. Before the game Johnny Lindell's bat was auctioned off and raised $2,600 in war bonds.

When 37-year-old Bill Dickey, the former Yankees catcher who was now a lieutenant in the Navy, watched the Boston Braves defeat the Washington Senators by a 2–1 score on March 26 in Washington, D.C., he was astonished to see how many of the players were unrecognizable to him. Dickey, who had last played in the big leagues in 1943, didn't know any of the players on the field. The game had changed so much since he had departed for military service. Clark Griffith, the Senators owner, assured Dickey that he shouldn't feel bad because nobody else knew who those players were either. Also on the 26th, the Signal Service Detachment filmed the Yankees perform their spring training drills and were going to send the film overseas so the servicemen could gain a glimpse of the Yankees preparing for the upcoming season.

Babe Ruth, the Yankees' revered former slugger, was still trying to draw adulation from sports crowds. During spring training he had taken a job as a wrestling referee but scoffed at suggestions that he was broke and in financial ruin, as long as he continued to receive money from his trust fund and his other investments kept paying out healthy dividends, then he was going to remain in good financial health. According to Ruth the reason that he agreed to referee in Portland and Boston was that he missed the crowds and wanted to keep in touch with his fans. Ruth was now fifty-one years old and declared that he weighed 240 pounds. Because of his throat problems his doctors advised him to cut down on smoking. Unfortunately, he also had to cut down on his visits to Army and Navy hospitals. When the war began he averaged about four visits a week but now he was down to one visit a week.

He had committed himself to do anything he could to help the wounded veterans. When he would see one of the wounded soldiers it reminded him of his baseball trip to Japan. He talked poignantly and honestly about the decline of Japan. Ruth remembered fondly his 1934 trip to that country with a group of first-rate American players that included Lou Gehrig, Jimmie Foxx, and Charlie Gehringer. There appeared to be a million Japanese who lined the streets to get a glimpse of the great American ballplayers. They proudly held both the American flag and the Japanese flag in their hands. They looked upon Ruth as a "god," but now things had changed so much that Ruth was pained just thinking about it.[9]

In the Pacific Islands the Japanese soldiers would scream "To hell with Babe Ruth!" when they got close to American troops. Ruth responded, saying, "I hope that every Jap who mentions my name gets shot — and to hell with all Japs anyway."[10] The Japanese eliminated American baseball slang from their lexicon during the war, and then they eliminated their professional league halfway through the 1944 season. Within baseball there were symbolic images of the newly-formed hatred towards the Japanese. This was the case, for example, when the Chicago White Sox pitchers warmed up by hitting cutouts of Japanese soldiers.

As the season approached, Al Laney wrote a column in the *New York Herald Tribune* encouraging people to come out for the exhibition game at the Stadium to benefit the Red Cross. In a similar game at Ebbets Field on April 11, the Dodgers raised $27,409.70 as they played against the Giants. Besides raising money for a good cause, that Giants/Dodgers game would not easily be forgotten by the estimated 12,000 fans that got to see their ball club before the curtain was raised on the new season. The Giants defeated the Dodgers, 9 to 7, despite three errors by their unspectacular but stable shortstop, Buddy Kerr. The Giants took an early 3–0 lead until Kerr's errant throw to second on a double-play grounder in the fourth inning led to a sequence in which the Dodgers pushed across three runs to tie the game. In the sixth inning he dropped a routine fly ball that would have ended the inning. Finally, in the ninth, the Dodgers scored three runs to tie the game, thanks to Kerr's inability to handle an easy grounder that was hit by Mike Sandlock. The comedic performance continued when the Dodgers also joined in on the ineptitude: George Hausmann, New York's second baseman, reached second when Red Durrett muffed a fly ball in the eleventh inning. The Giants went on to score three runs during the frame and held on for the victory. Harry Cross suggested that the best playing was done by Gladys Gooding, the Ebbets Field organist, and not by the men on the field.

Before the game a check was handed to Red Barber, the chairman of the New York Red Cross and Brooklyn broadcaster. The comedy pair of Olsen and Johnson entertained the crowd: when they played an inning against the baseball writers, they used exploding bats and movable bases, and they shot the opposition with toy guns. The fans were also entertained by Eli Danzig's orchestra and songs by such luminaries as Sue Ryan, Marion Leveridge, and Harry Stockwell, who performed "Oklahoma!" Al Schacht was also there. Plenty of Giants fans elbowed their way into Ebbets Field, and they vigorously booed Leo Durocher when his name was announced in the starting lineup.

Meanwhile, on that same day, the Yankees were beating up their Newark farm club in Plainfield, 8–2. Bill Bevens pitched five scoreless innings to earn the win while Steve Roser worked the final four innings. In his second major league season in 1945, the 27-year-old Roser would appear in eleven games, pitch 27 innings, and have a 3.67 ERA. Joe Buzas, the Yankees shortstop, who would bat .262 in 65 at-bats in 1945, his only big league season, went 3 for 5 in this exhibition game and had a great spring season. Up to this juncture of the training season he was able to collect a hit in eleven of the twelve games and led the team with 16 RBIs. However, it was Johnny Lindell who was leading the team in hits with 21.

Al Laney tried desperately to get people to attend the Red Cross game at Yankee Stadium on the following day. He was mildly critical of those persons who bought tickets but did not attend the game at Ebbets Field. Those people felt like they were simply giving a donation to the Red Cross and did not have to attend the game since their charitable donation was sufficient. Laney characterized their decision as a "mistake." There would have been a lot more spectators in the stands if they showed up, which would have shown more support for the Red Cross and for baseball. They should have given their tickets to servicemen if they did not plan to attend, which some of them did. The show that was put on by the comedians was worth the $1.20 price by itself. Laney implored fans to go see the game at Yankee Stadium. Ticket sales were weak and this was a "pity." Furthermore, he was discouraged by the fact that these charitable games drew more fans and support at Ebbets Field than at Yankee Stadium. This was going to be the first game in Yankee Stadium since Larry MacPhail became part of the new ownership group. Another attraction was going to be Ben Chapman, who would pitch for Brooklyn but who once wore the famous pinstripes for the Yankees. Laney wanted the "Bronx to outdo Brooklyn," and wanted to see a large number of sailors and soldiers in the stadium. As a reflection of the times, he urged people to call and tell the Sports Committee, Red Cross Fund, that they'd be sending a check, and then allow a serviceman to see the game in their place. According to Laney, they will "trust" that you'll send the money.[11]

They attracted about 13,000 fans for that game and raised approximately $22,400. Duke Ellington played music, and Milton Berle and Al Schacht were among the other notables there. There were thousands of soldiers and sailors in attendance. The wounded soldiers sat behind the screen of home plate. The Olsen and Johnson gang entertained the crowd just as they had done at Ebbets Field. Robert Patterson, the Undersecretary of War, watched the game from a field box. Larry MacPhail and fellow owner Del Webb were there but the final member of the ownership group, Dan Topping, was on duty with the Marines. The Brooklyn Dodgers defeated the Yankees, 3–1, in a one hour and thirty-six minute affair. The game took place on the same day, April 12, that President Roosevelt died.

Al Laney's appeal to raise money appeared to have had some effect: MacPhail announced on the following day that the final total he would hand over to the Red Cross was $22,837.20, including $2,788.70 that was sent to the Yankee offices to pay the admission for the servicemen who wished to see the game. Furthermore, some people sent pledges to the Red Cross headquarters directly, so the total money raised from this game was even higher. The paid attendance of 16,538 was significantly higher than the actual number of people in the stadium. This must have been a disappointment to Laney because he had admonished those people who bought tickets but never bothered to show up.

The Yankees' .259 batting average was the third best in the American League in 1945. They led the league with 93 home runs, 676 runs scored, 618 walks, a .343 on-base percentage and a .373 slugging average. Snuffy Stirnweiss was not only skilled in baseball but also in football; in 1940 he was drafted by the Chicago Cardinals of the National Football League. In 1945 he would lead the league in batting (.309), at-bats (632), slugging (.476), total bases (301), runs scored (107), hits (195), triples (22), and stolen bases (33). John Lardner quoted Babe Ruth in *Newsweek* as saying, "That sawed-off runt playing second base is the only ballplayer who could've gotten a uniform when the Yankees really had a ball club."[12] In 1944 first baseman Nick Etten led the American League with 22 homers, and then hit .285 with 18 homers and a league-leading 111 RBIs in 1945. Hersh Martin played with the Philadelphia Phillies from 1937 to 1940 and came back to the big leagues for two wartime seasons with the Yankees in 1944 and 1945. He batted .267, with 7 homers in 1945. Oscar Grimes batted .265 and Bud Metheny hit .248 with 8 homers.

In 1942 Charlie "King Kong" Keller led the team in homers with 26, batted .292 and drove home 108 runs. He was given the nickname "King Kong" because of his great strength but did not like it. Keller could hit for average and power: he batted .353 with 13 homers for the Newark Bears in 1937 and the following year batted .365 with 22 homers and 129 RBIs. The 1937 Newark Bears of the International League are considered by most to be the best minor league team in baseball history. In 1939 he made his Yankee debut, batting .334 with 11 homers and then .286 with 21 homers the following year. It had been Keller who in the 1939 World Series knocked out Ernie Lombardi at home plate in the fourth and final game. Keller would miss all of 1944 because of his obligations to the Merchant Marine and played only 44 games in 1945. In his first seven big league seasons, including his shortened 1945 season, he averaged 23.1 homers a year but he hurt his back in 1947 and that hindered his abilities for the rest of his career as he smacked only 27 more long balls in six seasons.

New York's 3.45 ERA was the fifth best in the league. Bill Bevens led the staff with a 13–9 record and a 3.67 ERA. Ernie Bonham was 8–11; Al Gettel was 9–8; Monk Dubiel was 10–9; Hank Borowy was 10–5 with a 3.13 ERA before going over to the Cubs; and Red Ruffing was 7–3 with a 2.89 ERA. After two and a half years in the Army, Ruffing rejoined the team near mid-season and was significantly overweight. In a July 16 game against Detroit he got a base hit as a pinch-hitter and drove in a run. Rud Rennie wrote, "Ruffing strode with unhurried dignity to bat in place of Joe Page. A good producer would have had a boy carry the stick to the plate for him so that Ruffing could have taken it as if it were a sword, because he was truly a regal figure." After his single, Don Savage ran for him and he "walked with the same unhurried dignity to the bench."[13] Ruffing would have a Hall of Fame career that ended with the White Sox in 1947 with a 273–225 record. He played in seven World Series with the Yankees and was 7–2 with a 2.63 ERA in the fall classic.

Joe Page would eventually prove himself to be one of the better relievers in the game. In 1945, his second year, he was 6–3 with a 2.82 ERA. He pitched in 20 games and started 9 of them. John Lardner would say, "Joe had a lot of stuff. He drank a lot of stuff so he had a lot of stuff. He was a left-handed pitcher, but a switch drinker. He could raise a glass with either hand."[14] Page threw hard pitches that sank in the strike zone. During his career he would be accused of throwing spitballs.

Paul Schreiber pitched in a total of ten games for the Brooklyn Dodgers in 1922 and 1923. Later he became a batting practice pitcher for the Yankees and pitched in two regular season games in 1945. The 6'2", 180-pound right-handed pitcher was 20 years old the last time he toed the slab in a major league game, but in 1945 he was approaching his 43rd birthday. The first of his two appearances was on September 4 as the Tigers were blowing out the Yankees. Surprisingly, when he came in to relieve the starting pitcher, the fans at Yankee Stadium recognized him and gave him a tempered ovation. What made the ovation a pleasant surprise was that Al Gettel, who had started for New York, exited the game with the Tigers winning 10–0. To say that he got his ears pinned back was an understatement: he allowed fifteen hits, one walk, and struck out five in five and two-thirds innings. Gettel pitched as if he were the batting practice pitcher and Schreiber pitched as if he were a starting pitcher. Paul Richards, the veteran Tigers catcher, was the first batter to face Schreiber and he struck out with a ball that fluttered to the plate. Schreiber pitched three and one-third innings without allowing a hit or a run, keeping the Tiger hitters off balance with his "nothing ball." He struck out one and walked two. Jesse Abramson of the *New York Herald Tribune* insisted that Schreiber's presence was an indication of the poor shape of the Yankees pitching staff. He also wrote that his pitches were so slow that he made Jim Tobin, the Tigers' slow-throwing knuckleball pitcher, look like Walter Johnson when compared to Schreiber.[15]

Schreiber had been a batting practice pitcher with the Yankees since 1937. And every time they went to a World Series since then he was voted a full share by the players. This gesture showed Schreiber and others how valuable he was to the ball club by rewarding him with the same amount of money that was given to a Joe DiMaggio, Joe Gordon, Tommy Henrich, or Bill Dickey for making it to the fall classic. Joe Williams of the *New York World-Telegram* believed the Yankees were the first team to carry a batting practice pitcher. Before this strategy was used by the Yankees, batting practice was often thrown by relief pitchers or coaches. In his capacity as a batting practice pitcher, Schreiber did an outstanding job. He had exceptional control and took his job seriously, incessantly throwing good batting practice pitches onto the hitter's bat. But this was a monotonous job that went largely unacknowledged by the fans or writers and he didn't get to experience that great rush of adrenaline that a pitcher feels when he faces batters in a major league game. When he was given this opportunity to pitch in a junior league game it was a great reward for the services he gave the ball club. While Joe Williams was impressed by Schreiber's performance on September 4, he thought the rest of the team was lousy. If they had played worse earlier in the season he was glad that he was not present to observe it.[16]

New York's durable batting practice pitcher admitted that he was slightly nervous in that first game he pitched. Perhaps the hardest obstacle to overcome was that for years he had trained himself to serve up fat pitches to batters that could easily be hit over the fence, but now he had to deliver balls that were difficult to hit. His second outing of the season was not so pleasant and he finished his final big league season by throwing four and one-third relief innings, yielding two runs, four hits, and two walks, and finishing with a 4.15 ERA.

The Yankees were baseball's aristocracy and nothing symbolized this more than the ballpark that they played in. After the New York Yankees left Hilltop Park at the conclusion of the 1912 season, they spent the next ten years playing in the Polo Grounds from 1913 through 1922. For most of these years the Giants drew significantly more fans than their tenants, but in 1920, with Babe Ruth in pinstripes, the Yankees became the first team in major league history to draw over one million fans for a season. John McGraw and the Giants organization cringed at the idea of having the Yankees crush them in attendance year in and year out. So in 1921, the Yankees received their eviction notice and were forced to look for a new home. McGraw said, "If we kick them out, they won't be able to find another location on Manhattan Island. They'll have to move to the Bronx or Long Island. The fans will forget about them and they'll be through."[17]

After a thorough search process the Yankees settled on a $675,000 lot, directly across the river from the Polo Grounds, that belonged to the William Waldorf Astor estate. Colonel Jacob Ruppert, the owner of the Yankees, was pleased that it was within view of the Polo Grounds. Therefore he would find great pleasure in watching his Yankees draw overflowing crowds and hope the Giants would struggle in attendance. The original dimensions were 295 feet to right field, 490 to center, and 281 to left. Center field became known as "Death Valley," since many mammoth drives died in the outfielder's glove.[18] The ballpark was the first to be called a "stadium," in acknowledgment of its massive structure, and as a reflection that it had not been named after the playing field within the ballpark, but after the structure that surrounded the playing field.[19] Yankee Stadium was a massive triple-decked structure. It reportedly seated 67,224, but it could hold thousands of more standing spectators.

The *New York Times* reported that a crowd of 74,200 paid spectators showed up for the ballpark's first game on April 18, 1923. Many of the dignitaries were there, John Philip Sousa led the Seventh Regiment band in entertaining the crowd. There were military processions and Al Smith, the governor of New York, threw out the first ball. Ruth christened the new stadium by hitting a home run in the fourth inning. Fred Lieb called the new structure "the House That Ruth Built," and the name stuck.[20] It would also become known as simply "the Stadium." The phrase "the House That Ruth Built" did not necessarily come about simply because Ruth hit a homer in the opening game. It was given the name because Ruth, in his first three seasons with the Yankees at the Polo Grounds, helped draw over a million fans each season, and that success forced them to find a new ballpark. Donald Dewey wrote, "The phrase was actually born before construction on Yankee Stadium was completed and refers more properly to the fact that the Stadium had to be built because the Giants booted the Yankees out of the Polo Grounds."[21]

Ironically, the Giants and Yankees met in the 1923 World Series with the Yankees winning four games to two. McGraw disallowed his club from dressing in the visiting clubhouse at the Stadium. Instead he had his team dress in the Polo Grounds clubhouse and then take cabs to the game. Babe Ruth would later say he preferred hitting at the Polo Grounds because of the poor hitting background at Yankee Stadium.

Laura Cunningham, in her book *Sleeping Arrangements*, provides her observations of seeing Yankee Stadium for the first time: "The old stadium had a biblical look. I assumed it had been standing on 161st Street since before Christ. Years later, when I saw the actual Roman Coliseum, I couldn't suppress an inner gasp of recognition. 'Ahhhh! It's like Yankee Stadium.'"[22] Yankee Stadium was so imposing that it served as the basis of much laudatory praise.

Those who attended Yankee games were in many ways sophisticated, particularly when compared with the unruly Dodger fans. They came from affluent communities and were very controlled when viewing the ball game, not prone to disorderly conduct. "They were refined people for the most part," said Eddie Lopat. "You'd hear the cheering, but they were kind of sedate, generally people with character."[23] Before the 1953 World Series between the Yankees and Dodgers, Arthur Daley wrote, "Because of Brooklyn's raffish past a Yankee fan automatically assumes an air of aristocratic superiority on the eve of any World Series."[24] That's what the Yankees were: "aristocrats," with their winning ball clubs, highbrow fans, and cathedral-like ballpark. In 1958 *Life* magazine reaffirmed a popular slogan that "cheering for the Yankees [is] somewhat like cheering for U.S. Steel."[25] The previous forty years up to 1958, the Yankees won 24 pennants and 17 World Series titles.

The New York Yankees made extra money by renting out their ballpark to the Black Yankees of the Negro Leagues during the 1930s and 1940s.

During the first game of the 1943 World Series the spectators at the Stadium were suddenly awakened by a B-17 Flying Fortress bomber that flew dangerously close to the upper deck. The game was halted while the bomber made three passes, one of which cleared the roof by only ten feet. New York Mayor Fiorello LaGuardia was beside himself in anger over the stunt. Lieutenant Jack Watson, who had flown the bomber, had no regrets. Later in Europe his bomber was hit and he made a courageous landing after every other crewmember bailed out.[26]

❖ 15 ❖

The Boy Manager and the Holdout

During the war the Cleveland Indians conducted their spring training activities at Purdue University in West Lafayette, Indiana. They had a giant field house that was covered with dirt which was used when the weather was poor. Allie Reynolds said, "Spring training at Purdue was tough. Working on the soft ground outside and hard ground inside gave me a beautiful case of shin splints. Because so many players were going into the service, several of us worked out at two positions. My second position was center field."[1]

In 1942 the Indians finished in fourth place (75–79); in '43 third place (82–71); in '44 tied for fifth place (72–82) and in '45 they again finished in fifth place (73–72).

Interestingly, Cleveland played their home games from 1934 to 1946 in both League Park and the cavernous Municipal Stadium. The intimate League Park held only about 22,000 fans while Municipal Stadium could accommodate nearly four times as many. It had 78,189 seats. The lower deck had 37,896 seats alone, which was more than several other ballparks, including Fenway Park, Wrigley Field, and Ebbets Field. Weekday games were played at League Park, and weekend, holiday, and night games at Municipal Stadium. League Park was never fitted with lights. Despite the fact that the two ballparks had different configurations, the Indians gained the home-field advantage because of a skilled groundskeeper named Emil Bossard. He would speed up the infield or slow it down if he thought it benefited the Indians. He could prepare the foul lines in a way that would make it more likely to keep bunts in fair territory. And he could alter the playing field in a number of other ways to help the home team. Bossard said, "This is a game of inches. An inch is often the difference between a base hit and an out. We try to have the inches go our way."[2] When Bill Veeck became the owner of the team during the 1946 season he soon abandoned the smaller park: starting in 1947 the Indians played all their home games at Municipal Stadium. The huge stadium on the banks of Lake Erie needed 5,100 tons of steel to build; in comparison, Braves Field needed only 750 tons.

Player/manager Lou Boudreau was arguably the most accomplished hitter on the team and batted .307 in 1945. However, injuries limited him to just 97 games and 345 at-bats, which was a sharp decline from the 150 games and 584 at-bats he accumulated in 1944. In fact, during the previous five seasons from 1940 to 1944, he played at least 147 games a season. Despite having feeble ankles, and being one of the slowest infielders in the game, Boudreau compensated for his lack of physical skills with great instincts and was a very good major league shortstop. He batted .295 lifetime, and led the league in batting in 1944 (.327) and also hit a career-best .355 in 1948. Despite his limited foot speed, Boudreau collected 385 doubles in his career, including a high of 46 in 1940. In 1941, 1944, and 1947 he led the American League in doubles, hitting 45 during each of those seasons. He hit 68 homers during his Hall of Fame career, including a career high of 18 in 1948. Boudreau hit 66 triples in his career, a somewhat impressive accomplishment for a player that Rob Neyer aptly described as being "slower than pond water."[3] Lou would steal an occasional base, swiping 51 in his career, but he was also caught stealing 50 times. Boudreau was among the best shortstops in the game despite his bad ankles. At the shortstop position he would gracefully glide after the ball and performed exceptionally at the position. During eight seasons he led the junior league in fielding average: from 1940 to 1944 and from 1946 to 1948. He spent thirteen of his fifteen seasons with the Indians from 1938 to 1950 and then finished his playing career with the Boston Red Sox in 1951 and 1952.

Lou became the manager of the club in 1942 at the age of twenty-four, which made him the youngest skipper in American League history. He was often referred to as the "boy manager." But things did not go smoothly for Boudreau early in his managerial career and he was often ridiculed because of his age. During the spring of 1942 he was reportedly approached by several players, including Gee Walker and Hal Trosky, who informed him that they wanted the managerial position and that they would do a better job as the Indians skipper than Boudreau. Jim Bagby, Jr., who was the son of a major league pitcher, was riding high in 1942, compiling a 17–9 record and a 2.96 ERA on the season. He would tear into Boudreau if he booted a ball behind him: Bagby would tell his young manager, using harsh words, that he should return to college and learn the intricacies of the shortstop position. Boudreau would overcome his trials and tribulations and become comfortable in his role as the manager of the ball club. The values that were instilled in him by his father, a competent semi-pro third baseman, helped him overcome his difficulties. Boudreau was born on July 17, 1917, in Harvey, Illinois, a town that wanted to be led and influenced around a capitalistic ethic and Christianity.[4]

When Bill Veeck became the owner he wanted to make Al Lopez the skipper and tried to trade Boudreau to the Browns. However, Veeck could not meet the Browns' demands, and soon the fans found out about the negotiations and became outraged. After an outpouring of support by the fans, Veeck renewed

Boudreau's contract for two more years. Veeck said, "Lou was determined to prove I was a jerk.... He did."[5] Boudreau received an additional two-year extension to his contract after the Indians won the 1948 World Series. However, at the end of the 1949 campaign, Cleveland's innovative owner sold the club to a group of Cleveland businessmen. Boudreau was replaced as the Tribe skipper after the 1950 season with Al Lopez, who was a reticent and stern personality who would occasionally reveal his nasty temper when provoked. But away from the playing field Lopez was well liked. He had an exceptional career as a major league manager and consistently got his ball club to perform up to their full potential. Lopez won two pennants and finished in second place ten times during his seventeen-year managerial career with the Indians and White Sox. The fact that Boudreau was able to hold the managerial position in Cleveland for so long and hold off Al Lopez, a talented and well-respected baseball man, was a testament to Boudreau's popularity with the fans and skill as the leader of the ball club.

After leaving the Indians in 1950, Boudreau later became the manager of the Boston Red Sox (1952–1954), the Kansas City Athletics (1955–1957), and the Chicago Cubs (1960). He led the 1948 Indians to a World Series title, but that was the only year he won the pennant and World Series as manager. However, in 1948 Boudreau was assisted by an exceptional coaching staff that consisted of Bill McKechnie, Muddy Ruel, and Mel Harder. McKechnie had spent twenty-five seasons as a major league manager. He played an integral role as a consultant to Boudreau in 1948 and was a coach for Lou for three seasons with the Indians (1947–1949) and two seasons with the Red Sox (1952–1953). Ruel had managed the 1947 St. Louis Browns to a last-place finish with a 59–95 record. He was an intelligent man who was trained in the legal profession. Later in his life he worked for commissioner Happy Chandler and then became director of the Detroit Tigers' minor league system. Harder had retired after the 1947 season and finished his twenty-year major league career, in which he spent the entire time with Cleveland, with a 223–186 mound record. During the 1961 and 1962 seasons he would manage a total of three major league games and won all three of them as skipper. Boudreau managed for sixteen years in the majors and had a 1,162–1,224 record for a .487 percentage.

The Indians' slick-fielding shortstop originally broke his right ankle in high school and then started practicing his basketball skills before the ankle healed, injuring it again. The ankle had bothered him ever since, and he later developed complications with the other ankle as well. At the University of Illinois he was known more for his basketball prowess than his baseball skills. He was the captain of the basketball team and in 1937 led them to a Big Ten title and then earned All-American honors the following year. As a baseball player he was solid but unspectacular. He was originally a third baseman but was moved to shortstop by Indians manager Ossie Vitt, who informed him that Ken Keltner, another young and talented player, was going to patrol the hot corner for a long time in Cleveland. Vitt's prediction was prescient, as Keltner gained a reputation as an excellent defensive third baseman who also handled the bat well. He played one game in 1937 and then was inserted into the starting lineup the following season when he hit .276 with 26 homers and 113 RBIs. In 1939, Keltner batted a career-high .325, and later he compiled a career-high 31 homers and 119 RBIs during Cleveland's world championship 1948 season. He played at least 149 games for five consecutive seasons from 1938 to 1942, proving to be a durable player. In 1944 he batted .295 with 13 homers and then was in the military during the 1945 campaign.

In 1938, Boudreau played in one game for Cleveland, going 0 for 1 with one walk. When he showed up at the Indians' 1939 spring training facility in New Orleans he shocked a newspaper man named Ed McAuley. When McAuley gazed upon the diamond he observed an apparently healthy young man who wasn't of large build but who ran the bases with the speed, grace, and style of Shanty Hogan. That was not a compliment. Hogan was a catcher in the major leagues for the Boston Braves, New York Giants, and Washington Senators from 1925 to 1937. He had a booming voice that reportedly could be heard by the fans who were situated in the bleachers. While he put together six seasons with a batting average of .300 or better, he was also known as being painfully slow. He tipped the scales somewhere in the vicinity of 240 pounds and battled weight problems his entire career. During the nineteenth century and the first half of the twentieth century, statistical records were often compiled in an erroneous fashion and the statistics in various encyclopedias from this period have been called into question throughout the years. The baseball encyclopedia insists that Hogan stole six bases in his thirteen-year career, which consisted of 989 games. It also credits another slow runner, Ernie Lombardi, with eight stolen bases in a seventeen-year career and 1,853 games. The spectator who witnessed any of these fourteen steals by Lombardi or Hogan was observing a rare feat. For Boudreau at the age of twenty-one to be compared to Shanty Hogan in the speed department was about as bad as it got. The only thing that may have been worse was to be compared to Ernie Lombardi.

Boudreau tried hard to become a faster runner but was largely unsuccessful. When he showed up for the 1940 training season at Ft. Myers, he was still slow before and after listening attentively to the advice of Speedy Rush, the longtime coach of the Princeton track team. Boudreau was ticketed for Buffalo of the International League in 1939, where he batted .331 and formed a solid double play combination with second baseman Raymond James Mlckovsky, who went by the name Ray Mack. Lou's double-play partner was from Cleveland and was hoping to play with his hometown team. Like Boudreau, he was a college graduate, earning a degree from Cleveland's Case Institute of Technology, which later became known as Case Western Reserve. Both Boudreau and Mack were called up towards the tail end of the 1939 season, Boudreau batted .258 in 225 at-bats and Mack batted .152 in 112 at-bats. In 1940 they were inserted into Cleveland's starting lineup and formed the team's middle infield combination until Mack went into the military and missed the entire 1945 season. When he returned he would only play briefly in 1946 and 1947, and then his big league career was over with a .232 batting average and a .301 on-base percentage.

Boudreau's right ankle was inspected for the second time at the Cleveland induction center on June 12, 1945, and once again he was rejected for military service. Even when the government was targeting professional athletes for the draft, they still did not want the services of Lou Boudreau. Boudreau told a reporter that there was an unnatural curve in his ankle bone and arthritis had developed as a result. The left ankle was also in poor condition. However, it was the right ankle that continued to be the most problematic. Boudreau showed great courage in putting on the uniform and playing hurt, serving as a positive example to his teammates. If the skipper was going to play hurt, then they better expect to do the same. Boudreau taped his ankles before every game. Despite this practice his right ankle would occasionally become so swollen that he had great difficulty tying his shoes. Additionally, in 1945 he also suffered from an ulcerated right eye during the season. It developed because of a vitamin deficiency which weakened his immune system and allowed an infection to develop. He was taking three different vitamins in hopes that the ulcers did not come back. Ed McAuley of the *Cleveland News* wrote, "Anyone know where the Indians can get eight more invalids?"[6]

Jeff Heath, Mickey Rocco, Pat Seerey, Felix Mackiewicz, and Les Fleming also contributed offensively. Mickey Rocco batted .264 with 10 homers and Les Fleming hit .329. Jeff Heath (.305, 15 homers), Felix Mackiewicz (.273) and Pat Seerey (.237, 14 homers) formed a muscular trio which prompted Stan Baumgartner to write that they "never have had their names inscribed on a police docket, and as far as we know have never had the 'Crime Doctor' put the finger on them, but they have done some of the fanciest clubbing and bludgeoning in New York, Boston, Cleveland, Detroit and Chicago that baseball has known since the days when another gang of ash ruffians, named the Bronx Bombers, terrorized the junior league."[7] Heath believed he would hit more homers if he didn't have to play in the spacious Municipal Stadium.

Jeff Heath suffered a knee injury in high school and had surgery while in college. He turned down an offer from the University of Washington athletic department to pay for the surgery, since in return he would have had to play halfback for their football team. He went to a Seattle surgeon instead because he didn't want to owe anyone anything. In 1944 he began to have problems when his knee began to lock up. He batted .331 in 60 games and some sportswriters thought he wasn't putting out his best effort. One Cleveland sportswriter wrote, "There is nothing the matter with his knee. Jeff just doesn't want to run out popups and easy grounders."[8] During the winter he had a second surgery in Seattle. Heath was a holdout during the first six weeks of the 1945 season and didn't make his first start until June 13 in Chicago. When he signed his contract with the Indians he predicted that the ball club would see a rise in attendance in his first game back, insisting that his presence upon the diamond would draw a few thousand additional fans to see him play and "to throw rocks at me."[9] However, Heath's fears were unfounded because when he made his first appearance of the season as a pinch-hitter he received an ovation from the home crowd. For much of the early part of the season it was rumored that he would be traded because of his uneasy relationship with the front office. But the only credible offer the Indians received was from Washington and they only offered to pay cash for Heath's services. It wasn't until 1946 that he would leave the team, splitting the season between the Senators and Browns. Heath was concerned about his knee during the 1945 season, and cautiously maneuvered after fly balls. Sliding was his biggest concern.

Felix Mackiewicz had only played twenty major league games for the Philadelphia Athletics before joining the Indians in 1945. He was not a home run hitter but sprayed line drives around the field. In 1945 he hit the only two homers of his six-year major league career in which he had 672 at-bats. Mackiewicz was born in Chicago on November 20, 1917, and went to college at Purdue, where he played baseball, basketball, and football. Pat Seerey had 14-inch forearms and in a seven-year major league career hit eighty-six homers. On July 13, 1945, he hit three homers and a triple against the New York Yankees. Seerey was not a disciplined hitter and would chase a lot of pitches outside the strike zone. Indians coach Burt Shotton and center fielder Myril Hoag were trying to get him to concentrate on making better contact. He was a right-handed batter and stood at 5'10", 200 pounds. Stan Baumgartner described him as a "stocky, brick schoolhouse type, with powerful shoulders, arms and wrists."[10]

Cleveland had a good pitching staff led by Steve Gromek (19–9) and Allie Reynolds (18–12). Jim Bagby (8–11), Al Smith (5–12), Ed Klieman (5–8), Pete Center (6–3), and Mel Harder (3–7) also made contributions. Bob Feller made a triumphant return late in the season, going 5–3 with a 2.50 ERA. He led the league in wins his last three seasons before going off to war, with 24, 27, and 25. And then he continued to dominate American League hitters in the post-war period as he led the league in wins his first two full seasons back, chalking up 26 wins in 1946 and then recording 20 victories in 1947. His lifetime record was 266–162 with a 3.25 ERA and 2,581 strikeouts. Feller was a 2-C classification because he was a farmer; he didn't have to go to war, but he went, and would not accept non-combat responsibilities, instead finding his way onto the USS *Alabama* and seeing the fighting at Tarawa, Kwajlein, and Iwo Jima. He said, "If I was in, I might as well be in all the way."[11]

Conventional wisdom reasonably and in most cases accurately suggests that those players who missed several seasons to military service would have had significantly better career statistical records if they had played during the war years and augmented their final tally. For example, one statistician crunched the numbers and declared that Bob Feller would have had 107 more victories

15. The Boy Manager and the Holdout 219

Left to right: Emmett Mueller, Morrie Arnovich, Mickey Harris, Johnny Sturm, John Grodzicki, Cecil Travis, Ken Silvestri, Pat Mullin, George Earnshaw, Fred Hutchinson, Vince Smith, Bob Feller, and Sam Chapman. Feller voluntarily joined the Navy a few days after Pearl Harbor and initially served in heavyweight champion Gene Tunney's physical fitness program. But after six months he demanded that he be prepared for sea duty and went to gunnery school. He led an anti-aircraft gun crew on the USS *Alabama*, which saw action in the North Atlantic and South Pacific. When he returned stateside in 1945, he managed the Great Lakes Naval Center team. When he was discharged in mid–August he promptly rejoined the Indians (George Brace photograph).

and 1,070 more strikeouts if he had not chosen to fight bravely to defend his country from encroaching totalitarian and murderous regimes and instead pitched for the Indians in the junior league. Rob Neyer, however, challenges this thesis when it comes to Bob Feller and puts forward a conjecture that should at least be considered. Feller threw 1,448 innings before the age of twenty-three. Neyer suggests that Feller's arm may have been overused and "hanging by a thin thread" by 1942. Neyer believes that Feller's decline in productivity would have begun earlier if he had continued to pitch in the major leagues and he may have actually won fewer games in his career than he did.[12] Before going off to war Feller threw an exorbitant number of innings from 1938 to 1941: 1938 (277.2 innings), 1939 (296.2), 1940 (320.1), and 1941 (343). Feller led the American League in innings pitched during his final three seasons before going to war (1939–1941) and during the first two postwar seasons (1946–1947). From 1939 to 1941 he had ERAs of 2.85, 2.61, and 3.15. After he returned from the war, in 1946 and 1947 his ERA was somewhat lower at 2.18 and 2.68. During each of those five seasons his ERA was well below the league average. In 1946 Lou Boudreau rode Feller like an expendable mule as he threw 371.1 innings and then threw 299 innings the following year. He never again would have an ERA below three, and from 1948 to 1956 his earned run averages were as follows: 3.56, 3.75, 3.43, 3.50, 4.74, 3.59, 3.09, 3.47, and 4.97. When his precipitous decline began in 1948 with inflated ERAs he was only twenty-nine years old.

After seeing little playing time in three major league seasons, Steve Gromek went 10–9 in 1944 and then went 19–9 with a 2.55 ERA in 251 innings pitched in 1945. He was well conditioned due to the fact he worked ten hours a day, and occasionally seven days a week during the off-season. He had other responsibilities outside of baseball as well. Gromek was determined to become a major league player and take advantage of whatever opportunities came in his direction. The money he earned in baseball and in his other jobs went to support his family: his father hadn't worked in twelve years because of an illness and his sister was also sick. If he was going to play baseball he felt that he had to make it in the major leagues because the minor league paycheck was not enough to pay the doctor bills.

Gromek threw a sharp curve and a moving fastball. He began his career in organized baseball in 1939 as a shortstop and became a pitcher when he injured his left shoulder. When he was at the plate, Gromek swung from his heels, and that was why he tore his shoulder. As a pitcher he initially threw overhand, straight fastballs, but the coaches got him to throw sidearm, which put more movement on the ball. George Susce was a coach for the Indians and a former catcher who had taken Gromek under his wing and taught him much about the game. Susce, whose nickname was "Good Kid," played in 146 major league games during eight seasons for five teams. His final season was in 1944 with Cleveland when he batted .230 in 61 at-bats.

Gromek was predominantly a relief pitcher until midway through the 1944 campaign when he relieved Allie Reynolds in the first inning of a game in which Reynolds had been hit hard for three markers. Gromek came in and shut the opposition down, yielding just two hits the rest of the way. Once in the starting rotation, Gromek ran into some tough luck, losing his first four starts by one run. He was one of the best-conditioned players on the 1944 Indians and this helped him to be effective late in ball games and work into extra innings. After those first four starts, Gromek's conditioning helped him win a 14-inning affair against the Browns by a 3–2 score; he drove in the winning run with his bat.[13]

He was 6'2" and in 1945, 190 pounds. Gromek was a right-handed pitcher and a switch-hitter. When he first started in organized ball he weighed 145 pounds. Bob Yonkers wrote, "He drinks beer and smokes an occasional cigar, but is addicted to neither, and he keeps regular hours. He is single, and 4-F."[14] In a seventeen-year major league career Gromek had a 123–108 record with a 3.41 ERA.

Al Smith and Jim Bagby were the two pitchers who ended Joe DiMaggio's 56-game hitting streak on July 17, 1941. They were helped out by their talented third baseman, Ken Keltner, who made two outstanding defensive plays to rob DiMaggio on the day. Smith was pitching the final season of his twelve-year big league career in 1945: he compiled a 5–12 record and a 3.84 ERA while starting nineteen of the twenty-one games he appeared in during the campaign. His final career record stood at 99–101 with a 3.72 ERA. Smith was a southpaw while his teammate, Jim Bagby, was a right-handed pitcher. Bagby had a better record in 1945, at 8–11, but his ERA of 3.73 was almost equivalent to Smith's. He was participating in his eighth major league season in 1945. In 1946 (7–6, 3.71 ERA) he pitched for the Boston Red Sox and in 1947 for the Pittsburgh Pirates (5–4, 4.67 ERA), and then his career was over with a 97–96 lifetime mark and a 3.96 ERA.

Allie Reynolds would play his final season for Cleveland in 1946 and then pitch for the Yankees for eight seasons, ending his career with a 182–107 record and a 3.30 ERA. After the 1946 campaign Reynolds was traded to the Yankees for Joe Gordon and Eddie Bockman. During Reynolds's four full seasons with the Indians from 1943 to 1946 he compiled a 51–47 record. He was a remarkably consistent and durable pitcher: after pitching in two games for the Indians in 1942 he then won between 11 and 20 games for the remaining twelve seasons of his major league career. He was a hard-throwing, 6-foot, 195-pound right-hander. Opposing batters did not dig a firm toehold in the batter's box because Allie had a reputation of throwing inside, and he threw that hard fastball that left a painful mark if it hit the batter. He also possessed a great curveball in his repertoire. When Reynolds was with the Yankees, Eddie Joost, the Philadelphia Athletics shortstop, recalled that his team visited Yankee Stadium to open the season and he got a rude awakening. Joost was having a conversation with Yogi Berra near home plate right before he was going to stand in the batter's box as the lead-off hitter to start the game. Reynolds was warming up and became perturbed when he witnessed Joost fraternizing with his catcher. Suddenly Joost heard Berra's voice yell "Look out!" and he quickly hit the deck, just avoiding a pitch delivered with harmful intent to send a message. Reynolds didn't want Joost standing near the batter's box, a territory that he had marked for himself, unless the game had commenced.[15] Those batters who were guess hitters and anticipated the curveball but got the high, inside fastball, were fortunate to leave the batter's box without getting hit and therefore without a severe injury. The intimidating hurler would occasionally be used late in a game for a relief appearance: when it started to get dark, Reynolds was the perfect moundsman to prevent a late-inning rally and close out a ball game because of his excellent fastball and the sense of uncertainty that a hitter felt against him. He was credited with 49 saves during his career. Reynolds was nicknamed "Superchief," and after he'd struck out Jackie Robinson three times during a World Series contest, manager Casey Stengel said, "Before that black sonofabitch accuses us of being prejudiced, he should learn how to hit an Indian."[16] Jackie had gone on a popular television show and accused the Yankees of being prejudiced towards blacks, while Reynolds was part Creek Indian. The Yankees were one of the last teams to allow a black man to wear their uniform; Elston Howard finally did so on April 14, 1955.

By mid–June the season began to fall apart for the Tribe. They lost seven of eight on the road against western opponents, culminating in a 5–1 loss to Detroit on June 21 at Briggs Stadium. Because of the apathetic and uninspiring performance by several of the Cleveland players, manager Boudreau felt compelled to hand out fines. Paul O'Dea, the right fielder; Dutch Meyer, the second baseman; and Mickey Rocco, the first baseman, were each fined for their nonchalant play. These players were not alert and ready to play, and worse yet, they did not always hustle. Meyer, for example, was late covering second base on an attempted steal. Boudreau was also displeased when a pop fly to short right field was not caught. This kind of play was not an isolated event but had become commonplace with the Indians.[17] Cleveland's hitting had also gone into hibernation: before scratching out a run against Stubby Overmire in the ninth inning on the 21st to end his shutout bid, the Indians had gone twenty consecutive innings without scoring a run. After the game the Indians had a 21–29 record and were situated in seventh place, only two games ahead of last-place Philadelphia and nine and a half games behind the first-place Tigers. By season's end they were able to finish one game above .500 but they failed to break into the first division.

❖ 16 ❖

Jimmy Dykes and the Pale Hose

Jimmy Dykes had managed the White Sox with limited success since 1934. His playing career ended in 1939 with a .280 lifetime average. He developed a reputation as a skilled bench jockey and, unlike his behavior as a player, got into some memorable arguments and was often fined and occasionally suspended. When Dykes got new players on his team he was not concerned about their past history but instead how they performed under him. He gave a lot of troubled players a final chance to prove they could stick in the big leagues. The ownership of the White Sox was quite frugal and did not spend a lot of money on personnel. But John P. Carmichael of the *Chicago Daily News* insisted that the White Sox were competitive during many seasons because of the great eye for talent that Dykes possessed. The White Sox relied heavily on troubled players that other teams were eager to discard. Dykes sanctioned the acquisition of players who were disgruntled, angry, complaining, unruly, or disobedient, and those that had a drinking problem. If Jimmy Dykes and his White Sox did not give these players another opportunity they may well have been playing in the bush leagues or worse yet, a semi-pro outfit. When these recalcitrant players joined the Pale Hose they were confronted by Dykes and told that what had happened in the past will remain in the past and they would be given a clean slate with the White Sox. Dykes did not penalize them for previous misbehavior even when he knew specifically what the player had done and objected to it. Dykes insisted that most of the players who had bad reputations before coming to his team were not as bad as they were portrayed.[1]

When Carmichael interviewed Dykes, the manager had a calm disposition, a somewhat rare sight for the animated skipper. Dykes was smoking a cigar, which he was wont to do. He candidly admitted that he was surprised to be managing his twelfth season for the Pale Hose in 1945. He thought that he would last two or three seasons but considered himself fortunate that he got the breaks. He didn't have a problem with most of his players, even those that had a bad reputation before joining the team. He estimated that 95 percent of his players had given their best effort since he assumed the title of manager.

When Dykes fined a player it generally did not stick. Up to this juncture of his managerial career, only on two occasions did he make a fine permanent and not rescind it. The first time was when Jake Wade told his teammates that nothing had been taken out of his check and fines are not something to be concerned about on the White Sox. The second time was with John Whitehead, who was fined for not being in proper shape. Dykes insisted that the 6'2", 195-pound right-handed hurler could have been among the greatest pitchers to ever toe the slab in a big league ballpark. He had baseball smarts and was a surprisingly cerebral hurler, according to Dykes, despite the fact that he was not intelligent away from the playing field. The fact that Whitehead never became a great pitcher was somewhat tragic. He had burst onto the big league scene in 1935, going 13–13 for the White Sox. He had the same record in 1936 and then went 11–8 and 10–11 during the next two seasons. During his final three seasons he would win only two more major league games. Dykes felt sorry that Whitehead had wasted his ability. The opinionated skipper allowed his players to provide feedback but insisted that when the game started he was the "boss." Umpire Bill Summers told a group of soldiers while overseas that Dykes is "one of our greatest managers." However, this opinion of Dykes was not universal; many hated him because he was a persistent bench jockey. John P. Carmichael wrote, "He is loud, sarcastic and blunt ... but never unapproachable."[2]

When asked about sign stealing by J.G. Taylor Spink, Dykes provided a response which was also a criticism of wartime baseball. He scoffed at the suggestion that players of the wartime ilk were engaged in the art of sign stealing and reading pitchers, although this had occurred quite frequently in the "dim past," when there were terrific ball players in the major leagues. But the times had changed: hitters now tried to hit knuckleball pitchers by holding their hands at the bottom of the bat and taking healthy cuts instead of simply choking up on the bat and trying to make contact. By 1945, hitters had begun to guess about what pitch would be delivered and this made them vulnerable to striking out. Dykes cited Art Fletcher and Del Baker as two players of the past who were excellent sign stealers.[3]

Dykes did not have a good history concerning race relations. Peter Bjarkman wrote the following concerning his time as manager of the Philadelphia Athletics in the early 1950s when he jeered Minnie Minoso: "Dykes was a special thorn.... It was treatment paralleling that meted out in the City of Brotherly Love against [Jackie] Robinson by Phillies skipper Ben Chapman.... In one disgraceful incident tensions were apparently especially high after Dykes revealed publicly that he had ordered pitcher Mario Fricano to fire the baseball directly at Minoso's head."[4] Minoso said that Dykes would act in a two-faced manner because after racially taunting him during the game and encouraging his players to join in, he would say hello to Minoso in a very polite manner at the hotel. Dykes was trying to distract Minoso and make him lose his concentration at the ballpark but did so in an unconscionable way. The talented White Sox outfielder, who was born in Havana, was trained by his parents to ignore the racial taunts. He would often reply with an "insincere grin," and retaliate by speaking Spanish.[5] It wasn't just the blacks who were verbally abused by Dykes. George Kell recalls, "He was nasty to everybody."[6]

The White Sox' manager was born James Joseph Dykes in Philadelphia on November 10, 1896. Despite playing for some awful teams with the Philadelphia Athletics during his first few seasons in the big leagues, he never lost his enthusiasm for the game. Connie Mack saw potential in the young prospect and allowed him to begin his career with the Athletics' 1918 contingent, where he batted .188 in 186 at-bats as a second baseman. The following year he batted .184 in 49 at-bats and then stabilized to a respectable .256 batting average in 546 at-bats during the 1920 season. In Dykes's first four seasons with the Athletics from 1918 to 1921 they finished in last place in the American League with records of 52–76, 36–104, 48–106, and 53–100. (The Athletics actually finished in last place for a streak of seven years starting in 1915.) Jimmy played through the lean years in Philadelphia but hung around until Mack had turned Philadelphia's American League outfit into a pennant-winning ball club. Philadelphia won the American League flag from 1929 to 1931 and won the World Series in 1929 and 1930. When the Depression decimated the country, Mack, like others, fell on hard times and needed to raise funds. Therefore Jimmy Dykes, Al Simmons and Mule Haas were traded to the Chicago White Sox on September 28, 1932, for about $150,000. The 5'9", 185-pound right-handed hitter played for the White Sox from 1933 to 1939 and ended his twenty-two-year major league career with a .280 batting average, 108 home runs, and 1,071 RBIs. He had a .365 on-base percentage and a .399 slugging percentage. Dykes's primary positions were third base and second base, but he played all four infield positions during his career, played the outfield, and even pitched in two games. Some fans are adamant that he even caught in the big leagues but there are no records to prove that he did.[7]

Dykes began his managerial career as a playing manager with the White Sox in 1934 and managed them with moderate success until 1946. Then he managed the Philadelphia Athletics from 1951 to 1953; the Baltimore Orioles in 1954; the Cincinnati Reds for part of the 1958 campaign; the Detroit Tigers in 1959 and 1960; and finally ended his managerial career as the skipper of the Cleveland Indians in 1960 and 1961. He had a 1,406–1,541 record in twenty-one seasons as a manager. Dykes drew headlines in 1960 when he was involved in the first trade between managers: On August 10, 1960, Dykes was traded to Cleveland from Detroit for Joe Gordon. The trade didn't spark either team to finish high in the standings: Cleveland finished in fourth place with a 76–78 record, while Detroit had a sixth-place conclusion at 71–83. In addition to managing in the major leagues he also managed Hollywood of the Pacific Coast

League for part of the 1946 season and in 1947 and 1948. When he wasn't managing in the majors he was often on someone's coaching staff, with the Philadelphia Athletics, Cincinnati Reds, Pittsburgh Pirates, Milwaukee Braves, and Kansas City Athletics. Dykes was a baseball lifer who truly loved the game.[8]

During Dykes's first eleven years as the manager of the White Sox they finished in the first division six times despite having limited home run power in their lineup. During many seasons they were one good hitter away from competing for the pennant. When Comiskey Park first opened for business on July 1, 1910, the spacious dimensions (362–420–362) helped the ballpark earn the reputation as a pitcher's park. Future Hall of Fame pitcher Ed Walsh helped design the ballpark and therefore gave a considerable advantage to his pitching brethren.[9] The dimensions were altered occasionally throughout the years but it still remained a pitcher's park for most of its existence. The large dimensions were the primary reason why there was a power outage on the South Side of Chicago.

The following chart shows where the White Sox finished in the American League in home runs during Dykes's tenure as the Pale Hose manager. It also provides the number of home runs hit and the team's record and position in the junior circuit for each season.

Year	Position (HRs)	Home Runs	Position and Record (AL)
1934	5th	71	8th (53–99)
1935	5th	74	5th (74–78)
1936	8th	60	3rd (81–70)
1937	7th	67	3rd (86–68)
1938	8th	67	6th (65–83)
1939	7th	64	4th (85–69)
1940	7th	73	4th, tie (82–72)
1941	8th	47	3rd (77–77)
1942	8th	25	6th (66–82)
1943	7th	33	4th (82–72)
1944	8th	23	7th (71–83)
1945	8th	22	6th (71–78)
1946	8th	37	5th (74–80)

During the 1934 season (137 games) and the 1946 season (30 games) Dykes did not manage the South Siders for the entire campaign. During the thirteen seasons in which Dykes managed all or part of the season for Chicago's American League representative, they averaged 51 homers a season. And in the following years after Dykes's departure they still had problems hitting the long ball. When the White Sox hit 116 homers in 1955, that was the first time in the team's history that they had hit over 100 home runs. In a spacious ballpark like Comiskey Park it would behoove a team to take advantage of the dimensions and build their team around speed, pitching, and defense. During Dykes's tenure they often tried to manufacture runs by utilizing small-ball strategies. They led the American League in stolen bases during four seasons: 1939 (113),

1941 (91), 1942 (114), and 1943 (173). And they led the AL in sacrifice bunts during three seasons: 1937 (111), 1939 (154), and 1940 (110). When the 1943 White Sox stole 173 bases, that was truly an exorbitant total for that time period. The 1925 Pittsburgh Pirates were the last team to steal over 150 bases before the 1943 White Sox accomplished the feat. After 1943 it took nineteen seasons until another team stole over 150 bases. The 1962 Los Angeles Dodgers stole 198 and sparked a revival in the running game.

There are a myriad of stories about Dykes and the memorable antics that he engaged in. In June of 1940 the Cleveland Indians were saddled with the nickname "Cry Babies" when they pleaded with team president Alva Bradley to fire their manager Ossie Vitt. When word got out about the Indians' predicament, fans around the league threw baby bottles at their players instead of the customary pop bottles.[10] When they arrived in Chicago the mischievous White Sox manager was waiting for them. A baby buggy was placed in front of the dugout and diapers were scattered everywhere. And, of course, Dykes let them have it with his effective, vicious, and often racist bench-jockeying skills.[11]

The players who were managed by Dykes had varying opinions about him. Joe DeMaestri, who batted a career-high .255 under Dykes with the 1953 Philadelphia Athletics, said, "Jimmy Dykes was like a father to me and everybody else. He was a good guy." DeMaestri also had fond memories of Dykes's coaches Bing Miller and Chief Bender.[12] Puerto Rican ballplayer Vic Power had an acrimonious relationship with Dykes and said, "He was like an army sergeant. He was the only manager I didn't get along with." Dykes would rip into Power over the most minor details, such as when Power ordered food at a rest stop when they were only supposed to use the bathroom. Or when Power went outside his hotel room at 3 o'clock in the morning to witness a lunar eclipse. He was subsequently fined for missing curfew. Dykes tried to intimidate Power but did offer some support and advice when he told the talented young player that it was okay to continue to catch the ball one-handed despite what the critics said. The writers and fans thought Power was showboating but Dykes quipped, "Don't argue with success."[13]

Like many managers, Dykes favored experience over youth. As he became older he would give the players more freedom. Dykes was almost always seen with a cigar in his mouth away from the ballpark. The clubhouse men around the league respected him and when his teams came into town he would find boxes of cigars waiting for him. Eddie Joost was one player who warned Dykes that smoking was a bad habit but the advice was disregarded.[14] Jimmy Dykes, who was born in Philadelphia, played and managed for that city's American League team, would also die in Philadelphia on June 15, 1976. He died of cancer.

During the war the White Sox never finished above fourth place. In 1942 they were in sixth place (66–82); in '43 they were in fourth place (82–72); in '44, seventh place (71–83); and in '45 they finished in sixth place (71–78). By

1944 the Sox had lost Luke Appling, Don Kolloway, Eddie Smith, Ted Lyons, Bob Kennedy, and Dario Lodigiani to the service.

They had the fewest homers in the majors (22) but the best batting average (.262) in the American League in 1945. Tony Cuccinello (.308), Johnny Dickshot (.302), Wally Moses (.295), Oris Hockett (.293), Guy Curtright (.281), Kerby Farrell (.258), and Cass Michaels (.245) led the hitters. Cuccinello was in his final major league season. He had played since 1930 with the Reds, Dodgers, Braves, Giants, and White Sox. "Cooch" finished his career with a .280 batting average, 334 doubles and 94 home runs. In 1945 he batted .308, but Snuffy Stirnweiss batted .309 to win the American League batting crown. "It was a big disappointment," admitted the 5' 7", 160-pound right-handed batter.[15] He was a line drive hitter who excelled in executing the hit-and-run. Tony was more of a pull hitter but would occasionally go the other way and drop a hit into right field. Cuccinello was also considered an excellent fielder: he played third base in 112 games in 1945 but was predominantly a second baseman during his career. He also played five games at shortstop during his life in the big leagues.

Tony was 37 years old in 1945, having been born in Long Island City, New York, on November 8, 1907. The Cuccinello brothers honed their skills by playing on the sand lots of Astoria, Long Island. Tony began playing for a semi-pro team as a teenager and then caught the eye of a member of the organized baseball community. His neighbor was the catcher for Syracuse in the International League and he persuaded Tony to work out with the team in Jersey City, where they had traveled for a series. He was offered a contract at 16 years old and he got his older brother to sign for him because he was too young to do so himself. He played briefly for Syracuse, which was part of the St. Louis Cardinals' vast farm system. Then he was sent to Lawrence, Massachusetts, and then to Danville of the Three-I League. The Cincinnati Reds purchased his contract after his sensational 1929 campaign with the Columbus Red Birds of the American Association when he batted a robust .358 with 20 homers and 111 RBIs. In 1930 he was patrolling the hot corner at Crosley Field as the Reds third baseman and hit .312 with a .380 on-base percentage in his rookie year. In 1931 he was shifted to second base and remained at that position until his final few seasons. He batted over .300 during five seasons in his career: 1930 (.312), 1931 (.315), 1936 (.308), 1939 (.306) and 1945 (.308). In 1935, when Tony was playing for the Brooklyn Dodgers, his brother Al was playing his only major league season with the New York Giants, batting .248 in 165 at-bats. During one game between the hated National League rivals the two brothers each hit a home run. Tony was Sam Mele's uncle. Mele played in the major leagues for six teams from 1947 to 1956. He later became the manager of the Minnesota Twins from 1961 to 1967.

Before Dykes settled on Cuccinello to handle the third-base responsibilities in 1945, he was planning to give the job to, first, Grey Clarke, and then to

Left to right: Tony Cuccinello, Vince Castino, unidentified player, Guy Curtright, Thornton Lee, and Orval Grove. These players made contributions to the 1945 Chicago White Sox. Cuccinello batted .308 and finished one point behind New York's Snuffy Stirnweiss for the American League batting title. Remarkably, he was not given a chance to play in the big leagues in 1946. Castino was a catcher who batted .222 in 36 at-bats in his third and final big league season. Curtright played all three outfield positions and batted .281 with 324 at-bats. Southpaw Thornton Lee led the club in victories, compiling a 15–12 record with a 2.44 ERA. Grove, a right-handed pitcher, was 14–12 on the season with a 3.44 ERA (George Brace photograph).

Bill Nagel. During the training season and the evaluation process, Dykes was unimpressed with Clarke's limited abilities, while Nagel was eventually moved to first base. After the 1945 season, Cuccinello thought that his good performance during the campaign would earn him a spot on the roster in 1946. "When the season ended, Jimmie Dykes definitely assured me I'd be back with the White Sox," said Cuccinello. He wasn't, and when released in January of 1946 he said, "I'm the most surprised guy in baseball."[16]

Cuccinello was the manager of the Jersey City Giants of the International League in 1941. He had batted a combined .226 for the Braves and Giants in 1940 and it appeared that he was going to start a new chapter in his baseball life as a manager and coach. He learned a lot from his experience in Jersey City and was pulled in two directions: the fans wanted him to play the best talent and win as many games as they could. However, Bill Terry, the Giants manager, ordered him to develop the young, inexperienced infielders, and the other talented prospects on the team. He was set to return to Jersey City in 1942 until Casey Stengel persuaded him to come to Boston to be a player-coach for the Braves. He was a third base coach and also a batting practice pitcher. At the plate he batted only .202 in 104 at-bats.

Tony was also a player-coach with Boston for part of the 1943 season, when he also played for the White Sox. After failing to get a hit in 19 at-bats for Boston he batted .272 in 103 at-bats for the Pale Hose. In 1944 he batted .262 in 130 at-bats for the White Sox. During the 1945 season he was having trouble with his legs, a problem that had developed after he had stopped playing every day following the 1940 season. He was given a backup role in the subsequent seasons until 1945, when the manpower shortage allowed him to start once again. Cuccinello stated that he never had problems with his legs when he was getting a lot of playing time and was in the lineup every day. But when he was a part-time player his legs were not so active, and that's when the problems began. When he felt a pull in his legs he would ask Dykes to take him out of the lineup. Dykes insisted that as long as the club put large quantities of "adhesive tape and crutches" in the clubhouse, Cooch would be patrolling the hot corner for the White Sox. During the first month and a half of the 1945 campaign, Cuccinello was the best hitter on the team and the most clutch, according to Dykes. Cuccinello was also helpful to the club in imparting advice to the younger players, especially shortstop Cass Michaels, his partner on the left side of the diamond. In 1945 he expressed interest in returning to coaching and managing once his playing days were over.[17] And that is precisely what he did, managing with Tampa of the Florida International League (1947) and coaching with Indianapolis of the American Association (1948). He also coached in the major leagues with several teams including the Cincinnati Reds (1949–1951); Cleveland Indians (1952–1956); and Chicago White Sox (1957–1965). For fourteen consecutive seasons from 1952 to 1965 he was on manager Al Lopez's coaching staff with the Indians and White Sox. In total he coached for twenty-one big league seasons, and was a coach on three pennant winners: the 1954 Cleveland Indians, 1959 Chicago White Sox, and the 1968 Detroit Tigers. The Tigers were the only team to win the World Series, defeating the St. Louis Cardinals, four games to three. Cuccinello never participated in the World Series as a player. However, his biggest regret during his career was never managing in the big leagues. Cuccinello claimed he was offered four managerial jobs with major league teams and he turned down all four. He had not graduated from high school and felt he was not a good speaker and therefore he didn't want to be embarrassed by the speaking engagements that a big league manager is required or expected to participate in.[18]

During spring training he suffered from a sinus condition and a cold. He was a 4-F, not because of his legs but because of a recurring laryngitis condition. Cuccinello had lost his voice for a three-year time period when he was younger. He pulled off the hidden-ball trick in 1945 as he had done in the past. This time he embarrassed Indians player-manager Lou Boudreau with the trick. There are many observations of Tony Cuccinello, and Milt Woodard provided his own in 1945: "If baseball men were like horse trainers, Anthony (Poosh-'Em Up Tony) Cuccinello would be so full of bullet holes that he'd never be able to hold even a plate of Italian spaghetti, let alone the numerous line drives which White Sox' opponents are firing at him these days."[19] Cuccinello had played most of his career in the National League. He said that in the senior circuit the offense plays for one run by executing the fundamentals while in the American League the teams played for the big inning.

Although Cuccinello had spent most of his career in the National League, getting to play in Comiskey Park during his final three major league seasons was somewhat of a homecoming. At 25 years old, Cuccinello was selected to play in the inaugural All-Star game as a member of the Brooklyn Dodgers. The contest was dubbed the "Game of the Century" by some scribes and played at Comiskey Park on July 6, 1933.[20] Babe Ruth, the aging hero, christened the game with a home run and helped the American League defeat the senior circuit by a 4–2 score. Cuccinello struck out as a pinch-hitter for Carl Hubbell in the ninth inning, while his future manager, Jimmy Dykes, went 2 for 3 with a run scored as the third baseman for the American League. Cuccinello was the only player from the National League team that was still playing in 1945. The American League team had three players who made an appearance in the inaugural All-Star game and were still active in 1945: Ben Chapman, Rick Ferrell, and Joe Cronin, who played his final three big league games during the season.

The predicament of Lou Novikoff, "The Mad Russian," was causing considerable friction between the two Chicago clubs in 1945. The Chicago Cubs affiliate in the Pacific Coast League, the Los Angeles Angels, repeatedly put Novikoff on the waiver list during the first half of the season; he was claimed by the White Sox twice, and other clubs also had an interest in him. During one waiver request nobody claimed him, and this was the Cubs' opportunity to banish Novikoff to permanent minor league status. Don Stewart, president of the Angels, insisted that the White Sox had never made an offer but merely inquired about his situation and his potential availability. However, it was reported that the White Sox ownership was willing to pay $15,000 for his rights. Jack Ryan of the *Chicago Daily News* intervened and wrote a letter to Commissioner Happy Chandler that was printed in the newspaper. Ryan and his colleagues at the paper demanded to know if Chandler wanted baseball to be known as a sport that tramples on a person's right to make a living and restricts him from achieving his potential and playing at the highest level. With old-timers like Dolph Camilli, Ben Chapman, Babe Herman, and Clyde Sukeforth still playing in the big leagues in 1945, then there certainly should have been a place for a player like Novikoff. This entire situation became somewhat irrelevant when the California Selective Service Appeal Board ordered Novikoff to report to Fort MacArthur on July 11. Novikoff had been previously deferred from service because his wife was ill.[21]

The Lou Novikoff situation illustrates the unjust nature of the game. Here was a man who some people predicted would be another Babe Ruth. In the bushes he won batting titles in the Pacific Coast League, the American Association, the Texas League and the Three-I League. By the end of June 1945, he was batting .316 with 45 RBIs for Los Angeles. He had underachieved in the big show but was a decent player nonetheless: in 1941, his first season, he batted .241 and then hit .300 with 25 doubles, 5 triples, 7 home runs, and 64 RBIs for the 1942 Cubs. In 1943 he hit for a .279 clip and then hit .281 in 1944. He would return for one final major league season in 1946, batting .304 for the Phillies in 23 at-bats. Certainly there should have been a place for Novikoff on a major league roster in 1945 when the talent level was somewhat abysmal. The Cubs didn't use him in 1945 because they had some talented outfielders on the roster and perhaps they had grown tired of his antics. Novikoff patrolled left field for the Cubs and insisted that he didn't field well because the left field foul line was crooked and not straight as in other parks. He was also wary of approaching the unyielding outfield wall at Wrigley Field. Apparently, his apprehension wasn't because he feared a serious injury like the one that befell Pete Reiser when he slammed into the wall at full speed and lay unconscious on the ground. Instead manager Charlie Grimm suspected that Novikoff thought the vines caused hay fever or poison ivy. Another problem for Novikoff was that he stayed out late and therefore wasn't in the proper shape to play day games at Wrigley Field. He was well liked by his teammates and a terrific storyteller.[22]

Novikoff was an eccentric personality, but there were many eccentric personalities in the big leagues in 1945. Certainly he was good enough to play in the big leagues during the final wartime season and he probably would have performed well. After his big league career ended with the 1946 campaign he continued to play in the minors with Seattle in the Pacific Coast League (1946–1948), Newark (1948–1949), Houston in the Texas League (1949), and then for both Yakima and Victoria in the Western International League in 1950.

The White Sox pitching staff was led by Thornton Lee (15–12) and Orval Grove (14–12), while Ed Lopat (10–13), Johnny Humphries (6–14), Bill Dietrich (7–10), and Earl Caldwell (6–7) also made contributions. Lee started his career in 1933 and would finish in 1948 with a 117–124 record and a 3.56 ERA. In a ten-year career Grove was 63–73 with a 3.78 ERA. "Steady Eddie" Lopat started his career in 1944, going 11–10 with a 3.26 ERA, and the following year he was 10–13 with a 4.11 ERA. Lopat was a southpaw hurler with limited abilities, but he knew how to make the most of them. He was considered a "junkballer" who had excellent control, and changed speeds effectively to keep the batters off balance. His screwball was his money pitch but he also threw a spitter during his career. Later he would be known for pitching for Casey Stengel's great Yankee teams. His career record was 166–112 with a 3.21 ERA. As for his time with the White Sox, he said, "Ted Lyons really put the finishing touches on my pitching. He polished me off and helped me become a real pro."[23] After a great career, Lyons took over for Jimmy Dykes as the manager of the Pale Hose during the 1946 season and remained in that capacity through the 1948 campaign. Lyons had pitched for the White Sox, from 1923 to 1942 before becoming a Marine at the age of forty-one. In 1942 he was still in fine form, compiling a 14–6 record and leading the American League with a 2.10 ERA. He was also remarkably durable that season as he completed all of his twenty starts. Lyons missed the next three seasons while in the military and then pitched the final five games of his outstanding career in 1946, going 1–4 but with a good 2.32 ERA. He completed his Hall of Fame career with a 260–230 record and a 3.67 ERA. His three years in the military may have cost him a legitimate chance at 300 career wins.

The White Sox played their home games on the South Side of Chicago at Comiskey Park. The park was built very rapidly on what had previously been a city dump. During the 1930s, Luke Appling tried to remove what he thought was a rock and found an antique. "I started digging with my spikes, and, lo and behold, I uncovered a blue-and-white teakettle.... The ground crew had to fill in the hole before play could continue."[24] After 1927, seating capacity was 52,000 and the dimensions were 352 feet down the lines and 440 feet to straightaway center field. There was a lot of room behind home plate to catch pop-ups. Comiskey Park was also the venue for many Negro League World Series and All-Star games. It was a pitcher's park and the wind blew in most of the time. However, Tony Cuccinello said, "when you could smell the stockyards, that meant the wind was blowing out, blowing with the hitter."[25]

❖ 17 ❖

Catfish, Boo, and Mr. Yawkey

Among the owners, Boston's Tom Yawkey was a whole different breed altogether. He had inherited twenty million dollars from his wealthy father and that sum grew exponentially over the years. In 1933 he bought the team and vowed that money would not be an issue in trying to develop a championship contingent. He brought stars like Jimmie Foxx, Lefty Grove, and Joe Cronin to Boston. Cronin cost him the exorbitant sum of $225,000. Heading into the 1945 season he had spent 3.5 million dollars on the Red Sox. Yawkey was a munificent owner, paying his players well, and even enjoying their company. The players loved him and Joe Dobson said, "He was the best man that ever walked." He even took batting practice with them, and those backup players who accommodated him during the pregame activities were often kept on the roster and were collectively known as the "ass-kissers squad."[1] However, such coddling of ballplayers gave Boston a "reputation as a haven for lazy players."[2] Leo Durocher believed that a hungry ballplayer was a better ballplayer and his success certainly supports such views. It was also believed that the Red Sox assembled power-laden squads that were too one-dimensional and not well rounded to succeed within the dimensions of Fenway Park. The Red Sox hadn't won a pennant since Babe Ruth graced their uniform in 1918 and many thought the baseball gods had cursed them for selling Ruth to the Yankees before the 1920 season. Yawkey's legacy may ultimately be his unwillingness to bring blacks to the Red Sox. They were the last team to put a black man in uniform; it happened on July 21, 1959, thirteen seasons after Jackie Robinson integrated the sport.

The Red Sox owner was born in Detroit and graduated from Yale in 1925. Ward Morehouse, the *New York Sun* dramatic critic, interviewed him and wrote that Yawkey, "stocky, blue-eyed and 42, sat at his flat-topped desk, looked up at the giant moose, and grinned amiably." Yawkey had a huge moose hanging on the wall that he obtained during a hunting trip to Alberta. Morehouse also added, "Words flow as fast as they do from Tallulah Bankhead, who, except for

Ethel Barrymore, is baseball's keenest feminine fan." Yawkey was a big game hunter and was also fond of bird shooting. He owned a 35,000-acre estate in South Carolina. He was an active outdoorsman and had shot brown and black bear in Alaska, and bear and elk in Wyoming. In New York he stayed at the Hotel Pierre and in Boston the Ritz. In his New York office he had a large oil painting of his father, W.H. Yawkey, who died in 1919. Scattered on the walls were also photographs of great ballplayers like Babe Ruth, Lefty Grove, and Jimmie Foxx.[3] He desperately tried to bring a world championship to Boston but never accomplished his goal despite pouring an exorbitant amount of money into player personnel.

During the war the Red Sox were hurt by the departure of players like Bobby Doerr, Tex Hughson, Jim Tabor, and Hal Wagner. Yawkey reminisced fondly about the terrific teams before the war. In 1938, 1939, and 1941, the Red Sox finished in second place behind the hated Yankees. And in 1940 they were tied for fourth place with Chicago, and even though New York failed to win the flag they still finished one notch above Boston in third place. Teams such as the St. Louis Cardinals had a great advantage during the war because of their deep and talented farm system. By 1945 the Red Sox were also trying to build up their minor league organization.

The Red Sox trained at Tufts College in Medford, Massachusetts, during their first two northern spring training camps. The players stayed at the Hotel Kenmore in downtown Boston and they had to travel six miles to their training facilities at the college. And then in 1945 they trained in Pleasantville, New Jersey, and stayed at the Claridge Hotel in Atlantic City. In 1942 the Red Sox finished in second place (93–59) but the remaining war years were a disappointment for the Fenway faithful. In 1943 they were in seventh place (68–84); in 1944 it was a fourth-place finish (77–77). They would finish in seventh place (71–83) in 1945 and then finally win that elusive pennant in 1946, only to lose the World Series to the St. Louis Cardinals.

In 1944 it appeared that Boston was going to win their first pennant since 1918 and perhaps bring the world championship back to Boston. They entered the final month of the campaign in fourth place, but they were only three and a half games behind the league-leading St. Louis Browns. But late in the season they lost Doerr, Hughson, Tabor, and Wagner to the military and the team never recovered, failing to take the flag. Before going into the service late in the 1944 season, Bobby Doerr, the team's second baseman, was batting .325 with a .399 on-base percentage. He had hit 30 doubles, 10 triples, and 15 home runs. The future Hall of Famer had driven in 81 runs and scored 95 in 468 at-bats and 125 games. The Red Sox' third baseman, Jim Tabor, was batting .285 with 13 homers and 72 RBIs in 116 games before Uncle Sam came calling. Hal Wagner, a left-handed hitting catcher, had started the 1944 season with the Philadelphia Athletics and in early May was traded to the Red Sox for Ford Garrison. He was the most improved catcher in the junior league, batting .332 for Boston with a .418 on-base percentage in 66 games and 223 at-bats before fulfilling his military obligations. Not only did the Sox lose three everyday players who were performing well, but then the military also took ace pitcher Tex Hughson. The 6'3", 198-pound right-handed pitcher had gone 22–6 in 1942 with a 2.59 ERA. In 1943 he had a 12–15 record but an ERA that was well below the league average at 2.64. In 1944 he was 18–5 with an excellent 2.26 ERA before he left the team. No team could survive losing four players of the quality of Doerr, Hughson, Tabor, and Wagner and expect to win the pennant. Predictably, Boston collapsed down the stretch, losing twelve of thirteen during a miserable stretch in September, and finishing the season twelve games off the pace. Furthermore, the departures in 1944 left their roster in a poor condition for the 1945 campaign.

With the acute manpower shortage in 1945, Tom Yawkey was receiving letters from Lefty Grove, who was willing to suit up and join the pitching corps once again. After nine seasons with the Philadelphia Athletics, including seven consecutive twenty-win seasons from 1927 to 1933 when he compiled a 172–54 record, Grove was traded to Boston along with Rube Walberg and Max Bishop. The Athletics received Bob Kline, Rabbit Warstler, and $125,000 in the deal. By the time he came to Boston, Grove was 34 years old. He still had several great seasons in him but his numbers began to decline as he aged. The 6'3", 190-pound flamethrower pitched his final major league season in 1941, going 7–7 with a 4.37 ERA. The Hall of Fame pitcher had a 300–141 lifetime record with a 3.06 ERA. He had 298 complete games, including 35 shutouts, and struck out 2,266 batters. With manpower decimated during the war, he could have undoubtedly come back and put up some decent numbers. But despite Grove's generous offer, Yawkey didn't want him to return and perhaps perform poorly against inferior talent and become embarrassed in his advanced age. Yawkey insisted that Grove should remain in the mountains of Maryland, where he lived peacefully. He surmised that neither Grove nor the club would benefit if Grove limped back during the final wartime season.[4]

Joe Cronin had been the Red Sox' skipper since 1935 and finished in second place to the Yankees four times during his reign. He made his last appearance as a player in 1945, playing in three games and batting .375 (3 for 8), before breaking his ankle. Cronin ended his twenty-year playing career with a .301 batting average and 170 homers. Cronin's father was born in Ireland and when he came to the United States he lived through the 1906 San Francisco earthquake, though he lost everything. That was the same year Joe was born. He started his big league career with Pittsburgh in 1926 and then played for Washington from 1928 to 1934. When Clark Griffith purchased Cronin's contract from Kansas City he was not only getting a good young player, but his scout Joe Engel informed Griffith's niece Mildred, who was employed by the Senators, that Cronin would become her husband. Joe eventually married Clark Griffith's niece Mildred in 1934.[5] In 1930 he had his highest batting average for a full season, .346. He was a good shortstop but did make 62 errors in 1929, which was by far the most in his career. When Tom Yawkey became the Red Sox' owner he desperately wanted to obtain Cronin's services as a player/manager and paid $225,000 to get him in October of 1934. Yawkey also sent Lyn Lary to the Senators in the deal. Cronin had been the Senators' player-manager in 1933 and 1934, winning the pennant in '33, but with the Red Sox he won only one pennant, in 1946. Many felt that Joe didn't know how to handle his pitching staff. He had been a hitter, so he knew hitting and talked about hitting constantly, but he didn't show the same kind of interest in the pitchers. When he had positive inclinations concerning a hurler he often stayed with that pitcher even when he was ineffective.[6]

During the seasons affected by World War II, Cronin put up some decent numbers. In 1942 he batted .304 with a .415 on-base percentage in 79 at-bats, and then in 1943 he batted .312 with a .398 on-base percentage. He inserted himself into games primarily as a pinch-hitter during those two seasons. However, in 1944 he played 49 games at first base and 76 total, batting .241 with 5 home runs, which was the same number of long balls that he had hit in 1943. Cronin was a shortstop during most of his career (1,843 games) but played mainly third base in his few games during the early wartime seasons. But in 1944 he was beginning to show his age, his reflexes had weakened, and worst of all he had gained a significant amount of weight. He was no longer fit to play shortstop or third base so he shifted to the gateway station.[7]

Bob Johnson (.280), Skeeter Newsome (.290), Tom McBride (.305), Johnny Lazor (.310), George "Catfish" Metkovich (.260), and Eddie Lake (.279) were among the team's hitting leaders. Their .260 batting average was second in the league in 1945. Johnson led the club in homers (12) and RBIs (74). "Indian" Bob Johnson was born on November 26, 1905, and had played big league ball since 1933. In a thirteen-year career he batted .296 with 288 homers but never got widespread recognition for his talents because he played ten seasons with Connie Mack's Athletics. The A's went through a tough stretch while he was there, finishing in last place six times. He was a solid defensive outfielder with a strong arm, but with a crowded Boston outfield in 1946 he couldn't make the team. Johnson was a prodigious run producer who drove in over 100 runs during eight seasons, including seven consecutive seasons from 1935 to 1941. He also scored over one hundred runs during six seasons. He had 1,283 RBIs in his career and 1,239 runs scored. His brother Roy also had a fine big league career with the Tigers, Red Sox, Yankees, and Braves from 1929 to 1938. Roy batted .296 lifetime with a .369 on-base percentage and a .437 slugging average. He collected 275 doubles in his career, 83 triples, and 58 home runs. During one game, Bob placed a bird under his brother's glove and when Roy ran onto the field and picked up his mitt he was startled to see the bird fly out from under his glove.

Twenty-four-year-old George Metkovich made his big league debut in

1943, batting .246 with 5 homers. In 1944 he hit .277 with 9 homers, and in 1945 he batted .260 with 5 homers. George had a ten-year big league career, hitting .261 with 47 home runs. After the final game in 1945 he looked at his teammates and declared that many of them would not return because the "real" players were coming home.[8] Metkovich was born in Angels Camp, California, on October 8, 1920. When he played in the Pacific Coast League he was known as the "Clubbing Croat." His parents came to the country from Austria but they were Croations. His father was a gold miner who had a large family of five sons and one daughter. George was six years old when he died.

After the spring of 1940 George Metkovich would henceforth be known as "Catfish." Casey Stengel, who was generally disposed to joke around and see the humor in various situations, could not find the humor in the predicament that befell George Metkovich during the 1940 Boston Braves training camp. Stengel was the manager of the Braves then and Metkovich was trying to make the ball club. Casey was apoplectic when he heard that Metkovich was in the hospital because he had been attacked by a catfish. The incident happened when Metkovich and Wilbur McElroy, who was a pitching prospect, went fishing. They were situated on a bridge over the Manatee River. McElroy hooked a three-foot catfish and the catfish swallowed the hook. Metkovich, at the urging of McElroy, tried to pull the hook out but was unsuccessful. He then placed the catfish on the bridge, placed his foot on it and pulled. According to Metkovich, the catfish raised its fin while it gyrated violently, fighting to stay alive, and the fin went through the bottom of his shoe. McElroy came to the aid of his friend but couldn't remove the fin from his foot. Metkovich was taken to Bradenton Hospital and was unable to play baseball for a week. When he did return to the diamond he had to play with a sponge on his foot.[9]

Despite his setback, Metkovich participated in a few spring training games in 1940 as a late-inning, first base replacement for Buddy Hassett. His bad luck continued in 1940 when he was farmed out to Evansville in the Three-I League as the Braves moved north to prepare for the season opener. At Evansville he played in only ten games before injuring his knee when he caught his spikes while sliding into second base. During the 1941 spring training he was warned by Stengel to keep away from catfish. He reinjured his knee in an exhibition game against the St. Louis Browns. He returned to Evansville for the 1941 season and impressed their manager, Bob Coleman, who made Metkovich an outfielder. Evansville won the pennant that year as Metkovich batted .287 with 30 doubles. After an unimpressive 1942 campaign with Hartford and Evansville, Metkovich was classified 1-A and expected to be called up by the Army. However, that call never came, and in 1943 he played in the Pacific Coast League for Lefty O'Doul's San Francisco Seals. After he tore up the circuit at a .325 clip, the Boston Red Sox purchased him for $25,000 on July 6, 1943. He made his major league debut for the Red Sox in 1943, and when Tony Lupien was traded to the Phillies after the 1943 campaign, it paved the way for Metkovich

George Metkovich acquired the nickname "Catfish" when he was injured by a catfish during the 1940 spring training with the Boston Braves. George was trying to remove the hook when suddenly the catfish fought back. Its fin penetrated George's shoe and injured his foot so severely that he had to go to the hospital. Casey Stengel, the Braves manager, was not amused when he found out his nineteen-year-old prospect was sidelined by a catfish (George Brace photograph).

to become their everyday first baseman.[5] Things didn't actually go as planned because Metkovich played in 82 games as an outfielder and 50 games as a first baseman in 1944. He played more games in the outfield (644 games) during his career than at first base (289 games). Metkovich had a great throwing arm, firing balls with excellent speed and accuracy. Lefty O'Doul said that he had witnessed players who threw harder than Metkovich, but he had never seen anybody with more accuracy, and therefore Metkovich's left-handed throwing arm was the greatest he had ever seen.[10] Metkovich was 6'1" and about 185 pounds. He was a left-handed hitter.

When shortstop Skeeter Newsome went down with a thumb injury in late May, Eddie Lake filled in admirably. In fact he played so well at the shortstop position that when Newsome returned to the lineup he played second base. In addition to his .279 average, Lake clubbed 11 homers and drove in 51 runs during the 1945 campaign. Lake also drew 106 walks and led the American League with a .412 on-base percentage. From 1939 to 1941 he played with the St. Louis Cardinals before playing with Sacramento of the Coast League. With Johnny Pesky marked for the service, he was acquired by Boston late in 1942. Lake had a strong arm and even pitched in six games in 1944 for a 4.19 ERA in nineteen and a third innings pitched. Lake was a right-handed batter and stood at 5'7", 159 pounds. He was signed by Cardinal scout Charley Remmers and began his pro career with Grand Island in the Nebraska State League in 1937. Lake explained the wartime predicament in Boston as follows: "Skeeter Newsome ... had asthma. Most of the guys had hernias or were color blind or wore glasses. When Tex [Hughson] was taken, our pennant chances were gone. We had to dip down to bring up replacements from Triple A, bring up our kids, and they couldn't handle the pressure."[11]

After Dave "Boo" Ferriss's twenty-one victories, the second most on the club was eight by Emmett O'Neill (8–11). Ferriss was 21–10 with a 2.96 ERA. The other Boston hurlers making contributions on the mound were Jim Wilson (6–8), Clem Hausmann (5–7), Mike Ryba (7–6), and Vic Johnson (6–4). The Red Sox had the worst ERA (3.80) in the American League; however, that was better than four National League teams.

Ferriss joined the club a week after the season had started and pitched his first game on April 29. He became the first American League rookie pitcher to win twenty games since Monte Weaver had done so for the Washington Senators in 1932. Before joining the Red Sox, Ferriss had spent a little over two years in the Army Air Forces and was discharged because of hay fever asthma. He was born in Shaw, Mississippi, on December 5, 1921, and went to Mississippi State. When he got out of the service he was told by the doctors not to play baseball because of his asthma condition. "But," Ferriss once said, "I had a ball in my hands as long as I can remember, and I like baseball. All I ever wanted to be was a ball player. I never wanted to be a fireman or engineer, just a ball player."[12] In August he had difficulty breathing when the humid weather began to aggravate his asthma and it began to affect his performance. He began the season remarkably strong, yielding only five runs in his first sixty-four innings. Ferriss had only one more great season, in 1946, when he was 25–6 with a 3.25 ERA and then his numbers fell off dramatically. In 1947 he was 12–11, and then he compiled a 7–3 record with a 5.23 ERA in 1948, his last meaningful major league season. The 6'2", 208-pound right-handed pitcher but left-handed batter became the first pitcher since Wes Ferrell to win twenty games in his first two seasons. In an otherwise disappointing season he gave the Red Sox fans something to cheer for in 1945.

The 23-year-old rookie pitcher caused quite a sensation in Boston in 1945. The attendance was very good when he pitched, and he was becoming the most popular Red Sox player since Ted Williams, who was still in the service. Ed Rumill of the *Christian Science Monitor* wrote that he was "Modest, clean living and dead serious about his pitching and hitting, he mingles with his mates with his eyes and ears open and his mouth shut." Ferriss was very polite and referred to manager Joe Cronin, the coaches, and scribes with the moniker "Mister" or "Sir." Not only was he impressing the spectators with his pitching, but he was a good hitter as well. In 1945 he batted .267 with one homer in 120 at-bats. He had a .250 lifetime batting average in 372 at-bats. This effective offensive prowess had many fans speculating whether he would eventually leave his pitching career behind and become a full-time position player like Babe Ruth, George Sisler, and Lefty O'Doul had done during their careers.[13]

In 1945 Ferriss made quite an impression on Donald Murray, a resident of Massachusetts, who was temporarily located in Battle Creek, Michigan, receiving treatment at a military hospital after losing his leg in combat in Germany. After perusing the schedule he noticed that his beloved Red Sox and his new favorite player would be traveling to Detroit for an upcoming series. Murray then contacted Red Sox employees, told them about his predicament, and inquired if they could help him persuade the hospital officials to allow him to travel to Briggs Stadium to watch the Sox. Manager Joe Cronin and the Red Cross helped arrange the trip to Briggs Stadium. Furthermore, Cronin made sure that Ferriss was on the hill the day Murray was at the game despite the fact it was not his turn in the rotation.[14]

During the war many baseball fans, writers, coaches, managers and front office personnel wondered if those ballplayers that went into the service would perform effectively once they were discharged and joined their major league teams. Ferriss's early season performance had convinced Red Sox coach Del Baker that they would be able to return successfully. While in the service Ferriss had played for the Randolph Field Ramblers and won a reported twenty games while batting .417. Baker insisted that Ferriss's military league was probably better than any minor league and perhaps even better than the major leagues. He also correctly predicted that some players who were in the service would be better when they returned to their big league team than when they left.[15] The 53-year-old Baker was a wise and knowledgeable baseball man for the 38-year-old Cronin to consult. Baker played three major league seasons from 1914 to 1916, batting .209 as a catcher for the Detroit Tigers. He would spend twenty years as a big league coach and managed during nine seasons, most of which were with Detroit in 1933 and from 1936 to 1942. Baker's best year as manager was in 1940 when the Tigers captured the pennant but then lost the World Series to the Cincinnati Reds, four games to three. Manager Joe Cronin was also able to utilize Baker's unique skill as a talented sign stealer in 1945. Baker was a coach for the Red Sox from 1945 to 1948 and then later from 1953 to 1960. In 1960 he even managed seven games for them, going 2–5 after Billy Jurges was let go and before Pinky Higgins was named the skipper.

Before the war Tom Yawkey saw more than two-thirds of the Red Sox home games from his rooftop box at Fenway Park. But because of his interests in aiding the war effort he was lucky to see one-third of the home games as he spent most of his time at his New York office.[16] Perhaps it was better for the young owner's health to remain away from the ballpark as much as possible instead of watching his ball club stumble to a seventh-place conclusion, 17.5 games off the pace in 1945.

❖ 18 ❖

Connie Mack, Bobo, and the No-Hit Wonder

As the Philadelphia Athletics prepared for the season in Frederick, Maryland, manager Connie Mack publicly criticized his team for their poor play in the first few exhibition games. He unleashed his rebuke during a dinner that was set up by the community leaders of Frederick. Mack was particularly upset over his team's play against the Curtis Bay Coast Guard. He told the gathering that his players were not giving their best effort, that they were disloyal to him, that they were cheating the fans of Philadelphia, that they had wasted twelve great days for training, and that no member of his team would be ready when the season began.[1] The team responded to Mack's criticisms, working hard for six hours the next day, and then took their frustrations out on the Norfolk Naval Training Sailors in a game. As the season was about to commence, Mack was not happy about how spring training had progressed, and the baseball prognosticators had them picked to finish in the second division.

Owner/manager Connie Mack was a Philadelphia institution, having managed the team since 1901. In 1945 he was 82 years old and prone to making mistakes at his advanced age. Therefore he allowed Al Simmons, the third base coach, to handle most of the managerial decisions. He would last through 1950, managing the team for fifty years and managing in the big leagues for fifty-three. Mack assembled some powerful ball clubs only to destroy them on two different occasions for financial reasons. He was a skinflint like Clark Griffith but would protect his players when necessary. Mack was born during the Civil War in 1862 to Irish immigrants and in the tough game of baseball developed a reputation of being a gentleman. He managed in civilian clothing, wearing a suit, holding a scorecard, and did his strategizing from the dugout, not in the coach's box like other managers. He believed the best kind of ballplayer was college educated but knew how to handle those who were not. In later years he found it hard changing with the times: in 1947, when the Athletics were scheduled to play an exhibition game against Jackie Robinson's Dodgers, Mack reportedly said, "I'm not putting my team on the same field with that nigger."[2] They did play that game as scheduled, but the press did not write the story.

Like the National League Phillies, the Athletics were dismal, directly before, during, and after the war. In 1942 they were in the cellar (55–99); again in '43 they finished last (49–105); in '44 they managed to finish tied for fifth place (72–82); and in '45 (52–98) they finished last yet again. As the manager of the Athletics, Mack won nine pennants, but finished in last place seventeen times. The Athletics finished in last place for seven consecutive seasons from 1915 to 1921 and again during ten of Mack's final sixteen seasons as the manager of the team from 1935 to 1950.

The hitters on the 1945 Athletics were led by Bobby Estalella, George Kell, Hal Peck, and Dick Siebert. Their .245 batting average was last in the major leagues. Joe Cambria, Clark Griffith's Cuban scout, originally signed Estalella. He played a total of 28 games with the Senators in 1935 and 1936, and then batted .275 for them with 8 homers in 1939. In 1941 he played with the Browns after not playing big league ball in 1940. In 1942 he was with the Senators again and came to Philadelphia in 1943. He batted .299 in 1945 with an impressive .399 on-base percentage and slugged 8 homers. The following year he would jump to Jorge Pasquel's Mexican League and was not able to return to organized ball until 1949, when he played in eight games for the Athletics, and then was never to play big league ball again. His career ended with a .282 average. He was listed at 5' 8" and 180 pounds but some said he was closer to 5' 6". Estalella had a muscular frame and was capable of hitting the long ball despite his small stature. Peter Bjarkman wrote that "Washington fans of the late 1930s had so much fun watching the gritty Estalella knock down enemy grounders with every part of his anatomy save his glove hand that they often phoned the park in advance to find out if the Cuban was in the lineup before making the trek to the Griffith Stadium grandstands."[3] He was a sideshow in Washington and when he walked out onto the field the fans could not suppress their laughter.

George Kell made his big league debut at the age of 21 in 1943, appearing in one game, going 1 for 5; in 1944 he batted .268 in 514 at-bats but did not hit a home run. In 1945 he improved to .272 and hit four homers. Kell always showed potential as a good fielder at third base but many thought he wouldn't develop into much of a hitter, although in 1943 he led the Inter-State League with a .396 average with Lancaster. "When I got to the majors, I felt like I was in over my head," said Kell. "The A's had Al Simmons as a coach, and some of the other greats like Bing Miller and Jimmy Dykes were around. They all tried to change my stance at the plate. Mack said, 'Leave him alone. He's hit everywhere he's played. He'll hit up here, too.'"[4] It is even doubtful that Mack thought he would be a good hitter. Bill Gilbert, in his book *They Also Served: Baseball and the Home Front, 1941–1945*, quotes Mack telling Kell: "You'll be a great fielder, but you'll never be a hitter."[5] Kell did go on to become a great hitter, with a lifetime batting average of .306 in fifteen seasons during his Hall of Fame career. His best year may have been 1949, when he tied Ted Williams with a .343 batting average to lead the majors while playing for the Detroit Tigers. The batting title was given to Kell as the statisticians calculated that his average was slightly better on the fourth decimal point. In 1950 (218 hits and 56 doubles) and 1951 (191 hits and 36 doubles) he led the American League in hits and doubles. If there had been no manpower shortage because of the war, Kell would have remained in the minor leagues. But because of the war he got the opportunity to learn the game at the big league level.

Kell wasn't in the service because of bad knees, and Hal Peck was a 4-F because he had blown off two of his toes in a shotgun accident while hunting. In 449 at-bats Peck batted .276 with 5 homers. He played in seven major league seasons but never received as many at-bats as he did in 1945. The Athletics hit only 33 homers for the season but that was still more than the Washington Senators (27) and the Chicago White Sox (22). Estalella led the club with eight homers.

Dick Siebert hit .267 with 7 homers and 51 RBIs. He had bounced around the minors for nearly ten years and saw brief playing time for the Dodgers and Cardinals before joining the Athletics in 1938. By the time he joined Philadelphia's American League representative, the championship seasons that were once a frequent occurrence for Mack's ball clubs were well in the past. The Athletics had been a consistent second-division occupant since 1934. During six of the eight seasons during which Siebert was a member of the ball club from 1938 to 1945, the Athletics finished in last place in the junior circuit. Their records during this time period were 53–99, 55–97, 54–100, 64–90, 55–99, 49–105, 72–82, and 52–98. Despite Siebert's unfortunate predicament of playing for a poor ball club, he considered himself "lucky" to be able to play for the Athletics. He went on to say that having Connie Mack as his manager was an "education and inspiration," and that he was "fortunate" to play for such a "wonderful character."[6]

Siebert was a 6-foot, 170-pound left-handed hitting first baseman. He was the son of a Lutheran minister and had the perfect background and disposition that Connie Mack was looking for in a ball player. Siebert graduated from Concordia Junior College of St. Paul, Minnesota, in 1930 and then spent two years at the Concordia Seminary in St. Louis. There was a debate in the Siebert household as to whether he should pursue a professional baseball career. After serious deliberations it was agreed upon that Dick would pursue his baseball career but he would play only during the summer during his first few minor league seasons so he could continue to pursue his educational goals. He received his B.A. from the University of Minnesota in 1934, took courses in business and journalism at the University of Missouri, and as of 1945 was working on a master's degree in physical education from the University of Minnesota. Later he would come back to the University of Minnesota and be the baseball coach for thirty-one years. Siebert decided to follow a different path from his father when he found out

18. Connie Mack, Bobo, and the No-Hit Wonder

Bobo Newsom was a loquacious, free-spirited, and extremely confident pitcher who was a major source of entertainment on the Philadelphia Athletics' limping expedition through the American League cities. After his win on April 21 he had a 1–1 record but then lost twelve consecutive games. The losses did not bother him because he felt he had pitched well and the breaks would eventually go his way. By season's end he had lost twenty games for the third time in his career, finishing the campaign with an 8–20 record but with a respectable 3.29 ERA. Bobo pitched for nine different teams during his twenty-year career (George Brace photograph).

he was a good player, and he received inspiration in knowing that former big leaguers Max Carey and Bill Wambsganss had also attended Concordia Seminary.

In June 1925 he signed with the St. Louis Cardinals. The left-handed throwing Siebert was a pitcher in the Cardinals' minor league system until he hurt his arm during the latter portion of the 1930 campaign. At two different times in his minor league career he asked Commissioner Landis to intervene and make clear his playing situation. The second time was when the Dodgers were making him play for both Dayton and Albany in 1934. The commissioner ruled that Siebert could not play for two teams at the same time and sent him to Dayton.[7] Dick had his best major league season in 1941, batting .334 with 28 doubles, 8 triples, 5 homers, and 79 RBIs. He played most of his big league career at first base but when a leg injury took him out of the lineup in 1944, Connie Mack called up Bill McGhee to play first base. McGhee batted .289 in 287 at-bats in the first season of his two-year major league career. When Siebert returned he was shifted to the outfield and played 58 games in the outer garden. However, in 1945 Siebert returned to first base and McGhee played most of his games in the outfield. Siebert ended his eleven-year major league career in 1945 with a .282 lifetime average. His son Paul had an unspectacular five-year major league career, pitching mostly in relief with the Houston Astros, San Diego Padres, and New York Mets from 1974 to 1978.

Louis Norman "Bobo" Newsom was the most prolific pitcher the Athletics had on the mound. He had an 8–20 record but with a good 3.29 ERA in 1945. To say Newsom bounced around the majors is an understatement. He started his career with the Brooklyn Dodgers in 1929, went to the Chicago Cubs, then to the St. Louis Browns, then to the Washington Senators, then to the Boston Red Sox, then back with the Browns, then off to the Detroit Tigers, then back to the Senators, then back to Brooklyn, then back to the Browns for the third time, then to the Senators for the third time, then to the Philadelphia Athletics, then a fourth go-around with the Senators, then to the New York Yankees, then to the New York Giants, then back to the Senators for the fifth time, and then to the Athletics once again, where he ended his career in 1953. He finished his twenty-year career with a 211–222 record and a 3.98 ERA. Newsom was a character: he would constantly argue with his managers. He had a superstition that he wouldn't tie his shoelaces on the day of the game and had someone else do it. The talented pitcher had a number of other superstitions as well, such as picking up a handful of dirt on the inside and outside part of the foul line as he advanced towards the mound. Newsom completed a game despite shattering his kneecap in the third inning as a result of a scorching line drive by Earl Averill. In another game the third baseman hit him in the back of the head with a throw to first. Newsom was knocked unconscious by the throw and didn't wake up till they poured a bucket of ice on him, but he went on to pitch a shutout. He pitched the Detroit Tigers to a victory in game one of the 1940 World Series, but tragically his father, who had been at the game, died of a heart attack the following night.[8]

Newsom was loquacious and wanted to be well liked. He was sympathetic to the plight of those who were in a bad situation and would help others. When people challenged the factual accuracy of his stories he said, "Who are you going to believe, Bobo, me or the record book?"[9] The stories about Bobo were so outrageous, entertaining, and tragic that they didn't need hyperbole to make them exciting.

Newsom would often refer to himself in the first person, saying, for example, "Ol' Bobo is on the mound today and you can put it in the win column." Newsom was never lacking for confidence and had an optimistic view of the world. He was saddled with his nickname "Bobo" because that is what he called other people when he forgot their names and soon others referred to him by that moniker. As a member of the Tigers he showed up at their spring training facility in Lakeland, Florida, in 1941 with a new car: the horn played "Hold That Tiger," and there was also a flashy neon sign on the automobile that said "Bobo." In 1941 he went 12–20 for a Detroit Tigers team that finished tied for fourth place with a 75–79 record. That was one of three times he lost twenty games in his career, the first time was with the 1934 St. Louis Browns when he went 16–20 with a 4.01 ERA, and the last time was with the 1945 Athletics. However, Newsom also won twenty or more games during three seasons: in 1938 with the St. Louis Browns (20–16 with a 5.08 ERA); in 1939 with the Browns and Tigers (20–11 with a 3.58 ERA); and in 1940 with the Detroit Tigers (21–5 with a 2.83 ERA). He was a member of the Washington Senators during five different occasions as he traveled around the major leagues: 1935–1937, 1942, and then after pitching for the Dodgers and Browns he returned in 1943, 1946–1947, and 1952. This prompted him to say that he had more terms in Washington than President Roosevelt. He started the 1947 season with Washington, going 4–6, and then was sent to the New York Yankees on July 11 for the waiver price; he went 7–5 with a 2.80 ERA. Newsom was hit hard as the starting pitcher in the third game of the 1947 World Series and failed to make it through the second inning. The Yankees lost that game, 9–8, but won the World Series from Brooklyn in seven games. The Yankee players did not vote Newsom a full share and gave him three-quarters of a share instead. Bobo informed the jeweler that his ring should be three-quarters the size because "that's all I'm worth in this city."[10]

The 6'2", right-handed pitcher weighed between 195 and 220 pounds during his career. If he saw any injustices befall his pitching brethren he was quick to defend them. Newsom came to the defense of Bill Voiselle of the Giants in 1945 when he was fined for throwing the ball across the plate on a 0 and 2 pitch. He felt that he was speaking for the pitching community when he confidently declared that the managers could not and should not restrict a hurler's tactical maneuvers and they would be more intelligent once they found this out. Newsom said if a good pitcher threw his best pitch over the plate it didn't matter what the count was because the hitters would have difficulty making good contact. A manager also needed to realize that some hitters couldn't hit a specific type of pitch. A knuckleball pitcher should be lauded and not reprimanded if he throws his erratic offering over the plate on an 0 and 2 count. As for his own pitching repertoire, Newsom said, "Some of the hitters in this league couldn't hit my change of pace if they were swinging a park bench." Newsom acknowledged that there were times when it would behoove a pitcher to waste an 0 and 2 delivery but it should not be prohibited under all circumstances. He praised Connie Mack for not interfering with his pitching tactics. However, Bobo recalled that when he had played under Rogers Hornsby, the St. Louis Browns manager, he also fined his players when they failed to waste an 0 and 2 pitch. It was well known around the league that Hornsby would fine his pitchers in that situation. Newsom disobeyed Hornsby's orders one day when he faced Wes Ferrell of the Boston Red Sox. When an 0 and 2 fastball was called a strike, Ferrell argued with the umpire and informed him that it couldn't have been a strike because Hornsby would fine his pitcher. When Jim Walkup was a rookie with the Browns he inadvertently threw an 0 and 2 pitch over the plate. When the umpire called the batter out, Walkup argued with the umpire, insisting that the ball was outside, because he did not want to get a $100 fine.[11]

When Newsom began piling up losses in 1945 he insisted that the losing did not bother him. On July 1 the Athletics lost their thirteenth consecutive game as they dropped a doubleheader to the Detroit Tigers at Briggs Stadium by scores of 9–5 and 5–3 before 47,729 spectators. In the opener Hank Greenberg made his return to the Tigers lineup after a four-year stint in the Army and smashed a homer, going 1 for 4. Newsom was burdened with his eleventh consecutive loss when he relieved Jesse Flores in the seventh inning and gave up a three-run homer to Rudy York. Philadelphia's losing streak would extend to fourteen games before they defeated the St. Louis Browns 3–2 in the opening game of a twin bill on July 4. On July 12, the Athletics returned home after an abysmal road trip and won two games from the Browns by 4–0 and 11–0 scores. Newsom's four-hit shutout in the opener ended his twelve-game losing streak that began on April 29 when he lost the first game of a doubleheader against Boston before a robust Shibe Park crowd of 23,828. His record now stood at 2–13. The Athletics were 24–49 and buried in last place in the American League, 11 games behind seventh-place Cleveland and 19 and a half games behind the first-place Tigers. The only consolation they could take was to peruse the National League standings, where the Philadelphia Phillies were 20–60, 27 games behind first-place Chicago. At this juncture of the season the Athletics were clearly the best team in Philadelphia.

Newsom informed J.G. Taylor Spink of *The Sporting News* that he wasn't losing sleep about losing those ball games. After all, it wasn't like Bobo was not accustomed to losing. He insisted that he had pitched well and had been hit hard only a few times all season. Furthermore, the high number of losses that the team was accumulating did not bother him. He felt the breaks had gone

18. Connie Mack, Bobo, and the No-Hit Wonder

against him and sooner or later his luck, and the team's, would change for the better. When he was in the minor leagues he once invited his entire hometown of Hartsville, South Carolina, to a game in Charlotte. He got knocked around in the first few innings and believed that he never had pitched well in the vicinity of his hometown. One time while Bobo was pitching with the bases loaded in the minors, the batter hit a liner that hit Newsom in the knee and was caught by the third baseman without hitting the ground; the third baseman then stepped on third for a double play.[12] Newsom was one of the most colorful players in baseball's long history and there are countless humorous stories about him.

Russ Christopher led the team in wins with a 13–13 record and a 3.17 ERA. Jesse Flores (7–10), Joe Berry (8–7), Lou Knerr (5–11), and Don Black (5–11) also made contributions on the mound. Christopher, who stood at 6' 3½", was a 170-pound right-handed pitcher who began his major league career in 1942 with the Athletics, going 4–13. He was 5–8 with a 3.45 ERA in 1943 and 14–14 with a 2.97 ERA in 1944. He got off to a terrific start in 1945 and by June 17 he had compiled an 11–2 record. Stan Baumgartner wrote in June 1945, "He is the 'Philadelphia Story.' There ain't nothin' else to talk about in this town."[13] However, he would struggle in the remaining games in 1945, going 2–11 the rest of the way. An impressive Shibe Park crowd of 34,716 showed up on Sunday, June 17, to watch the doubleheader between the Athletics and Yankees. For the three-day series, 61,612 fans made their way through the turnstiles to observe the activities on the greensward. Bobo Newsom lasted only four innings in the opener as his record fell to 1–8 in the 7–1 Yankees victory. Bobo had lost seven straight; his only victory had come early in the season on April 21 when the Athletics defeated the Red Sox, 8–2, at Fenway Park. In the nightcap, Christopher yielded eight hits and three walks, and hit Frankie Crosetti with a pitched ball, but New York was only able to push across two runs as they lost 4–2. This was the sixth straight victory for Christopher and he had won eleven of Philadelphia's twenty victories at this juncture of the season. Russ also had two hits in the game and would bat .171 on the season with one home run.

In the minor leagues Christopher had a reputation of not working long into games. But in both 1944 and 1945 he pitched well over 200 innings and had a combined 30 complete games in those two seasons. Christopher's career had taken off in 1944 when he began to throw "underhand" which put better movement on his pitches. He insisted that was the pitch he had been looking for since he became a hurler. The hitters were fooled by the way he delivered the pitch and by the movement of the ball. His underhand and sidearm delivery was developed under the guidance of catcher and coach Earle Brucker. Brucker first taught him how to pace himself so he could work deeper into ball games. Then, when Christopher hurt his arm late in the 1943 season and Connie Mack was ready to give up on him, Brucker saved his career by teaching him the sidearm delivery.[14] After the 1945 campaign, Russ pitched two more seasons for the Athletics in 1946 (5–7) and 1947 (10–7). Then he pitched his final big league season for the 1948 Cleveland Indians, going 3–2 with a 2.90 ERA and 17 saves. He made a brief appearance in game five of the World Series against Boston.

He had a rheumatic heart and suffered from a sore arm throughout much of his career. He had the rheumatic fever when he was young and this left him in a weakened condition. Christopher also survived a career-threatening hunting injury. Russ went hunting with his two brothers and insisted that his brother Lloyd was a poor shot who couldn't hit a big target from a short distance. The two brothers argued and Russ was so certain that Lloyd was a poor shot that he volunteered to hide behind a rock and have Lloyd try to shoot him. Lloyd's shot wasn't off target, and he shot his brother in the leg. To make matters worse he had accidentally shot him with the more lethal pellets. Lloyd played briefly for the Boston Red Sox in 1945, going 4 for 14 (.286), and also appeared in one game for the Chicago Cubs during the season. In 1947 he returned to the big leagues, going 5 for 23 (.217) in seven games for the Chicago White Sox. The baseball encyclopedia spells his name as "Loyd"; however, a 1945 article in *The Sporting News* refers to him as "Lloyd."[15]

Russ Christopher was originally an outfielder in the minors but in 1938 with El Paso he became a pitcher. He was batting only .163 a few weeks into the season and was demoted to batting practice pitcher. The hitters raved about Christopher's pitching prowess during batting practice. Soon after, manager Zinn Beck, a former major league player with the St. Louis Cardinals (1913–1916) and the New York Yankees (1918), wanted to see for himself how good Christopher was as a pitcher. He stepped into the batter's box, watched a few pitches sail by, and then encouraged Christopher to throw harder. Christopher subsequently hit Beck in the back, and when he inquired as to whether his manager was hurt he was informed that his pitch couldn't hurt anybody so he shouldn't be concerned. On the next day he was released to a team in Clovis, New Mexico, where he pitched well until injuring his arm and then decided to stop pursuing a professional baseball career. He worked in a fish oil plant at home and then decided to give baseball another shot, playing semi-pro ball over the winter, and then impressing scouts at a Yankees spring training camp, which resulted in another tour with El Paso in 1939. The spring training camp was for younger players from the west coast: Christopher was born in Richmond, California, on September 12, 1917, and would die there on December 5, 1954, at the young age of 37. He had his breakout year in 1939, going 18–7. Before making his major league debut in 1942 he played in Wenatchee, Washington, and for Newark.[16]

Jesse Flores was a 5'10", 175-pound right-hander from Mexico. He pitched in four games (0–1) for the 1942 Chicago Cubs, and then during his next five seasons with the Athletics he went 12–14, 9–11, 7–10, 9–7, and 4–13. In 1950 he compiled a 3–3 mark for the Cleveland Indians and then his big league career was over with a 44–59 record and a 3.18 ERA. His lowest ERA during his career was in 1946 (2.32) and his highest was during his final season in 1950 (3.74). "Jittery Joe" Berry pitched two games for the 1942 Chicago Cubs, and then in 1944 went 10–8 with an impressive 1.94 ERA for the Athletics. In 1945 he was 8–7 with a 2.35 ERA and an American League-leading 52 games. He pitched a total of 26 games for the Athletics and Indians in 1946 (3–7, 3.22 ERA) and then his four-year career was over with a 21–22 record and a 2.45 ERA. Berry pitched in 133 big league games, all in relief. Lou Knerr, a 6'1", 210-pound right-hander went 5–11 with a 4.22 ERA in his rookie year in 1945. He was 3–16 with a 5.40 ERA for Connie Mack's 1946 squad and then he pitched six games for the 1947 Washington Senators in his final season. Don Black, another right-handed pitcher for the Athletics, started his career in 1943, compiling a 6–16 record with a 4.20 ERA. In 1944 he improved to 10–12 with a 4.06 ERA. During his 5–11, 5.17 ERA, 1945 season he started 18 of his 26 games and had 8 complete games. He pitched three more seasons in the major leagues with the Cleveland Indians, going 1–2, 10–12, and 2–2 from 1946 to 1948. His six-year career ended with a 34–55 record and a 4.35 ERA.

Phil Marchildon and Dick Fowler made brief appearances with the club but they had a large impact on those who saw them. Marchildon pitched in three games in 1945 and then made a significant contribution in 1946 (13–16, 3.49 ERA) and 1947 (19–9, 3.22 ERA). Despite his good performance, everything was not well with Marchildon, as the Canadian-born pitcher had his thoughts somewhere else. George Kell said he had a "funny look in his eye" that made it appear that "his thoughts were about the war and not baseball." His teammates noticed that he was extremely nervous and lacking composure on the hill. After the 1947 campaign he went downhill, going 9–15 with a 4.53 ERA in 1948, and then pitching seven games (0–3, 11.81 ERA) in 1949 and one game for the 1950 Boston Red Sox. Eddie Joost recalled that after the 1947 season Phil would freeze up on the mound; start thinking too much; walk behind the hill; and waste time with the resin bag and hitting his glove with his palm for about thirty seconds. Something was not right and the next pitch would be significantly off the mark. According to Joost the fans at Shibe Park wouldn't voice their displeasure in his direction because they had a feeling that something was wrong.[17]

Teenager Carl Scheib pitched in four games for the 1945 Athletics. He was sixty-four years younger than his manager. Scheib pitched in a total of twenty-five games during the final three wartime seasons, having made his major league debut at the age of sixteen on September 6, 1943. Unlike Joe Nuxhall, who was unsuccessful in his one game in 1944, Scheib actually pitched quite well. In 1943 he had a 4.34 ERA in 18.2 innings; in 1944 his earned run average stood at 4.21 in 36.1 innings; and in 1945 he had a 3.12 ERA in 8.2 innings. During each season his ERA was significantly below his career 4.88 earned run average.

On September 9, Dick Fowler, who had been recently discharged from the Canadian Army, hurled the third no-hitter in the history of Shibe Park. It would be his only win of the season. The tall right-hander was about thirty pounds overweight and not necessarily in playing condition when he joined the team. In the Army he worked mainly as a postal clerk. After his discharge he did not join the A's right away because his wife was ill. Before his no-hit game he had been knocked around in the few appearances he made in relief. When Fowler recorded the final out, the bleacher fans rushed the field and carried him off on their shoulders. His catcher Buddy Rosar said, "And I never saw another kid with such confidence. He wasn't cocky. Just sure of himself. Stood out there and never shook me off on a sign. Just reared back and threw it where he wanted it."[18] Fowler had complete confidence in his catcher calling the signs and said, "I figured he knew more about it than I did."[19] In another dreadful season for Philadelphia's American League representative, Dick Fowler gave the spectators at Shibe Park something to cheer about.

❖ 19 ❖

The American League Campaign

Babe Ruth was among the 13,923 fans at Yankee Stadium to witness the opener on April 17. The Yankees defeated the Boston Red Sox, 8–4, behind two homers by Russ Derry, one of which was a grand slam. George "Catfish" Metkovich made three errors in an inning to set an American League record and tie Dolph Camilli's National League mark. Rex Cecil, Boston's starting hurler, had given up only two hits through the first six innings, a single to Johnny Lindell and a solo homer to Derry, and had held New York hitless in the middle innings before the Yankees exploded for seven runs in the seventh inning. The opening ceremonies were simple and solemn: a band played the national anthem, and then the flag was raised to full staff and then lowered halfway. The crowd silently honored the late President Franklin D. Roosevelt, and the bugler played taps. Some of the prominent people at the game included Fiorello H. LaGuardia, mayor of New York; Fulgencio Batista, former president and future dictator of Cuba; and Herbert Leary, Vice Admiral.

While the Yankees opened the season in the Stadium, the League for Equality was picketing outside and protesting against "Jim Crowism in Baseball." They were attempting to get blacks to boycott this game and future games, and for the most part the boycott appeared to have worked, because it was reported that there were "only a few Negroes inside the park."[1] The picketers said it was their intention to boycott an upcoming game at the Polo Grounds.

By this fourth wartime season the fans had become accustomed to witnessing the poor quality of play that was ubiquitous around the majors. Al Laney described the Yankees' opener in the *New York Herald Tribune* as having an inauthentic feeling, as if it were an ordinary contest played in the middle of the season. The anticipation, excitement, and "holiday mood" that were palpable on previous opening days were missing. Also absent were the cheers that resonated around the stadium on the first day of the season when fans cheered not necessarily because of the play on the field but because of the importance of the occasion. The enthusiasm may have been diminished for this event because the country was still mourning the loss of President Roosevelt. The customary opening day ceremonies were canceled at Yankee Stadium. The crowd did not become excited and inspired to cheer until the Yankees' offense came to life. The threat of rain may also have kept the attendance low. It had rained intermittently in the morning, just enough to make people question whether there would be a ball game that afternoon. Considering the circumstances under which this game was played, the 13,923 (12,249 paid) fans that showed up represented a "pretty good crowd" and an indication that the fans would turn out in fairly large numbers in 1945. Al Laney and some of his colleagues sat among the soldiers and sailors in right field for some of the game. Despite the cajoling by Laney, they did not show anger over the fact that seemingly well and fit men were playing baseball instead of being in the military. Some of the soldiers and sailors tried to argue that Laney's position was mistaken. However, this was all in good humor: Laney exited the premises before they became aware that "their legs were being pulled."[2]

The temperature was in the low 50s at Sportsman's Park as only 4,167 fans braved the elements and watched the Browns defeat the Tigers, 7–1. Sig Jakucki scattered six hits in the route-going performance. The victory gave the Browns nine straight opening-day triumphs. Pete Gray went 1 for 4 and scored a run in his major league debut. His one hit was an infield single. Doc Cramer, Detroit's center fielder, robbed him of a two-base hit in the game, much to the consternation of the fans who groaned with displeasure.

In Philadelphia, the Senators collected fifteen hits to defeat the Athletics, 14–8, before 7,846 fans. Joe Kuhel and George Binks had four hits apiece. Dutch Leonard earned the victory while Bobo Newsom was charged with the defeat. Connie Mack used five pitchers on the day, including eighteen-year-old Carl Scheib. Before the game, the fans stood silent for five minutes to honor President Roosevelt. Stan Baumgartner wrote about some of the pregame festivities in the *Philadelphia Inquirer*:

> The Moose Band and the Police and Firemen's Band had preceded both teams to the flagpole in center field; Old Glory had been hoisted; then, while the crowd — its collective spirit matched by the untoward elements — stood in silence and the bugler sounded taps, it had been lowered to half-mast; Nicholas E. Rodecker, water tender first class, who lost a leg when a Jap plane attacked his destroyer and is now convalescing at the Philadelphia Naval Hospital, had tossed out the first ball when the Nats, supposedly weakened by the loss of Stan Spence to the Navy broke forth.[3]

In Cleveland, 20,588 spectators watched the White Sox beat the Indians, 5–2. Both teams made a pair of errors on the day and the Pale Hose were buoyed by timely hitting to give Thornton Lee the victory. Allie Reynolds started for Cleveland and took the loss. Ray Mack, the Indians' starting second baseman for the last five years, was inducted into the Army on opening day. He had been anticipating this and had not gone to spring training but instead worked as an engineer at a war plant.

19. The American League Campaign

The Yankees swept their three-game series from Boston on April 19 as they won, 4–3, behind the strong pitching of Monk Dubiel. Joe Cronin, the Red Sox' 38-year-old manager, caught his spikes as he was advancing to second base in the seventh inning and broke his ankle. Boston's center fielder, Leon Culberson, hit a grounder to New York's third baseman, Don Savage, who could not field it cleanly; therefore there was no play at second when Cronin was hurt. It was just an unfortunate accident as he collapsed to the ground and fell on the bag. He was carried off the field into the clubhouse and later left Yankee Stadium with the aid of Red Sox owner Tom Yawkey. Cronin went 0 for 2 and scored a run in what would be the last game of his illustrious career. In the second inning, Culberson drove the ball into the outfield and center fielder Johnny Lindell dropped it after a long run, colliding with left fielder Hersh Martin. As the two Yankee outfielders rolled on the ground, Lindell cut Martin's nose with his cleats; Martin needed several stitches. Mike Ryba, a 41-year-old relief pitcher, hit Lindell with the bases loaded and no outs in the last of the ninth to force home the winning run.

Boston used several players in this game who were fortunate to be playing in the big leagues, including Cronin's replacement at third base, 28-year-old Nick Polly. Polly was born Nicholas Joseph Polachanin in Chicago on April 18, 1917. He batted .222 for the 1937 Brooklyn Dodgers in 18 at-bats and 10 games and then wore a big league uniform for one last time in 1945, batting .143 in 7 at-bats and 4 games for Boston. Billy Holm, who went 0 for 2 as Boston's starting catcher, was also born in Chicago on July 21, 1912. As a big leaguer he was consistently bad at the plate, batting .067 in 15 at-bats for the 1943 Chicago Cubs, and then hitting .136 for them in 132 at-bats the following year. In 1945 he batted .185 in 135 at-bats for Boston's American League representative. His lifetime slugging average was a paltry .177 in 282 at-bats. Catcher Fred Walters went 1 for 1 on the 19th with a double and an RBI. Like his teammate, Dave Ferriss, he also attended college at Mississippi State, but at 32 years of age was much older than his young batterymate. In 1945, his only major league season, he batted .172 in 93 at-bats and 40 games. Ben Steiner led off for Boston and went 1 for 4. He was a 5'11", 165-pound left-handed hitting, but right-handed throwing second baseman who batted .257 in 304 at-bats as a rookie in 1945. He only played a total of four more major league games, with the 1946 Red Sox and the 1947 Tigers. The starting pitcher for Boston on the 19th was Clem Dreisewerd, who made his big league debut in 1944 with Boston, going 2–4 with a 4.07 ERA. In 1945, his second of four major league seasons, he went 0–1 in two starts with a 4.66 ERA and then went into the military. Dreisewerd shocked his teammates when he joined Boston in 1944 and insisted that his wife be his bullpen catcher, a tradition that had served him well in the Pacific Coast League.

It was reported that Ed Barrow, former president of the Yankees, turned down the opportunity to become commissioner. He said that he informed

William Harridge, the president of the American League, that he was "too old and my health was not good. Ten years ago it would have been different." Barrow was approaching his 77th birthday and had been in poor health for many years. He never got the opportunity to play in the big leagues, but he managed the Detroit Tigers in 1903 and 1904, and then later managed the Boston Red Sox from 1918 to 1920. In 1918 the Sox defeated the Chicago Cubs in the World Series, four games to two. Barrow joined the Yankees' front office as their business manager in 1921 and remained with the club until 1947. Barrow was the president of the club from 1939 until January 1945, when the new ownership group took over. During the final two years he was a member of the board. The commissioner's job was offered to Barrow on a temporary basis while the owners sought to find someone to fill it permanently. The new commissioner would receive a $50,000 salary. Barrow recommended that they hire Ford Frick or Jim Farley for the position.[4]

There was widespread speculation as to who would get the job. In addition to Happy Chandler, some of the names that were rumored for the job included Ford Frick, president of the National League; Leslie O'Connor, Commissioner Landis's secretary; and John W. Bricker, former Governor of Ohio. Horace Stoneham and Larry MacPhail, owners of the Giants and Yankees respectively, insisted that someone be named to the position right away. This was a different time from when Kenesaw Mountain Landis was named to the position. Stoneham was less concerned with finding a "policeman" but instead wanted someone who could promote the game to the baseball public and expand its popularity. While some owners were eager to name a replacement for Landis as quickly as possible, others insisted that they should take their time, and perhaps even name someone to the position on a temporary basis and for a short-term contract, because many of the best baseball minds who were qualified for the job were helping their country win the war and were unavailable to assume the position right away. The owners came close to selecting a commissioner at the February meeting as Frick received ten of the twelve votes needed to become commissioner. A four-man committee was established with the responsibility of finding a candidate, and then 12 of the 16 owners, or three-quarters, would have to vote in favor of electing that man to the position. The four-man committee consisted of owners Alva Bradley of the Cleveland Indians; Don Barnes of the St. Louis Browns; Sam Breadon of the St. Louis Cardinals; and Philip Wrigley of the Chicago Cubs.[5] On April 24, Chandler was named Landis's replacement as commissioner.

Also on the 19th, the Tigers got three singles in the ninth inning by Eddie Mayo, Rudy York, and Doc Cramer to push across the only run of the game in a 1–0 win over St. Louis. Al Benton allowed only four hits, but walked seven, as he escaped trouble a few times to earn a complete-game win. Nelson Potter was the hard-luck loser for the Browns. They were also without the services of Vern Stephens, who had jammed his thumb in the previous game. Only 1,641 fans paid their way into Sportsman's Park to watch the game. At Shibe Park, Marino Pieretti worked twelve innings as the Senators won, 4–3, on George Case's extra inning homer. The White Sox defeated Cleveland, 14–6, on the day.

On April 20 the Yankees won their fourth straight game to open the season, a 6–3 victory over the Senators in Washington. It was the home opener at Griffith Stadium and a crowd of 24,494 showed up. There was red, white, and blue bunting draped over the stands. The flag was lowered to half-staff to honor President Roosevelt, who had died eight days earlier. It was a somber day, not one for celebrations. Those who participated in lowering the flag were Robert Patterson, Undersecretary of War; Will Harridge, American League president; and the great hurler Walter Johnson. Sam Rayburn, the Speaker of the House, threw out the first ball. Additionally, the military display that was often recognizable at wartime games was missing. The Yankees won the game despite committing four errors in the field. Bill Bevens pitched five innings for the win but received some help from Al Gettel, who worked the final four.

At Comiskey Park, Ed Lopat worked ten innings and also hit a homer as the White Sox defeated St. Louis, 3–2, before 3,649 freezing fans. Despite batting only .211 lifetime, Lopat was collecting plenty of hits during his first three major league seasons from 1944 to 1946: in 1944 he batted .309 in 81 at-bats; then he hit for a .293 clip in 82 at-bats the following year; and when the postwar era began in 1946 he batted a respectable .253 in 87 at-bats. Al Hollingsworth took the loss for the Browns and Ellis Clary hit the only homer of his major league career. Pete Gray was out of the Browns lineup nursing a shoulder injury. Luke Sewell said, "His shoulder has been hurting him and I decided to give him some rest."[6] The Tigers played their home opener before 28,357 fans but lost, 4–1, to the Indians. Cleveland won their first game of the season behind the fine hurling of Steve Gromek. It was a cold day at Fenway Park for the home opener as only 3,489 spectators showed up to watch the Red Sox drop their fourth straight game to begin the season. The Athletics got the better of them, 5–3. Catcher Frankie Hayes hit a home run for Philadelphia. Del Baker was the acting manager for Boston while Joe Cronin was out with his injury.

Only 4,374 fans showed up at Briggs Stadium on April 21 as the Tigers defeated Cleveland, 3–2, in 42-degree weather. Hal Newhouser went the distance in the eleven-inning affair for his first victory. At the plate he collected two hits and drove in two runs. He won the game when he slashed a single through the right side of the drawn-in infield in extra innings. In Boston, Frankie Hayes hit a grand slam homer to lead the Athletics to an 8–2 victory. Bobo Newsom went the distance for the win. Elsewhere, Roger Wolff hooked up in a pitcher's duel with Ernie Bonham as the Senators scored two in the first inning and held on for a 2–1 win over New York before 3,553 spectators at Griffith Stadium. St. Louis and Chicago were rained out on the day.

A Sunday crowd of 13,781 was on hand, and the temperature was 50 degrees as the White Sox improved to 5–0 with a doubleheader victory over St. Louis by scores of 4–3 and 5–3 at Comiskey Park on April 22. Joe Haynes and Orval Grove earned victories. In Washington, Hank Borowy yielded only three hits and walked one as the Yankees defeated the Senators, 5–2. The Red Sox got only five hits off Russ Christopher and lost to the Athletics, 6–1, at Fenway Park. At Briggs Stadium, the Indians committed four errors, including one by third baseman Bob Rothel. He played in four games for Cleveland in 1945, his only big league season, going 2 for 10 with three walks. Detroit won, 6–3, as Dizzy Trout earned the victory with a complete-game performance.

Happy Chandler attended his first game as commissioner on April 26 as he watched the Senators defeat Boston, 4–1, at Griffith Stadium. Before the game he visited with players from both sides, autographed baseballs, and posed for the cameras and newsreels. It was Boston's seventh straight loss to begin the season despite collecting ten hits. The 5–0 White Sox were rained out on the day against Detroit. In Philadelphia, 5,680 patrons were on hand to watch the Yankees blow a five-run lead and lose, 7–5. Joe Berry earned the win while Monk Dubiel took the loss. In Cleveland, Nelson Potter's single brought in the go-ahead run in the ninth inning as the Browns won, 4–3. The second game on the day was postponed because of the rain.

On Friday, April 27, the Yankee Stadium crowd numbered 5,497 (2,089 paid), but only 181 women showed up for the ladies' day game. It was reported that 2,563 children brought fourteen tons of old clothing to the ballpark and were given free admission. There were trucks located outside the ballpark to collect the clothing for the National Clothing Collection. Washington won the game, 6–4, behind the pitching of knuckleballer Mickey Haefner. The only other junior league game that was played on the day was between Philadelphia and Boston. The Shibe Park spectators were delighted to watch Russ Christopher collect his third win of the short season, going the distance in a 5–3 win. On April 28, the Red Sox won their first of the season after losing eight straight. It was an 8–4 win over the Athletics behind the pitching of Rex Cecil. On the same day, Al Benton pitched a two-hitter to propel Detroit to a 5–1 win over Cleveland. Chicago and St. Louis were rained out, while the Yankees defeated Washington, 2–1, in thirteen innings. There were four doubleheaders in the American League on April 29. New York and Washington split two games, as did Cleveland and Detroit. Meanwhile, Boston and St. Louis won both ends of their doubleheader, defeating Philadelphia and Chicago respectively.

On May 1, the American League standings stood as follows:

	W L	PCT	GB
Chicago White Sox	5–2	.714	—
Detroit Tigers	6–3	.667	—
New York Yankees	7–4	.636	—
Philadelphia Athletics	6–5	.545	1

19. The American League Campaign

	W L	PCT	GB
Washington Senators	6–5	.545	1
St. Louis Browns	4–5	.444	2
Boston Red Sox	3–8	.273	4
Cleveland Indians	2–7	.222	4

Al Benton won his third straight game as the Tigers defeated the White Sox, 2–1, on May 2 at Briggs Stadium. The Yankees received strong pitching from rookie Al Gettel, who led the team to a 6–4 victory over Philadelphia in his first major league start. Russ Christopher dropped his record to 3–1 as he lost his first game of the season. At Fenway Park, rookie Jim Wilson threw a four-hit shutout as the Red Sox put down the Senators, 4–0. Boston won their fifth straight game after losing their first eight to begin the season. Paul "Big Poison" Waner was released from the Yankees on May 3. He played in what would be his last major league game on April 26 when he drew a walk in his only at-bat. Donald Honig wrote that men like Paul Waner "were stretching out the flaccid elastic of exhausted careers almost as a patriotic service."[7] In a twenty-year Hall of Fame career, Waner had a lifetime .333 batting average.

New York pushed across five runs in the first inning on May 5 at Fenway Park as they went on to defeat the Red Sox, 7–3. In Detroit, Jack Kramer pitched a four-hit shutout as the Browns put down the Tigers, 5–0. In the fourth inning, Vern Stephens hit his third homer of the season off Dizzy Trout. It was the first homer served up by Detroit pitching this season. In Chicago, Earl Henry of the Indians came in to pitch in the ninth inning and threw one pitch to Johnny Dickshot, who promptly knocked it into center field for a double. Allie Reynolds relieved Henry, who then allowed a sacrifice and then a single to Tony Cuccinello to push home the winning run in a 3–2 White Sox victory. Henry was charged with the loss. Thornton Lee won his second game for the White Sox. Al Cihocki, the Indians rookie second baseman, had three hits on the day, including a double. The Senators also defeated the Athletics, 7–3, on the day. The White Sox were leading the major leagues in batting at .288, while St. Louis had the best fielding percentage at .979.

Hal Newhouser pitched a one-hitter in the first game of a doubleheader on May 6 to defeat St. Louis, 3–0. The Tigers also won the second game, 1–0, on Roy Cullenbine's ninth-inning homer to give Al Benton the victory. The White Sox had a half-game lead over the Yankees after winning two from the Indians, 3–2 and 6–4, at Comiskey Park. Ed Lopat and Joe Haynes were the winning pitchers. The Senators won the second game of a doubleheader, 2–0, behind the shutout pitching of Dutch Leonard. The Athletics won the first game, 3–2, as Russ Christopher earned the win. At Fenway Park, Dave Ferriss won the first of two by a 5–0 score over the Yankees. This was Ferriss's second major league start and in each game he tossed a shutout. In his first two games, Ferriss was 5 for 6 at the plate and Rud Rennie boasted that he had outhit Enos Slaughter while in the Army. Hank Borowy returned the favor in the nightcap as the Yankees shutout Boston,

2–0. It was Borowy's fourth consecutive win to begin the season and his first shutout of the campaign. Only one game was scheduled on May 7, the day Germany surrendered at Rheims, France, but it was rained out.

By May 10 there were twenty-one playing days in the regular season and already there had been forty-five postponements. The Chicago White Sox, Boston Braves, and Cincinnati Reds were already washed out eight games apiece. It was reported that 125 of the 254 starting pitchers in the major leagues had pitched complete games. This was a .492 percentage, which was ahead of the previous year's tally of .455. The American League pitchers were proving to be more durable early in the season, completing 72 of their 126 games, while the senior circuit pitchers completed 53 of their 128 games.

After the contests on May 12, New York held a one-game lead on both Chicago and Detroit, while Washington and St. Louis were three games out. On May 14 the Yankees were in Chicago to play the Pale Hose. It was rainy and cold, the game for the day had been postponed, and McCarthy sat in the lobby of the Del Prado, holding a cigar and expressing his anger to a reporter. Despite the Yankees' early success, they were leaving too many runners on base. Joe McCarthy said, "I lay awake at night, dreaming of warm, sunny days and [Johnny] Lindell coming up with the bases full and knocking the ball out of the park." Ironically, while he would curse out his cleanup man Johnny Lindell for failing to hit in the clutch, he only had positive words of encouragement for Mike Garbark, who was batting .024. He saw great potential in Lindell and drove him hard. Furthermore, Lindell was confident in his ability and could take the harsh criticism that McCarthy sent in his direction. Garbark, on the other hand, was at the breaking point, unsure as to whether he belonged here. To verbally criticize him or to bench him may shatter his confidence beyond repair. McCarthy observed Garbark's unfortunate predicament in Cleveland: he popped up with the bases loaded and then came back to the bench filled with anger at himself. McCarthy said, "He kicked the bats, he kicked his shin guards. He gritted his teeth.... He was making me nervous. I said to him 'Mike, take it easy. Just try not to hit at bad balls.... You're pressing. You're all tightened up. You're worrying. Don't worry, I got confidence in you.... You'll snap out of it and it will be all over, like a bad dream.'"[8] When he came to the bench he would sit up and then sit down, unable to stand still, steaming with anger. At this juncture of the season, Garbark had batted forty-one times and stranded thirty-five base runners. The Yankees had lost Bill Dickey, their exceptional but aging catcher, to the service in 1944 and 1945. In 1944 Garbark batted .261 in 89 games and 299 at-bats, helping to make up for the loss of Dickey behind the plate. However, in 1945 Garbark batted only .216 in 60 games and 176 at-bats. Mike's older brother Bob also played during the war. Bob Garbark played briefly as a catcher for the Cleveland Indians (1934–1935) and Chicago Cubs (1937–1939) before the war. In 1944 he played eighteen games for Connie Mack's Philadelphia Athletics, batting .261 in 23 at-bats. And then in 1945 he played his last big league season with the Boston Red Sox, batting .261 in 68 games and 199 at-bats.

There was some hostility between Clark Griffith and Branch Rickey over Rickey's insistence that players in the Negro National and American Leagues join his planned United States League. It was in May of 1945 that Rickey proposed the new league, and his Brooklyn Brown Dodgers would be a member. He would use the Brown Dodgers as a cover to scout black players for the National League Dodgers, already having committed himself to the integration of baseball. Griffith rebuked Rickey for proposing the new league because he insisted it would lead to the death of the Negro Leagues.

In an interview with the *Pittsburgh Courier*, Griffith was adamant in his belief that Rickey was making himself the "dictator" of black baseball since he was insisting that the well-established Negro Leagues join his new league "or else." The destruction of the Negro Leagues would be the outcome of Rickey's actions. Griffith also said that Rickey was being manipulated by those who had failed or had been dishonest in the two black leagues and he was falling for their "propaganda." The 75-year-old owner of the Washington Senators hoped and believed that the owners and players of the two Negro Leagues who were being ordered by Rickey to join the U.S. League "or die" would reject and resent the proposal. At a time when the United States had committed all of its resources to end the reign of murderous dictators around the world, Griffith insisted, "This is not the age of dictators." Perhaps he was suggesting that dictatorial tendencies would no longer be tolerated henceforth. He said people should resist Rickey's grand scheme to destroy the Negro Leagues. He also urged those major and minor league teams that rented out their ballparks to the Negro League clubs to continue to do so.[9] Griffith had a financial interest in seeing the Negro Leagues remain intact because he rented out his ballpark to the Homestead Grays of the Negro National League.

Griffith was a skinflint and was most likely lashing out because he thought Rickey and the Brooklyn Dodgers would reap a hefty financial reward from the endeavor. When Griffith helped legitimize the American League, he succeeded in getting National League players to jump their contracts, showing no concern for the viability of the rival league. When he got his scouts to sign Cubans and Mexicans, he also got them to jump their contracts with local leagues, showing no concern for their fiscal health. However, Griffith was accurate in predicting the inevitable death of the Negro Leagues, although that death would not be abrupt but systematic. If the owners had known of Rickey's true intentions it would have set off a firestorm, but for now it was temporarily delayed as he meticulously looked for the right person to open up the door of integration in the major leagues.

From May 14 to May 17 there were eighteen postponements in the American League, including two doubleheaders on the 17th. There were no junior league games played during those four days because of either cold, rain, or wet grounds. On May 18, Dave Ferriss pitched his third shutout and won his fourth game as the Red Sox blanked Chicago, 2–0. In thirty-six innings pitched, Ferriss had worked thirty-four scoreless innings. Joe Haynes was the tough-luck loser for the White Sox. After five days without playing a game, New York finally took the field at Sportsman's Park but lost, 4–1, as Vern Stephens accounted for the Browns' runs with a grand slam in the third inning. Hank Borowy became unnerved when he walked Pete Gray, who subsequently stole second. The Yankee right-hander then walked the next two batters before serving up the gopher ball to Stephens, who slammed it into the left field bleachers. The other two games on the day were rained out.

The White Sox had a two-game lead in the junior circuit after sweeping a doubleheader from the Red Sox on May 20. Thornton Lee and Orval Grove earned the victories before a home crowd of 12,773. The Yankees played their first twilight game of the season at Yankee Stadium on May 22. They won 3–0 despite having the game halted on two occasions, first because of darkness and then rain. Hank Borowy earned the win, while Steve Gerkin took the loss for Philadelphia. In his only major league season in 1945, Gerkin compiled a 0–12 record with a 3.62 ERA. New York won the following day when they scored five in the first to support Bill Bevens, who led them to a 5–3 victory against Chicago. At Fenway Park, Dave Ferriss won his fifth in a row, defeating St. Louis, 4–1. Hal Newhouser was working on a shutout in Philadelphia before Bobby Estalella connected for a solo shot in the ninth inning. Detroit won, 7–1, as the Tigers' southpaw hurler was in complete control, scattering seven hits, walking one, and striking out eleven. Elsewhere on the 23rd, Cleveland defeated Washington, 3–2.

On the 24th not only did the Tigers lose to the Athletics, 7–2, at Shibe Park, but their starting pitcher, Al Benton, fractured a bone above his right ankle when Estalella nailed him with a line drive. He had to be carried off the field and attended to by Athletics' club physician Dr. James E. Pugh. George Kell, Philadelphia's 22-year-old third baseman, batted out of order in the second inning and was called out by umpire Eddie Rommel, who instructed him to lead off the third inning. As a result, five batters made six putouts in the first two frames. At Yankee Stadium, Tony Cuccinello went 3 for 5 to increase his American League leading batting average to .366. However, the Yankees starting pitcher, Atley Donald, withstood a twelve-hit attack by Chicago to win, 6–3. The White Sox committed four errors in the game, including two by shortstop Cass Michaels, who would accumulate 47 errors in 1945 and had a .936 fielding average. At Fenway Park, the Red Sox scored five runs in the sixth inning and held on for an 8–6 win over St. Louis. Pinky Woods, a huge, 6'5", 225-pound right-handed pitcher, earned his first win of the campaign. He played for Boston during the final three wartime seasons and compiled a 13–21 lifetime mark with a 3.97 ERA. In Washington, Pat Seerey and the little-used catcher Jim McDonnell hit doubles in the tenth inning to give the Indians a 1–0 win. Steve Gromek outdueled Roger Wolff for the win.

19. The American League Campaign

The Yankees completed a four-game sweep over Chicago on May 26, winning 13–0 before 16,604 fans at Yankee Stadium. The White Sox were now in third place, a game and a half behind the first-place Yankees. Detroit was in second, a half game out. Jimmy Dykes rearranged his lineup to no avail and Monk Dubiel pitched the shutout for McCarthy's club. Rud Rennie wrote, "The Sox ran into one another, played grounders as if they were rattlesnakes and fly balls as if they carried signs: 'Please do not handle while in the air.'"[10] Because of the lenient scoring they were only charged with two errors, one by third baseman Tony Cuccinello, and the other by catcher Vince Castino. The Yankees collected eighteen hits, the most they had made that year. Snuffy Stirnweiss, the Yankees leadoff hitter, had three hits, including a home run. In Boston, the Browns defeated the Red Sox, 9–2, behind the pitching of Tex Shirley. The Tigers defeated the Athletics, 5–4, as Walter Wilson won what would be his only major league game. Cleveland and Washington were rained out.

On Sunday, May 27, a crowd of 38,378 attended the doubleheader at Yankee Stadium despite the rainy weather that hovered over the area. The Yankees were six runs behind St. Louis going into the bottom of the seventh; they had a three-run deficit in the ninth; and they also overcame a one-run deficit in the fourteenth inning to win, 10–9, in a three hour and twenty-four minute extra-inning marathon. Pete Gray went 0 for 2 and committed one error in the field. Gray's parents traveled to the stadium from Nanticoke, Pennsylvania, to see their son play. Pete also received a $50 war bond between the games. He had a big smile on his face when a picture was taken with his parents, who were dressed impeccably but gazed into the camera with a serious look, perhaps unaccustomed to the attention. The Yankees increased their winning streak to seven with a 3–1 win in the nightcap, which ended after seven and a half frames because of darkness and wet grounds. Gray hit a pinch-hit single in the seventh inning. At Fenway Park, the White Sox got a total of three hits in a doubleheader and lost to the Red Sox, 7–0 and 2–1. Dave Ferriss pitched a one-hitter in the opener, while Emmett O'Neill yielded only two hits in the second game. Detroit and Washington split their doubleheader at Griffith Stadium. Lou Boudreau connected for a two-run homer in the fifth inning to lead the surging Indians to their fifth straight win in an 8–3 triumph over Philadelphia at Shibe Park. Red Embree earned the victory with a route-going performance. The second game was postponed because of rain.

Three American League games were postponed due to rain or wet grounds on May 28. In the midst of a six-game losing streak, Jimmy Dykes had a meeting with his men before taking the field at Fenway Park. There was no batting practice for the Pale Hose players. They appeared motivated by Dykes' speech and collected fifteen hits against four Boston pitchers to win, 8–6. Cuccinello led the attack, collecting three singles and a double.

Philadelphia pulled the trigger on a surprising trade on May 29 as they sent catcher Frankie Hayes to Cleveland for Buddy Rosar. Hayes had caught in 189 consecutive games for the A's and was only twenty-eight short of the major league record for catchers. Ray Mueller of the Cincinnati Reds set the mark in 1943 and 1944 with 217. In 1944 Hayes caught all 155 games for the Athletics and batted .248. In 1945 he batted a combined .234 for the season. Buddy Rosar was also a catcher and had yet to play with Cleveland in 1945 because he was holding out for a better contract. He batted .210 for Philadelphia in 92 games. The previous two years he had a .263 (1944) and .283 (1943) average. He was considered an excellent defensive catcher and had once quit the Yankees in the heat of a pennant race to seek out employment with the Buffalo police force.

On June 1 the American League standings stood as follows:

	W L	PCT	GB
New York Yankees	22–13	.629	—
Detroit Tigers	19–12	.613	1
Chicago White Sox	17–16	.515	4
St. Louis Browns	16–16	.500	4.5
Boston Red Sox	16–19	.457	6
Cleveland Indians	14–17	.452	6
Washington Senators	15–19	.441	6.5
Philadelphia Athletics	14–21	.400	8

The Boston Red Sox secured a 6–4 win over Detroit on June 1 with two bases-loaded walks in the fifth inning at Fenway Park. Emmett O'Neill earned the win. Walter Wilson took the loss. Eighteen-year-old Billy Pierce pitched three and a third innings in relief of Wilson. He walked the first batter he faced to force in a run, then settled down, giving up just one hit, yielding no runs and striking out four the rest of the way. Pierce appeared in only five games and pitched ten innings on the season but did have an excellent 1.80 ERA. He wouldn't pitch in the big leagues again till 1948 and would retire in 1964 after an eighteen-year career with a 211–169 record. Also on the first day of the month, the Yankees got a fine pitching performance from Bill Bevens to defeat Cleveland, 9–2, before a ladies' day crowd of 4,193 at Yankee Stadium. Rud Rennie wrote, "The contest was neither close nor exciting. There was no suspense."[11] Mike Garbark had two hits on the day, which was a major accomplishment because he entered the game 1 for 50 on the season. Walter Holborow, the Senators' fifth pitcher in the game, allowed two runs to score in the eleventh on three consecutive walks as the White Sox defeated Washington, 11–9. Holborow pitched in only twenty-one major league games over three seasons. In 1945 he was 1–1 with a 2.30 ERA in 15 games. Before getting mound assignments with the 1945 Senators, Holborow was pitching for the Department of Sanitation in New York. Elsewhere, Sig Jakucki pitched a three-hit shutout to give St. Louis a 4–0 win over Philadelphia at Shibe Park. At the plate, Jakucki went 1 for 4 with a triple and two runs scored. Larry Rosenthal, Philadelphia's left fielder, crashed into the outfield wall trying to run down Jakucki's drive in the sixth inning and suffered a leg injury. Don Gutteridge, the Browns leadoff man and second baseman, hit his first homer of the season and drove in three runs.

The Indians started the month of June by finding out that Red Embree would soon be leaving for California to be inducted into the Army. He made eight starts for the Tribe in 1945 and had a 4–4 record and a 1.93 ERA. On June 2, Lou Boudreau was in his hotel room and unable to manage the team because of his ulcerated right eye. Burt Shotton was the manager in his stead as the Indians defeated the Yankees, 4–0, behind the fine pitching of the bespectacled right-hander, Ed Klieman. Cleveland also received some good news when they found out that Mel Harder, the accomplished but aging pitcher, was going to leave his job at the Cleveland Steel Company and rejoin the team. Harder also held a position as an expeditor at the Ohio Rubber Company.

New York split two games with the Senators at Griffith Stadium on June 5. The Yankees won the opener, 12–3, behind the pitching of Atley Donald. The Senators won the nightcap, 7–3, as Marino Pieretti scattered nine hits and three walks. Red Embree made his final start before joining the military and tossed a shutout for Cleveland in a 9–0 win over Detroit. A crowd of 10,214 were on hand for the first night game of the season at Comiskey Park. Joe Schultz's pinch-hit single in the ninth inning gave the Browns a 2–1 win over Chicago. Philadelphia and Boston were rained out on the day. The St. Louis Browns roster was boosted on June 6 when Mark Christman joined the team on a permanent basis. Previously he had only been available for home games because he worked in a war plant but then he lost his job when they cut back. Christman batted .271 in 1944 as the everyday third baseman and then batted .277 in 78 games in 1945. The Yankees roster was hurt by the loss of Johnny Lindell on the following day when he passed his physical examination and then was inducted into the Army on June 8. Lindell batted .300 in 1944 and led the league in triples (16) and total bases (297). In 1945 he batted .283 in 41 games.

The Tigers were tied with the Yankees in first place after they defeated Chicago, 2–1, before 14,385 fans in a twilight affair at Briggs Stadium on June 8. Dizzy Trout earned the win. Boston defeated the Yankees, 6–4, before a ladies' day crowd of 8,674 at Yankee Stadium. Clem Hausmann earned the victory and George Metkovich had three hits, including a home run. Steve Gromek won his seventh game in Cleveland as the Indians defeated St. Louis, 2–1. At Shibe Park, Russ Christopher won his league-leading ninth game by tossing a six-hit shutout, defeating Washington, 4–0. Irv Hall, the Athletics second baseman, went 2 for 4 with a triple and three runs scored. Hall played in 151 games during the season and batted .261. His double-play partner in this game was the 22-year-old Bobby Wilkins. The 5'9", 165-pound right-handed hitting Wilkins had a two-year big league career, batting .240 in 25 at-bats in 1944 and then hitting .260 in 154 at-bats in 1945. He played most of his games at shortstop and had a .923 fielding average during the final wartime season. On June 8 he batted eighth and went 1 for 3 with one RBI. The Red Sox were leading the

American League in batting with a .267 average. Cleveland was last at .225 but the Indians had the best fielding percentage at .977.

Dave Ferriss lost his first game of the season after eight victories as Boston fell to New York, 3–2, before a Sunday crowd of 41,216 at Yankee Stadium on June 10. Hank Borowy improved to 8–1 with the win and had the same record as Ferriss. The second game was rained out. Cleveland and St. Louis split two games on the day, as did Detroit and Chicago. The Senators and Athletics were rained out. Both New York teams were in first place in their respective leagues. The Philadelphia Athletics and the Philadelphia Phillies played an exhibition for the city championship on June 11. The Nationals took the seven-inning game by a 3–1 score as about 25,000 showed up and purchased a reported half-million dollars' worth of war bonds.

Steve O'Neill's Tigers took over first place on June 12 with a 2–1, eleven-inning victory over the Browns before a Tuesday crowd of 19,943 at Briggs Stadium. Hal Newhouser went the distance for the win. Dutch Leonard led Washington to a 5–3 win over New York despite not having his best stuff at Yankee Stadium. Roger Wolff worked an inning in relief to close the door. Fred Vaughn had three hits for the Senators: a single, double, and triple. The loss dropped the Yankees to second place, a half game behind Detroit, while Washington was in a fifth-place tie, five and a half games behind. Bing Crosby watched the game with Del Webb in the royal box. But when Crosby was identified by a throng of school children, he needed police protection and had to leave the game before it concluded, during the ninth inning. Dick Siebert hit a two-run homer in the twelfth inning in Philadelphia, giving the home team a 7–5 win over Boston. Thornton Lee tossed a three-hit shutout and struck out thirteen at Comiskey Park as the White Sox defeated the Indians, 1–0. Al Smith was the tough-luck loser for Cleveland.

The Tigers received news that Hank Greenberg would be discharged from the Army. Cleanup hitter Rudy York had two singles and a three-run homer to lead the Tigers to a 6–4 win over St. Louis on June 13. Joe Orrell, a 6'4", 210-pound right-hander, earned the win. In the only other junior league game that was played on the day, Chicago gave up fourteen hits to Cleveland but won 5–3 before 2,314 fans at Comiskey Park. Joe Haynes lasted only five innings as the White Sox starter but earned the win despite giving up ten hits.

Leon Culberson hit a two-run double in the sixth inning of the first game of a doubleheader on June 17 to lead the Red Sox to a 2–1 victory over Washington at Griffith Stadium. Jim Bucher had three hits for Boston, while Ben Steiner and Culberson had two apiece. Emmett O'Neill went the distance for his fourth win. In the second contest, Jim Wilson pitched five scoreless innings before leaving the game with heat exhaustion. Frank Barrett then pitched the final four innings and yielded only one run as Boston won, 7–1. The Red Sox had eighteen hits in the game and George Metkovich had a single, double, and triple. Bob Johnson also had three hits for Boston. The Yankees and Athletics split a doubleheader at Shibe Park. Cleveland and St. Louis were rained out. But in Chicago the White Sox took two games from Detroit by scores of 6–1 and 7–5. It only took 1:31 and 1:47 to complete the two games. In the second game, Joe Haynes, Chicago's starting pitcher, had allowed only one run on one hit and one walk after five innings before disaster struck. In the bottom of the fifth he singled for the second time, and when Guy Curtright hit a one-base hit to right field, Haynes slid into third and suffered a severe leg fracture. He was rushed to the hospital, where Dr. John Claridge observed that the injury was so bad that Haynes's baseball career may be over. Haynes had started his big league career with Washington in 1939, going 8–12 with a 5.36 ERA. During the war he pitched well for Chicago, predominantly in relief. In 1942 he was 8–5 with a 2.62 ERA. In 1943 he compiled an impressive 7–2 mark and a 2.96 ERA. In 1944 he was 5–6 with a 2.57 ERA and then in 1945 he went 5–5 with a 3.55 ERA. Haynes would resume his baseball career in 1946 and pitched seven more big league seasons after the 1945 campaign. In 1947 he had his best year, compiling a 14–6 record for the Pale Hose with an American League-leading 2.42 ERA. In fourteen major league seasons he had a 76–82 record and a 4.01 ERA. Haynes was Clark Griffith's son-in-law, having married his adopted daughter, Thelma R. Griffith, in 1941. After his playing career ended in 1952 he became a coach for the Senators from 1953 to 1955 and then became their vice president after Clark died in October of 1955. He also held an executive position when the club moved to Minnesota in 1961.

In the bottom of the ninth inning on June 18, catcher Mike Tresh executed the squeeze bunt and sent pinch runner Joe Orengo across the plate with the winning run as the White Sox defeated Detroit, 1–0. Bill Dietrich was the winning pitcher while Dizzy Trout was burdened with the loss. On the following day, the Tigers took a two-game lead in the American League flag race with a 4–3 win over Cleveland. Zeb Eaton was the winning pitcher. Hal Newhouser tossed a five-hit shutout for his tenth win on June 20 as Detroit defeated the Indians, 5–0. The Tigers' ace hurler had two hits on the day and drove in three runs. At Sportsman's Park the White Sox defeated St. Louis, 4–1, in the game where a brawl was started when George Caster fired the ball into the White Sox dugout. In Philadelphia, the Senators benefited from five errors by the opposition and held on to win, 7–5, behind the pitching of Mickey Haefner. The New York versus Boston game was rained out at Fenway Park.

A disappointed Fenway Park crowd watched Dave Ferriss fail to make it out of the fifth inning as the Yankees walloped Boston by a 14–4 score on June 21. New York scored thirteen runs in the fifth inning, their biggest inning since 1920, when they scored fourteen runs during an inning on July 6. The only other junior circuit game played on the day was between Detroit and Cleveland, as Stubby Overmire led the Tigers to a 5–1 triumph in front of the home fans. Hank Greenberg worked out with the team before the game both at first base and in the outfield but was not expected to play in a league game for several more days.

Bill Bevens tossed a four-hit shutout on June 22 as New York defeated Philadelphia, 2–0, at Yankee Stadium. There were 6,297 fans in the stadium but only 4,241 paid. The Yankee players attended a cocktail party at the Concourse Plaza after the game as the Bronx War Bond Committee celebrated a special day honoring the Yankees. In St. Louis, the Browns knocked Dizzy Trout out of the box in the fifth inning and won, 8–4, over Detroit. Eddie Lake connected for a three-run homer in the third inning to help Boston defeat Washington, 10–5, at Fenway Park. Boston scored nine of their runs in the first three innings. The White Sox and Indians split two games in Cleveland. Larry MacPhail returned from his fishing trip in Canada and watched New York score in the last of the ninth to win, 7–6, on the 23rd. Washington and Detroit also emerged victorious on the day.

Hal Newhouser and Dizzy Trout pitched the Tigers to a doubleheader victory over the Browns on June 24. In Boston, Dave Ferriss gave up ten hits and walked three but held on to win his tenth game as the Red Sox defeated Washington, 6–5, in the first of two. The Senators won the nightcap, 5–2, behind the pitching of Marino Pieretti. A Sunday crowd of 31,469, the Red Sox' largest of the season, was on hand to watch the game. In Cleveland, Steve Gromek won his eighth game in a 7–3 win over Chicago. The White Sox won the second game, 7–4, behind Ed Lopat. A Yankee Stadium crowd of 37,745 were on hand to watch the Yankees sweep the four-game set from Philadelphia with a doubleheader victory. Hank Borowy and Ernie Bonham were the winning pitchers.

Newhouser won his twelfth game on June 28 at Briggs Stadium as Detroit defeated Washington, 5–2. Roger Wolff dropped to 8–4 with the loss. He struck out six batters but two of his victims reached first base as catcher Rick Ferrell was unable to handle his knuckleball. The Yankees dropped to second place, a game behind Detroit, with their 9–4 loss to the Browns. In Cleveland, the Indians scored four runs in both the third and fourth innings and their sixteen-hit attack helped them secure an 11–0 win over the Athletics. The Boston at Chicago game was postponed due to the wet grounds at Comiskey Park. On the following day, Dave Ferriss won his eleventh game when he hit a two-run homer in the ninth inning to give the Red Sox a 4–2 win over Chicago. Cleveland also won by a 4–2 score as Allie Reynolds earned the win and the Athletics lost their tenth consecutive game. In Detroit, the Senators collected fifteen hits to win 8–3 as Marino Pieretti went the distance.

On July 1 the American League standings looked as follows:

	W L	PCT	GB
Detroit Tigers	37–24	.607	—
New York Yankees	35–24	.593	1
Boston Red Sox	32–27	.542	4
Washington Senators	30–29	.508	6
Chicago White Sox	31–30	.508	6
St. Louis Browns	26–31	.456	9

19. The American League Campaign

	W L	PCT	GB
Cleveland Indians	26–32	.448	9.5
Philadelphia Athletics	20–40	.333	16.5

After four years away from the game, Hank Greenberg returned to the Tigers lineup on July 1 and triumphantly hit a home run in the first game of a doubleheader as they defeated Philadelphia, 9–5, before a Sunday crowd of 47,729 at Briggs Stadium. Dizzy Trout earned the win, while Bobo Newsom lost his eleventh straight game. Al Benton, in his first game back since his leg injury, pitched two scoreless innings in relief. Philadelphia dropped their thirteenth straight contest when they lost the second game, 5–3. Greenberg was out of the lineup in the nightcap. The largest home crowd (36,751) of the season showed up at Comiskey Park to watch the White Sox sweep the doubleheader from New York, 11–4 and 6–5. Bill Dietrich and Thornton Lee earned the wins. The Red Sox scored five in the ninth in the nightcap at Sportsman's Park to win 7–4 after dropping the opener 7–3. Bob Muncrief won the opener for St. Louis while Dave Ferriss earned a relief victory for Boston. In Cleveland, the Senators and Indians split a doubleheader by identical 6–5 scores. Dutch Leonard won the opener for Washington while Allie Reynolds improved his record to 8–6 with a relief victory in the second game.

Jim Wilson of Boston tossed a five-hit shutout to lead the Red Sox to a 4–0 win over Detroit before 22,528 spectators at Briggs Stadium on July 3. After winning seven straight, Hal Newhouser was saddled with the loss. Despite the setback, Detroit had a three-and-a-half-game lead over the second-place Yankees. On the 4th of July, Dave Ferriss earned a 4–3 victory in the opener against the Tigers. Al Benton made his first start since May 24 in the nightcap, and earned the win as Detroit prevailed 5–2. The Senators were showing signs of life as they took two games from Chicago, 5–4 and 11–2, before 21,996 witnesses at Comiskey Park. Harlond Clift had three homers on the day. Marino Pieretti and Mickey Haefner earned the victories. Cleveland and New York split two games on the day, as did Philadelphia and St. Louis.

On July 5, Jeff Heath hit an eleventh-inning homer to propel the Indians to a 2–1 win over New York at League Park. At Briggs Stadium, Hank Greenberg hit a two-out pinch-hit single to drive in two runs in the ninth inning that gave the Tigers a 9–8 triumph. Boston had fourteen hits in the game but stranded twelve runners. Detroit had seventeen hits and stranded eleven in the slugfest. Bobo Newsom walked home the winning run in the eleventh inning in St. Louis that gave the Browns a 4–3 win. Dutch Leonard had his knuckleball working before only 1,548 fans at Comiskey Park as the Senators won, 5–2. Hank Greenberg struck out as a pinch-hitter in the ninth inning on the 6th as Bill Bevens went the distance to give New York a 5–4 win before a crowd of 31,288 at Briggs Stadium. Greenberg admitted that he had rushed back to the game too soon after being discharged and was now suffering from a charley horse and a problem with his elbow. Pete Gray went 0 for 4 for St. Louis out of the leadoff spot and he was also charged with an error as the Browns lost to Washington, 6–3. In Cleveland, Allie Reynolds got the final out in the opener and then got the final three outs in the nightcap as the Indians defeated Boston, 3–2 and 4–2. Jim Bagby and Mel Harder earned victories as the starting pitchers. On July 7, George Case was leading the American League in hitting at .336. Tony Cuccinello was second at .333, followed by Vern Stephens (.317); Snuffy Stirnweiss (.311); and Bob Johnson (.296). By July 11, during the mid-season break, the Tigers had a four-and-a-half-game lead over both Washington and New York.

After the three-day mid-season break the Indians defeated the Yankees, 7–4, as New York stranded thirteen runners on July 12. Jeff Heath had three hits including a double and a three-run home run for Cleveland. He had also connected for a circuit shot the last time he faced New York on July 5. Rud Rennie wrote, "The reunion with the Indians was like a hangover."[12] Joe Buzas, who had done a bangup job for McCarthy's squad during the spring training season, was sent down to Kansas City of the American Association. However, he refused to report and attended this game in hopes of speaking to Larry MacPhail and perhaps persuading him to orchestrate a trade. The Indians were missing their veteran right-hander, Jim Bagby, who returned to his home in Atlanta to care for his wife, who was ill. In Boston, Jim Wilson outdueled Hal Newhouser as the Red Sox won, 2–1. Philadelphia took two games from St. Louis, 4–0 and 11–0, as Bobo Newsom ended his twelve-game losing streak with his opening-game triumph. Washington moved to within three and a half games of Detroit when Dutch Leonard led them to a 4–2 win over Chicago.

On the following day Dave Ferriss won his fifteenth game as the Red Sox put down Detroit, 5–1. The Senators gained another game on Detroit when George Case drove in the winning run with a ninth-inning single for a 3–2 win over the White Sox. In Philadelphia, Mike Kreevich broke a 2–2 tie with an eleventh-inning RBI double to propel the Browns to a 4–2 win. New York Governor Thomas E. Dewey was among the spectators at Yankee Stadium who saw the Indians slug the Yankees, 16–4. Pat Seerey had three homers and a triple while Jeff Heath hit two homers on the day. Steve Gromek defeated the Yankees for the fourth time on the season. Gromek was a fly-ball pitcher and the infielders only fielded four grounders on the day. In the previous game he faced New York he got twenty-three fly balls and pop-ups and no Indian had an assist.

Detroit lost to Boston, 7–1, on July 14. The Senators were rained out but picked up a half game to inch two games behind the Tigers in the standings. New York defeated Detroit, 5–4, the following day before 40,808 rain-soaked Yankee Stadium fans. Again Washington was rained out and picked up a half game in the standings. The Senators dropped two games on July 16 to the Browns while the Tigers snapped a four-game losing streak behind the pitching of Stubby Overmire. The final score was Detroit 9, New York 4. Left-handed pitcher Stubby Overmire went the distance for Detroit and also helped himself at the bat. He laid down a successful squeeze bunt and also reached base four times on the day via a single, an error, a double and a walk. Rud Rennie wrote that the Yankees were in a magnanimous mood and treated their opponent "Like good Samaritans." Overmire, the "enemy pitcher," was treated by the Yankees "as if he were a captured German spy, and for seven innings did everything but buy him hot dogs and cigarettes."[13] Overmire had surrendered only three one-base hits until the Yankees' bats came alive and pushed across four runs in the eighth inning. In Boston, Pat Seerey's seventh homer of the season, a two-run shot in the sixth inning, led the Indians to a 3–2 win at Fenway Park.

At Shibe Park on the 16th, Bobo Newsom tossed a two-hitter in the second game of a twin bill to give the Athletics a 7–1 win in the nightcap after losing the first game to Chicago. Philadelphia was paced by Bobby Estalella's two home runs and Newsom won his second game in a row since ending his twelve-game losing streak. Bobo surrendered both of his hits in the game to Johnny Dickshot, and at the plate he went 2 for 4 with a run scored. Johnny Humphries outdueled Russ Christopher to lead the Pale Hose to a 6–2 win in the first game. Speedy leadoff man Wally Moses led the White Sox in the opener, going 3 for 4, with a double, a triple, and two runs scored. Moses was in his fourth season with the White Sox after spending seven seasons with the Philadelphia Athletics. He batted .295 with a .373 on-base percentage and led the junior circuit with 35 doubles. In 1943 he was tied with Johnny Lindell for the American League lead with 12 triples. He stole 56 bases that season, finishing second to Washington's George Case. His last big league season was in 1951, as he finished his seventeen-year major league career with a .291 batting average and a .364 on-base percentage. He collected 435 doubles, 110 triples, 89 home runs, and stole 174 bases. Moses' best season was in 1937 when he batted .320 and had 48 doubles, 13 triples, 25 homers, 113 runs scored and 86 RBIs. He also had 208 hits for his second consecutive season with more than 200 hits. Two different times in his career he had a game-ending steal of home: the first time was on August 20, 1940, in the tenth inning of the second game of a doubleheader with Thornton Lee on the mound for Chicago. The second time was when he stole home against the Boston Red Sox' right-handed pitcher, Mace Brown. It occurred on July 7, 1943, in the fourteenth inning. Moses was a 5'10", 160-pound left-handed hitter.

On July 17 there were three postponements in the junior league, including the game between Chicago and Philadelphia at Shibe Park, which was postponed because the White Sox had to catch a train for Boston so they would be there in time to play the Red Sox on the following day. White Sox officials said they were complying with the Office of Defense Transportation ruling that disallowed them to use a Pullman car for distances of 450 miles or less. As a result they had to take a day coach. Meanwhile, Boston played their game on the 17th, losing to the Indians, 6–1, at Fenway Park. Steve Gromek won his eleventh game of the season. Then, with Chicago in town on the following day, the Red Sox defeated the White Sox, 6–2, as Dave Ferriss won his sixteenth game. St. Louis and New York had their doubleheader postponed on the day because of the wet grounds at Yankee Stadium. Meanwhile, the Athletics and Indians were set to play a twin bill in Philadelphia; they only played twelve innings of the opener before it was halted at 2–2 when the rain came in. Detroit took two games from Washington by 6–4 and 5–0 scores and were four and a half games ahead of both New York and Boston, who were tied for second place. The only game played in the American League on the 19th was between Chicago and Boston as there were two doubleheaders and one single contest postponed. Thornton Lee allowed nine hits and seven walks, and hit a batter. But the Red Sox stranded fourteen runners on the bases and Chicago won, 5–3.

Despite making a triple play on July 20, the Tigers lost two games to knuckleballers Dutch Leonard and Roger Wolff by scores of 4–3 and 3–1 at Griffith Stadium. New York finally took the field at Yankee Stadium after being idle for three days because of the rain and the wet field. Sig Jakucki led St. Louis to a 4–3 win in the opener with a complete-game effort and a home run, while Al Hollingsworth earned a 3–2 victory in the nightcap. Babe Martin also hit a long ball in the opener and Milt Byrnes hit one in the nightcap. Because of the transportation difficulties, both teams agreed that no inning would start past 5:45 so that the St. Louis Browns ball club could catch a train to Boston. Jesse Flores and Bobo Newsom earned victories as Philadelphia took two games from Cleveland at Shibe Park by 8–3 and 3–2 scores. In Boston, Clem Hausmann failed to make it through the third inning as Chicago scored five runs in the third and held on for a 6–3 triumph. On the following day Washington defeated Cleveland, 7–4. The Tigers and Athletics hooked up in an endurance battle as they fought to a 1–1, twenty-four-inning stalemate that was called on account of darkness only two innings shy of a major league record. Les Mueller, Detroit's starter, lasted nineteen and two-thirds innings, while Russ Christopher, Philadelphia's starter, lasted thirteen innings. A crowd of 4,325 fans showed up at Shibe Park for the game. Ernie Bonham had pitched well for the Yankees but had a 1–8 record because of little run support. But the Yankees offense helped rectify the problem by scoring twelve runs on thirteen hits against Chicago. Bonham did his part and New York won, 12–3. Elsewhere, St. Louis defeated Boston, 4–1.

Dave Ferriss won his seventeenth game with a 3–2 win over the Browns before 34,810 fans at Fenway Park on July 22. Tex Shirley led St. Louis to a 5–1 win in the nightcap. Joe McCarthy was advised to stay away from the ballpark on the 22nd because he had become depressed and nervous over the Yankees' recent play. Art Fletcher was the acting manager as the Yankees kicked away a game to Chicago, 6–5, in twelve innings. Larry MacPhail, the Yankees president, said that McCarthy wanted to resign after the 1944 season but "after we bought the club, he changed his mind because it might look as if he was resigning because he could not get along with me." MacPhail said he was not dissatisfied with the Yankees manager and insisted that he didn't have the personnel to be successful and he should not be blamed for that.[14] Elsewhere on the day, the Tigers and Athletics split two games, as did Washington and Cleveland.

Joe McCarthy offered his resignation to MacPhail on July 23, but the Yankees president refused to accept it. McCarthy was heading to his farm in Buffalo, New York, to recuperate. He said, "I can't sleep. I can't eat. I haven't been well for the last two years. I'm going home to see my own doctor." A reporter asked him whether he would return to the club. McCarthy responded, "I don't know. I don't know. I'm awfully sick right now."[15] By early September a rumor was circulating that Leo Durocher would replace McCarthy for the 1946 season. The *New York World-Telegram* felt compelled to contact MacPhail to find out the veracity of the rumor. MacPhail vehemently denied it and insisted that McCarthy would serve out his contract and finish the 1945 season and then return for the 1946 campaign.[16]

Not only did the Yankees lose their manager for part of the season because of an illness, but coach Art Fletcher suffered a heart attack in September and had to leave the team. Fletcher played for the New York Giants during twelve of his thirteen big league seasons and played for the Philadelphia Phillies during two seasons as well. He batted .277 lifetime and was predominantly a shortstop in the major leagues from 1909 to 1920 and 1922. He managed the Phillies for four seasons from 1923 to 1926 and managed the Yankees for eleven games (6–5) in 1929. Fletcher spent nineteen seasons as a coach for the Yankees; 1945 was his final season in that capacity.

On July 27, MacPhail seemed quite happy to get rid of Hank Borowy but acknowledged that the Cubs had gotten a pitcher who may lead them to a pennant. The Yankees received a reported $100,000 in the waiver deal, according to the *New York Herald Tribune*, but the actual sum was $97,000. And although MacPhail implied that the Yankees were going to receive players in the trade, there were none coming. When the reporters asked him which players he received, MacPhail tried to change the subject. Furthermore, the Yankees front office, perhaps fearful of the fan reaction, came prepared to discredit Borowy: he had only pitched three complete games since April. The last time he went the distance in a game was June 24, when he defeated the Athletics and improved his record to 9–3. Despite finishing the 1944 season with a 17–12 record, Borowy had weakened down the stretch, going 5–8 after July 15. MacPhail may have also thought he had pulled a fast one on the Cubs: he grinned when asked if he had informed the Cubs general manager about a problem with Borowy's pitching arm.[17]

While Larry MacPhail was busy on July 27 explaining his deal with the Cubs, the Yankees defeated Philadelphia, 2–0, behind the route-going performance of Bill Bevens. The ladies' day crowd of 8,826 at Yankee Stadium watched Russ Christopher pitch a superb game for the Athletics in the losing effort. He gave up two unearned runs on four hits and three walks. He struck out twelve: he fanned every Yankee batter in the lineup, and Hersh Martin, Oscar Grimes, and Tuck Stainback struck out twice. The game started ominously when shortstop Edgar Busch booted leadoff man Snuffy Stirnweiss's grounder in the opening inning. Stirnweiss stole second and scored on Martin's single to plate the first run. Busch had two errors on the day, and when third baseman George Kell was unable to handle Oscar Grimes's grounder in the eighth inning, the Yankees scored their second run. In Boston, Dave Ferriss had his second eight-game winning streak of the season snapped as Washington defeated the Red Sox, 3–1, at Fenway Park. Steve Gromek won his twelfth game of the season for Cleveland as they downed St. Louis, 3–1. In Detroit, Johnny Humphries of the White Sox and Hal Newhouser hooked up in a pitcher's duel. It was a scoreless game after eight frames. Humphries had yielded only two hits when he served up a home run to Eddie Mayo in the bottom of the ninth.

By July 28, Larry MacPhail was on the attack against the critics of the Borowy trade. Clark Griffith accused the Yankees of foul play and of asking waivers on the entire Washington ball club. Branch Rickey claimed he was unaware that Borowy was available and shocked that he had gone to the National League-leading Cubs. MacPhail was indignant and wasn't going to listen to Rickey's whining. MacPhail said that Rickey had claimed three players via a waiver deal and suggested that he should get his eyes checked and get himself a new pair of glasses. Will Harridge, the president of the American League, backed up MacPhail, and said that the deal was legitimate and that no team put in a claim for Borowy, which allowed the Yankees to deal him to any team that they wanted.

On the 28th, Philadelphia and New York were rained out, and Detroit, Boston, and Cleveland emerged victorious in their ball games. The Yankees swept their four-game series with the Athletics when they took both ends of a doubleheader on July 29 by 2–1 and 11–3 scores. Ernie Bonham and Bill Zuber were the winning pitchers for New York. Bonham was known as "Tiny" but he was anything but small in stature, standing at 6'2" and weighing 215 pounds. In Cleveland, the Browns and Indians split a pair: St. Louis won the opener, 4–0, behind the ten-hit shutout by Tex Shirley. Then Jim Bagby pitched a six-hit shutout for the Indians in the second game as they won 3–0. In Boston, Bob Johnson went 4 for 4 with two doubles, three runs scored, and one RBI while batting in the cleanup spot. In the fifth inning he led off with a single, the 2,000th hit of his career, and then the game was halted as Johnson was presented with the baseball. Emmett O'Neill pitched a complete game for the Red Sox as they defeated Washington, 8–4. In Detroit, the White Sox collected thirteen hits and two walks against Al Benton but pushed across only two runs. The Tigers won the game, 4–2.

On August 1 the American League standings looked as follows:

	W L	PCT	GB
Detroit Tigers	51–36	.586	—
New York Yankees	47–40	.540	4
Washington Senators	45–41	.523	5.5
Boston Red Sox	46–43	.517	6
Cleveland Indians	44–44	.500	7.5
Chicago White Sox	44–45	.494	8
St. Louis Browns	42–44	.488	8.5
Philadelphia Athletics	30–56	.349	20.5

Roy Cullenbine hit a three-run double in the last of the ninth and scored on Vern Stephens's throwing error, his third of the game, as the Tigers defeated St. Louis, 9–8, on August 1 at Briggs Stadium. Lou Finney, who had been traded to the Browns from Boston on July 27, hit a grand slam homer. Washington was tied with New York in second place, five games back, when they won two games from the Athletics, 2–1 and 3–0, at Griffith Stadium. Dutch Leonard and Roger Wolff earned victories. Bobo Newsom's five-game winning streak was snapped when he took the loss in the second contest. In Boston, left fielder Hersh Martin had to avoid a bottle that was thrown at him by a fan while fielding a double in the fifth inning. He successfully avoided the bottle but injured his right leg while doing so and had to leave the game in the sixth inning. The Yankees lost to the Red Sox, 7–5. Vic Johnson earned the win in relief. In Cleveland, Floyd Baker squeezed home the winning run in the ninth inning to give the White Sox a 2–1 win. Ed Lopat defeated Steve Gromek in a pitchers' duel.

Washington won another doubleheader against Philadelphia by identical 2–1 scores on August 2. Mickey Haefner and Marino Pieretti went the distance in the two games with the contests lasting 1:43 and 1:27. In Cleveland the Indians won two of the three games in the series against Chicago when they took the rubber game by a 13–7 score. Cleveland pushed across eight runs in the third inning, which was highlighted by Pat Seerey's grand slam homer. They used four pitchers in the game to secure the victory: Allie Reynolds, Jack Salveson, Ed Klieman and the winner Pete Center. Salveson pitched a few innings in relief. He followed starter Allie Reynolds to the hill when Reynolds failed to make it through the second inning. Salveson also went 3 for 3 in the game with two doubles, two runs scored, and two RBIs. The six-foot and one-half-inch, 180-pound right-handed pitcher made his major league debut at the age of 19 for the 1933 New York Giants. After going 0–2 with a 3.82 ERA during his first year for Bill Terry's pennant-winning ball club, he improved to 3–1 with a 3.52 ERA in 1934. In 1935 he split the season between the Pittsburgh Pirates (0–1, 9.00 ERA in 5 games) and Chicago White Sox (1–2, 4.86 ERA in 20 games) as his productivity decreased. He didn't return to the majors until 1943, going 5–3 with a 3.35 ERA for Cleveland. In 1945, the 31-year-old Salveson pitched in his final big league season, failing to collect either a win or a loss, and compiling a 3.68 ERA in 19 relief appearances. Also on August 2 in the American League, the Yankees defeated Boston, 3–1, and first-place Detroit blanked St. Louis, 6–0.

The surging Senators once again won a doubleheader on August 3, this time defeating the Red Sox by scores of 7–3 and 3–1. Alex Carrasquel went the distance in the opener to improve his record to 3–3 and Johnny Niggeling surrendered only six hits to win the nightcap. After the first game, the Fenway Park patrons were entertained with a ceremony honoring the 155th anniversary of the United States Coast Guard. Additionally, manager Joe Cronin accepted the 1944 MVP award for Bobby Doerr, who was serving in the Coast Guard. In 1944, the BBWAA (Baseball Writers Association of America) voted Hal Newhouser, the American League MVP. However, *The Sporting News* named Bobby Doerr as their player of the year. New York defeated Philadelphia on the 3rd by a 4–1 score as Ernie Bonham yielded six hits and walked none in the complete-game effort. It was Bonham's third straight victory and he improved to 4–8 on the campaign. In St. Louis the Browns pushed across four runs in the sixth inning and defeated Cleveland, 6–5. A Comiskey Park crowd of 26,919 watched the White Sox defeat the Tigers, 5–0. Roy Schalk, who was born Le Roy John Schalk in Chicago on November 9, 1908, continued his hot hitting, going 3 for 5 with a double, one run scored and three runs batted in. The 5'10", 168-pound right-handed hitting second baseman made his big league debut in 1932, appearing in three games for the New York Yankees and going 3 for 12. He didn't return to the big leagues until 1944, when he was the everyday second baseman for the White Sox, batting .220 with one homer and 44 RBIs in 587 at-bats. Like many wartime players, 1945 was his final big league season as he batted .248 with one homer and 65 RBIs in 513 at-bats.

While the White Sox fans were enjoying their team's victory on August 3, the game was held up for five minutes when an intruder made its way into center field in the bottom of the fourth inning. It was a red hen, and center fielder Doc Cramer pursued the fowl and caught it, but before handing it off to someone else he noticed that the animal was accompanied with a tag. It stated that the winning team would be given the hen as a gift. By this time Packy Schwartz, the White Sox trainer, was running towards Cramer to take possession of the animal. Cramer was moving in Schwartz's direction until he read the tag, and then he suddenly changed course and gave the animal to Dr. Roy Forsyth, the Tigers trainer. When Earl Caldwell, the winning pitcher for Chicago, had tossed a shutout and secured the victory, Cramer obeyed the order that was on the animal and gave it to the White Sox' winning pitcher as a reward for his fine effort.[18]

In addition to beating Philadelphia, 5–1, on August 4, the Yankees received news that Joe McCarthy would soon rejoin the team. Tom McBride, the Red Sox outfielder and first baseman, tied a major league record by driving in six runs in one inning during the second game of a doubleheader, which the Red Sox won, 15–4, over Washington. The six-foot, 190-pound right-handed hitter would have his best season in 1945, batting .305 in 344 at-bats. Boston scored twelve runs in the fourth inning. Dave Ferriss won his eighteenth game and the Cuban-born Sandy Ullrich took the loss for Washington as the starting pitcher. Bert Shepard worked the final five and one-third innings in relief and gave up one run on three hits and one walk, and he hit one batter. Also making a relief appearance in the second game for Washington was Joe "Fire" Cleary, who was born in Cork, Ireland, on December 3, 1918. This was the only major league game he ever pitched in and it was an outing that made Joe Nuxhall's 1944 appearance look good by comparison. Cleary only recorded one out during Washington's disastrous fourth inning and he allowed seven runs on five hits and three walks. He also threw a wild pitch. His ERA in the baseball encyclopedia stands at 189.00. Walter Holborow tossed a 4–0 shutout to give the Senators the opening game victory. Meanwhile, the White Sox got strong pitching from Orval Grove and defeated Hal Newhouser and the Tigers, 3–2. Chicago was leading the American League in both batting (.284) and fielding percentage (.981). St. Louis defeated Cleveland, 8–2, in the other game of the day.

Connie Mack's Athletics defeated the Yankees in two games on August 5 by scores of 6–3 and 4–3 to end their ten-game losing streak. A Sunday Shibe Park crowd of 25,319 watched Bobo Newsom and Jesse Flores pitch their way into the victory column. On August 7 the Athletics sent Charlie Metro, an outfielder who batted .210 in his third and final major league season in 1945, and two players to be named later to the Oakland Oaks of the Pacific Coast League for shortstop Jake Caulfield. Caulfield never did play for the 1945 Athletics, but he made his big league debut in 1946, batting .277 on the season with 94 at-bats during the only major league campaign he ever participated in. On August 8, the Senators picked up Mike Kreevich on waivers to give them an extra hitter for the pennant drive. Kreevich finished his career with Washington in 1945, batting .278 in 45 games. Detroit bolstered their mound corps when they picked up George Caster on waivers from St. Louis. Caster had been ineffective for the Browns (1–2, 6.89 ERA) but with the Tigers he compiled a 5–1 record with a 3.86 ERA in twenty-two relief appearances.

On August 9, Joe McCarthy rejoined the Yankees at League Park and watched his club defeat the Indians, 3–2. Rud Rennie wrote that McCarthy was "a little nervous" but appeared "fit" in his return to action. He had some color in his face and appeared in much better condition than when he had left. McCarthy had not managed a game since July 20 and got to watch the recently discharged battery consisting of Red Ruffing and Aaron Robinson for the first time. Ruffing was in the service despite the fact that he was missing four toes because of a mining accident as a teenager. He gained a significant amount of weight in the service as he played ball for the courageous troops in Long Beach and Honolulu to give them a respite.[19] Ruffing outdueled Jim Bagby for the victory. He surrendered seven hits and walked one: Dutch Meyer, Cleveland's leadoff hitter and second baseman, went 4 for 5 with two doubles and a run scored. But with two out in the last of the ninth and runners on first and second, Meyer flew out to end the game. Aaron Robinson went 1 for 2 in the contest. Prior to 1945 he had appeared in one major league game with the 1943 Yankees. He made quite an impression towards the tail end of the 1945 season, batting .281 with a .368 on-base percentage. He hit 8 homers and had 24 RBIs in 50 games and 160 at-bats.

In Chicago on August 9, Mike Kreevich played his first game for the Senators and hit a two-run double in the fifth inning to lead Washington to a 7–2 win. Rudy York hit two two-run homers for Detroit as the Tigers collected fifteen hits to defeat Boston, 11–5, at Briggs Stadium. Dizzy Trout won his tenth game. The Athletics and Browns were rained out in St. Louis.

The Tigers bolstered their pitching staff once again by acquiring Jim Tobin on waivers. The Red Sox feared that they had lost pitcher Jim Wilson for the season when he suffered a fractured skull in the second game of a doubleheader on August 8 when Hank Greenberg hit him with a scorching line drive. Wilson had to have an operation at Henry Ford Hospital in Detroit. Manager Joe Cronin said, "I hardly think there's a chance he'll recover fully before the race is over."[20]

As a harbinger of things to come and a glimpse into the postwar world, it was reported on August 9 that United Air Lines had signed contracts with eleven major league teams for significant travel time that would commence when wartime conditions were loosened. The eleven teams that were signed were the New York Yankees, New York Giants, Chicago White Sox, Chicago Cubs, Cleveland Indians, Washington Senators, Boston Braves, Philadelphia Phillies, Philadelphia Athletics, Pittsburgh Pirates, and St. Louis Browns. The train was the preferred mode of transportation by many players and apparently safer as well, but in September 1945, the Brooklyn Dodgers were involved in a train accident as they were traveling from St. Louis to Chicago. Outfielder Luis Olmo and coach Chuck Dressen had minor injuries as a result. But Charlie Tegtmeyer, the train's engineer, was burned to death.[21]

The Yankees were making McCarthy's return as stress-free as possible as they clobbered Cleveland pitching for a 10–4 win on August 10. Al Gettel was the winner while Hersh Martin and Nick Etten hit homers. Elsewhere, St. Louis took two games from Philadelphia. Nelson Potter gave up five hits and two walks as the Browns won the opener, 2–1, in only one hour and twenty-four minutes. The nightcap took three hours and twenty minutes as the Athletics rallied from a 12-to-6 deficit and scored seven runs in the eighth inning to take the lead. However, the Browns scored one run in the last of the ninth on Vern Stephens's RBI single and Milt Byrnes hit a home run in the eleventh to give them a 14–13 victory. Rookie right hander Randy Heflin tossed a four-hit shutout for Boston as they defeated the Tigers, 9–0. It was Heflin's first major league win. The White Sox beat the Senators, 6–3, before 3,732 fans at Comiskey Park behind the pitching of Thornton Lee. The game took only one hour and thirty-one minutes to complete. Chicago was situated in fourth place, four and a half games behind first-place Detroit, while second-place Washington was only a game behind in the American League flag race.

On August 12, the Tigers took two from New York, 9–6 and 8–2, at Briggs Stadium. The Yankees made two errors in the opener and four errors in the nightcap. Rud Rennie wrote, "The Brooklyn Dodgers today lost the exclusive rights to dizzy baseball when the Yankees ... confused themselves and 54,969 persons so thoroughly they had everybody laughing except Joe McCarthy, their manager."[22] The Senators split their doubleheader with the Browns on the day. Dave Ferriss pitched a complete game to lead the Red Sox to a 7–1 victory over Cleveland in the first game of a doubleheader. But Pete Center went the distance for the Indians in the nightcap as they won, 8–2. At Comiskey Park a crowd of 19,442 witnessed their White Sox lose their first home game of the season on a Sunday. Jesse Flores pitched a four-hit shutout for Philadelphia in the opener as the Athletics won, 7–0. Chicago won the second game by a 5–3 score.

New York made five more errors on the following day as Detroit won 15–4 and 11–9. Dizzy Trout and the recently acquired George Caster were the winners. Rud Rennie wrote that the Yankees' poor performance for the second consecutive day contributed "to the negative side of the argument that baseball is a game of skill." The performance was much worse than the five errors that showed up in the box score and he felt sympathy for the "impressionable" children who may come to the conclusion that this is the way baseball is to be played.[23] Washington and St. Louis again split two games. Al Hollingsworth was the winner for St. Louis and Alex Carrasquel for the Senators. When the Sportsman's Park fans disagreed with an umpire's decision in the eighth inning of the nightcap, they threw pop bottles and seat cushions on the field and held up play for fifteen minutes. Tony Cuccinello's pinch-hit RBI single in the eleventh inning propelled the White Sox to a 4–3 win over Philadelphia. In Cleveland, Al Smith pitched his second consecutive shutout as the Indians defeated Boston, 10–0.

Detroit was rained out on V-J Day, August 14, while the Senators lost to the Browns, 5–4. Roger Wolff lost his control in the fourth inning, leading to a four-run St. Louis rally. Nelson Potter failed to record an out in the first inning and got an early hook after surrendering three runs. Weldon West, who was known as "Lefty," relieved him and pitched the entire nine innings, earning one of the three wins in his two-year big league career. Philadelphia was rained out in Chicago. Meanwhile, in Cleveland the Indians defeated Boston, 3–0, as Jim Bagby tossed a three-hit shutout. Al Laney wrote that "on the first day of peace everyone in sports appeared to be in a happy dream of future bliss."[24] The new era of sports which Laney was referring to began on August 15. However, the Yankees continued their poor play as they fell into the second division with a 10–4 loss to St. Louis at Sportsman's Park. A crowd of 15,304 gleefully watched the Yankees lose their sixth consecutive game as Red Ruffing suffered his first defeat of the season. Tex Shirley pitched six and one-third innings to earn the win, and Earl Jones, a southpaw who recently got called up from Toledo, went the rest of the way. Jones made ten relief appearances for the Browns in 1945, the only major league games he ever pitched in, and he had a 2.54 ERA despite giving up 18 hits and 18 walks in 28.1 innings. Chicago continued to play well at home since returning from their terrible road trip as they defeated Boston by 5–1 and 11–0 scores as Bill Dietrich and Orval Grove emerged victorious. Cleveland and Washington also won their games on the day.

Hal Newhouser led the Tigers to a 9–2 victory on August 16 at Briggs Stadium against the Senators. Detroit was drawing large crowds to their ball games: the 35,681 fans who paid their way into Briggs Stadium on Thursday the 16th was their smallest crowd in four days. The Tigers had a three-and-a-half-game lead over second-place Washington. Washington bounced back the following day, winning 3–1 behind the pitching of Mickey Haefner. In St. Louis, the Yankees' losing streak extended to eight games as they fell to the Browns, 4–1. It was tied for the longest losing streak since Joe McCarthy assumed the managerial duties in 1931: New York also lost eight straight games from May 4 to May 11, 1940. The losing had gotten to the Yankees skipper and he was tossed out of this game when he argued a decision at first base. New York's losing streak would extend to nine games before they defeated Chicago, 4–2, in the first game of a doubleheader on August 19. A fifteen-hit Boston attack propelled them to an 8–2 win over Chicago at Comiskey Park on the 17th. In Cleveland, Phil Marchildon pitched in his first game since 1942, and was the losing pitcher in a relief appearance as the Indians won, 6–4.

On August 18, the Senators won 11–5 as Roger Wolff earned the win. The Cleveland Indians received news that Bob Feller would be discharged. Feller rejoined his team right away, and before 46,477 enthusiastic partisans at Cleveland's Municipal Stadium on August 24, he led the Indians to a 4–2 win over Detroit. He gave up four hits and struck out twelve. On August 26, the Yankees won a doubleheader from Washington for the second consecutive day at Yankee Stadium before a Sunday crowd that numbered at 57,315. The Fenway Park crowd watched Dave Ferriss win his twentieth game when he drove in the winning run with a tenth-inning double to lead Boston to a 4–3 victory in the first of two. The Red Sox defeated Philadelphia by an identical 4–3 score in game two as Vic Johnson was the winning pitcher. Allie Reynolds and Steve Gromek led the Indians to a double defeat of Detroit by 3–1 and 5–4 scores. A Sportsman's Park crowd watched the third-place Browns win two games from Chicago, 3–2 and 4–1. Gene Moore celebrated his 36th birthday in grand style by winning the first game with an inside-the-park home run in the tenth inning.

On August 28, Philadelphia received news that outfielder Sam Chapman would be discharged by the Navy. He only got into nine games on the season

19. The American League Campaign

and batted .200. New York, Washington, Detroit, and Cleveland won their games on the 28th. The Yankees won their fifth straight on the day with an 8–7 win over Boston. McCarthy's squad collected eleven hits, drew nine walks and also was helped by two passed balls and a wild pitch. Home runs by Roy Cullenbine, Hank Greenberg, and Bob Maier, along with fine pitching by Hal Newhouser, gave Detroit a 10–1 win over St. Louis. In the ninth inning at Shibe Park, Rick Ferrell hit a low liner into the lower left field stands for his first long ball of the season to give Washington a 6–5 win. It was his twenty-eighth homer of his career and it would be his last. Bob Feller won his second game as Cleveland downed Chicago, 8–2, at Comiskey Park.

As the end of the month approached, the Senators were desperately trying to stay close to Detroit to set up a thrilling final month of baseball.

On September 1, the American League standings were as follows:

	W L	PCT	GB
Detroit Tigers	69–53	.566	—
Washington Senators	69–56	.552	1.5
St. Louis Browns	65–56	.537	3.5
New York Yankees	64–56	.533	4
Cleveland Indians	63–57	.525	5
Chicago White Sox	60–61	.496	8.5
Boston Red Sox	59–66	.472	11.5
Philadelphia Athletics	38–82	.317	30

When Douglas MacArthur moved into Japan, he set up his headquarters at the New Grand Hotel in Yokohama, the same hotel used by a group of major league baseball All-Stars as they toured the country fourteen years earlier. In 1945 Japan was a defeated country, its spirit broken, its intentions misguided, and its citizens frightened to see American soldiers walking down their streets while brandishing weapons. The cold reception the Americans received as conquerors was in stark contrast to the enthusiasm that was bestowed upon the American ballplayers in 1931 when an estimated two million Japanese crowded on the Ginza, Tokyo's Broadway, to witness the American All-Stars. Some of the players on that trip included Lou Gehrig, Lefty Grove, Frankie Frisch, Mickey Cochrane, Al Simmons and Lefty O'Doul. The Japanese fans were desperate for a glimpse of the All-Star players, who were paraded through the streets in open cars.

Frederick G. Lieb of *The Sporting News* called the Japanese a "gullible people," insisting that these two starkly different receptions teach us a lesson of what happens to a nation when people abandon the game of baseball for destructive weapons and totalitarian desires. When the Americans visited Japan and participated in those exhibition games against the Japanese, the American teams would not let up even when they were blowing out their opponents. This should have warned the Japanese of how the Americans would act in combat, not giving up until there was a complete victory and a vanquished opponent. Once on Japanese soil, the Americans would have no problem finding a baseball field, despite the fact that the best fields in Tokyo, Osaka, Nagoya, Mayebashi and Sendai were destroyed by the bombing.

When the American All-Stars made their trip to Japan in 1931 they drew 500,000 fans for seventeen games. They played against college teams and All-Star teams whose players were selected by the Japanese fans. It was this trip that sparked tremendous interest in the game throughout the country. There had been several other trips by American players before this, including the round-the-world tour in 1913–1914, led by Charles Comiskey and his White Sox and John McGraw and his Giants. In 1923 former major leaguer Herb Hunter led an All-Star team that consisted predominantly of players from the 1922 World Series participants: the New York Giants and New York Yankees. Hunter was integral in establishing relations with the Japanese and with persuading American players to go to Japan. He played for four major league teams in 1916–1917 and 1920–1921 and had a .163 lifetime average in 49 at-bats. In addition to spearheading the 1923 tour he also brought American stars like Ty Cobb, Lefty O'Doul and Ted Lyons to Japan so they could teach the game at colleges. He made several trips to Japan and along with Frederick G. Lieb was largely responsible for setting up the 1931 trip as well.

In 1934 the Americans made their last organized trip to the country before hostilities broke forth. This trip was led by Connie Mack, manager of the Philadelphia Athletics, and consisted of only American League players. Babe Ruth went along as a playing manager and was given $25,000 to show up by the Japanese. The Americans won all 18 games they played. Despite the fact that the Japanese once again showed great enthusiasm for the American players there were indications that things weren't all right. Connie Mack said he was being followed by the Japanese secret police throughout the trip. Japanese baseball improved dramatically over time as a result of these collective visits by the Americans. The Japanese college teams had gotten so good that they were competitive with the American teams.[25]

Alex Carrasquel tossed a five-hit shutout on September 1 to give the Senators a 3–0 win over New York at Griffith Stadium. In Detroit, Rudy York drove home the winning run in the last of the ninth, sending the Tigers home triumphant with a 5–4 victory against the Indians. Both Hal Newhouser and Bob Feller lasted only six and one-third innings. Jim Tobin earned the win in relief and Ed Klieman was the losing pitcher. Detroit's second baseman, Red Borom, went 5 for 5 and scored the winning run in the ninth after he legged out a bunt. Cleveland won the following day, 3–2, behind the pitching of Jim Bagby while the Senators split two games with New York. On September 3 the Tigers swept a doubleheader from the White Sox before 53,953 fans at Briggs Stadium by identical 6–5 scores. Tommy Bridges and Jim Tobin were the winning pitchers. Washington split their doubleheader with Boston. The real action on the day took place in Philadelphia's Shibe Park, where the Athletics were hosting the Yankees. It occurred in the tenth inning of the second game of the doubleheader. Athletics pitcher Jesse Flores had just recorded a strikeout when Philadelphia catcher Charlie George and umpire Joe Rue "were flying at each other like wild men."[26] George landed a vicious punch to Rue's right eye. The blow sent the umpire to the clubhouse, where everyone had to wait till his eye was attended to before play could proceed. Before making it back to the big leagues in 1945, George had not played since 1941. He was a weak-hitting catcher and the last wartime season was his final big league campaign; he batted .174, which was not far off his .177 lifetime average.

On September 6, New York and Detroit split two games and Joe McCarthy was thrown out of the second contest for arguing a controversial call. The Senators won their two games from St. Louis, 2–0 and 3–2, at Griffith Stadium. Hal Newhouser tossed a four-hit shutout on September 7 as the Tigers defeated New York, 5–0, before 13,607 paid spectators at Yankee Stadium. With Detroit's pitching staff overworked, Newhouser was forced to start despite a lame shoulder. He had been left behind in Detroit as the team traveled east and his left shoulder was evaluated by doctors at the hospital. They couldn't find anything wrong with Newhouser and Detroit's ace pitcher insisted that they were incompetent because they could not properly diagnose the problem. Washington kept pace and defeated St. Louis, 3–2, on the day, remaining one and a half games out of first. At Fenway Park, the Red Sox defeated Cleveland, 1–0, behind a three-hit shutout by Mike Ryba. The last-place Philadelphia Athletics took both ends of a doubleheader against the White Sox at Shibe Park by scores of 4–3 and 9–2. Connie Mack's club pushed across three runs in the ninth inning of the opener to secure the come-from-behind victory. They were assisted by two errors by Chicago center fielder Bill Mueller. Mueller had made his big league debut in 1942, batting .165 in 85 at-bats for the Pale Hose. In 1945 he appeared in thirteen games and was 0 for 9. In the second game, Charlie Gassaway was the beneficiary of a seven-run seventh inning, as Philadelphia collected seven hits and Chicago made three errors in the inning.

Not since 1930 had an American President attended a game outside of opening day. That all changed on September 8 when President Harry Truman threw out the first ball with a left-handed delivery and then watched the Senators defeat St. Louis, 4–1. The President said that he was not rooting for any one team and that he was "neutral!" Before the game the crowd of 24,000 at Griffith Stadium watched his limousine enter the ballpark while the Navy band tuned in with "Hail to the Chief."[27] On the following day, Dick Fowler pitched his no-hitter for Philadelphia. The Sunday crowd at Yankee Stadium numbered 72,152 as they packed in to watch Bob Feller win the opener, 10–3. The Yankees did Feller a favor by sending the soon-to-be-discharged Spud Chandler to the mound with only a few days of practice. Officially, Chandler was set to be discharged from the Army on Tuesday or Wednesday. He had not pitched since 1944, when he appeared in one game, and his last complete major league season was in 1943, when he tied for the American League lead in wins, going 20–4, and also led the majors with a 1.64 ERA. Jeff Heath and Mickey Rocco hit circuit clouts in the opener for the Indians. And then Les Fleming and Rocco hit home runs in the nightcap and Allie Reynolds earned the victory as Cleveland won, 4–3, in a game that was called after seven innings because of darkness. The Senators took two from Chicago as Mickey Haefner and Sandy Ullrich earned the victories. Detroit defeated Boston, 6–3, in the opener. The second game went eleven innings and was tied at three before play could no longer continue at Fenway Park because of darkness.

On Monday, September 10, there were 65,958 fewer fans at Yankee Stadium than the previous day. The crowd numbered at 6,194 as New York defeated Cleveland, 5–1, thanks to Charlie Keller's seventh-inning grand slam homer. In the ninth inning of the opening game, Dick Fowler hit a pinch-hit triple and scored on an infield out, but the Athletics came up short against St. Louis, 3–2. The Athletics' pitcher also got to pinch-hit in the nightcap but was unsuccessful. Fowler batted .444 on the season, although he only had 18 at-bats. Philadelphia won the second game, 5–3, as Lou Knerr earned the win. At Fenway Park, the Tigers and the Red Sox split a doubleheader. Washington and Chicago also split their twin bill.

On September 11, the White Sox scored two in the ninth to defeat Washington, 2–1. Meanwhile, in Boston, Dizzy Trout hurled a two-hitter for a 5–0 Tiger victory. One writer observed, "Unfortunately, however, Hank Greenberg is wearing a cane and dark glasses; Eddie Mayo, strapped so tightly around the chest he can hardly speak, is a candidate for his uncle's clinic, and Hal Newhouser, top left-hander, who is scheduled to start in Philly tomorrow, is moaning about dorsal damage which baffles the medical fraternity."[28] Steve O'Neill, the Tigers manager, predicted that the American League pennant race would go into the final week of the season. The team was strengthened with the return of Greenberg and he had given the club a "tremendous lift." Greenberg, Mayo, and Roy Cullenbine were each hitting well in early September and had impressed their manager.[29]

The Yankees swept the White Sox in a doubleheader at the Stadium on September 12 by scores of 3–1 and 9–8. Both starting pitchers, Red Ruffing and Orval Grove, went the distance in a pitchers' duel in the opener. But back-to-back homers by Russ Derry and Charlie Keller in the fourth inning gave Ruffing all the support he needed. Shortstop Mike Milosevich led off the fifth inning with a single and came around to score the final run for New York. Milosevich was a wartime player who batted .247 in 94 games and 312 at-bats in 1944, and then in his final big league season in 1945, he batted .217 in 30 games and 69 at-bats. New York won the second game as well, as both starting pitchers, Ed Lopat for the White Sox, and Bill Bevens for the Yankees, were pulled from the game in the early innings. Frank Papish, a southpaw pitcher for the Pale Hose, was the loser. In 1945, the rookie went 4–4 with a 3.74 ERA. Ken Holcombe, the third Yankee pitcher, who followed Steve Roser to the mound, was the winner. Nick Etten went 3 for 5 for New York with a home run and three runs driven in while Frankie Crosetti also hit a circuit shot.

On the following day the White Sox scored seven runs in the tenth inning to win, 7–0, against the Yankees. In Boston, the Browns scored what would be the winning run against the Red Sox when Skeeter Newsome, the second baseman, made a bad throw to first as he tried to turn a double play in the ninth inning. St. Louis won, 2–1. In more meaningful action on the day, the Athletics defeated Detroit, 3–2, at Shibe Park. Jim Tobin took a 2–1 lead into the ninth but the Athletics pushed two across the plate in the final frame to win the contest. Joe Rue was the home plate umpire for the first time in Philadelphia since his altercation with the Athletics catcher, Charlie "the Greek" George. This time it was Buddy Rosar, another Athletics catcher, who exploded when Rudy York was called safe on a close play in the fourth inning at home plate. While Rosar verbally tore into Rue, no punches were thrown and Rosar remained in the game. Jim Tobin also had problems with Rue, complaining about his strike zone. The Tigers held a half-game lead over Washington, who defeated the Indians, 4–0, before 24,606 Griffith Stadium fans. Walt Masterson tossed a two-hit shutout to defeat Bob Feller.

The Senators rallied for six runs in the final three innings on September 14 to defeat the Indians, 6–5, before 11,255 fans at Griffith Stadium. The Tigers beat Philadelphia, 1–0, behind the pitching of Les Mueller in a rain-shortened five-inning game. Red Smith observed, "An error by Buddy Rosar, a decision by Art Passarella and a couple of cloudbursts combined to get the Detroit Tigers out of town tonight with the battered remnant of their pennant pretensions moist, but intact."[30] Detroit was clinging to a half-game lead over Washington. Then the Tigers struck a severe blow to Washington's pennant hopes by sweeping a doubleheader on the 15th by scores of 7–4 and 7–3 at Griffith Stadium. Dutch Leonard earned a relief victory over Detroit on September 18 and the Senators were a game and a half behind Detroit. Rud Rennie wrote, "The lordly Tigers went out of here head over tea-kettle this afternoon defeated, 12 to 5. They didn't fall; they were tripped."[31] Detroit used nineteen players on the day, including six pitchers. George Caster took the loss.

Bob Feller of Cleveland predicted that Detroit would take the flag. He observed that the Tigers win in the clutch. Feller made this prediction despite the fact that Detroit often performed poorly against the second-division occupants. However, they were able to pull out a victory when things looked bleak and when it was necessary for them to win.[32] On Wednesday, September 19, only 2,500 spectators showed up on an overcast day to watch the Indians defeat the Tigers, 2–0, in Cleveland. Feller showed no mercy against the league-leading Tigers and tossed a one-hit shutout. Detroit's third baseman, Jimmy Outlaw, got the only safety, a Texas leaguer that fell gently upon the outfield grass in shallow right field. Steve O'Neill sent three pitchers to the hill and they collectively almost matched the masterful pitching of Feller. They were Les Mueller, George Caster, and Tommy Bridges. However, Jeff Heath hit a two-run homer against starting pitcher Mueller in the third inning. Heath's blast was a towering shot that pierced through the inward-blowing wind and landed over the right center field wall. Hank Greenberg and Eddie Mayo were back in the lineup after missing time with injuries.

Elsewhere around the junior league, the Red Sox won a doubleheader from Philadelphia by scores of 11–10 and 3–0 at Fenway Park. The second game was rather uneventful compared to the opener as Otis Clark pitched a seven-hit shutout. Clark would compile a 4–4 record and a 3.07 ERA in his only major league season in 1945. In the top of the third inning of the opening game, Boston center fielder Tommy McBride went after a pigeon instead of the baseball when Sam Chapman hit the ball off the wall. And then in the bottom of the third inning, Philadelphia right fielder Hal Peck killed a pigeon when he was throwing the ball back into the infield on Skeeter Newsome's double. Jim Bucher had three hits for Boston, while George "Catfish" Metkovich, Bob Johnson, Skeeter Newsome, and Johnny Tobin each had two. Relief pitcher Frank Barrett earned the win in relief. In New York, rookie pitchers Sam Zoldak and Ox Miller earned victories for St. Louis as they won 6–5 and 4–3. Both games were completed in ten innings.

On September 20, Detroit lost to Cleveland, 6–1, and Washington lost to New York by an identical score. The Tigers still had a one-game lead over the Senators. And then on the following day the Yankees defeated Washington, 5–3, in the only game scheduled in the junior league. Bill Zuber was the winning pitcher, while Walt Masterson was burdened with the loss. The Yankees' offensive attack was effective as Nick Etten and Snuffy Stirnweiss hit home runs. On September 22, Roger Wolff outdueled Russ Christopher as the Senators defeated Philadelphia, 2–0. But in Detroit a crowd of 30,354 watched Hal Newhouser win his twenty-third game of the season and pitch his seventh shutout as the Tigers blanked the Browns, 9–0.

Clark Griffith had not expected his team to be in the race. They finished the season a week before the rest of the league since the frugal owner had rented their stadium to the Washington Redskins for that week. The Tigers were stumbling to the finish line with injuries to key position players and Newhouser pitching with a sore shoulder.

The Senators closed their season on September 23 with a doubleheader in Philadelphia. There was a tense atmosphere around the club, for they needed to win both games to realistically have a shot to win the pennant. In the eighth inning of the opener, right fielder Buddy Lewis squeezed a fly and while running in tried to flip it to his second baseman, but the ball fell to the ground. The umpire, who had turned his back, heard the crowd cheer, then turned around and called the batter safe. It had been 3–0 but the Athletics pushed across three unearned runs to tie the game. In the twelfth inning George Binks

Fittingly, it was "George Stirnweiss Day" at Yankee Stadium on September 29. Snuffy Stirnweiss's friends ordered an automobile on his behalf and manager Joe McCarthy gave him an engraved pen and pencil set. Stirnweiss had an outstanding 1945 season, leading the junior league in several categories, including batting average (.309), slugging average (.476), runs scored (107), hits (195), triples (22), and stolen bases (33). When *The Sporting News* named Eddie Mayo as the AL Player of the Year in 1945, it was a major injustice. Stirnweiss collected three hits on both the 29th and 30th to win the batting crown (George Brace photograph).

went out to center field without his sunglasses and lost an easy fly ball that dropped for a double and led to the winning run. There was dead silence in the Senators' dressing room. They did win that second game but they really needed both. It came down to the final day of the season, September 30, with the Tigers in front by one game. But Hank Greenberg's grand slam homer in the ninth inning in the first game of two that were scheduled sealed the pennant for Detroit. A reporter asked Detroit's hero what was the pitch that he hit the home run on. Greenberg responded, "It was just a baseball. I kinda liked it."[33]

A couple of days before the end of the season, Red Smith tore into Griffith: "In a sport that is supposed to be a model of sustained competitive action, the Senators' war of nerves is an unsightly spectacle. Losing the revenue that home games would provide at this stage of the race only serves Griff right. But it would be altogether outrageous if his virile athletes should win the championship squatting on their hunkers, like Schmeling cringing before Sharkey, without striking a ball in anger."[34]

The final American League standings stood as follows:

	W L	PCT	GB
Detroit Tigers	88–65	.575	—
Washington Senators	87–67	.565	1.5
St. Louis Browns	81–70	.536	6
New York Yankees	81–71	.533	6.5
Cleveland Indians	73–72	.503	11
Chicago White Sox	71–78	.477	15
Boston Red Sox	71–83	.461	17.5
Philadelphia Athletics	52–98	.347	34.5

❖ 20 ❖

The World Series

The 1945 World Series was tough for true baseball fans to bear, particularly because many of the real big leaguers had come home and baseball in 1946 would return to normalcy as best it could. So knowing they would soon be seeing authentic major league baseball once again, they had to sit through an inferior series, with the teams stacked with wartime players who would shortly be gone. Warren Brown, a Chicago sportswriter, was asked whom he thought would win the series and he replied, "Really, I can't conceive of either team winning a single game!" Writer Frank Graham said it was "the fat men against the tall men at the annual office picnic."[1] As predicted, the games were horribly played, perhaps the worst ever, and the Detroit Tigers needed seven games to take care of Charlie Grimm's Cubs. Thankfully, many thought, ersatz baseball was now over.

On the day before the World Series, Shirley Povich wrote in the *Washington Post*:

> The temptation is to haul off and pick the Tigers to beat the Cubs in this World Series, and for that temptation we are a push-over. We think the Tigers will win in five games, maybe six, but lest you are assailed by any get-rich-quick ideas we remind you that our opinion has been retailing at the ceiling price of a nickel in recent years.
>
> You could almost boil it down to a case of Hal Newhouser vs. Hank Borowy. Certainly those two pitchers will meet in at least two games of the series, and the final outcome will be wrapped up in their comparative success. If you like Newhouser, you have to take the Tigers and we have a liking for a guy who can win 54 games in two seasons.[2]

Povich went on to say how the National League was weaker than the junior circuit. He insisted that some of the National League clubs were "rank counterfeits." The American League was not that strong in itself, but the Cubs "were operating in even cheaper company." For example, the Cubs had a 21–1 record against the woeful Cincinnati Reds on the season. Against the Reds and Phillies they were 38–6, but played only slightly above .500 baseball against the more formidable first-division teams. Contrarily, Detroit was well over .500 against the first-division American League clubs and won the pennant the more "creditable way."[3]

The opening game of the World Series wasn't the much-anticipated pitchers' duel. Instead, the Cubs jumped on the Tigers for a 9–0 victory before 54,637 fans at Briggs Stadium on October 3. This was the worst defeat in the opening game of the fall classic since 1919, when the Reds defeated the White Sox, 9–1. There had never been a more lopsided opening game score in World Series history and their nine-run margin of victory was not surpassed until 1959, when the White Sox defeated the Dodgers, 11–0. Furthermore, it was the first time a National League club had won the opening game of the World Series since the 1936 New York Giants defeated the Yankees, 6–1. The temperature was in the high 50s but the sun was shining bright throughout the game. Chicago had thirteen hits against four Detroit pitchers. Phil Cavarretta had three hits including a homer, scored three runs, and drove in two. Hal Newhouser lasted only two and two-thirds innings. He allowed seven runs on eight hits and one walk. Hank Borowy pitched brilliantly, tossing a six-hit shutout. It was the first time a pitcher had thrown an opening-game shutout since 1935, when Lon Warneke, the Cubs' twenty-game winner, whitewashed the Tigers. Tigers catcher Paul Richards had a tough day in the 1945 opener, allowing two passed balls and two stolen bases while going 0 for 2 at the plate. Eddie Mayo had two hits for Detroit. Shirley Povich wrote that the Tigers were "a hapless bush-league outfit today. Not only were they punchless at the plate, but their fielding was ragged enough to cause a wonder as to how the club ever got into the World Series."[4] Connie Mack, Philadelphia's manager, was among those at the game and said, "Our league didn't look so good. Fortunately, there are other games."[5]

In game two on the following day, the game was deadlocked at 1–1 when Hank Greenberg stepped into the box with two runners on base in the fifth inning. Hank Wyse promptly brushed him back with the first pitch. Greenberg was unperturbed and stepped back into the batter's box, hitting a curveball on the inner half of the plate for a three-run homer that propelled the Tigers to a 4–1 win. Shirley Povich wrote, "No ball was ever labeled home run so quickly. The ball took on the dimensions of a marble as it streaked toward the center field fence near the 400-foot sign, a long line drive." Greenberg said, "I know everything is back to normal for me, they're beginning to knock me down at the plate."[6] Virgil Trucks went the distance for Detroit. He had rejoined the team at the end of the season after being discharged from the Navy and only pitched in one regular season game for five and one-third innings and a 1.69 ERA. Charlie Grimm, the Cubs manager, was among those surprised by the velocity of his pitches and said, "Virgil Trucks was faster than anybody we saw all year in the National League."[7] Hank Wyse was the losing pitcher for Chicago. Doc Cramer had three hits for the Tigers and Stan Hack of Chicago went 3 for 3. The crowd at the second game was 53,636 in Detroit and it was significantly warmer than the previous day. Thus far in the series the Cubs had proven they were better defensively and had a lot more speed than their opponents.

A crowd of 55,500 showed up at Briggs Stadium on October 5 for game three and watched Claude Passeau give the Cubs the series lead with a 3–0, one-hit shutout. Stan Hack and Peanuts Lowrey had two hits apiece for Chicago. Rudy York got the lone Tiger safety. Stubby Overmire took the loss for Detroit. A campaign was initiated to persuade the Tiger fans to give their tickets to injured veterans who couldn't obtain seats to the sold-out game. As a result, three hundred disabled veterans made their way into Briggs Stadium and in a touching tribute were acknowledged by the fans. Jerry Liska wrote, "In they came — cases of double amputees and lads otherwise hacked by shellfire — to root and toot for their champions."[8]

The series shifted to Wrigley Field on October 6, and 42,923 fans were on hand to watch the Tigers even the series at two with a 4–1 win. Dizzy Trout went the distance to earn the victory, while Ray Prim was the losing pitcher. Trout allowed one unearned run, five hits, and one walk. Shirley Povich wrote that Trout "was literally strutting his stuff and show-boating all afternoon. Deliberately he provoked Cub fans with his stalling tactics, impishly halting the game a half dozen times to wipe his spectacles, and he grinned in high glee when he made a hit for himself in the ninth."[9] After the final out, Trout took his hat off and bowed. He also shook hands with the plate umpire in appreciation of his work before exiting the field. Hank Greenberg, Roy Cullenbine, Jimmy Outlaw, and Paul Richards each drove in one run for the victors. Doc Cramer had two hits and scored a run. Don Johnson had two hits for the Cubs, which included a triple and a run scored.

The Tigers took a three-games-to-two lead in the series with an 8–4 win on October 7. Hal Newhouser earned the victory as he bounced back from his disappointing first-game performance. He allowed the four runs on seven hits and two walks. Four of the hits were wind-blown pop-ups that eluded the fielders. Detroit's excellent southpaw hurler also fanned nine hitters on the day. Hank Borowy was the losing pitcher as he lasted only five innings. Hank Greenberg was 3 for 5, with three runs scored and one driven in. Each of his three hits was a double. Eddie Mayo and Roy Cullenbine had two hits apiece.

On the following day, before 41,708 Wrigley Field fans, Stan Hack's single took a wicked hop over Greenberg's shoulder and pinch runner Bill Schuster raced across the plate with the winning run in the twelfth inning for an 8–7 Cubs victory. Initially the official scorer gave Greenberg an error in what Shirley Povich called an "unpardonably brutal piece of official scoring."[10] Later the ruling was reversed and Hack was credited with a double. Greenberg was playing left field in this game and throughout the series. The Cubs kept themselves alive with the win but it came with a price. Four of their starting pitchers made an appearance in the game: Claude Passeau, Hank Wyse, Ray Prim, and Hank Borowy. Greenberg hit a homer and scored two runs. Stan Hack went 4 for 5 for the Cubs. Borowy pitched four innings for the relief victory. Dizzy Trout pitched well for four and two-thirds innings in relief but took the loss. Detroit had Hal Newhouser ready to go for game seven, albeit on only two days of rest. However, it was unclear whom the Cubs would start in the decisive game.

The Tigers scored five runs in the first inning to propel them to a 9–3 victory before 41,590 disappointed Wrigley Field fans in the decisive final game of the World Series. Hal Newhouser went the distance and led Detroit to the world championship. Hank Borowy started for Chicago but failed to record even a single out in the first inning before being taken out of the game. He threw only eight pitches and gave up three hits. Paul Derringer relieved Borowy and served up a two-out bases-loaded double to Paul Richards that scored three runs. Richards added an RBI double later in the game. Doc Cramer went 3 for 5 and Eddie Mayo went 2 for 5 for the world champions. Leadoff man Skeeter Webb, along with Mayo, Cramer, and Cullenbine, each scored two runs. A new World Series attendance record was set for the seven games (333,457). Frederick G. Lieb wrote in *The Sporting News*, "Though the play at times was ordinary, and some players made the box scores who never again will bask in the World's Series spotlight, the classic was one which will be remembered and talked about for years."[11] Shirley Povich wrote in the *Washington Post*: "Detroit and Chicago had a long look at this 1945 World Series, and that was fair enough, because a World Series may not be coming their way again for several years. Neither club stacks up as a pennant winner in the near future when baseball again becomes war-free, and the talent starts flowing to other teams."[12] Detroit didn't make it back to the World Series until 1968, when they defeated the Cardinals, four games to three. Through the 2008 season, the Cubs had failed to win a National League pennant and return to the World Series.

❖ 21 ❖

Return to Normalcy

The off-season served as a harbinger of the changes to come in the subsequent years. Branch Rickey announced in October that he had signed Jackie Robinson, who would first play with the Montreal Royals of the International League before coming to the big leagues. *The Sporting News* was one of the many critics of the signing and implied that the move was doomed to failure. However, Al Laney wrote in the *New York Herald Tribune*, "The matter of the Negro in baseball is no longer something that might happen in the future. It is a fact. Brother Rickey has signed a Negro to a contract and from all accounts a player who is very likely to make the grade."

Ludlow Werner, the editor of the *New York Age*, wrote:

> I'm happy over the event, but I'm sorry for Jackie. He will be haunted by the expectations of his race. To 15,000,000 Negroes he will symbolize not only their prowess in baseball, but their ability to rise to an opportunity. Unlike white players, he can never afford an off-day or an off-night. His private life will be watched, too, because white America will judge the Negro race by everything he does. And Lord help him with his fellow Negroes if he should fail them.[1]

Dan Burley, the sports editor of the *Amsterdam News,* wrote, "It is a silly and un–American practice which has deprived an entire race of the opportunity of contributing its share of talent to a great pastime."[2] Rickey's signing sent shock waves around organized baseball and was the primary conversation piece during the off-season.

The assault on Commissioner Happy Chandler was well underway. At the winter meetings the bush league owners voted to restrict the powers that Chandler had over minor league ball. Chandler fired back, "You have resolutions before you that are offensive and obnoxious to me personally."[3] But by the end of the meetings both the owners and Chandler made some concessions to leave on a somewhat harmonious note. The Pacific Coast League put in a proposal to make them a "major league," but that was voted down. Chandler did cast the deciding vote that allowed for unlimited night games.

The spring training camps were overflowing with ballplayers in 1946: the wartime players weren't given much of a look and were squeezed out. Many of them decided to take Jorge Pasquel's money and play in the Mexican League. The prewar players who had lost their skills also found it difficult to crack the rosters for an extended period of time despite the fact that the G.I. Bill of Rights obligated the owners to give the veterans their old jobs back for a year unless they were unable to fulfill their duties. Owners attempted to circumvent the law whenever possible.

Dan Daniel wrote in *The Sporting News* towards the conclusion of the '45 season that it was "incredible" that baseball had survived with stars like Ted Williams, Enos Slaughter, Joe DiMaggio, Spud Chandler, Johnny Beazley, Charlie Keller, Johnny Mize, Babe Young, Pee Wee Reese, Pete Reiser, and Terry Moore away from the game. The list of players who had left for the service appeared to be "endless." But big league baseball would once again be at a level that was worthy of the title "major leagues."[4] Bushers like Danny Gardella and Sig Jakucki were no longer needed or wanted. Mel Ott said of Gardella, "The time has passed when we have to worry about players like that."[5]

Major league club owners were encouraged by the flourishing attendance figures in many of the big league cities in 1945. The National League drew 5,260,703 customers to their ballparks, while 5,580,420 attended American League games. The Tigers led the majors by drawing 1,280,341 to Briggs Stadium. The Cubs, Giants and Dodgers also drew over a million fans. The attendance boom continued into the first postwar season as 18.5 million fans attended games in 1946. It represented a 71 percent increase over the 1945 numbers.

The wartime players ultimately helped give Americans a pleasant diversion when it was much needed. But by 1946 authentic major league baseball had returned. As the curtain rose on the first postwar major league season in 1946, the *Detroit News* wrote about Opening Day: "This was a day to forget about nylon lines, black marketeers, high rents, low beer supply, sugar rationing, shortage of shorts, shirts, suits.... It was a day even to forget about the Iranian question and the atom bomb." This was because baseball had returned and it was the "genuine pre-war brand."[6]

The major leaguers who went into the service had no regrets about sacrificing several big league seasons to win the war. It was estimated that Bob Feller sacrificed about 100 wins during the nearly four seasons he missed while in the service. Feller said, "You'll never hear me cry about that or those lost four years. I've always felt that one big win — World War II — and being a part of that was a heck of a lot more important than winning another 100 ball games."[7]

Appendix A: The National League Teams

The 1945 National League Standings

	W L	PCT	GB
Chicago Cubs	98–56	.636	—
St. Louis Cardinals	95–59	.617	3
Brooklyn Dodgers	87–67	.565	11
Pittsburgh Pirates	82–72	.532	16
New York Giants	78–74	.513	19
Boston Braves	67–85	.441	30
Cincinnati Reds	61–93	.396	37
Philadelphia Phillies	46–108	.299	52

1. Chicago Cubs (98–56)

Team Leaders

Hitting		Pitching	
Phil Cavarretta	.355,* 6 homers, 97 RBIs	Hank Wyse	22–10, 2.68 ERA
Don Johnson	.302, 2 homers, 58 RBIs	Claude Passeau	17–9, 2.46 ERA
Stan Hack	.323, 2 homers, 43 RBIs	Paul Derringer	16–11, 3.45 ERA
Bill Nicholson	.243, 13 homers, 88 RBIs	Ray Prim	13–8, 2.40 ERA
Andy Pafko	.298, 12 homers, 110 RBIs	Hank Borowy	11–2, †2.13 ERA
Peanuts Lowrey	.283, 7 homers, 89 RBIs	Paul Erickson	7–4, 3.32 ERA

*Phil Cavarretta's .355 average led the major leagues.
†Hank Borowy's 2.13 ERA led the National League.

Manager: Charlie Grimm

Oldest player to play for the '45 Cubs:
Johnny Moore, born: March 23, 1902.
1945 stats: 7 games, 6 at-bats, 1 hit, 2 RBIs, .167 batting average.

Youngest player to play for the '45 Cubs:
Andy Pafko, born: February 25, 1921.
1945 stats: 144 games, 534 at-bats, 159 hits, 110 RBIs, .298 batting average.

Chicago Cubs opening day lineup:
3B Stan Hack
SS Lennie Merullo
1B Phil Cavarretta
RF Bill Nicholson
LF Ed Sauer
CF Andy Pafko
2B Don Johnson
C Mickey Livingston
P Paul Derringer

3–2 victory over the St. Louis Cardinals.
Ed Sauer and Hank Sauer were brothers. Ed batted .258 while Hank batted .293 for the Reds.

2. St. Louis Cardinals (95–59)

Team Leaders

Hitting

Whitey Kurowski	.323, 21 homers, 102 RBIs
Buster Adams	.292, 20 homers, 101 RBIs
Johnny Hopp	.289, 3 homers, 44 RBIs
Augie Bergamo	.316, 3 homers, 44 RBIs
Ray Sanders	.276, 8 homers, 78 RBIs
Emil Verban	.278, 0 homers, 72 RBIs

Pitching

Red Barrett	21–9,* 2.74 ERA
Ken Burkhart	18–8, 2.90 ERA
Blix Donnelly	8–10, 3.52 ERA
Harry Brecheen	15–4, 2.52 ERA
George Dockins	8–6, 3.21 ERA
Ted Wilks	4–7, 2.93 ERA

*Red Barrett led the National League with 23 wins. He began the season with the Boston Braves and was 2–3 for them in nine games before being traded to St. Louis on May 23.

Manager: Billy Southworth

Oldest player to play for the '45 Cardinals:
Pep Young, born: August 29, 1907.
1945 stats: 27 games, 47 at-bats, 7 hits, 4 RBIs, .149 batting average.

Youngest player to play for the '45 Cardinals:
Red Schoendienst, born: February 2, 1923.
1945 stats: 137 games, 565 at-bats, 157 hits, 47 RBIs, .278 batting average.

St. Louis Cardinals opening day lineup:
RF Augie Bergamo
CF Johnny Hopp
LF Red Schoendienst
C Walker Cooper
1B Ray Sanders
3B Whitey Kurowski
SS Marty Marion
2B Emil Verban
P Ted Wilks

3–2 loss to the Chicago Cubs.

3. Brooklyn Dodgers (87–67)

Team Leaders

Hitting

Dixie Walker	.300, 8 homers, 124 RBIs*
Goody Rosen	.325, 12 homers, 75 RBIs
Luis Olmo	.313, 10 homers, 110 RBIs
Augie Galan	.307, 9 homers, 92 RBIs
Eddie Stanky	.258, 1 homer, 39 RBIs
Mike Sandlock	.282, 2 homers, 17 RBIs

Pitching

Hal Gregg	18–13, 3.47 ERA
Vic Lombardi	10–11, 3.31 ERA
Curt Davis	10–10, 3.25 ERA
Art Herring	7–4, 3.48 ERA
Tom Seats	10–7. 4.36 ERA
Ralph Branca	5–6, 3.04 ERA

*Dixie Walker's 124 RBIs led the major leagues.

Manager: Leo Durocher

Oldest player to play for the '45 Dodgers:
Clyde Sukeforth, born: November 30, 1901.
1945 stats: 18 games, 51 at-bats, 15 hits, 1 RBI, .294 batting average.

Youngest player to play for the '45 Dodgers:
Erv Palica, born: February 9, 1928.
1945 stats: 2 games, 0 at-bats.

Palica compiled a 41–55 record as a pitcher in his career but did not pitch in '45. His first action on the mound came in 1947, when he appeared in 3 games.

Brooklyn Dodgers opening day lineup:
LF Frenchy Bordagaray
CF Luis Olmo
1B Augie Galan
RF Dixie Walker
3B Bill Hart
C Mickey Owen
SS Mike Sandlock
2B Leo Durocher
P Curt Davis

8–2 win over the Philadelphia Phillies.

4. Pittsburgh Pirates (82–72)

Team Leaders

Hitting

Bob Elliott	.290, 8 homers, 108 RBIs
Frankie Gustine	.280, 2 homers, 66 RBIs
Al Gionfriddo	.284, 2 homers, 42 RBIs
Jim Russell	.284, 12 homers, 77 RBIs
Johnny Barrett	.256, 15 homers, 67 RBIs
Babe Dahlgren	.250, 5 homers, 75 RBIs

Pitching

Preacher Roe	14–13, 2.87 ERA
Nick Strincevich	16–10, 3.31 ERA
Rip Sewell	11–9, 4.07 ERA
Max Butcher	10–8, 3.03 ERA
Al Gerheauser	5–10, 3.91 ERA
Ken Gables	11–7, 4.15 ERA

Manager: Frankie Frisch

Oldest player to play for the '45 Pirates:
Jack Saltzgaver, born: January 23, 1903.
1945 stats: 52 games, 117 at-bats, 38 hits, 10 RBIs, .325 batting average.

Youngest player to play for the '45 Pirates:
Bill Rodgers, born: December 5, 1922.
1945 stats: 1 game, 1 at-bat, 1 hit, 0 RBIs, 1.000 batting average.

Pittsburgh Pirates opening day lineup:
SS Frankie Zak
CF Johnny Barrett
LF Jim Russell
3B Bob Elliott
RF Frank Colman
1B Babe Dahlgren
2B Frankie Gustine
C Al Lopez
P Fritz Ostermueller

7–6 loss to the Cincinnati Reds.

5. New York Giants (78–74)

Team Leaders

Hitting

Mel Ott	.308, 21 homers, 79 RBIs
Ernie Lombardi	.307, 19 homers, 70 RBIs

Pitching

Bill Voiselle	14–14, 4.49 ERA
Harry Feldman	12–13, 3.27 ERA

Appendix A

	Hitting		Pitching
Danny Gardella	.272, 18 homers, 71 RBIs	Van Lingle Mungo	14–7, 3.20 ERA
Phil Weintraub	.272, 10 homers, 42 RBIs	Jack Brewer	8–6, 3.83 ERA
Johnny Rucker	.273, 7 homers, 51 RBIs	Ace Adams	11–9, 3.42 ERA
Nap Reyes	.288, 5 homers, 44 RBIs	Slim Emmerich	4–4, 4.86 ERA

Manager: Mel Ott

Oldest player to play for the '45 Giants:
Ray Berres, born: August 31, 1907.
1945 stats: 20 games, 30 at-bats, 5 hits, 2 RBIs, .167 batting average.

Youngest player to play for the '45 Giants:
Whitey Lockman, born: July 25, 1926.
1945 stats: 32 games, 129 at-bats, 44 hits, 18 RBIs, .341 batting average.

New York Giants opening day lineup:
CF Johnny Rucker
2B George Hausmann
RF Mel Ott
LF Steve Filipowicz
1B Phil Weintraub
C Ernie Lombardi
SS Buddy Kerr
3B Nap Reyes
P Bill Voiselle

11–6 victory over the Boston Braves.

6. Boston Braves (67–85)

Team Leaders

	Hitting		Pitching
Tommy Holmes	.352, 28 homers,* 117 RBIs	Jim Tobin	9–14, 3.84 ERA
Chuck Workman	.274, 25 homers, 87 RBIs	Bob Logan	7–11, 3.18 ERA
Butch Nieman	.247, 14 homers, 56 RBIs	Johnny Hutchings	7–6, 3.75 ERA
Phil Masi	.272, 7 homers, 46 RBIs	Nate Andrews	7–12, 4.58 ERA
Carden Gillenwater	.288, 7 homers, 72 RBIs	Ed Wright	8–3, 2.51 ERA
Whitey Wietelmann	.271, 4 homers, 33 RBIs	Bill Lee	6–3, 2.79 ERA

Tommy Holmes' 28 homers led the major leagues.

Manager: Bob Coleman (42–51) and Del Bissonette (25–34)

Oldest player to play for the '45 Braves:
Joe Heving, born: September 2, 1900.
1945 stats: 1–0 record, 3 games, 5.1 innings pitched, 3.38 ERA.

Youngest player to play for the '45 Braves:
Hal Schacker, born: April 6, 1925.
1945 stats: 0–1 record, 6 games, 15.1 innings pitched, 5.28 ERA.
That was the only season he ever pitched in the big leagues.

Boston Braves opening day lineup:
SS Dick Culler
LF Tommy Holmes
RF Chuck Workman
1B Joe Mack
CF Carden Gillenwater
2B Eddie Joost
C Phil Masi
3B Steve Shemo
P Al Javery

11–6 loss to the New York Giants.

7. Cincinnati Reds (61–93)

Team Leaders

Hitting		Pitching	
Dain Clay	.280, 1 homer, 50 RBIs	Ed Heusser	11–16, 3.71 ERA
Frank McCormick	.276, 10 homers, 81 RBIs	Joe Bowman	11–13, 3.59 ERA
Steve Mesner	.254, 1 homer, 52 RBIs	Bucky Walters	10–10, 2.68 ERA
Al Libke	.283, 4 homers, 53 RBIs	Howie Fox	8–13, 4.93 ERA
Al Lakeman	.256, 8 homers, 31 RBIs	Vern Kennedy	5–12, 4.00 ERA
Eric Tipton	.242, 5 homers, 34 RBIs	Frank Dasso	4–5, 3.67 ERA

Manager: Bill McKechnie

Oldest player to play for the '45 Reds:
Hod Lisenbee, born: September 23, 1898.
1945 stats: 1–3 record, 31 games, 80.1 innings pitched, 5.49 ERA.

Youngest player to play for the '45 Reds:
Herm Wehmeier, born: February 18, 1927.
1945 stats: 0–1 record, 2 games, 5 innings pitched, 12.60 ERA.

Cincinnati Reds opening day lineup:
CF Dain Clay   2B Woody Williams
LF Eric Tipton   SS Kermit Wahl
RF Gee Walker   C Joe Just
1B Frank McCormick   P Bucky Walters
3B Steve Mesner

7–6 win over the Pittsburgh Pirates.

8. Philadelphia Phillies (46–108)

Team Leaders

Hitting		Pitching	
Vince DiMaggio	.257, 19 homers, 84 RBIs	Dick Barrett	*8–20, 5.38 ERA
Vance Dinges	.287, 1 homer, 36 RBIs	Andy Karl	8–8, 2.99 ERA
John Antonelli	.256, 1 homer, 28 RBIs	Charley Schanz	4–15, 4.35 ERA
Coaker Triplett	.240, 7 homers, 46 RBIs	Charlie Sproull	4–10, 5.94 ERA
Jimmy Wasdell	.300, 7 homers, 60 RBIs	Dick Mauney	6–10, 3.08 ERA
Glenn Crawford	.295, 2 homers, 24 RBIs	Oscar Judd	5–4, 3.81 ERA

*Dick Barrett tied Bobo Newsom of the Philadelphia Athletics with the most losses in the majors with 20. However, Newsom's 3.29 ERA was significantly better.

Manager: Freddie Fitzsimmons (18–51) and Ben Chapman (28–57)

Oldest player to play for the '45 Phillies:
Gus Mancuso, born: December 5, 1905.
1945 stats: 70 games, 176 at-bats, 35 hits, 16 RBIs, .199 batting average.

Youngest player to play for the '45 Phillies:
Putsy Caballero, born: November 5, 1927.
1945 stats: 9 games, 1 at-bat, 0 hits, 1 RBI, .000 batting average.

Philadelphia Phillies opening day lineup:
3B Bitsy Mott   1B Jimmy Wasdell
LF Vance Dinges   CF Vince DiMaggio
RF Rene Monteagudo   2B Garvin Hamner

Appendix A

C Johnny Peacock P Ken Raffensberger
SS Granny Hamner

8–2 loss to the Brooklyn Dodgers.

Garvin Hamner and Granny Hamner were brothers, and Garvin was making his major league debut on opening day. This was Garvin's only big league season, while Granny went on to play in seventeen major league seasons.

Appendix B: The American League Teams

The 1945 American League Standings

	W L	.PCT	GB
Detroit Tigers	88–65	.575	—
Washington Senators	87–67	.565	1.5
St. Louis Browns	81–70	.536	6
New York Yankees	81–71	.533	6.5
Cleveland Indians	73–72	.503	11
Chicago White Sox	71–78	.477	15
Boston Red Sox	71–83	.461	17.5
Philadelphia Athletics	52–98	.347	34.5

1. Detroit Tigers (88–65)

Team Leaders

Hitting		Pitching	
Rudy York	.264, 18 homers, 87 RBIs	Hal Newhouser	25–9,* 1.81 ERA*
Eddie Mayo	.285, 10 homers, 54 RBIs	Dizzy Trout	18–15, 3.14 ERA
Roy Cullenbine	.277, 18 homers, 93 RBIs	Al Benton	13–8, 2.02 ERA
Doc Cramer	.275, 6 homers, 58 RBIs	Stubby Overmire	9–9, 3.88 ERA
Bob Maier	.263, 1 homer, 34 RBIs	Les Mueller	6–8, 3.68 ERA
Hank Greenberg	.311, 13 homers, 60 RBIs	Jim Tobin	4–5, 3.55 ERA

Hal Newhouser led the majors in both wins and ERA.

Manager: Steve O'Neill

Oldest player to play for the '45 Tigers:
Chuck Hostetler, born: September 22, 1903.
1945 stats: 42 games, 44 at-bats, 7 hits, 2 RBIs, .159 batting average.

Youngest player to play for the '45 Tigers:
Art Houtteman, born: August 7, 1927.
1945 stats: 0–2 record, 13 games, 25.1 innings pitched, 5.33 ERA.

Detroit Tigers opening day lineup:
SS Skeeter Webb   RF Jimmy Outlaw
2B Eddie Mayo   1B Rudy York

CF Doc Cramer
LF Bob Maier
3B Don Ross

C Paul Richards
P Hal Newhouser

7–1 loss to the St. Louis Browns.

2. *Washington Senators (87–67)*

Team Leaders

Hitting		Pitching	
Buddy Lewis	.333, 2 homers, 37 RBIs	Roger Wolff	20–10, 2.12 ERA
Joe Kuhel	.285, 2 homers, 75 RBIs	Mickey Haefner	16–14, 3.47 ERA
George Myatt	.296, 1 homer, 39 RBIs	Marino Pieretti	14–13, 3.32 ERA
George Binks	.278, 6 homers, 81 RBIs	Dutch Leonard	17–7, 2.13 ERA
George Case	.294, 1 homer, 31 RBIs	Johnny Niggeling	7–12, 3.16 ERA
Rick Ferrell	.266, 1 homer, 38 RBIs	Alex Carrasquel	7–5, 2.71 ERA

Manager: Ossie Bluege

Oldest player to play for the '45 Senators:
Johnny Niggeling, born: July 10, 1903.
1945 stats: 7–12 record, 26 games, 176.2 innings pitched, 3.16 ERA.

Youngest player to play for the '45 Senators:
Armando Roche, born: December 7, 1926.
1945 stats: 0–0 record, 2 games, 6 innings pitched, 6.00 ERA.
This was Roche's only big league season.

Washington Senators opening day lineup:
LF George Case
2B George Myatt
1B Joe Kuhel
RF George Binks
3B Harlond Clift

SS Gil Torres
CF Walt Chipple
C Al Evans
P Dutch Leonard

14–8 victory over the Philadelphia Athletics.

3. *St. Louis Browns (81–70)*

Team Leaders

Hitting		Pitching	
Vern Stephens	.289, 24 homers,* 89 RBIs	Nelson Potter	15–11, 2.47 ERA
George McQuinn	.277, 7 homers, 61 RBIs	Jack Kramer	10–15, 3.36 ERA
Mark Christman	.277, 4 homers, 34 RBIs	Sig Jakucki	12–10, 3.51 ERA
Gene Moore	.260, 5 homers, 50 RBIs	Tex Shirley	8–12, 3.63 ERA
Milt Byrnes	.249, 8 homers, 59 RBIs	Al Hollingsworth	12–9, 2.70 ERA
Frank Mancuso	.268, 1 homer, 38 RBIs	Bob Muncrief	13–4, 2.72 ERA

Vern Stephens led the American League in homers.

Manager: Luke Sewell

Oldest player to play for the '45 Browns:
Pete Appleton, born: May 20, 1904.
1945 stats: 0–0 record, 2 games, 2.1 innings pitched, and a 15.43 ERA with the St. Louis Browns. Later in the season he played with the Washington Senators for 6 games. His combined record was 1–0 with a 4.56 ERA in 8 games and 23.2 innings pitched. He was

born Peter William Jablonowski and from 1927 to 1933 played as Pete Jablonowski before he changed his name.

Youngest player to play for the '45 Browns:
Cliff Fannin, born: May 13, 1924.
1945 stats: 0–0 record, 5 games, 10.1 innings pitched, 2.61 ERA.

St. Louis Browns opening day lineup:
2B Don Gutteridge
LF Pete Gray
CF Mike Kreevich
SS Vern Stephens
RF Milt Byrnes
1B George McQuinn
3B Len Schulte
C Frank Mancuso
P Sig Jakucki

7–1 win over the Detroit Tigers.

4. New York Yankees (81–71)

Team Leaders

	Hitting		Pitching
Snuffy Stirnweiss	.309,* 10 homers, 64 RBIs	Bill Bevens	13–9, 3.67 ERA
Nick Etten	.285, 18 homers, 111 RBIs*	Ernie Bonham	8–11, 3.29 ERA
Oscar Grimes	.265, 4 homers, 45 RBIs	Al Gettel	9–8, 3.90 ERA
Hersh Martin	.267, 7 homers, 53 RBIs	Monk Dubiel	10–9, 4.64 ERA
Charlie Keller	.301, 10 homers, 34 RBIs	Hank Borowy	10–5, 3.13 ERA
Bud Metheny	.248, 8 homers, 53 RBIs	Red Ruffing	7–3, 2.89 ERA

Snuffy Stirnweiss led the American League in batting. Nick Etten led the American League in RBIs.

Manager: Joe McCarthy

Oldest player to play for the '45 Yankees:
Paul Schreiber, born: October 8, 1902.
1945 stats: 0–0 record, 2 games, 4.1 innings pitched, 4.15 ERA.

Youngest player to play for the '45 Yankees:
Bill Drescher, born: May 23, 1921.
1945 stats: 48 games, 126 at-bats, 34 hits, 15 RBIs, .270 batting average.

New York Yankees opening day lineup:
2B Snuffy Stirnweiss
LF Hersh Martin
RF Russ Derry
CF Johnny Lindell
1B Nick Etten
SS Joe Buzas
3B Don Savage
C Mike Garbark
P Atley Donald

8–4 win over the Boston Red Sox.

5. Cleveland Indians (73–72)

Team Leaders

	Hitting		Pitching
Jeff Heath	.305, 15 homers, 61 RBIs	Steve Gromek	19–9, 2.55 ERA
Lou Boudreau	.307, 3 homers, 48 RBIs	Allie Reynolds	18–12, 3.20 ERA
Mickey Rocco	.264, 10 homers, 56 RBIs	Jim Bagby	8–11, 3.73 ERA
Pat Seerey	.237, 14 homers, 56 RBIs	Al Smith	5–12, 3.84 ERA

	Hitting		Pitching
Felix Mackiewicz	.273, 2 homers, 37 RBIs	Ed Klieman	5–8, 3.85 ERA
Les Fleming	.329, 3 homers, 22 RBIs	Pete Center	6–3, 3.99 ERA

Manager: Lou Boudreau

Oldest player to play for the '45 Indians:
Gene Desautels, born: June 13, 1907.
1945 stats: 10 games, 9 at-bats, 1 hit, 0 RBIs, .111 batting average.

Youngest player to play for the '45 Indians:
Hank Ruszkowski, born: November 10, 1925.
1945 stats: 14 games, 49 at-bats, 10 hits, 5 RBIs, .204 batting average.

Cleveland Indians opening day lineup:
1B Mickey Rocco
CF Myril Hoag
RF Eddie Carnett
SS Lou Boudreau
LF Pat Seerey
3B Roy Cullenbine
2B Al Cihocki
C Hank Ruszkowski
P Allie Reynolds

5–2 loss to the Chicago White Sox.

6. Chicago White Sox (71–78)

Team Leaders

	Hitting		Pitching
Tony Cuccinello	.308, 2 homers, 49 RBIs	Thornton Lee	15–12, 2.44 ERA
Johnny Dickshot	.302, 4 homers, 58 RBIs	Orval Grove	14–12, 3.44 ERA
Oris Hockett	.293, 2 homers, 55 RBIs	Ed Lopat	10–13, 4.11 ERA
Guy Curtright	.281, 4 homers, 32 RBIs	Johnny Humphries	6–14, 4.24 ERA
Kerby Farrell	.258, 0 homers, 34 RBIs	Bill Dietrich	7–10, 4.19 ERA
Wally Moses	.295, 2 homers, 50 RBIs	Earl Caldwell	6–7, 3.59 ERA

Manager: Jimmy Dykes

Oldest player to play for the '45 White Sox:
Clay Touchstone, born: January 24, 1903.
1945 stats: 0–0 record, 6 games, 10 innings pitched, 5.40 ERA.

Youngest player to play for the '45 White Sox:
Cass Michaels, born: March 4, 1926.
1945 stats: 129 games, 445 at-bats, 109 hits, 54 RBIs, .245 batting average.
He was born Casimir Eugene Kwietniewski. He changed his name in 1944, partially so it could fit into the box score.

Chicago White Sox opening day lineup:
RF Wally Moses
CF Oris Hockett
LF Johnny Dickshot
1B Bill Nagel
3B Tony Cuccinello
2B Roy Schalk
SS Cass Michaels
C Mike Tresh
P Thornton Lee

5–2 win over the Cleveland Indians.

7. Boston Red Sox (71–83)

Team Leaders

Hitting		Pitching	
Bob Johnson	.280, 12 homers, 74 RBIs	Dave Ferriss	21–10, 2.96 ERA
Skeeter Newsome	.290, 1 homer, 48 RBIs	Jim Wilson	6–8, 3.30 ERA
Tom McBride	.305, 1 homer, 47 RBIs	Emmett O'Neill	8–11, 5.15 ERA
Johnny Lazor	.310, 5 homers, 45 RBIs	Clem Hausmann	5–7, 5.04 ERA
George Metkovich	.260, 5 homers, 62 RBIs	Mike Ryba	7–6, 2.49 ERA
Eddie Lake	.279, 11 homers, 51 RBIs	Vic Johnson	6–4, 4.01 ERA

Manager: Joe Cronin

Oldest player to play for the '45 Red Sox:
Mike Ryba, born: June 9, 1903.
1945 stats: 7–6 record, 34 games, 123 innings pitched, 2.49 ERA.

Youngest player to play for the '45 Red Sox:
Jim Wilson, born: February 20, 1922.
1945 stats: 6–8 record, 23 games, 144.1 innings pitched, 3.30 ERA.

Boston Red Sox opening day lineup:
2B Ben Steiner
1B George Metkovich
RF Pete Fox
LF Bob Johnson
3B Joe Cronin
CF Leon Culberson
SS Skeeter Newsome
C Fred Walters
P Rex Cecil

8–4 loss to the New York Yankees.

8. Philadelphia Athletics (52–98)

Team Leaders

Hitting		Pitching	
Bobby Estalella	.299, 8 homers, 52 RBIs	Bobo Newsom	8–20*, 3.29 ERA
Dick Siebert	.267, 7 homers, 51 RBIs	Russ Christopher	13–13, 3.17 ERA
Irv Hall	.261, 0 homers, 50 RBIs	Jesse Flores	7–10, 3.43 ERA
George Kell	.272, 4 homers, 56 RBIs	Joe Berry	8–7, 2.35 ERA
Ed Busch	.250, 0 homers, 35 RBIs	Lou Knerr	5–11, 4.22 ERA
Hal Peck	.276, 5 homers, 39 RBIs	Don Black	5–11, 5.17 ERA

*Bobo Newsom tied Dick Barrett of the Philadelphia Phillies for the most losses in the majors.

Manager: Connie Mack

Oldest player to play for the '45 Athletics:
Joe Berry, born: December 16, 1904.
1945 stats: 8–7 record, an American League leading 52 games pitched, 130.1 innings pitched, 2.35 ERA.

Youngest player to play for the '45 Athletics:
Carl Scheib, born: January 1, 1927.
1945 stats: 0–0 record, 4 games, 8.2 innings pitched, 3.12 ERA.

Philadelphia Athletics opening day lineup:
LF Charlie Metro
RF Hal Peck
CF Bobby Estalella
C Frankie Hayes

1B Dick Siebert 3B George Kell
2B Irv Hall P Bobo Newsom
SS Ed Busch

14–8 loss to the Washington Senators.

Chapter Notes

Introduction

1. Goldstein, *Spartan Seasons*, 15.
2. Tindall and Shi, *America*, 1068–69.
3. Goldstein, *Spartan Seasons*, 15.
4. Honig, *Baseball America*, 91.
5. Zingg, *Harry Hooper*, 172–74.
6. Wood, *1918*, 355–57, 368.
7. Robinson, *Matty*, 188.
8. Scheinin, *Field of Screams*, 144.
9. Goldstein, *Spartan Seasons*, 10.
10. Kavanagh and Macht, *Uncle Robbie*, 105.
11. Marshall, *Baseball's Pivotal Era*, 6.
12. Hynd, *The Giants of the Polo Grounds*, 322.
13. Goldstein, *Spartan Seasons*, 19.
14. Hynd, *The Giants of the Polo Grounds*, 322.
15. Ritter, *Lost Ballparks*, 194.
16. Oakley, *Baseball's Last Golden Age*, 3.
17. Echevarria, *The Pride of Havana*, 145.
18. *The Sporting News*, 17 July 1957.
19. Bjarkman, *Baseball with a Latin Beat*, 198.
20. Alexander, *Our Game*, 190.
21. Bjarkman, *Baseball with a Latin Beat*, 201.
22. Ibid., 194.
23. Zoss and Bowman, *Diamonds in the Rough*, 342–43.
24. Alexander, *Our Game*, 193.
25. Turner, *When the Boys Came Back*, 48.
26. Mead, *Baseball Goes to War*, 32.
27. Scheinin, *Field of Screams*, 207.
28. Kahn, *The Era*, 47.
29. Kaufman, "The Life and Times of Hank Greenberg."
30. Scheinin, *Field of Screams*, 208.
31. Marshall, *Baseball's Pivotal Era*, 9.
32. Oakley, *Baseball's Last Golden Age*, 41.
33. Ibid., 42.
34. Kahn, *The Era*, 84.
35. Mead, *Baseball Goes to War*, 97–98.
36. Scheinin, *Field of Screams*, 278.
37. Turner, *When the Boys Came Back*, 8.
38. Marshall, *Baseball's Pivotal Era*, 10.
39. Ibid., 9.
40. Durocher with Linn, *Nice Guys Finish Last*, 432.
41. Linkugel and Pappas, *They Tasted Glory*, 31–32.
42. Goldstein, *Spartan Seasons*, 213.
43. Pietrusza, *Baseball's Canadian-American League*, 80.
44. Turner, *When the Boys Came Back*, 24.
45. Mead, *Baseball Goes to War*, 76.
46. Goldstein, *Spartan Seasons*, 117.
47. Oakley, *Baseball's Last Golden Age*, 6.
48. Mead, *Baseball Goes to War*, 78.
49. Schlesinger, *The Almanac of American History*, 488.
50. Mead, *Baseball Goes to War*, 80.
51. Goldstein, *Spartan Seasons*, 89.
52. Mead, *Baseball Goes to War*, 2.
53. Goldstein, *Spartan Seasons*, 92.
54. Oakley, *Baseball's Last Golden Age*, 5.
55. Mead, *Baseball Goes to War*, 1–2.
56. Ibid., 10; Moskowitz, "The Sporting News During WWII," 44–54.
57. Moskowitz, "The Sporting News During WWII," 46; Goldstein, *Spartan Seasons*, 90–91.

Chapter 1

1. Goldstein, *Spartan Seasons*, 201.
2. *The Sporting News*, 1 March 1945.
3. Ibid.
4. Oakley, *Baseball's Last Golden Age*, 151.
5. Voigt, *American Baseball: Vol. 3*, 95.
6. *New York Herald Tribune*, 15 April 1945.
7. Mead, *Baseball Goes to War*, 50.
8. *New York Herald Tribune*, 13 March 1945.
9. *The Sporting News*, 12 April 1945.
10. Ibid.

Chapter 2

1. Krah, "The Limestone League: Spring training in Indiana during WWII," 119.
2. Karst and Jones, *Who's Who in Professional Baseball*, 386.
3. *The Sporting News*, 6 September 1945.
4. Peary, *We Played the Game*, 319.
5. Golenbock, *Wrigleyville*, 283.
6. Karst and Jones, *Who's Who in Professional Baseball*, 385.
7. *The Sporting News*, 6 September 1945.
8. *The Sporting News*, 27 September 1945.
9. Karst and Jones, *Who's Who in Professional Baseball*, 385.
10. Westcott, *Diamond Greats*, 135.
11. *The Sporting News*, 7 June 1945.
12. Peary, *We Played the Game*, 251.
13. *The Sporting News*, 19 July 1945.
14. *The Sporting News*, 27 September 1945.
15. *The Sporting News*, 16 August 1945.
16. *The Sporting News*, 26 July 1945.
17. *The Sporting News*, 27 September 1945.
18. *New York Herald Tribune*, 13 September 1945.
19. Mead, *Baseball Goes to War*, 231.

Chapter 3

1. Turner, *When the Boys Came Back*, 58.
2. Honig, *Baseball America*, 253.
3. Karst and Jones, *Who's Who in Professional Baseball*, 99.
4. Dickey, *The History of the World Series Since 1903*, 141.
5. *The Sporting News*, 29 March 1945.
6. Ibid.
7. *The Sporting News*, 24 May 1945.
8. Mead, *Baseball Goes to War*, 16.
9. Pietrusza, *Baseball's Canadian-American League*, 159–60.
10. *The Sporting News*, 9 August 1945.
11. Durocher with Linn, *Nice Guys Finish Last*, 291–92.
12. Voigt, *American Baseball: Vol. 3*, 61.
13. *The Sporting News*, 6 September 1945.
14. Ibid.
15. Peary, *We Played the Game*, 219.
16. Obojski, *All-Star Baseball Since 1933*, 58.
17. James, *The New Bill James Historical Baseball Abstract*, 620.
18. Karst and Jones, *Who's Who in Professional Baseball*, 634; Mead, *Baseball Goes to War*, 121.
19. Westcott, *Diamond Greats*, 363; Turner, *When the Boys Came Back*, 56.
20. *The Sporting News*, 31 May 1945.
21. *The Sporting News*, 30 August 1945.
22. Quigley, *The Crooked Pitch*, 19.
23. Turner, *When the Boys Came Back*, 172.
24. *The Sporting News*, 14 June 1945.

Chapter 4

1. Karst and Jones, *Who's Who In Professional Baseball*, 270.
2. Durocher with Linn, *Nice Guys Finish Last*, 14.
3. Turner, *When the Boys Came Back*, 78–79.
4. *New York Herald Tribune*, 14 June 1945.
5. *New York Herald Tribune*, 15 June 1945.
6. Prince, *Brooklyn's Dodgers*, 88–89.
7. Goldstein, *Superstars and Screwballs*, 267.
8. James, *Bill James' Guide to Baseball Managers*, 121.
9. Golenbock, *Bums*, 54.
10. Ibid.
11. *New York Times*, 10 September 1952.
12. James, *Bill James' Guide to Baseball Managers*, 121.
13. *The Sporting News*, 29 March 1945.
14. Durocher with Linn, *Nice Guys Finish Last*, 84.
15. Kiernan, *The Miracle at Coogan's Bluff*, 33.
16. Durocher with Linn, *Nice Guys Finish Last*, 14.
17. Gutman, *It Ain't Cheatin' If You Don't Get Caught*, 119.
18. Mead, *Baseball Goes to War*, 122.
19. Turner, *When the Boys Came Back*, 158.
20. Gilbert, *They Also Served*, 141.
21. Oakley, *Baseball's Last Golden Age*, 4.
22. *New York Times*, 13 August 1945.
23. Mead, *Baseball Goes to War*, 108.
24. Karst and Jones, *Who's Who in Professional Baseball*, 432.
25. Goldstein, *Superstars and Screwballs*, 153.
26. "July's Contenders," 80.
27. *New York Herald Tribune*, 11 July 1945.
28. *New York Herald Tribune*, 8 June 1945.
29. *New York Times*, 8 June 1945.
30. *Brooklyn Eagle*, 19 June 1945.
31. *New York Herald Tribune*, 19 June 1945.
32. Karst and Jones, *Who's Who in Professional Baseball*, 338–39.
33. *New York Herald Tribune*, 2 September 1945.

Chapter 5

1. *The Sporting News*, 5 April 1945.
2. James, *The New Bill James Historical Baseball Abstract*, 492.
3. Honig, *Baseball America*, 146.
4. James, *The New Bill James Historical Baseball Abstract*, 492.
5. Goldstein, *Spartan Seasons*, 59.
6. *The Sporting News*, 7 June 1945.
7. Karst and Jones, *Who's Who in Professional Baseball*, 576.

8. Dickson, *The New Dickson Baseball Dictionary*, 175.
9. Quigley, *The Crooked Pitch*, 125.
10. Ibid., 130.
11. Dickson, *The New Dickson Baseball Dictionary*, 175–76.
12. Kahn, *The Era*, 231.
13. Oakley, *Baseball's Last Golden Age*, 187.
14. Kahn, *The Boys of Summer*, 305.
15. Roberts and Rogers, *The Whiz Kids and the 1950 Pennant*, 19.
16. Honig, *Baseball America*, 51.

Chapter 6

1. Kart and Jones, *Who's Who in Professional Baseball*, 729.
2. Honig, *Baseball America*, 192–93.
3. Gilbert, *They Also Served*, 31.
4. Durocher with Linn, *Nice Guys Finish Last*, 14.
5. Stein, *Mel Ott*, 148.
6. Goldstein, *Spartan Seasons*, 111.
7. Stein, *Mel Ott*, 133.
8. *New York Herald Tribune*, 13 March 1945.
9. Gilbert, *They Also Served*, 64.
10. Graham, "The Great Mexican War of 1946," 119.
11. "'The Luck,'" 93.
12. Karst and Jones, *Who's Who in Professional Baseball*, 687.
13. Gilbert, *They Also Served*, 192.
14. Goldstein, *Superstars and Screwballs*, 183.
15. *New York Herald Tribune*, 13 March 1945.
16. Gutman, *It Ain't Cheatin' If You Don't Get Caught*, 63.
17. Prince, *Brooklyn's Dodgers*, 51.
18. Durocher with Linn, *Nice Guys Finish Last*, 14.
19. Honig, *Baseball America*, 195.
20. Stein and Peters, *Giants Diary*, 95.
21. Goldstein, *Spartan Seasons*, 192.
22. *New York Times*, 12 August 1945.
23. Oakley, *Baseball's Last Golden Age*, 83.
24. *New York Herald Tribune*, 12 March 1945.
25. Dickson, *The New Dickson Baseball Dictionary*, 94.
26. *New York Times*, 12 August 1945.
27. Gilbert, *They Also Served*, 188.
28. *New York Herald Tribune*, 4 April 1945.
29. Stein, *Mel Ott*, 148.
30. Stein and Peters, *Giants Diary*, 94.
31. Durocher with Linn, *Nice Guys Finish Last*, 290.
32. Goldstein, *Spartan Seasons*, 140–41.
33. *New York Herald Tribune*, 28 April 1945.
34. Ibid.
35. Stein, *Mel Ott*, 151.
36. Frommer, *New York City Baseball*, 84–85.
37. Prince, *Brooklyn's Dodgers*, 106.
38. Ibid., 107.
39. Hynd, *The Giants of the Polo Grounds*, 182.
40. Gauthreaux, "Eddie Grant: Player On Two Fields," 2.
41. Hynd, *The Giants of the Polo Grounds*, 210–11.
42. Robinson, *Matty*, 197.
43. Ibid., 198.
44. Kahn, *The Era*, 21.
45. Mayer, "Bill Voiselle and the $500 Pitch," 136.
46. Stein and Peters, *Giants Diary*, 95.
47. Mayer, "Bill Voiselle and the $500 Pitch," 136.
48. Ibid., 137.
49. *New York Herald Tribune*, 5 June 1945.
50. *New York Herald Tribune*, 2 August 1945.
51. Stein, *Mel Ott*, 152.

Chapter 7

1. *The Sporting News*, 2 August 1945.
2. Ibid.
3. Karst and Jones, *Who's Who in Professional Baseball*, 75.
4. Goldstein, *Spartan Seasons*, 135–36.
5. Gilbert, *They Also Served*, 246.
6. Ibid., 249.
7. Peary, *We Played the Game*, 7–8.
8. *The Sporting News*, 13 September 1945.
9. Ibid.
10. *The Sporting News*, 21 June 1945.
11. *The Sporting News*, 9 August 1945.
12. Kavanagh and Macht, *Uncle Robbie*, 167–68; *The Sporting News*, 9 August, 1945.

Chapter 8

1. *New York Herald Tribune*, 15 August 1945.
2. *New York Herald Tribune*, 13 September 1945.
3. *The Sporting News*, 31 May 1945.
4. Werber and Rogers, *Memories of a Ballplayer*, 147–48.
5. Ibid., 146–47, 149.
6. *Christian Science Monitor*, 19 May 1945.
7. Gershman, *Diamonds*, 156.
8. Karst and Jones, *Who's Who in Professional Baseball*, 586–87; Werber and Rogers, *Memories of a Ballplayer*, 43–44, 166.
9. Goldstein, *Spartan Seasons*, 213; Mead, *Baseball Goes to War*, 213.
10. *Christian Science Monitor*, 19 May 1945.
11. Alexander, *Breaking the Slump*, 256.
12. Ibid., 257.

13. Werber and Rogers, *Memories of a Ballplayer*, 174–75.
14. Peary, *We Played the Game*, 71.
15. Ibid., 37.
16. *The Sporting News*, 14 June 1945.

Chapter 9

1. *The Sporting News*, 5 April 1945.
2. Ibid.
3. *The Sporting News*, 14 June 1945.
4. *The Sporting News*, 3 May 1945.
5. Gershman, *Diamonds*, 85–86.
6. *New York Times*, 2 May 1945.
7. Finoli, *For the Good of the Country*, 55.
8. Scheinin, *Field of Screams*, 219.
9. Oakley, *Baseball's Last Golden Age*, 54.
10. Roberts and Rogers, *The Whiz Kids and the 1950 Pennant*, 50.
11. Ibid., 52.
12. *The Sporting News*, 5 July 1945.
13. Mead, *Baseball Goes to War*, 108.
14. Roberts and Rogers, *The Whiz Kids and the 1950 Pennant*, 27.
15. Jordan, Gerlach, and Rossi, "A Baseball Myth Exploded," 3–13.
16. Oakley, *Baseball's Last Golden Age*, 56.
17. Roberts and Rogers, *The Whiz Kids and the 1950 Pennant*, 38.
18. Goldstein, *Spartan Seasons*, 169.
19. Scheinin, *Field of Screams*, 220.
20. Oakley, *Baseball's Last Golden Age*, 20.
21. Pappas, "Jake Powell: The John Rocker of the 1930s."
22. Alexander, *Breaking the Slump*, 156–57.
23. Karst and Jones, *Who's Who in Professional Baseball*, 772.
24. Gilbert, *They Also Served*, 12.
25. Oakley, *Baseball's Last Golden Age*, 2.
26. *Christian Science Monitor*, 8 May 1945.

Chapter 10

1. *Philadelphia Inquirer*, 18 April 1945.
2. *New York Herald Tribune*, 21 April 1945.
3. *New York Herald Tribune*, 28 April 1945.
4. *New York Herald Tribune*, 22 July 1945.
5. Westcott, *Diamond Greats*, 105.
6. Scheinin, *Field of Screams*, 227.
7. *New York Herald Tribune*, 25 April 1945.
8. *New York Herald Tribune*, 26 April 1945.
9. *New York Herald Tribune*, 2 May 1945.
10. Karst and Jones, *Who's Who in Professional Baseball*, 155.
11. Ibid., 156.
12. Voigt, *American Baseball: Vol. 3*, 92.
13. Oakley, *Baseball's Last Golden Age*, 150.
14. Ibid., 52.
15. *New York Herald Tribune*, 8 May 1945.
16. *New York Herald Tribune*, 13 May 1945.
17. *Christian Science Monitor*, 18 May 1945.
18. *New York Herald Tribune*, 24 May 1945.
19. *New York Herald Tribune*, 28 May 1945.
20. Goldstein, *Spartan Seasons*, 217.
21. *New York Herald Tribune*, 20 June 1945.
22. Ibid.
23. Goldstein, *Spartan Seasons*, 53.
24. *New York Herald Tribune*, 24 June 1945.
25. *New York Herald Tribune*, 25 June 1945.
26. *New York Herald Tribune*, 4 July 1945.
27. Goldstein, *Spartan Seasons*, 138; *New York Herald Tribune*, 12 July 1945.
28. *New York Herald Tribune*, 16 July 1945.
29. *New York Herald Tribune*, 20 July 1945.
30. Mead, *Baseball Goes to War*, 83–84.
31. *New York Herald Tribune*, 21 July 1945.
32. *Christian Science Monitor*, 25 May 1945.
33. *The Sporting News*, 13 September 1945.
34. *New York Herald Tribune*, 15 August 1945.
35. *New York Herald Tribune*, 16 August 1945.
36. *New York Herald Tribune*, 17 August 1945.
37. *New York Herald Tribune*, 18 August 1945.
38. *New York Herald Tribune*, 28 August 1945.
39. *New York Herald Tribune*, 11 September 1945.
40. *New York Herald Tribune*, 13 September 1945.
41. Goldstein, *Spartan Seasons*, 139.
42. *The Sporting News*, 20 September 1945; *New York Herald Tribune*, 13 September 1945.
43. *New York Herald Tribune*, 16 September 1945.
44. *New York Herald Tribune*, 26 September 1945.
45. *New York Herald Tribune*, 30 September 1945.
46. *New York Herald Tribune*, 1 October 1945.

Chapter 11

1. Goldstein, *Spartan Seasons*, 119.
2. Krah, "The Limestone League: Spring training in Indiana during WWII," 120.
3. Turner, *When the Boys Came Back*, 67.
4. *The Sporting News*, 5 July 1945.
5. Ibid.
6. Jordan, *A Tiger in His Time*, 135.
7. *New York Times*, 17 June 1945.
8. *The Sporting News*, 13 September 1945.
9. Jordan, *A Tiger in His Time*, 145.
10. Ibid., 164.
11. *The Sporting News*, 13 September 1945.
12. Jordan, *A Tiger in His Time*, 149.
13. Ibid., 267.
14. Peary, *We Played the Game*, 46–47, 166.
15. Ibid., 166.

16. *New York Herald Tribune*, 1 October 1945.
17. Jordan, *A Tiger in His Time*, 269.
18. Peary, *We Played the Game*, 239.
19. Jordan, *A Tiger in His Time*, 269.
20. Peary, *We Played the Game*, 166.
21. *The Sporting News*, 30 August 1945.
22. *The Sporting News*, 17 May 1945.
23. Ibid.
24. *The Sporting News*, 13 September 1945.
25. Ibid.
26. Ibid.

Chapter 12

1. Karst and Jones, *Who's Who in Professional Baseball*, 69.
2. Gilbert, *They Also Served*, 157–61.
3. Goldstein, *Spartan Seasons*, 249–50.
4. *The Sporting News*, 2 August 1945.
5. Gilbert, *They Also Served*, 230.
6. Schlesinger, *The Almanac of American History*, 499.
7. Newell, "Boys of Summer Head to War: Baseball's rising stars didn't hesitate when duty called them for World War II," 66.
8. *The Sporting News*, 22 March 1945.
9. *The Sporting News*, 24 May 1945.
10. Turner, *When the Boys Came Back*, 24.
11. *The Sporting News*, 23 August 1945.
12. Karst and Jones, *Who's Who in Professional Baseball*, 669.
13. *The Sporting News*, 23 August 1945.
14. Mead, *Baseball Goes to War*, 114.
15. Westcott, *Diamond Greats*, 357–58.
16. *The Sporting News*, 12 July 1945.
17. Ibid.
18. Westcott, *Diamond Greats*, 354.
19. Ibid., 354, 356.
20. *The Sporting News*, 13 September 1945.
21. Karst and Jones, *Who's Who in Professional Baseball*, 498.
22. *The Sporting News*, 13 September 1945.
23. *The Sporting News*, 20 September 1945.
24. Bjarkman, *Baseball with a Latin Beat*, 199–200.
25. Quigley, *The Crooked Pitch*, 111.
26. Mead, *Baseball Goes to War*, 228–29.
27. Gilbert, *They Also Served*, 207.
28. *The Sporting News*, 13 September 1945.
29. *The Sporting News*, 2 August 1945.
30. *The Sporting News*, 14 June 1945.
31. Ibid.
32. *The Sporting News*, 9 August 1945.
33. Ibid.
34. Alexander, *Breaking the Slump*, 192–93.
35. *The Sporting News*, 9 August 1945.

Chapter 13

1. Mead, *Baseball Goes to War*, 18.
2. Ibid., 68.
3. Gilbert, *They Also Served*, 116.
4. Phillips, *The Mexican Jumping Beans*, 32.
5. Ibid., 39.
6. Mead, *Baseball Goes to War*, 150.
7. *The Sporting News*, 22 March 1945.
8. Pietrusza, *Baseball's Canadian American League*, 156.
9. Ibid., 156–57.
10. *The Sporting News*, 22 March 1945.
11. Mead, *Baseball Goes to War*, 209–10.
12. *Christian Science Monitor*, 23 May 1945.
13. Mead, *Baseball Goes to War*, 210–11.
14. *The Sporting News*, 6 September 1945.
15. *The Sporting News*, 28 June 1945.
16. Ibid.

Chapter 14

1. Henrich and Nickas, "Joe Gordon: A Reliable view of Flash," 42.
2. Ibid., 43.
3. Kahn, *The Era*, 189.
4. Karst and Jones, *Who's Who in Professional Baseball*, 612.
5. Violanti, *Miracle in Buffalo*, 63.
6. *New York Herald Tribune*, 1 March 1945.
7. *New York Herald Tribune*, 12 March 1945.
8. *New York Herald Tribune*, 14 March 1945.
9. *New York Herald Tribune*, 3 April 1945.
10. Oakley, *Baseball's Last Golden Age*, 68.
11. *New York Herald Tribune*, 12 April 1945.
12. Spatz, "Snuffy Stirnweiss: Not Just a Wartime Player," 48.
13. *New York Herald Tribune*, 17 July 1945.
14. Kahn, *The Era*, 85.
15. *New York Herald Tribune*, 5 September 1945.
16. *The Sporting News*, 13 September 1945.
17. Gershman, *Diamonds*, 134.
18. Ibid., 134, 138.
19. Benson, *Ballparks of North America*, 269.
20. Gershman, *Diamonds*, 138.
21. Dickson, *The New Dickson Baseball Dictionary*, 264.
22. Gershman, *Diamonds*, 132.
23. Frommer, *New York City Baseball*, 128.
24. Prince, *Brooklyn's Dodgers*, 107.
25. Oakley, *Baseball's Last Golden Age*, 278.
26. Goldstein, *Spartan Seasons*, 54.

Chapter 15

1. Krah, "The Limestone League: Spring training in Indiana during WWII," 119.
2. Gershman, *Diamonds*, 147.
3. Neyer, *Rob Neyer's Big Book of Baseball Lineups*, 71.
4. Berger, "Lou Boudreau."

5. Karst and Jones, *Who's Who in Professional Baseball*, 91.
6. *The Sporting News*, 21 June 1945.
7. *The Sporting News*, 2 August 1945.
8. Ibid.
9. *The Sporting News*, 21 June 1945.
10. *The Sporting News*, 2 August 1945.
11. Honig, *Baseball America*, 212.
12. Neyer, *Rob Neyer's Big Book of Baseball Lineups*, 78.
13. *The Sporting News*, 29 March 1945.
14. *The Sporting News*, 19 July 1945.
15. Peary, *We Played the Game*, 82.
16. Scheinin, *Field of Screams*, 272.
17. *The Sporting News*, 28 June 1945.

Chapter 16

1. *The Sporting News*, 29 March 1945.
2. Ibid.
3. *The Sporting News*, 24 May 1945.
4. Bjarkman, *Baseball with a Latin Beat*, 226.
5. Peary, *We Played the Game*, 207.
6. Ibid., 47.
7. Karst and Jones, *Who's Who in Professional Baseball*, 277.
8. Ibid.
9. Ritter, *Lost Ballparks*, 31–32.
10. Scheinin, *Field of Screams*, 241–42.
11. Karst and Jones, *Who's Who in Professional Baseball*, 277.
12. Peary, *We Played the Game*, 227.
13. Ibid., 479.
14. Ibid., 159.
15. Westcott, *Diamond Greats*, 98.
16. Spatz, "Snuffy Stirnweiss: Not Just a Wartime Player," 48.
17. *The Sporting News*, 24 May 1945.
18. Westcott, *Diamond Greats*, 99.
19. *The Sporting News*, 24 May 1945.
20. Obojski, *All-Star Baseball Since 1933*, 8.
21. *The Sporting News*, 12 July 1945.
22. Goldstein, *Spartan Seasons*, 193–94; Karst and Jones, *Who's Who in Professional Baseball*, 709–10.
23. Westcott, *Diamond Greats*, 284.
24. Ritter, *Lost Ballparks*, 30.
25. Gershman, *Diamonds*, 92.

Chapter 17

1. Turner, *When the Boys Came Back*, 105.
2. Voigt, *American Baseball: Vol. 3*, 83.
3. *The Sporting News*, 29 March 1945.
4. Ibid.
5. Karst and Jones, *Who's Who in Professional Baseball*, 208–09.
6. Turner, *When the Boys Came Back*, 70–71.
7. Ibid., 10.
8. Ibid., 16.
9. *The Sporting News*, 21 June 1945.
10. Ibid.
11. Golenbock, *Fenway*, 149.
12. Gilbert, *They Also Served*, 186.
13. *Christian Science Monitor*, 15 May 1945.
14. Goldstein, *Spartan Seasons*, 48.
15. *Christian Science Monitor*, 15 May 1945.
16. *The Sporting News*, 29 March 1945.

Chapter 18

1. *The Sporting News*, 5 April 1945.
2. Honig, *Baseball America*, 36.
3. Bjarkman, *Baseball with a Latin Beat*, 119.
4. Westcott, *Diamond Greats*, 34.
5. Gilbert, *They Also Served*, 139.
6. *The Sporting News*, 12 July 1945.
7. Ibid.
8. Karst and Jones, *Who's Who in Professional Baseball*, 703–04; Werber and Rogers, *Memories of a Ballplayer*, 122, 124; Berger, "Bobo Newsom."
9. Karst and Jones, *Who's Who in Professional Baseball*, 703.
10. Berger, "Bobo Newsom."
11. *The Sporting News*, 21 June 1945.
12. *The Sporting News*, 12 July 1945.
13. *The Sporting News*, 14 June 1945.
14. *The Sporting News*, 21 June 1945.
15. Ibid.
16. Ibid.
17. Peary, *We Played the Game*, 72–73.
18. *New York Herald Tribune*, 11 September 1945.
19. *New York Herald Tribune*, 10 September 1945.

Chapter 19

1. *New York Herald Tribune*, 18 April 1945.
2. Ibid.
3. *Philadelphia Inquirer*, 18 April 1945.
4. *New York Herald Tribune*, 20 April 1945.
5. *New York Herald Tribune*, 24 April 1945.
6. *New York Herald Tribune*, 21 April 1945.
7. Honig, *Baseball America*, 246.
8. *New York Herald Tribune*, 15 May 1945.
9. *New York Herald Tribune*, 16 May 1945.
10. *New York Herald Tribune*, 27 May 1945.
11. *New York Herald Tribune*, 2 June 1945.
12. *New York Herald Tribune*, 12 July 1945.
13. *New York Herald Tribune*, 17 July 1945.
14. *New York Herald Tribune*, 23 July 1945.
15. *New York Herald Tribune*, 24 July 1945.
16. *The Sporting News*, 13 September 1945.
17. *New York Herald Tribune*, 28 July 1945.
18. *The Sporting News*, 9 August 1945.
19. Finoli, *For the Good of the Country*, 70–71.

20. *New York Herald Tribune*, 10 August 1945.
21. Finoli, *For the Good of the Country*, 228; Goldstein, *Spartan Seasons*, 139–40.
22. *New York Herald Tribune*, 13 August 1945.
23. *New York Herald Tribune*, 14 August 1945.
24. *New York Herald Tribune*, 16 August 1945.
25. *The Sporting News*, 6 September 1945.
26. *New York Herald Tribune*, 4 September 1945.
27. *New York Herald Tribune*, 9 September 1945.
28. *New York Herald Tribune*, 12 September 1945.
29. *The Sporting News*, 13 September 1945.
30. *New York Herald Tribune*, 15 September 1945.
31. *New York Herald Tribune*, 19 September 1945.
32. *New York Herald Tribune*, 20 September 1945.
33. *New York Herald Tribune*, 1 October 1945.
34. *New York Herald Tribune*, 26 September 1945.

Chapter 20

1. Oakley, *Baseball's Last Golden Age*, 11.
2. *Washington Post*, 3 October 1945.
3. Ibid.
4. *Washington Post*, 4 October 1945.
5. *The Sporting News*, 11 October 1945.
6. *Washington Post*, 5 October 1945.
7. *The Sporting News*, 11 October 1945.
8. *Washington Post*, 6 October 1945.
9. *Washington Post*, 7 October 1945.
10. *Washington Post*, 9 October 1945.
11. *The Sporting News*, 11 October 1945.
12. *Washington Post*, 11 October 1945.

Chapter 21

1. *New York Herald Tribune*, 25 October 1945.
2. Ibid.
3. *New York Herald Tribune*, 7 December 1945.
4. Oakley, *Baseball's Last Golden Age*, 12.
5. Ibid., 32.
6. Jordan, *A Tiger in His Time*, 171.
7. Newell, "Boys of Summer Head to War: Baseball's rising stars didn't hesitate when duty called them for World War II," 69.

Bibliography

Newspapers

Brooklyn Eagle
Christian Science Monitor
Philadelphia Inquirer
New York Herald Tribune
New York Times
The Sporting News
Washington Post

Books

Alexander, Charles C. *Breaking the Slump: Baseball in the Depression Era.* New York: Columbia University Press, 2002.
_____. *Our Game: An American Baseball History.* New York: Henry Holt, 1991.
The Baseball Encyclopedia: The Complete and Definitive Record of Major League Baseball. 9th ed. New York: Macmillan, 1993.
Benson, Michael. *Ballparks of North America: A Comprehensive Historical Reference to Baseball Grounds, Yards, and Stadiums, 1845 to the Present.* Jefferson, NC: McFarland, 1989.
Bjarkman, Peter C. *Baseball with a Latin Beat: A History of the Latin American Game.* Jefferson, NC: McFarland, 1994.
Dickey, Glenn. *The History of the World Series Since 1903.* New York: Stein & Day, 1984.
Dickson, Paul. *The New Dickson Baseball Dictionary.* San Diego: Harcourt Brace, 1999.
Durocher, Leo, with Ed Linn. *Nice Guys Finish Last.* New York: Simon & Schuster, 1975.
Echevarria, Roberto Gonzalez. *The Pride of Havana: A History of Cuban Baseball.* New York: Oxford University Press, 1999.
Filichia, Peter. *Professional Baseball Franchises: From the Abbeville Athletics to the Zanesville Indians.* New York: Facts On File, 1993.
Finoli, David. *For the Good of the Country: World War II Baseball in the Major and Minor Leagues.* Jefferson, NC: McFarland, 2002.
Frommer, Harvey. *New York City Baseball: The Last Golden Age, 1947–1957.* New York: Macmillan, 1980.
Gershman, Michael. *Diamonds: The Evolution of the Ballpark.* Boston: Houghton Mifflin, 1993.
Gilbert, Bill. *They Also Served: Baseball and the Home Front, 1941–1945.* New York: Crown, 1992.
Goldstein, Richard. *Spartan Seasons: How Baseball Survived the Second World War.* New York: Macmillan, 1980.

_____. *Superstars and Screwballs: 100 Years of Brooklyn Baseball*. New York: Dutton, 1991.
Golenbock, Peter. *Bums: An Oral History of the Brooklyn Dodgers*. New York: G.P. Putnam's, 1984.
_____. *Fenway: An Unexpurgated History of the Boston Red Sox*. New York: G.P. Putnam's, 1992.
_____. *Wrigleyville: A Magical History Tour of the Chicago Cubs*. New York: St. Martin's, 1996.
Gutman, Dan. *It Ain't Cheatin' If You Don't Get Caught: Scuffing, Corking, Spitting, Gunking, Razzing, and Other Fundamentals of Our National Pastime*. New York: Penguin, 1990.
Honig, Donald. *Baseball America: The Heroes of the Game and the Times of Their Glory*. 1985. New York: Barnes & Noble, 1997.
Hynd, Noel. *The Giants of the Polo Grounds: The Glorious Times of Baseball's New York Giants*. 1988. Dallas, TX: Taylor, 1995.
James, Bill. *Bill James' Guide to Baseball Managers: From 1870 to Today*. New York: Simon & Schuster, 1997.
_____. *The New Bill James Historical Baseball Abstract*. New York: Free Press, 2001.
Jordan, David M. *A Tiger in His Time: Hal Newhouser and the Burden of Wartime Ball*. South Bend, IN: Diamond Communications, 1990.
Kahn, Roger. *The Boys of Summer*. New York: Harper & Row, 1971.
_____. *The Era: 1947–1957 When the Yankees, the Giants, and the Dodgers Ruled the World*. New York: Ticknor & Fields, 1993.
Karst, Gene, and Martin J. Jones, Jr. *Who's Who in Professional Baseball*. New Rochelle, NY: Arlington House, 1973.
Kavanagh, Jack, and Norman Macht. *Uncle Robbie*. Lincoln, NE: The Society for American Baseball Research, 1999.
Kiernan, Thomas. *The Miracle at Coogan's Bluff*. New York: Thomas Y. Crowell, 1975.
Linkugel, Wil A., and Edward J. Pappas. *They Tasted Glory: Among the Missing at the Baseball Hall of Fame*. Jefferson, NC: McFarland, 1998.
Marshall, William. *Baseball's Pivotal Era, 1945–1951*. Lexington: University of Kentucky Press, 1999.
McConnell, Bob, and David Vincent, eds. *SABR Presents The Home Run Encyclopedia: The Who, What, and Where of Every Home Run Hit Since 1876*. New York: MacMillan, 1996.
Mead, William B. *Baseball Goes to War*. 1978. Washington, D.C.: Broadcast Interview Source, 1998.
Meany, Tom. *The Incredible Giants*. New York: A.S. Barnes, 1955.
Neyer, Rob. *Rob Neyer's Big Book of Baseball Lineups: A Complete Guide to the Best, Worst, and Most Memorable Players to Ever Grace the Major Leagues*. New York: Simon & Schuster, 2003.
Oakley, J. Ronald. *Baseball's Last Golden Age, 1946–1960: The National Pastime in a Time of Glory and Change*. Jefferson, NC: McFarland, 1994.
Obojski, Robert. *All-Star Baseball Since 1933*. New York: Stein & Day, 1980.
Palmer, Pete, and Gary Gillette, eds. *The 2006 ESPN Baseball Encyclopedia*. New York: Sterling, 2006.
Peary, Danny, ed. *We Played the Game: 65 Players Remember Baseball's Greatest Era, 1947–1964*. New York: Hyperion, 1994.
Phillips, John. *The Mexican Jumping Beans: The Story of the Baseball War of 1946*. Perry, GA: Capital, 1997.
Pietrusza, David. *Baseball's Canadian-American League: A History of Its Inception, Fran-

chises, Participants, Locales, Statistics, Demise and Legacy, 1936–1951. Jefferson, NC: McFarland, 1990.
Prince, Carl E. *Brooklyn's Dodgers: The Bums, the Borough, and the Best of Baseball, 1947–1957*. New York: Oxford University Press, 1996.
Quigley, Martin. *The Crooked Pitch: The Curveball in American Baseball History*. Chapel Hill, NC: Algonquin, 1984.
Ritter, Lawrence S. *Lost Ballparks: A Celebration of Baseball's Legendary Fields*. New York: Penguin Studio, 1992.
Roberts, Robin, and C. Paul Rogers III. *The Whiz Kids and the 1950 Pennant*. Philadelphia: Temple University Press, 1996.
Robinson, Ray. *Matty: An American Hero: Christy Mathewson of the New York Giants*. New York: Oxford University Press, 1993.
Scheinin, Richard. *Fields of Screams: The Dark Underside of America's National Pastime*. New York: W.W. Norton, 1994.
Schlesinger, Jr., Arthur M., gen. ed. *The Almanac of American History*. New York: Barnes & Noble, 1993.
Simon, Tom, ed. *Deadball Stars of the National League*. Washington, D.C.: Brassey's, 2004.
Spatz, Lyle, ed. *The SABR Baseball List and Record Book: Baseball's Most Fascinating Records and Unusual Statistics*. New York: Scribner, 2007.
Stein, Fred. *Mel Ott: The Little Giant of Baseball*. Jefferson, NC: McFarland, 1999.
_____, and Nick Peters. *Giants Diary: A Century of Giants Baseball in New York and San Francisco*. Berkeley, CA: North Atlantic, 1987.
Szalontai, James D. *Close Shave: The Life and Times of Baseball's Sal Maglie*. Jefferson, NC: McFarland, 2002.
Tindall, George Brown, and David E. Shi. *America: A Narrative History*. 4th ed. New York: W.W. Norton, 1996.
Turner, Frederick. *When the Boys Came Back: Baseball and 1946*. New York: Henry Holt, 1996.
Violanti, Anthony. *Miracle in Buffalo: How the Dream of Baseball Revived a City*. New York: St. Martin's, 1991.
Voigt, David Quentin. *American Baseball: Vol. 3, From Postwar Expansion to the Electronic Age*. University Park: Pennsylvania State University Press, 1983.
Werber, William M., and C. Paul Rogers III. *Memories of a Ballplayer: Bill Werber and Baseball in the 1930s*. Lincoln, NE: The Society for American Baseball Research, 2001.
Westcott, Rich. *Diamond Greats: Profiles and Interviews with 65 of Baseball's History Makers*. Westport, CT: Meckler, 1988.
Wood, Allan James. *1918: Babe Ruth and the World Champion Boston Red Sox*. Lincoln, NE: iUniverse-Writers Club Press, 2000.
Wright, Marshall D. *The International League: Year-by-Year Statistics, 1884–1953*. Jefferson, NC: McFarland, 1998.
Zingg, Paul J. *Harry Hooper: An American Baseball Life*. Urbana: University of Illinois Press, 1993.
Zoss, Joel, and John S. Bowman. *Diamonds in the Rough: The Untold History of Baseball*. New York: Macmillan, 1989.

Articles

Bjarkman, Peter C. "First Hispanic Star? Dolf Luque, Of Course." *Baseball Research Journal* 19, 1990.
Gauthreaux, Jay. "Eddie Grant: Player on Two Fields." Unpublished article.

Graham, Frank, Jr. "The Great Mexican War of 1946." *Sports Illustrated*, September 19, 1966.
Henrich, Tom, with Richard Nickas. "Joe Gordon: A Reliable view of Flash." *Baseball Research Journal* 28, 1999.
Jordan, David M., Larry R. Gerlach, and John P. Rossi. "A Baseball Myth Exploded: Bill Veeck and the 1943 sale of the Phillies." *The National Pastime: A Review of Baseball History* 18, 1998.
"July's Contenders." *Newsweek*. July 16, 1945.
Krah, Steve. "The Limestone League: Spring training in Indiana during WWII." *Baseball Research Journal* 26, 1997.
Levin, Leonard. "Baseball in 1945 — The Pits." *Providence Journal-Bulletin*, February, 1995.
"'The Luck.'" *Newsweek*. May 28, 1945.
Mayer, Bob. "Bill Voiselle and the $500 Pitch: Ott enraged by 0–2 triple." *Baseball Research Journal* 26, 1997.
Moskowitz, Eric. "*The Sporting News* During WWII." *The National Pastime: A Review of Baseball History* 23, 2003.
Newell, Rob. "Boys of Summer Head to War: Baseball's rising stars didn't hesitate when duty called them for World War II." *The Retired Officer*, October, 2001.
Spatz, Lyle. "Snuffy Stirnweiss: Not Just a Wartime Player." *The National Pastime: A Review of Baseball History* 19, 1999.
Wysard, Paul L. "The World War II Years: A Re-Evaluation." From SABR Presentation, San Francisco, 6/98.

Internet Sources

www.baseballlibrary.com
www.baseball-reference.com
Berger, Ralph. "Lou Boudreau." *The Baseball Biography Project*. Society for American Baseball Research.
_____. "Bobo Newsom." *The Baseball Biography Project*. Society for American Baseball Research.
Kaufman, King. "'The Life and Times of Hank Greenberg.'" October 31, 2000. www.salon.com.
Kirkpatrick, Rob. "Cecil Travis." *The Baseball Biography Project*. Society for American Baseball Research.
Pappas, Doug. "Jake Powell: The John Rocker of the 1930s." Originally published in the March 2000 Boston Baseball Website, taken from www.roadsidephotos.com.

Index

Abramson, Jesse 91, 132, 139, 210
Acosta, Julio 32
Adams, Ace 59, 74, 79–80, 113, 118, 120, 133, 137
Adams, Buster 43, 45, 48, 107, 140–41
Aderholt, Morrie 138
Alexander, Charles 99
Alexander, Grover Cleveland 8
Alexander, Jess 197
Alexander, William D. 115
Allen, Johnny 204
Almada, Mel 180, 186
Almeida, Rafael 11
Andrews, Nate 87–89, 119, 124
Andrews, Stan 123
Antonelli, John 42, 48, 103, 107, 126
Appling, Luke 20, 228, 233
Arnovich, Morrie 219
Ashburn, Richie 77
Averill, Earl 246

Bagby, Jim, Jr. 214, 218, 221, 270, 274, 277, 279, 282
Bain, Loren 68
Baker, Bill 99
Baker, Del 151, 224, 241, 257
Baker, Floyd 275
Balinger, Ed 35
Bankhead, Tallulah 234
Barber, Red 207
Barnes, Don 177, 200, 256
Barnhart, Clyde 124
Barnhart, Vic 63, 124–25
Barr, George 34, 128, 142
Barrett, Dick 111, 140, 143
Barrett, Frank 266, 286
Barrett, Johnny 63–64, 120
Barrett, Red 1, 43, 45, 49–50, 86, 88, 92, 122, 124, 132, 137, 139–40, 146–48
Barrow, Ed 135, 205, 255–56
Barrymore, Ethel 235
Bartosch, Dave 121–22
Basinski, Eddie 57, 120, 124
Batista, Fulgencio 130, 253

Baumgartner, Stan 103, 217–18, 249, 254
Baumholtz, Frank 100
Beazley, Johnny 41, 294
Beck, Walter "Boom-Boom" 66, 100, 120, 123, 141
Beck, Zinn 250
Becker, Heinz 35–36, 139–42
Bender, Chief 227
Benton, Al 156–57, 163, 165, 168, 256, 258–59, 262, 269, 274
Berg, Moe 14, 172–73
Bergamo, Augie 42–43, 45, 89, 147
Berle, Milton 208
Berra, Yogi 221
Berry, Joe 249, 251, 258
Bevens, Bill 207, 209, 257, 262, 264, 268–69, 273, 284
Binks, George 175, 178, 183, 254, 286, 288
Bishop, Max 236
Bissonette, Del 81–83, 90
Bithorn, Hi 12, 55, 143
Bjarkman, Peter 224, 243
Black, Don 249, 251
Blair, Buddy 27
Blattner, Buddy 42
Bloodworth, Jimmy 154
Bluege, Ossie 30, 173–79
Bluege, Otto 178
Bockman, Eddie 221
Bonham, Ernie "Tiny" 209, 257, 268, 272, 274, 276
Bonura, Zeke 182
Bordagaray, Frenchy 56, 146–47
Borom, Red 164, 282
Borowy, Hank 38–40, 133, 137, 139–42, 145–49, 185, 209, 258–60, 262, 266, 268, 273–74, 289–92
Bossard, Emil 213
Bosser, Mel 100
Bottomley, Jim 154
Boudreau, Lou 2, 32, 64, 178, 192, 214–17, 220, 222, 231, 263, 265
Bowman, Bob 72
Bowman, Joe 91, 98, 124, 143

319

Bradley, Alva 227, 256
Bradley, Omar 178
Bragan, Bobby 54
Branca, Ralph 10, 57, 60, 132, 136, 146–47
Brancato, Al 27
Brannick, Eddie 77
Brazle, Al 15
Breadon, Sam 26, 42–45, 51–52, 86–87, 135, 146, 256
Brecheen, Harry 42, 45, 50–51, 141–42, 144, 148
Brewer, Forrest "Lefty" 15
Brewer, Jack 68, 80, 133
Bricker, John W. 256
Bridges, Tommy 167, 282, 286
Brissie, Lou 15–16
Brown, Jimmy 41
Brown, Joe E. 37
Brown, Mace 271
Brown, Tommy 2, 10, 56, 147
Brown, Warren 289
Brucker, Earle 191, 249
Bryant, Clay 153
Bucher, Jim 266, 286
Buker, Cy 57, 132, 142
Burkhart, Ken 45, 49–50, 120, 127, 129, 140, 148
Burley, Dan 293
Burr, Alex 77
Busch, Edgar 274
Bush, Donie 177
Bush, Guy 100
Butcher, Max 63, 132, 136
Buzas, Joe 2, 207, 270
Byerly, Bud 119, 132
Byrnes, James F. 9, 23
Byrnes, Milt 164, 180, 191–92, 196, 272, 278

Caballero, Putsy 110
Cain, Bob 163, 167
Caldwell, Earl 173, 232, 276
Cambria, Joe 11, 243
Camilli, Dolph 99, 231, 253
Camp, Walter 61
Campbell, Bruce 154
Carey, Max 64, 246
Carmichael, John P. 223–24
Carpenter, Robert R.M., Jr. 102–3
Carpenter, Robert R.M., Sr. 102–3, 106
Carrasquel, Alex 183, 276, 279, 282
Case, George 1–2, 16, 158, 173, 175–81, 183, 257, 270–71
Casey, Hugh 57, 116
Caster, George 200, 267, 277, 279, 285–86
Castino, Vince 229, 263
Caulfield, Jake 277
Cavarretta, Phil 31–32, 35–37, 83, 130, 136, 138, 140–42, 144, 148, 290
Cecil, Rex 253, 258
Center, Pete 218, 275, 279

Chandler, Albert B. "Happy" 23, 25, 116–17, 128, 131–33, 137, 178, 192, 215, 231, 256, 258, 293
Chandler, Spud 283–84, 294
Chapman, Ben 13, 104–6, 110, 118, 121, 126, 147, 186, 204, 207, 224, 231
Chapman, Sam 219, 280–81, 286
Chase, Hal 7, 34, 78
Chipman, Bob 32, 128, 149
Chipple, Walt 2
Christian, John 54
Christman, Mark 164, 191–92, 265
Christopher, Lloyd "Loyd" 250
Christopher, Russ 10, 249–50, 258–59, 265, 271–74, 286
Churchill, Winston 118
Cihocki, Al 176, 259
Claridge, John 267
Clark, Otis 286
Clarke, Grey 228–29
Clary, Ellis 200, 257
Clay, Dain 113
Cleary, Joe "Fire" 1, 277
Clift, Harlond 175, 177, 269
Cobb, Ty 66, 282
Cochrane, Mickey 19, 119, 281
Coleman, Bob 81, 88, 90, 127, 238
Coleman, George 59
Collins, Bill 76
Collins, Eddie 8
Comellas, Jorge 2, 121
Comiskey, Charles 7, 282
Conlan, Jocko 120
Cooper, Mort 43–45, 49, 86–87, 89, 96, 116, 118–19, 122, 132
Cooper, Walker 26, 29, 43–44, 49, 68, 114
Coscarart, Pete 144
Cox, William D. 106–7
Cozart, Charlie 88, 115
Cramer, Doc 1, 151–54, 164–65, 167, 254, 256, 276, 290–92
Crawford, Glenn 48, 107, 109, 126
Creel, Jack 79, 124
Crespi, Creepy 41
Cronin, Joe 2, 110, 154, 184, 188, 231, 234, 236–37, 240–41, 255, 257, 276, 278
Crosby, Bing 266
Crosetti, Frankie 188, 249, 285
Cross, Harry 60, 73, 80, 91, 114–15, 122, 127–28, 207
Croucher, Frank 154
Cuccinello, Al 228
Cuccinello, Tony 1, 228–31, 233, 259, 262–263, 270, 279
Culberson, Leon 255, 266
Cullenbine, Roy 151, 259, 275, 281, 284, 291–92
Culler, Dick 89, 120, 126–27, 137, 142
Cunningham, Laura 211–12
Curtright, Guy 228–29, 267

Dahlgren, Babe 63
Daley, Arthur 13, 56, 73, 117, 155, 212
Dallessandro, Dom 37
Daniel, Dan 20, 294
Daniels, Fred "Tony" 2, 103, 109, 126, 138
Danning, Harry 49, 76, 106
Dantonio, John "Fats" 2, 123
Danzig, Eli 207
Dark, Alvin 55, 74
Dasso, Frank 115, 124
Daubert, Jake 7
Davis, Crash 27
Davis, Curt 10, 57, 113, 119, 126, 128, 130
Davis, Spud 61
Dean, Dizzy 43, 45, 62
De la Cruz, Tommy 12, 98
Delahanty, Ed 154
DeMaestri, Joe 227
Derringer, Paul 10, 32, 38–39, 113, 118, 121, 133, 136, 139, 144, 292
Derry, Russ 253, 284
Devlin, Art 61
Dewey, Donald 211
Dewey, Thomas E. 270
Dickey, Bill 119, 203, 205, 210, 260
Dickshot, Johnny 228, 259, 271
Dickson, Murry 15
Dietrich, Bill 232, 267, 269, 280
Dihigo, Martin 10
DiMaggio, Dom 107, 154
DiMaggio, Joe 27–28, 63, 66, 82, 107, 166, 189, 203–4, 210, 221, 294
DiMaggio, Vince 61, 91, 102–3, 107, 118, 126, 141, 144
Dinges, Vance 107, 126
Dobson, Joe 234
Doby, Larry 107
Dockins, George 46, 51, 128, 137–38, 141, 143
Doerr, Bobby 235–36, 276
Donald, Atley 262, 265
Donatelli, Augie 15
Donnelly, Blix 45, 50, 121
Doolittle, James 172
Dorsey, Tommy 50
Douglas, John 114
Drebinger, John 59, 67, 110
Dreisewerd, Clem 255
Dressen, Chuck 53, 55–56, 143, 278
Dubiel, Monk 185, 209, 255, 258, 263
Dunn, Tom 60, 128, 139, 143–44
Durocher, Leo 2, 10, 12, 15, 35, 53–57, 59–61, 67–68, 72, 74–75, 78, 113, 115, 117, 121–22, 128, 143, 146, 207, 234, 273
Durrett, Red 207
Dyer, Eddie 46
Dykes, Jimmy 8, 31, 182, 200–1, 223–31, 233, 243, 263

Earley, Tom 88, 124
Early, Jake 175
Earnshaw, George 219

Eastman, Joseph B. 17
Eaton, Zeb 39, 267
Egan, Dave 13–14
Eisenhower, Dwight D. 118, 127–28, 178
Ellington, Duke 208
Elliott, Bob 63, 126, 142, 144
Embree, Red 166, 263, 265
Emmerich, Bill 68
Engel, Joe 236
Ennis, Skinny 50
Erickson, Paul 38, 122, 137, 149
Ermisch, Red 45
Estalella, Bobby 11, 243–44, 262, 271
Etten, Nick 43, 208, 278, 285–86
Evans, Al 175

Fannin, Cliff 199
Farley, Jim 172, 256
Farrell, Kerby 185, 228
Feldman, Harry 59, 68, 80, 129, 139, 141, 144
Feller, Bob 12–13, 27–28, 119, 156, 165–66, 176, 218–20, 280–83, 285–86, 294
Ferrell, Rick 1, 175–76, 178, 183–87, 231, 268, 281
Ferrell, Wes 186, 240, 248
Ferriss, Dave 1, 165, 173, 240–41, 255, 259, 262–63, 266–70, 272, 274, 277, 279–80
Filipowicz, Steve 115
Finney, Lou 164, 196, 275
Firpo, Luis 36
Fischer, Rube 68
Fitzsimmons, Freddie 90, 104, 106, 108–9, 112
Flager, Wally 126
Fleming, Sir Alexander 80
Fleming, Les 160, 162, 217, 284
Fletcher, Art 224, 272–73
Flores, Jesse 248–51, 272, 277, 279, 283
Forrestal, James 132–33
Forsyth, Roy 276
Fowler, Dick 251–52, 283–84
Fox, Howie 98, 143
Foxx, Jimmie 2, 10, 80, 102–3, 110, 122, 140, 172, 206, 234–35
Franklin, Jack 10
Fricano, Mario 224
Frick, Ford 5, 24–26, 60, 82, 105, 131, 140, 256
Frisch, Frankie 61–64, 124, 132, 142, 281

Gable, Clark 37
Gables, Ken 63, 132
Galan, Augie 56, 60, 122, 128, 137, 143, 146
Galehouse, Denny 29
Garbark, Bob 260–61
Garbark, Mike 10, 260, 264
Gardella, Al 120
Gardella, Danny 59, 72–73, 80, 120, 134, 137, 139, 294
Gardner, Glenn 147
Garms, Debs 42
Garner, Peggy Ann 131

Garrison, Ford 235
Gassaway, Charlie 283
Gedeon, Elmer 27
Gehrig, Lou 63, 141, 172, 193, 203–4, 206, 281
Gehringer, Charlie 206
George, Charlie "Greek" 283, 285
Gerheauser, Al 61, 63, 125
Gerkin, Steve 262
Gerlach, Larry 107
Gershman, Michael 104
Gettel, Al 209–10, 257, 259, 278
Gilbert, Bill 173, 243
Gillenwater, Carden 85, 89–90, 126, 132
Gillespie, Paul 32, 139
Gilmore, Leonard 63
Gionfriddo, Al 63, 124
Gleason, Jackie 131
Goldstein, Louis 54
Gomez, Lefty 204
Gonzalez, Mike 45
Gooding, Gladys 207
Gordon, Joe 202–3, 210, 221, 225
Gordon, Sid 68
Goslin, Goose 180
Goulish, Nick 103
Gowdy, Hank 5, 93
Grabiner, Harry 7
Graham, Frank 11, 121, 289
Grant, Eddie 77
Grant, Ulysses S. 77
Gray, Pete 1, 10, 27, 192–98, 200, 254, 257, 262–63, 270
Gray, Ted 47
Greenberg, Hank 9, 12–13, 27–28, 110, 119, 151–52, 155, 165–66, 248, 266–67, 269, 278, 281, 284, 286, 288, 290–91
Gregg, Hal 57, 114, 126, 130, 136, 138, 143, 146
Griffith, Clark 8–9, 11, 16, 28, 40, 135, 158, 175, 182–83, 188, 205, 236, 242–43, 261, 267, 274, 286, 288
Griffith, Thelma R. 267
Grimes, Burleigh 11, 195
Grimes, Oscar 208, 274
Grimm, Charlie 29, 31–35, 38–40, 140–41, 149, 232, 289–90
Grimm, Margaret 35
Grimm, William 35
Grodzicki, John 15, 219
Gromek, Steve 218, 220–21, 257, 262, 265, 268, 270, 272, 274–75, 280
Grove, Lefty 234–36, 281
Grove, Orval 229, 232, 258, 262, 277, 280, 284
Guerra, Mike 175
Guest, Edgar 117
Gumbert, Harry 98
Gustine, Frankie 63, 124–25
Gutteridge, Don 164, 197, 265

Haak, Howie 12
Haas, Mule 225

Hack, Stan 10, 32, 34, 36–37, 94, 133, 148, 290–91
Haefner, Mickey 30, 183–85, 187, 258, 267, 269, 275, 280, 284
Haight, Walter 174
Halas, George 168
Hall, Irv 265
Hamlin, Luke 55
Hamner, Garvin 103, 107–9
Hamner, Granny 2, 10, 103–4, 107–10
Handley, Lee 124
Haney, Fred 190–91
Hannegan, Robert 8
Hansen, Andy 68, 119–20, 122
Hanyzewski, Eddie 32
Harder, Mel 215, 218, 265, 270
Harrell, Ray 68
Harridge, William 24, 256–57, 274
Harris, Bucky 106, 175, 180
Harris, Mickey 219
Harris, Ned 153
Hart, Bill 120
Hartnett, Gabby 32, 49, 142
Hasenmayer, Don 109
Hassett, Buddy 27, 238
Hausmann, Clem 240, 265, 272
Hausmann, George 68, 120, 127, 133–34, 140, 207
Hayes, Frankie 158, 161–62, 176, 181, 186, 257, 264
Hayes, Ira 198
Haynes, Joe 258–59, 262, 266–67
Hearn, Barney 194
Heath, Jeff 1, 159, 162, 175, 217–18, 269–70, 284, 286
Heflin, Randy 278
Heilmann, Harry 8
Heisenberg, Werner 173
Hemingway, Ernest 71
Hendrickson, Don 142
Henrich, Tommy 27, 203, 210
Henry, Earl 259
Herman, Babe 1–2, 56–59, 90, 130, 138, 147, 231
Herman, Billy 55
Herring, Art 57, 128, 137
Hershberger, Willard 98–99
Heusser, Ed 98, 114–15, 118
Heving, Joe 10, 87, 123
Heydler, John 78
Higbe, Kirby 102
Higgins, Pinky 29, 241
Hitler, Adolf 14, 18, 55, 72, 111, 118, 173
Hoag, Myril 218
Hockett, Oris 228
Hofmann, Fred 199
Hogan, Shanty 216
Holborow, Walter 264, 277
Holcombe, Ken 284–85
Hollingsworth, Al 195, 198, 257, 272, 279
Holm, Billy 255

Index

Holmes, Tommy 1, 38, 56, 82–84, 120, 129–30, 144, 178
Honig, Donald 41, 66, 162, 259
Hooper, Harry 6
Hoover, J. Edgar 23
Hopp, Johnny 42–43, 45, 79, 123, 128–29, 137, 141
Hornsby, Rogers 45, 82, 191, 248
Hostetler, Chuck 155
Houtteman, Art 10
Howard, Elston 222
Hoy, William "Dummy" 10, 95
Hubbard, Cal 184
Hubbell, Carl 18, 76, 231
Hudson, Johnny 134
Hughes, Roy 120
Hughson, Tex 235–36, 239
Humphries, Johnny 232, 271, 274
Hunter, Herb 282
Hutchings, Johnny 80, 87, 123, 125, 132
Hutchinson, Fred 219
Hutchinson, Ira 126
Hyland, Robert 86

Jakucki, Sig 198–200, 254, 264, 272, 294
James, Bill 7, 202
Javery, Al 88–89, 113, 123, 137
Jethroe, Sam 12
Johnson, Ban 7
Johnson, Bob 237, 266, 270, 274, 286
Johnson, Chic 207–8
Johnson, Don 32, 35–37, 113, 122, 130, 142, 148, 291
Johnson, J. Monroe 23, 119
Johnson, Roy (manager) 35
Johnson, Roy (player) 237
Johnson, Vic 240, 275, 280
Johnson, Walter 150, 186, 210, 257
Jones, Earl 280
Joost, Eddie 83, 85–86, 89, 114, 221, 227, 251
Jorda, Lou 115
Jordan, David 107, 156
Judd, Oscar 111, 139
Judge, Joe 167, 177, 182
Jurges, Billy 10, 38, 73–74, 85, 116, 120, 142, 241
Jurisich, Al 89, 147
Just, Joe 96

Kahn, Roger 78, 203
Karl, Andy 111
Kaye, Sammy 50
Keaton, Buster 37
Kell, George 2, 225, 243–44, 251, 262, 274
Keller, Charlie 70, 156–57, 208–9, 284, 294
Keltner, Ken 215–16, 221
Kennedy, Bob 228
Kennedy, Vern 98, 132
Kerr, Buddy 68, 74, 80, 133–34, 142, 206–7
Kiernan, Thomas 55
Killefer, Bill 6

Kiner, Ralph 155
King, Clyde 57
King, Joe 73
Klein, Chuck 10
Klieman, Ed 192, 218, 265, 275, 282
Kline, Bob 236
Kluttz, Clyde 89, 134, 137
Knerr, Lou 249, 251, 284
Kolloway, Don 228
Konstanty, Jim 98
Kramer, Jack 10, 198–99, 259
Kreevich, Mike 192, 196, 270, 277–78
Kuhel, Joe 110, 175–76, 178, 181–83, 254
Kurowski, Whitey 41, 45, 48, 79, 141, 148

Laabs, Chet 196
LaGuardia, Fiorello H. 114, 127, 212, 253
Lake, Eddie 152, 237, 239, 268
Lakeman, Al 94–96
LaMacchia, Al 199
Lamanno, Ray 95
Landis, Kenesaw Mountain 8, 12, 17–18, 24–25, 28, 72, 94, 106–7, 111, 116–17, 246, 256
Laney, Al 40, 59, 79, 127, 135, 139, 145, 148, 206–8, 253–54, 279, 293
Lanier, Max 41–43, 116, 118
Lardner, John 77, 208–9
Lary, Lyn 237
Lauder, Bill, Jr. 59, 147
Layne, Hillis 177
Lazor, Johnny 237
Lazzeri, Tony 188, 204
Leary, Herbert 253
Lee, Bill 87–88, 122, 137, 140
Lee, Thornton 185, 229, 232, 254, 259, 262, 266, 269, 271–72, 278
Leon, Izzy 144
Leonard, Dutch 30, 183–85, 187, 254, 259, 266, 269, 270, 272, 275, 285
Leveridge, Marion 207
Lewis, Buddy 20, 173–74, 178, 286
Libke, Al 94–95
Lieb, Frederick G. 7, 12, 42, 46, 50, 64, 86, 195, 211, 281–82, 292
Lindell, Johnny 205, 207, 253, 255, 260, 265, 271
Lindstrom, Fred 67
Lisenbee, Hod 10, 91, 100–1, 113
Liska, Jerry 291
Litwhiler, Danny 26, 29, 42–43
Livingston, Mickey 32, 36, 38, 129
Lobert, Hans 34, 180–81
Lockman, Whitey 134
Lodigiani, Dario 228
Logan, Bob 87, 89–90, 93, 126
Lombardi, Ernie 10, 68–70, 75, 80, 95, 98, 113, 118, 121, 124, 129, 133–34, 137, 186, 209, 216
Lombardi, Vic 57, 121, 137, 146
Lopat, Ed 212, 232–33, 257, 259, 268, 275, 284

Index

Lopatka, Art 146
Lopez, Al 10, 64, 120, 124, 142, 214–15, 230
Louis, Joe 31
Lowrey, Peanuts 1, 36–37, 122, 133, 136, 141, 291
Lupien, Tony 103, 238
Luque, Dolf 10–11, 130
Lyman, Abe 50
Lyons, Ted 228, 233, 282

MacArthur, Douglas 139, 281
Mack, Connie 1, 16–17, 104, 151, 153–54, 161, 168, 198, 225, 237, 242–44, 246, 248–49, 251, 254, 277, 282–83, 290
Mack, Ray 216–17, 254
Mackay, Gordon 62
Mackiewicz, Felix 217–18
MacPhail, Larry 40, 135–36, 145, 203–4, 207–8, 256, 268, 270, 272–74
Maeso, Flora 189
Magerkurth, George 115–16, 137
Maglie, Sal 11, 60, 83, 91, 140–41, 143
Maier, Bob 2, 151, 155, 281
Malaney, Jack 89
Mallory, Jim 42–43, 144
Mancuso, Frank 10, 180, 191, 200
Mancuso, Gus 102, 110, 126, 191
Mann, Les 6
Mantle, Mickey 48
Maranville, Rabbit 8
Marchildon, Phil 15–17, 26–27, 251, 280
Marion, Marty 10, 42–43, 46, 48, 51, 74, 86, 141, 144, 148
Marion, Red 48
Marsans, Armando 11
Marshall, Willard 68
Martin, Babe 196, 272
Martin, Hersh 208, 255, 274–75, 278
Masi, Phil 85, 123, 137
Masterson, Walt 175–76, 285–86
Mathewson, Christy 7–8, 66, 78
Mauney, Dick 104, 111, 138
Mayo, Eddie 151, 154–55, 164, 256, 274, 284, 286–87, 290–92
Mays, Willie 66
McAuley, Ed 216–17
McAuliffe, Anthony 174
McBride, Tom 237, 276–77, 286
McCarthy, Joe 1, 45, 90, 111, 202, 204–5, 260, 263, 270, 272–73, 276–81, 283, 287
McCormick, Frank 91, 94, 120, 123, 131, 134
McCosky, Barney 151
McCoy, Benny 27
McDonnell, Jim 262
McElroy, Wilbur 238
McGhee, Bill 246
McGinnity, Joe 148
McGowan, Bill 173
McGowen, Roscoe 81
McGraw, John 53, 62, 66–67, 78, 211, 282
McKain, Archie 110

McKechnie, Bill 35, 50, 64, 81, 86, 91–96, 98–99, 115, 139, 215
McNair, Eric 110
McNutt, Paul V. 25
McQuinn, George 164, 191–92
Mead, William 19, 197
Medwick, Joe 45, 54, 68, 71–72, 74–75, 89, 121, 137
Mele, Sam 228
Merullo, Len 32, 38, 144
Mesner, Steve 115
Metheny, Bud 197, 208
Metkovich, George "Catfish" 1, 27, 237–39, 253, 265–66, 286
Metro, Charlie 277
Meusel, Bob 183
Meyer, Dutch 151, 159–60, 162, 222, 277–78
Michaels, Cass 10, 178, 228, 230, 262
Milan, Clyde 177
Miller, Bing 227, 243
Miller, Eddie 91, 94
Miller, John "Ox" 199–200, 286
Milosevich, Mike 2, 284
Minoso, Minnie 165, 224–25
Mize, Johnny 27, 49, 67–68, 72, 294
Modak, Mike 143
Monteagudo, Rene 109
Moore, Gene 191–92, 196, 280
Moore, Terry 41, 46, 294
Moore, Whitey 41, 92–93
Morehouse, Ward 234–35
Moses, Wally 153, 228, 271
Mott, Bitsy 103, 109
Muckerman, Dick 191
Mueller, Alvin 46
Mueller, Bill 283
Mueller, Emmett 219
Mueller, Heinie 46
Mueller, Les 156, 167, 272, 285–86
Mueller, Ray 95, 161, 264
Mulcahy, Hugh 9, 111–12
Mullin, Pat 219
Muncrief, Bob 166, 180, 198–99, 269
Mungo, Van Lingle 68, 71, 80, 118, 129, 133, 140
Munzel, Edgar H. 144
Murray, Donald 240–41
Musial, Stan 12, 14, 29, 42–43
Myatt, George 175–76, 178, 183
Myer, Buddy 105

Nagel, Bill 229
Navin, Frank 182
Nelson, Tommy 90
Newhouser, Hal 10, 29, 150, 156–58, 162–67, 257, 259, 262, 266–70, 274, 276–77, 280–84, 286, 289–92
Newsom, Bobo 54, 111, 186, 245–49, 254, 257, 269–72, 275, 277
Newsome, Skeeter 237, 239, 285–86
Neyer, Rob 214, 219

Nicholson, Bill 31–32, 36–38, 120, 122, 125, 140, 142
Nieman, Butch 85, 90, 108, 115, 118, 120, 129, 137
Niggeling, Johnny 30, 177, 183–84, 187, 276
Nimitz, Chester W. 132
Northey, Ron 25, 103
Novikoff, Lou 37, 231–32
Nugent, Gerry 106–7
Nuxhall, Joe 10, 101, 251, 277

O'Brien, Tommy 149
O'Connor, Leslie M. 24, 256
O'Dea, Ken 42, 49, 139
O'Dea, Paul 222
O'Doul, Lefty 64, 81, 188, 238–40, 281–82
Olmo, Luis 56, 120, 122, 129, 143, 278
Olsen, Ole 207–8
O'Malley, Walter 78
O'Neill, Emmett 240, 263–64, 266, 274
O'Neill, Frank 176, 183
O'Neill, Harry 27
O'Neill, Steve 29, 150–51, 155–58, 161–65, 167, 266, 284–85
Orengo, Joe 267
Orrell, Joe 266
Ortiz, Roberto 11
Ostermueller, Fritz 96, 137
Ostrowski, John 36
Ott, Mel 1, 59–60, 67–75, 78–80, 104, 115, 118, 120, 127, 134, 137–39, 294
Outlaw, Jimmy 285, 291
Overmire, Stubby 156–57, 163, 167, 222, 267, 270–71, 291
Owen, Marv 71–72
Owen, Mickey 57, 122
Owens, Jesse 181

Packard, Gene 7
Pafko, Andy 32, 36, 38, 120, 133, 139, 148
Page, Joe 209
Papish, Frank 284
Partenheimer, Stan 120
Partenheimer, Steve 120
Pascual, Camilo 11
Pasquel, Jorge 70, 117, 130, 191, 243, 294
Passarella, Art 285
Passeau, Claude 32, 38–39, 115, 122, 128, 133, 137, 141, 147, 291
Patterson, Robert 208, 257
Patton, George S. 174
Peacock, Johnny 126
Peck, Hal 243–44, 286
Pegler, Westbrook 111
Pennock, Herb 8, 102–4, 108–9, 112
Perini, Lou 169
Perkins, Ralph "Cy" 153
Pesky, Johnny 239
Pfund, Lee 120
Phelon, William 7
Phillips, Bill 93

Pierce, Billy 10, 264
Pieretti, Marino 30, 183, 186, 188–89, 257, 265, 268–69, 275
Pinelli, Babe 144, 148
Poland, Hugh 26
Polly, Nick 255
Potter, Nelson 164–65, 179, 198, 200, 256, 258, 278–79
Povich, Shirley 175, 178, 181–83, 289–92
Powell, Jake 110–11, 176, 204
Power, Vic 227
Prim, Ray 38–39, 122, 128, 132, 138, 140–41, 147–48, 291
Pugh, James E. 262
Pyle, Ewald 68, 89, 128

Quigley, Martin 183
Quinn, John 89, 124, 169

Raffensberger, Ken 26, 113
Rayburn, Sam 257
Rebel, Art 140
Reese, Pee Wee 56, 67, 294
Reiser, Pete 13–15, 232, 294
Remmers, Charley 239
Rennie, Rud 205, 209, 259, 263–64, 270–71, 277, 279, 285
Reyes, Nap 68, 72, 80, 130
Reynolds, Allie 162, 192, 213, 218, 220–22, 254, 259, 268–70, 275, 280, 284
Rice, Del 49
Rice, Sam 8
Richards, Paul 10, 156, 181, 210, 290–92
Rickey, Branch 41, 45, 53–54, 56–57, 78, 89, 106, 113, 118, 130–31, 261, 274, 293
Riddle, Elmer 96–98
Riddle, Johnny 96–97
Rizner, John 114
Rizzuto, Phil 27
Robinson, Aaron 277–78
Robinson, Jackie 10, 12, 25, 105–7, 203, 222, 224, 234, 242, 293
Robinson, Ray 78
Robinson, Wilbert 57, 64, 90
Rocco, Mickey 159–60, 162, 217, 222, 284
Rockefeller, John D. 68
Rodecker, Nicholas E. 254
Rodgers, Bill 63
Roe, Preacher 56, 63, 65–66, 116, 121, 136, 138
Rolfe, Red 129
Rommel, Eddie 262
Rooney, Mickey 46
Roosevelt, Franklin D. 2, 5, 8–9, 23, 28, 75, 118, 172, 208, 247, 253–54, 257
Root, Charlie 193
Rosar, Buddy 161, 252, 264, 285
Rosen, Al 165
Rosen, Goody 56, 82, 120, 122, 142, 146
Rosenthal, Larry 264–65
Roser, Steve 207, 285

Rosner, Max 194
Ross, Don 151, 155, 160, 162
Rossi, John 107
Rothel, Bob 258
Rothstein, Arnold 78
Rucker, Johnny 59, 68, 80, 128, 134, 139, 144
Rue, Joe 180, 283, 285
Ruel, Muddy 31, 215
Ruffing, Red 27, 209, 277, 280, 284
Ruhl, Oscar 50
Rumill, Ed 196–97, 240
Ruppert, Jacob 211
Rush, Speedy 216
Russell, Jim 63
Ruth, Babe 13, 66, 75, 80, 141, 172, 193–94, 204, 206, 208, 210–11, 231–32, 234–35, 240, 253, 282
Ryan, Jack 231
Ryan, Sue 207
Ryba, Mike 240, 255, 283

Salkeld, Bill 124–25, 149
Salkeld, Roger 125
Salsinger, H.G. 154, 156
Salveson, Jack 275
Salvo, Manny 75
Sanders, Ray 45, 49, 57, 79, 139, 148
Sandlock, Mike 207
Sauer, Eddie 37, 145
Sauer, Hank 100, 145
Savage, Don 209, 255
Sawyer, Eddie 104
Scarsella, Les 103
Schacht, Al 207–8
Schaefer, Willie 80
Schalk, Roy 276
Schanz, Charley 26, 103, 111, 115, 122
Scheel, Karl 200–1
Scheib, Carl 2, 10, 251, 254
Schmeling, Max 288
Schmidt, Fred 43
Schmitz, Johnny 165
Schoendienst, Joe 47
Schoendienst, Julius 47
Schoendienst, Red 1, 10, 29, 43, 45–47, 140, 148
Schofield, Dick 47
Schreiber, Paul 1, 209–10
Schulte, Frank 141
Schultz, Howie 25–26, 56, 59
Schultz, Joe 265
Schumacher, Hal 75–76
Schuster, Bill 122, 291
Schwartz, Packy 276
Scott, Lefty 2, 126
Sears, Ziggy 128
Seats, Tom 57, 118, 139, 141–43, 147
Secory, Frank 32, 37
Seerey, Pat 160–62, 217–18, 262, 270–71, 275
Seminick, Andy 39, 103, 110
Seward, Frank 68

Sewell, Joe 190–91
Sewell, Luke 164, 190–92, 195, 199–201, 257
Sewell, Rip 63, 65, 96, 114, 118, 132
Sewell, Tommy 190–91
Sharkey, Jack 288
Shean, Dave 6
Shemo, Steve 114, 126
Shepard, Bert 1, 15–16, 131, 277
Shirley, Tex 263, 272, 274, 280
Shor, Toots 80
Shotton, Burt 48, 218, 265
Shoun, Clyde 98
Shupe, Vince 137
Siebert, Dick 27, 243–44, 246, 266
Siebert, Paul 246
Silvestri, Ken 219
Simmons, Al 17, 180, 225, 242–43, 281
Sinatra, Frank 130
Sipek, Dick 10, 95–96
Sisler, George 240
Slaughter, Enos 41, 46, 51, 259, 294
Smith, Al (governor of New York) 211
Smith, Al (pitcher) 218, 221, 266, 279
Smith, Chester 104
Smith, Eddie 228
Smith, John L. 121
Smith, Red (Cubs coach) 31
Smith, Red (sportswriter) 117, 148–49, 285, 288
Smith, Vince 219
Sousa, John Philip 211
Southworth, Billy 18, 29, 43, 45, 47–48, 120, 142, 147–48
Southworth, Billy, Jr. 45
Spence, Stan 29, 175, 254
Spindel, Hal 103
Spink, J.G. Taylor 28, 30, 39, 224, 248
Sproull, Charlie 111, 122
Stainback, Tuck 274
Stalin, Joseph 118
Stanky, Eddie 49, 55–57, 59–60, 74, 82, 128–29, 137, 142
Steiner, Ben 255, 266
Stengel, Casey 64, 71, 81, 86, 222, 230, 233, 238–39
Stephens, Vern 129, 191–92, 200, 256, 259, 262, 270, 275, 278
Stettinius, Edward R. 178
Stevens, Ed 53, 138, 142, 146–47
Stevens, Mal 138
Stewart, Bill 122
Stewart, Don 231
Stirnweiss, Snuffy 208, 228–29, 263, 270, 274, 286–87
Stockwell, Harry 207
Stone, Johnny 180
Stoneham, Charles A. 77–78
Stoneham, Horace 74, 76–78, 127, 256
Stover, Dewey 64
Street, Gabby 186, 201
Strincevich, Nick 63, 116, 119, 129–30, 141, 143

Index

Sturm, Johnny 219
Sukeforth, Clyde 1–2, 114, 126, 231
Summers, Bill 224
Sunkel, Tom 10
Susce, George 220
Swanson, Evar 181
Sweetland, Leo 81

Tabor, Jim 235–36
Taylor, Luther "Dummy" 10, 95
Taylor, Zack 199
Tebbetts, Birdie 105, 119
Tegtmeyer, Charlie 278
Terry, Bill 62, 71, 98, 230, 275
Thomson, Bobby 68
Thorpe, Lester 21
Tierney, James 77
Tipton, Eric 94–95, 115, 124, 134
Tobin, Jim 1, 87–88, 114, 124, 127, 156, 168–70, 185, 210, 278, 282, 285
Tobin, Johnny 170, 286
Tobin, Maurice J. 113
Topping, Dan 203–4, 208
Torres, Gil 175–76
Touchstone, Clay 10
Travis, Cecil 15, 174, 219
Traynor, Pie 169
Treadway, Red 51, 68, 134
Tresh, Mike 267
Triplett, Coaker 103, 107, 121
Trosky, Hal 182, 214
Trout, Dizzy 29, 150, 156–57, 163–64, 166–67, 170, 258–59, 265, 267–69, 278–79, 284, 291
Trout, Steve 167
Troy, Bun 77
Trucks, Virgil 163–64, 167, 290
Truman, Harry 28, 116–18, 139, 174, 283
Tunney, Gene 219

Udel, S.C. 129
Ullrich, Sandy 2, 277, 284
Unser, Al 91, 96
Unser, Del 96

Vandenberg, Hy 132, 141, 147
Vaughan, Arky 54
Vaughn, Fred 176, 266
Veeck, Bill 25, 32, 35, 64, 107, 181, 213–15
Verban, Emil 45, 48, 145
Vitt, Ossie 215–16, 227
Voigt, David 25, 45
Voiselle, Bill 10, 68, 70, 79–80, 113, 115, 121, 123, 130, 137, 144–45, 247

Waddell, Rube 66
Wade, Jake 224
Wagner, Hal 235–36
Wagner, Honus 42, 66, 142
Wainwright, Jonathan M. 178
Waitkus, Eddie 185

Wakefield, Dick 29, 65, 155
Walberg, Rube 236
Walczak, Ed 145
Walker, Dixie 54, 56, 116, 128, 139, 143, 146
Walker, Gee 154, 214
Walker, Harry 12, 14–15, 56, 106
Walker, Hub 164
Walkup, Jim 248
Wallace, Jimmy "Lefty" 88
Wallen, Norm 114
Walsh, Ed 226
Walters, Bucky 98–100, 115, 122, 130, 132–33
Walters, Fred 2, 255
Walters, Sam 131
Wambsganss, Bill 246
Waner, Lloyd 10, 64–65, 87
Waner, Paul 10, 64–65, 83, 259
Warneke, Lon 128, 290
Warstler, Rabbit 236
Wasdell, Jimmy 107, 126
Watson, Jack 212
Wayne, John 13
Weaver, Harry 7
Weaver, Monte 240
Webb, Del 203–4, 208, 266
Webb, Skeeter 155, 164, 292
Webber, Les 57, 120
Wehmeier, Herm 101
Weingartner, Elmer 158, 162
Weintraub, Phil 51, 68, 72, 74–75, 80, 113–14, 118, 120, 134
Weiss, George 83, 205
Wendler, Doc 15
Werber, Bill 93–94, 99
Werner, Ludlow 293
West, Sam 180
West, Weldon "Lefty" 279
Westcott, Rich 180
Wheeler, Bert 131
Wheeler, Ralph 38
Whitcher, Bob 142
Whitehead, John 224
Whittlesey, Charles 77
Wietelmann, Whitey 85, 126
Wilhelm, Kaiser 40
Wilkins, Bobby 2, 265
Wilks, Ted 10, 42, 46, 51, 115, 124, 127
Williams, Dewey 32
Williams, Joe 157, 210
Williams, Marvin 12
Williams, Ted 12–14, 27, 65–66, 163, 166, 178, 186, 196, 240, 244, 294
Williams, Woody 134
Wilson, Jim 240, 259, 266, 269–70, 278
Wilson, Jimmie 35, 55, 139
Wilson, Walter 263–64
Winsett, Tom 71
Wolff, Roger 30, 157, 183–85, 187, 257, 262, 266, 268, 272, 275, 279–80, 286
Wood, Allan 7
Woodard, Milt 231

Woods, Pinky 262
Woodward, Stanley 76
Workman, Chuck 85, 129, 137
Wright, Ed 87–88, 137, 145
Wright, Taffy 180
Wrigley, Philip K. 32, 37, 256
Wyatt, Whitlow 102–3
Wynn, Early 29
Wyse, Hank 32, 38–39, 82, 119, 121, 129–30, 132–33, 137–38, 143, 147, 290–91

Yawkey, Tom 103, 105, 234–37, 241, 255
Yawkey, W.H. 235

Yonkers, Bob 221
York, Rudy 141, 151–52, 248, 256, 266, 278, 282, 285, 291
Yost, Ed 10
Young, Babe 294
Young, Dick 15, 66

Zardon, Jose 176
Zeller, Jack 150, 155
Zoldak, Sam 286
Zuber, Bill 274, 286

www.ingramcontent.com/pod-product-compliance
Lightning Source LLC
Chambersburg PA
CBHW021336230426
43666CB00006B/316